Rober

Robert Manne
A Political Memoir
Intellectual Combat in the Cold War and the Culture Wars

IN CONJUNCTION WITH BLACK INC.

Published by La Trobe University Press in conjunction with Black Inc.
Wurundjeri Country
22–24 Northumberland Street
Collingwood VIC 3066, Australia
enquiries@blackincbooks.com
www.blackincbooks.com
www.latrobeuniversitypress.com.au

La Trobe University plays an integral role in Australia's public intellectual life, and is recognised globally for its research excellence and commitment to ideas and debate. La Trobe University Press publishes books of high intellectual quality, aimed at general readers. Titles range across the humanities and sciences, and are written by distinguished and innovative scholars. La Trobe University Press books are produced in conjunction with Black Inc., an independent Australian publishing house. The members of the LTUP Editorial Board are Vice-Chancellor's Fellows Emeritus Professor Robert Manne and Dr Elizabeth Finkel, and Morry Schwartz and Chris Feik of Black Inc.

Copyright © Robert Manne 2024
Robert Manne asserts his right to be known as the author of this work.

ALL RIGHTS RESERVED.
No part of this publication may be reproduced, stored in a retrieval system, or transmitted in any form by any means electronic, mechanical, photocopying, recording or otherwise without the prior consent of the publishers.

9781760645069 (hardback)
9781760645625 (paperback)
9781743823873 (ebook)

 A catalogue record for this book is available from the National Library of Australia

Cover design by John Warwicker
Text design and typesetting by Tristan Main
Author photograph by Tom Ross

In memory of Kate and Henry, and Hans

*For Anne,
Kate, Daniel and Sophie; Lucy; and David*

Contents

Introduction: By Way of Explanation   ix

Part I: Education

1. Grandparents   3
2. Father   25
3. Childhood and Adolescence   45
4. University   65
5. From Oxford to Bundoora   93

Part II: Cold War

6. Cambodia   119
7. Wilfred Burchett   147
8. The Petrov Affair   169
9. The 1980s – My Conservative Decade   193

Part III: Quadrant

10.	Editing *Quadrant* (1989–1992)	227
11.	*Quadrant* 2: History Wars (1993–1995)	261
12.	*Quadrant* 3: The Politics of Race (1996–1997)	291

Part IV: Culture Wars

13.	Denialism and the Right	323
14.	"Howard Hater"	349
15.	"Oh Dear, Mr Rudd!"	383
16.	Good News, Bad News	411
17.	On Borrowed Time	439

Afterword	461
Acknowledgements	467
Previous Works by Robert Manne	471
Index	473

Introduction

By Way of Explanation

MY LIFE CAN BE DIVIDED INTO THREE PARTS. The first is as a son, brother, partner, husband, father, grandfather, father-in-law, uncle and friend. The second is as a teacher, beginning on Sundays at Temple Beth Israel when I was a teenager and continuing as a university lecturer and finally a professor at La Trobe University. The third is as what came to be called a "public intellectual", someone whose research and writing is responsive to the major questions facing their country and the world. This book is concerned with the third part. I would not be able to tell the whole truth about my private life. Nor is my memory reliable enough. University tutorials as a teacher were times of fierce concentration and moral intensity. I was more nervous entering a tutorial group for the first time than I was before an appearance on national television. Yet those moments have vanished from memory, like dreams.

There was porousness between my private life, as a friend and a husband, and my life as a political writer. My take on the world was influenced by conversations with former teachers who became friends, Frank Knopfelmacher and Vincent Buckley; with my closest friend, Raimond Gaita, from undergraduate days until the present; and later in almost daily email exchanges with the remarkable chief editor at Black Inc., Chris Feik. Most important were the conversations with my wife, Anne, that have lasted forty-five years. Anne deepened my understanding of intellectual courage and independence. She taught

INTRODUCTION

me about feminism and the cultural and psychological consequences of the neo-liberal age in which we live.

Wherever possible I have relied on publications – my own and others' – rather than on memory. I have spared readers details of the vendettas mounted over the decades by two political enemies, Gerard Henderson and Keith Windschuttle, principally because their lines of attack almost never concerned questions of any general significance or interest. The only exception was an argument with Henderson over Australian anti-communist intellectuals and the murder in 1965–66 of between 500,000 and 1 million Indonesian communists or supposed fellow travellers. I have tried to outline accurately what I believed at different times, and on the questions where I have changed my mind, why. Although my writing on communism in the 1980s positioned me on the right, and my writing on Indigenous dispossession and refugees in the 1990s and beyond on the left, I believe that there is a moral and political consistency between my earlier and later selves.

I decided to write this political memoir at the invitation of Morry Schwartz, the creator of Black Inc., *Quarterly Essay*, *The Monthly*, *The Saturday Paper* and La Trobe University Press. The invitation came at a difficult time for me, having lost my larynx in December 2016 to throat cancer, with my voice reduced to a whisper. For a while I tried to continue contributing to political life in my customary role. Before long I lost the hunger. I decided that an account of my political education, my arguments with the left during the final decade of the Cold War, my turbulent years as editor of *Quadrant* and my arguments with the right during the culture wars might be of interest to those who remember these years but also to curious younger readers. Morry invited me to write a long book. I am extremely grateful to him. I am especially pleased that the book is published by the press of the university to which I was appointed as a lecturer almost exactly fifty years ago, and to which, as a self-described La Trobe Patriot, I owe a great deal.

Part I
Education

[1.]

Grandparents

AS SOON AS I BEGAN THINKING ABOUT this political memoir, I realised that it must begin with my grandparents' last years, months and days. The reason is not that their end was unusual. Quite the contrary; it was shared by some 6 million others who were starved in ghettos, shot and then buried in mass graves, or driven into gas vans or chambers in the lands of Eastern Europe the Nazis had conquered following their invasions of Poland on September 1, 1939, and the Soviet Union on June 22, 1941. The soul-shock delivered by the recognition, when I was still a young child, that a few years before I was born the German state had attempted to rid the Earth of the Jewish people shaped my political life from first to last. That the Holocaust stands at the beginning of my political thought is neither a good nor a bad thing, or so it seems to me. It is just the way it was and is.

It took less than five minutes to discover what happened to my maternal grandparents, Otto Joseph Meyer and his wife, Friederike or Frida Meyer née Munter. Having typed their names into the electronic database of victims compiled at Yad Vashem, the Holocaust museum in Israel, I learned that they had both been deported from Berlin on October 18, 1941, to the ghetto in Lodz that the Germans had renamed Litzmannstadt in memory of a First World War general who had been killed nearby. Frida died on February 7, 1942, in the ghetto. Otto died on May 8, 1942, in Chelmno, an extermination site some 50 kilometres from Lodz. Because of a rich scholarly literature, that was all I needed to know to be able to reconstruct my maternal grandparents' last years, months, days and, in the case of Otto, last hours and minutes.

The Meyers were a bourgeois Berlin business family. One is tempted to add "typical" to that description. Otto and Frida had two children, Kate, my mother, and Hans, my uncle. The family were fully assimilated, patriotic Germans who observed the Passover Seder and the High Holy Days of Rosh Hashanah and Yom Kippur, but also ate ham and celebrated the secular parts of Christmas with gifts and a tree. So far as I can judge from what my mother told me, the Meyers were not wealthy but comfortable. Kathe (Kate in Australia) was for example brought up by a full-time, in-house nanny, Paulschen. Kate completed her qualification as a teacher of "domestic science". Her brother, Hans, did not go further than high school. Like so many assimilated and successful but not prominent German Jewish families, the Meyers appear only to have turned their minds to arranging for the escape of their adult children (but not themselves) more than five years after the Nazi seizure of power, in the shock of the nationwide anti-Jewish pogrom of November 9–10, 1938, *Kristallnacht*. Kate was accepted by Australia shortly before the outbreak of war following the German invasion of Poland. Hans managed to get to neutral Sweden during the war and to work there as a farmhand. He enjoyed the physical labour and treasured the kindness of the Swedes. These were, he once told me, the happiest years of his life.

What did my maternal grandparents observe and experience between the Nazi seizure of power on January 30, 1933, and their deportation to the Lodz Ghetto on October 18, 1941? The SA, the Nazi Storm Troopers, called for a boycott of Jewish businesses to begin on April 1, 1933. It had little effect and fizzled out that day. At much the same time, across German university campuses, books by Jewish and left-wing authors – and especially left-wing Jewish authors – were incinerated in great bonfires. As the Meyers were neither academics nor intellectuals, I doubt that this affected them greatly. Nor were they directly affected by either the April 1933 Law for the Restoration of the Professional Civil Service, which dismissed senior Jewish civil servants but also many Jewish judges, lawyers and doctors, or by Josef Goebbels' leadership of the Chamber of Culture from September 1933 and the systematic removal of thousands of Jews from every aspect of German cultural life. The Nuremberg Laws of 1935 – The Law for the Protection of German Blood and The Reich Citizenship Law – did of course affect them, and all German Jews, personally and directly. These laws divided Germans into Aryans and Jews. Jews were defined in law as a race, not as members of a faith. The race was formally stripped of citizenship. Not only marriage but all sexual relations between Aryans and Jews were forbidden. As insurance, Jews were no longer able to employ Aryan women under forty-five years to help at home. As a result of illegal copulation, an Aryan-Jewish half-caste, a *mischlinge* – whose legal position was also outlined in the Nuremberg Laws – might be born. Luckily, Paulschen, the nanny, was well over childbearing age. In these early years, Otto and Frida Meyer must have been aware of the existence of concentration camps – Dachau, Buchenwald and Sachsenhausen – but at first the inmates were principally political enemies, communists and socialists (among whom there were to be sure many Jews) rather than racial enemies, the Jews and Roma ("Gypsies").

What would almost certainly have affected my maternal grandparents in these early years were matters more intangible – the understanding that they had been brutally woken from the post-Enlightenment dream of Germany as a home for Jews and that in its aftermath what they faced was the ideologically conjured hostility of strangers and the opportunistic betrayal of former supposed friends. Marta Appel captured the psychological impact of living in a world of real or imagined hostility:

> I hated to go out, since on every corner I saw signs that the Jews were the misfortune of the people ... When I was waiting for a streetcar I always thought the driver would not stop if he knew I was Jewish ... I did not go into a theatre or a movie for a long time before we were forbidden to, since I could not bear to be among people who hated me so much.

In a few words Hannah Arendt captured the sickening shock of betrayal. "Our friends Nazified [*gleichschalteten*] themselves! The problem ... after all, was not what our enemies did, but what our friends did."

In January 1933 there were some 520,000 Jews living in Germany. At this time and for several years after, the German state's "solution" to its Jewish "problem" was encouraged or enforced migration, what one scholar has called the "territorial final solution". The policy was summarised with admirable clarity in a memorandum sent on May 24, 1934, from the SD (the security service of the secret police) to one of the leaders of the SS, Reinhard Heydrich:

> [T]he aim of Jewish policy has to be the emigration of all Jews ... The possibilities for Jewish life – not just in the economic sense – should be restricted. Germany must be a country with no future for them, a country in which the older generation may die off ... but in which the young cannot live. So that the appeal of emigration remains constant.

In the *Altreich* (Germany as established by the Treaty of Versailles) that policy was at best partially successful. In the first five years of the Nazi dictatorship – from January 1933 to December 1937 – only one-quarter of Germany's Jews departed. By early 1935, 10,000 Jews who had fled returned to Germany. Only the threat of the concentration camp ended that strange reverse migration flow. Like so many comfortable, non-prominent bourgeois families, Otto and Frida Meyer and their adult children, Kate and Hans, seem to have made no effort to leave Germany before late 1938. They must have found conditions bearable and, most likely, believed that the Hitler dictatorship would over time become more moderate or even perhaps collapse.

In early November 1938, a third secretary in the German embassy in Paris, Ernst vom Rath, was shot and killed by a young Jew, Herschel Grynszpan, whose family had been brutally uprooted and deported along with 12,000 other Polish Jews living in Germany, to a no-mans-land on the German–Polish border. In response, the Nazi state organised a nationwide anti-Jewish pogrom. Across Germany, Jewish shops and apartments were robbed and ransacked and their windows smashed (hence the eventual name of the pogrom, the Night of Broken Glass, *Kristallnacht*). Three major synagogues – Munich, Nuremberg and Dortmund – were completely destroyed and scores more defiled. One hundred Jews were murdered. Thirty thousand were arrested and sent to a concentration camp – Dachau, Buchenwald or Sachsenhausen – many on the understanding of release on proof that all their emigration taxes had been settled satisfactorily, and that both an entry visa and, if necessary, a berth on an ocean liner had been obtained. To cover the costs of the damage for which the insolent Jewish terrorist, Grynszpan, was deemed responsible, the Jewish community in Germany was presented with an "atonement" fine of 1 billion marks – which was paid.

This November pogrom did the trick. By now, the Germans had replicated in Berlin the kind of "conveyor belt" system of Jewish emigration that a middle-ranking member of the SS, Adolf Eichmann, had created in Vienna in mid-1938. At the Eichmann trial in Israel in 1960 the system was vividly described:

> At one end you put in a Jew who still has some property, a factory or a shop, or a bank account, and he goes through the building from counter to counter, from office to office, and comes out at the other end without any money, without any rights, with only a passport.

Tens of thousands of Jews, especially the young, now scrambled to get out, recognising finally, belatedly, that they had no future in Germany. In the year following *Kristallnacht*, 78,000 Jews emigrated from the *Altreich*. Because of the shock delivered to world opinion by the November pogrom, several countries, perhaps most significantly the United States and the United Kingdom, opened their doors at least a little wider to Jewish refugees.

One such country was Australia, a dominion of the British Empire. In July 1938, an international conference on Jewish refugees had been held in Evian, France, convened by President Roosevelt. The head of the Australian delegation was Lieutenant-Colonel Thomas White, the minister for Trade and Customs. In words widely reported at the time and remembered still, White explained with unusual candour his country's reluctance to take significant numbers of Jewish refugees: "[A]s we have no real racial problems, we are not desirous of importing one by encouraging any scheme of large-scale foreign migration." His words have, however, misled even the best historians. In his magnificent study "Jewish Emigration from Germany – Nazi Policies and Jewish Responses", Herbert A. Strauss, for example, claims that "the November *Kristallnacht* had no repercussions 'down under'". This is not quite right. At the time of *Kristallnacht*, Australia's high commissioner in London was the former prime minister Stanley Bruce. Bruce urged Joseph Lyons' government to offer sanctuary to 30,000 European refugees. In response, on December 1, 1938, to Bruce's bitter disappointment, Australia announced its willingness to accept not 30,000 but 15,000 refugees over the next three years. The offer did not specifically mention Jews, although it was understood that almost every refugee accepted would be a German or Austrian Jew. Colonel White supported this offer, as did the leader of the Opposition, John Curtin.

Interviews of potential Jewish refugees were conducted in Germany principally by members of organisations of British Jews. The names of those whose claims they supported were then passed to the non-government body with authority in such matters, the Australian Jewish Welfare Society. From there, the names went to the Ministry of the Interior in Canberra. One of the successful candidates was my mother. I have no idea how much the family needed to pay to get her out of Germany or why her brother, Hans, did not leave with her. Kate Meyer arrived in Perth in early September 1939. Her arrival coincided with the German invasion of Poland and the consequent British declaration of war, "as a result" of which, as the new prime minister, Robert Menzies, put it, Australia was also at war. One consequence was that the mail service between Australia and Germany now ended. Kate was truly alone.

GRANDPARENTS

I have tried to discover what my mother's parents must have experienced in the years before their deaths in 1942. In mid-1938, German Jews had to declare their assets if they were worth more than 5,000 marks. Almost certainly, the Meyers qualified. After *Kristallnacht* nearly all existing Jewish businesses in Germany were taken by the state in a process known as Aryanisation. The Meyer family's principal source of income must have dried up either then or sooner. Remaining Jewish bank accounts were blocked, meaning that Jews were permitted only to withdraw small sums each month, required to justify larger withdrawals and, if they needed foreign currency, to exchange their marks at a highly unfavourable rate. Jews had to surrender their driving licences and their automobiles, their radios and their private telephones. They were forbidden to walk in public parks, to sit on public benches, to attend theatres, concert halls or cinemas, to visit libraries or museums, or to use several kinds of public transport. In January 1939, Jewish men were obliged to add "Israel" to their name, and women, "Sarah". So, presumably, my grandfather now became, for official purposes, Otto Israel Meyer, and my grandmother, Frida Sarah Meyer. Jewish adults were conscripted to hard manual labour for eight or nine hours per day, which was frequently altogether beyond their physical capacity. In May 1939, labour service was required of Jewish men between the ages of eighteen and fifty-five. As Otto Meyer had just celebrated his fifty-fifth birthday, he might have been exempt. In September 1940, the upper age limit for men was raised to sixty, so he was most likely included. Frida, two years older than Otto, was above the age limit for female labour.

Throughout Germany, Jews lost the homes they owned and tenant rights, and were forced into impoverished neighbourhoods and overcrowded, sometimes squalid apartment buildings, some of which were collectives, known as *Judenhausen*, Jew Houses. According to a Gestapo letter of September 18, 1941: "The Jews must be assigned only the dirtiest and worst accommodation." Jews had to observe strictly enforced outdoor night-time curfews. Inside the Jew Houses, residents were forbidden from loitering in halls or on staircases. Staple foods were delivered through ration cards, considerably lower for

Jews than for Aryans, scarcely above semi-starvation levels. Clothing was rarely available. By 1941, Jews were forbidden from purchasing not only "luxuries" like tobacco, coffee and alcohol but also white bread and rolls, milk and even skim milk, poultry, fish, meat, fresh vegetables and fruit. In war-time Berlin, Jews were allowed to shop only between the hours of 4.00 and 5.00 p.m. Many shops discouraged or entirely forbade Jewish customers.

Rules governing Jewish behaviour continued to grow in number. Some rules were remarkably petty. Postgraduate students were advised that "Jews may only be cited in doctoral dissertations if this is unavoidable for academic reasons ... German and Jewish authors should be separated in the bibliography." Some rules were devastating. One month before they left Berlin, Otto Israel and Frida Sarah Meyer, were informed that, like every Jew in Nazi Germany over the age of six, they must not appear in public without a large yellow Star of David sewn onto the left breast of their clothing. Many of the rules and regulations were publicised in the official, state-controlled "Jewish Newspaper", the *Judisches Nachrichtenblatt*.

On October 23, 1941, the policy of enforced Jewish emigration was formally abandoned and replaced by a new policy, the deportation of the Jews of greater Germany to "the East". Josef Goebbels, the Gauleiter of Berlin, wanted Berlin to be the first German city to be *Judenfrei*, Jew-free. Goebbels discussed the question with Hitler. On August 18 he wrote in his diary that Hitler had promised "the Jews will be deported from Berlin as soon as possible". On September 24 an internal government message was sent to Munich: "The Fuhrer believes that the Jews must gradually be removed from throughout Germany. The first towns to be made free of Jews will be Berlin, Vienna and Prague. Berlin will be first." This policy shift and this choice of destination determined the lives of my maternal grandparents (and also, as we shall see, my paternal grandfather).

Until this moment I have only been able to understand what Otto and Frida Meyer, as elderly middle-class Berlin Jews, must have experienced, working with a rich historical literature and, from the subjective inside, the wonderful diary of the Dresden Jewish linguist

Professor Victor Klemperer. When I learned from the Yad Vashem database that Otto and Frida were deported to the Lodz Ghetto on October 18, 1941, the last months of their lives came into sharper focus. Because the October 18 train was the first of sixty-three trains to leave Berlin for the East, the circumstances surrounding it have been carefully studied. And because an extraordinary contemporary chronicle of the Lodz Ghetto has been published, written by several sensitive, observant and analytical Polish Jewish intellectuals, what happened to the 20,000 German Jews who were deported there in the last months of 1941 is painfully clear. It is possible now to replace surmising about my maternal grandparents with concrete evidence – not of what they must have experienced but of what they did.

Beate Meyer (no relation) has studied in minute detail the details of the first train leaving Berlin for the East. The Jewish community there had established an "advice centre" for Jews evicted from their apartments. On October 1 or 2, 1941, two or three members of the advice centre were summoned to appear at the office of the Gestapo and told about the so-called resettlement to Lodz. They were offered a choice between co-operating or allowing the work to be carried out instead by the SS, "and 'you know what that would be like'". That night the *Reichsvereinigung der Juden in Deutschland*, the Reich Association of Jews in Germany – the most important Jewish body in Germany, created and controlled by the state – held an emergency meeting. It decided to co-operate "because one hoped in this way to be able to do as much good as possible". Around this time its deputy chairman, Philipp Kozower, spoke to 200 assembled Jewish "marshals": "The Jewish community sees it as an honour to alleviate through personal commitment the circumstances of our emigrating comrades of Jewish faith." They had worked closely and amicably for years with the Gestapo and the SS in the enforced emigration program, so the co-operation of the *Reichsvereinigung* and other Jewish bodies in Berlin in the "resettlement" program was never in doubt.

The advice centre was obliged to forward the names of 3,000 Berlin Jews to the Gestapo. By using a tax register in its possession, it chose these 3,000 "at random". Those chosen were required to fill out a sixteen-page questionnaire supplied by the Gestapo. Of the 3,000, the Gestapo chose 1,000 for deportation. Otto and Frida Meyer were among the chosen. The thousand were summoned to appear in a few days' time at a synagogue that had been converted into an assembly camp. They arrived on October 16 and 17, and stood in pouring rain waiting to be allowed into the lobby. Their luggage was now checked carefully, with jewellery, money and other items of value stolen. People slept on straw or on the synagogue's bare marble. Inside the synagogue, according to one of those registering the assets, there were frightful scenes. "Some of the women threw themselves from the balcony and landed on the marble floor below." On October 18, those like my grandparents who were not young but not yet sixty, were ordered to walk in convoys, carrying their heavy suitcases – there was a suitcase allowance of 55 kilograms each – to the Grunewald railway station several kilometres away. They were seated not in the cattle trucks of popular Holocaust imagination but in third-class carriages of a passenger train. Some food and water were provided by Jewish women volunteers. Once safely on board, the Jews chosen for deportation were no longer treated with the earlier, calculatedly deceptive "studied politeness". According to the November 1941 Eleventh Decree to the Reich Citizenship Law, all property of those who had already left Germany or would leave in the future belonged to the state. What my grandparents and others on the first train from Berlin believed would happen to them on arrival in the East is not known.

Lodz was Poland's second-largest city. Thirty-five per cent of its population, and 50 per cent of its large or middle-sized businesses, were Jewish. Following the German invasion many Jewish factories and apartments were seized. By April 1940 all the Jews of Lodz had been forced into a ghetto in an impoverished quarter of the city, surrounded by barriers and barbed wire. Lodz had no sewerage system. This meant that unlike the Warsaw Ghetto, which had sewer pipes allowing food, clothing and, later, arms to be smuggled into its ghetto, the Lodz Ghetto was hermetically sealed from the city. The Germans appointed Chaim Rumkowski as the Jewish leader of the ghetto. As the editor of *The Chronicle of the Lodz Ghetto* puts it: "Everyone and everything was subordinate to him there, and his power ended only when German authority began." Rumkowski oversaw the state-owned factories and workshops that served the German war machine; managed the distribution of food and the social welfare system of hospitals and aged-care homes; and created a cult of personality, comical in other circumstances, with himself as the compassionate but stern father-protector of the ghetto residents. It was into the surpassingly strange world of some 153,000 Polish Jews that some 20,000 German Jews – disproportionately female, well educated (there were at least 500 lawyers and magistrates) and elderly (more than half over fifty; one-third over sixty; 1,400 over seventy; and one ninety-six) – were dumped in late 1941.

The German Jews were settled in an abandoned school building in the poor Baluty quarter of the ghetto without adequate bedding, heating, running water or toilet facilities. At first, some were haughty. They had been promised comfortable housing. They were offered only this. Was there a hotel in Lodz? They had been promised suitable work. They were now being asked to lug sacks of vegetables or dispose of garbage and human excrement for a pittance. Rumkowski was mock-humble to be ruling over such highly educated people. "It is not easy for me – a simple Jew from Lodz – to speak before … people who represent the western intellectual elite." But he was also exasperated and harsh. "I will teach you how to work. I will wean you off your arrogance." "Aren't you ashamed that I have to use policemen to force you to work?" The presence of the German Jews – "forever hungry and searching for food" – was the subject of the gently humorous Yiddish hit song: "Es Geyt a Yekke mit a Tekke" – "Here Goes a *yekke* (the derisive name the Polish Jews gave their German brethren) with a Case" – sung by Herszkowicz, a Polish Jewish tailor, and Rosenzweig, a Viennese travelling salesman. But it also occasioned real bitterness. On the arrival of the German Jews the daily ration of bread was reduced from 33 grams to 28. Their arrival also distorted the Lodz Ghetto's political economy. As one of the authors of the Lodz Ghetto chronicle explained, the German Jews sold the goods they brought with them – "clothing, shoes, linen, cosmetics, travelling accessories" – and exchanged money orders they received in the post for ghetto currency, "Rumkis". They used the money to buy food, thereby creating galloping inflation and driving "the mass of working people" from the market.

Before arriving in the ghetto the German Jews, including no doubt my grandparents, had experienced privation. They now began to witness starvation. One of them wrote:

> Children gather around the school buildings where we live ... for hours they stand in the courtyards by the windows, waiting for someone to pour some soup into the bowls and pots they had brought ... They do not talk, just stare at you ... You are hungry but for the first time in your life you understand the meaning of the word "hunger" by looking into those eyes.

But they did not merely witness starvation. The death rate among the German Jews from diseases, primarily caused by lack of food and heat, was extraordinarily high – far higher than it was among the locals. Of the 19,953 German Jews transported to the Lodz Ghetto, 3,418 died between October 1941 and early May 1942. This accounted for half of all the ghetto deaths during these months. And of the deaths of German Jews, the rate among Berlin Jews was the highest. One was my maternal grandmother, Frida Meyer, who died on February 7, 1942.

In January 1942 a "resettlement" action began in the Lodz Ghetto – at first involving only the local Polish Jews. A rabbi from a nearby village, Jakub Szulman, learned what was happening to the deportees from someone who escaped. He described what he learned in a letter dated January 19, 1942, whose circulation thereafter is uncertain:

> An eye witness who by chance was able to escape from hell has been to see me ... The place where everyone is being put to death is called Chelmno ... Do not think that a madman is writing; unfortunately, it is the cruel and tragic truth (Good God!). O Man, throw off your rags, sprinkle your head with ashes, or run through the streets and dance in madness ...

GRANDPARENTS

The Chronicle of the Lodz Ghetto makes clear that while terror about what might be happening to those chosen for resettlement was almost universal, no one was willing to admit that those chosen were being murdered. The April 10–14, 1942, entry of the chronicle disclosed that it had now been "irrefutably established" that the 44,000 Polish Jews from the Lodz Ghetto resettled since mid-January had been sent to a work camp near the town of Kolo, which the Germans had left in "perfectly decent order", with "furniture for the Jews to use" and an "apparently exemplary" food supply. When several large trucks from the Chelmno extermination site entered the ghetto with neatly parcelled clothing, "[t]he people of the ghetto" did not draw the obvious inference but were merely "tremendously puzzled".

In late April, Proclamation 380 announced that the time for the resettlement of German Jews had arrived. The chosen were told to make their way to the Radogoszcz railway station with 12.5 kilograms of luggage each. One of the chroniclers observed people wearing "a few suits, a few changes of underwear and, quite frequently, two overcoats". When the chosen were about to board their train, a German official ordered them to step back five paces and to drop all their luggage. The chronicler observed that while several Polish Jews on earlier resettlements had "found ways of evading orders" the German Jews were entirely obedient. "For them an order issued by a uniformed authority is sacred." On the other hand, in a later chronicle entry it was conceded:

> [I]n these tragic moments before another journey into the unknown, the exiles from the West preserved their equanimity to a greater degree than have their brothers ... Lamentation, screaming and wailing at the final assembly points were characteristic features of the previous deportations, whereas during this deportation the Western European Jews made an outward display of considerably greater self-control.

There is an extraordinary entry in the Lodz chronicle for May 7, written by Józef Klementynowski, on the question of what the once entitled, sometimes arrogant Jews of six months ago had become:

[T]he soups they had scorned became the height of their dreams. Once it had been others, but then it was they who prowled the "city" with a cup or canteen on a chain to *schnorn* [beg] a little soup ... [O]nly half a year ... had proven an eternity for them! Some of the metamorphoses could not be imagined, even in a dream ... Ghosts, skeletons with swollen faces and extremities, ragged and impoverished, they now left for a further journey on which they were not even allowed to take a knapsack.

Otto Meyer was one of the Jews chosen for resettlement on May 8, 1942. He was taken on a 55-kilometre journey by train and then truck, leading to a manor house near the village of Chelmno. According to what was by now standard practice, the Jews who arrived here were advised by SS officers disguised in physicians' white coats that they would be sent for labour in Germany but first had to be washed and their clothing disinfected. In lots of fifty to seventy, naked Jews were led into a sealed truck and killed by the carbon monoxide gas produced by the exhaust. No doubt this is what happened to my grandfather. The bodies of the murdered Jews were then taken by lorry to a nearby forest and buried in prepared graves by a detachment of Jewish prisoners. Eventually, an unpleasant stench reached nearby villages.

*

My father's father, Joachim Manne, or Chaim, as he was called, was a Galician Jew born in 1872 and raised in Cracow, in the Polish lands of the Habsburg Empire. His family owned a substantial furniture manufacturing business, The Cracow Furniture Company (*Krakowska Fabryka Mebli*), whose records go back to 1860. For some reason, unknown to me, Chaim Manne migrated to the United States in 1900. Not long after, he married Leonora Hötchner, his first cousin, which was not uncommon then. In January 1904 my father was born in New York, always Henry so far as I know, never Heinrich. Chaim Manne failed in business in the Promised Land of America – a surprising fact I like to think helps explain my own almost spectacular lack of commercial acumen – and returned to Europe in 1910, not to Cracow but to Vienna, the capital of the Habsburg Empire. There he established his own furniture business, in part, it appears, as an agency for the Mannes' Cracow company and in part as a designer and manufacturer of furniture for individual, wealthy bourgeois clients. My father was expelled from his school in late 1918 at the age of fourteen for a joke that mocked the aged Habsburg emperor, Franz Josef: "The crown (the currency) is no Crown (Emperor)." As a child I learned, as part of family folklore, that from a very early age he ran the Vienna business.

On March 9, 1938, Henry Manne visited Prague to look over the exhibits at the International Sample Fair. Two days later, because of the defiance of the Austrian chancellor, Kurt Schuschnigg, who proposed a plebiscite on the independence of his nation, Hitler ordered German troops to enter Austria, a move forbidden under the terms of the Treaty of Versailles. It is well known that the German occupation of Austria was not only unopposed but welcomed joyously. It is not so well known that the *Anschluss*, as it was called, unleashed in Vienna, where 90 per cent of the nearly 200,000 Austrian Jews lived, a violent, vicious and lawless pogrom that historians have characterised as an "open season" on the Jews. *The Times*' correspondent for Central Europe, G.E.R. Gedye, estimated that on the night following the arrival of German troops, between 80,000 and 100,000 Viennese Nazis and pro-Nazi citizens terrorised those who lived in the Jewish quarter, Leopoldstadt. In the next weeks very many Jews, especially but not exclusively the well-to-do and the Orthodox with their beards and side-locks, were openly and brutally attacked in the streets or in their apartments. This was a pogrom of a kind not seen in Central Europe for centuries and not yet witnessed in Nazi Germany. (*Kristallnacht* was still almost nine months away.) As the historian Paul Schatzberg, who was in Vienna and was twelve years old at the time, puts it: "[I]t was as if a medieval monster had been released from the sewers beneath Vienna." Learning of this, my father decided not to return home from Prague.

The Jews of Vienna had played a disproportionately large role in the professions, the universities and the arts and owned one-quarter of Austrian companies. According to the minister of the Economy and Labor, Hans Fischbock, at least 25,000 Jewish businesses in post-*Anschluss* Austria were temporarily taken over and almost bled dry of their assets by those who were called "the wild commissars", while 7,000 were forced to close permanently. Shop owners were frequently obliged to paint the word *Jude* in large, pseudo-Hebraic letters on their front windows as a supposed warning to potential customers. The homes of many wealthier Jews were entered unlawfully and robbed – of money, jewellery, artworks, furs, clothing and furniture. Even the Reich commissioner appointed by Hitler to oversee the unification of Germany and Austria, Josef Burckel, conceded that "the shining history of National Socialism and the uprising in Austria has been tarnished to a certain extent by the plunder and larceny of the first few weeks". Hitler eventually issued an order for the lawlessness to stop.

The purpose was not only plunder but also public humiliation. Gedye saw Jewish families forced to "put scrubbing brushes in their hands ... and made to go down on their knees to scrub away for hours". Sometimes they were forced to clean the pavements of pro-Schuschnigg independence slogans with toothbrushes or with buckets of water laced with acid. Thugs cut off the beards of Orthodox Jewish men or ordered them to cut off their own beards. Synagogues were ransacked and the sacred Torah scrolls burned or torn up. The US consul in Vienna saw several hundred elderly Jews driven onto the Prater parklands and ordered to perform "endless calisthenics" and even to "eat grass". Gedye described the demeanour of some Jews after they had been brutalised, as "grey faced, with trembling limbs, eyes staring with horror and mouths that could not keep still". Some sixty Jews were arrested and sent to the German concentration camp Dachau. Several thousands more followed in May and June, usually for brief periods before they provided evidence of imminent emigration. Quite suddenly, in this way in the weeks following the *Anschluss*, the Jews of Vienna learned what it meant to be living in a lawless state without protection from the police.

Contemporary observers were aware that in March 1938 something new and disturbing was taking place in Vienna. In April, after visiting Austria, the British Zionist Leo Lauterbach wrote of the "terrible shock" the Viennese Jews had experienced because of the jeering crowds that "revealed to [the Jews of Vienna] that they lived not only in a fool's paradise but also in a veritable hell. No one who till then had known the average Viennese would have believed that he could sink to such a level." The ultimate ambition, he argued with prescience, "may be the complete destruction of Austrian Jewry".

A fortnight after the *Anschluss* a member of the US Consulate in Vienna, John C. Wiley, wrote to the White House that "practically all of the Jewish population is in a state of acute anxiety and depression". On April 6 he received a letter from an anonymous Viennese Jew, who signed as "one of the unhappy people who went through it personally", claiming that "hundreds and thousands of suicides occur which are not published in the newspapers". Thousands might have been an exaggeration; hundreds was certainly not. One careful study estimates that 220 Jewish suicides occurred in Vienna in March 1938. Another that the Jewish suicide figure for the first two months after the *Anschluss* was 500. According to Gedye, suicide among the Viennese Jews had become so commonplace that it was openly discussed as an option in a tone that could easily be mistaken for nonchalance. Nor was suicide in Vienna only an individual choice. There were several cases where families decided to die together. In one terrible instance, seven members of a family took poison. One son survived. As soon as he was released from hospital, he hanged himself. Wiley wrote of another family: "[O]ut of desperation resulting from the savage mistreatment of Jews, a certain Herr Bergman, proprietor of a large furniture store in the Praterstrasse (which had been plundered and taken over) killed himself, his wife, son, daughter in law and grandchild." To what degree these suicides were driven by fear of violence and humiliation or by despair and the loss of hope, it is impossible to say.

I do not know what happened to my father's family – Chaim and Leonora Manne and their younger son, Siegmund – in the two months following the *Anschluss*. Was their furniture business, like that of Herr Bergman, taken over and robbed by some of the "wild commissars" and then closed down? Was their apartment ransacked?

Did they witness or experience or merely learn about the street violence? All I know is that on May 15, 1938, in reality at a time when the ferocity of the Viennese pogrom had died down, the family tried to commit suicide with kitchen gas, and that while Leonora succeeded in taking her own life, both Chaim and Siegmund did not. My father learned of what happened. In a statement he prepared in 1943 for the Australian government while he was seeking naturalisation, he wrote: "My family in Vienna, consisting of my mother, my father and one brother, Siegmund, attempted suicide in May 1938 in Vienna. My mother died." There can be no doubt that the events of May 15 would have been dreadful beyond imagining. I once tried gently to discuss what had happened with Siegmund, my uncle, who arrived in Australia as a migrant in 1946. He could not. My impression was that Uncle Sigi, as I called him, never recovered from what had happened in his parents' Vienna apartment on May 15, 1938.

Between May 1938 and December 1939 117,409 Jews emigrated from the *Ostmark* (German-occupied Austria). At first to emigrate from post-*Anschluss* Austria – before the Eichmann "conveyor belt" was introduced – Jews had to apply at the central police station in Vienna for a passport; to join queues and fill out many complicated forms from many different government departments; to pay a bewildering series of costly taxes and charges for the privilege of leaving, the "flight tax" for example, before being granted a tax clearance; to obtain an entry visa from a willing government at a time when most doors were closed; and to purchase a ticket on a shipping line if the visa obtained was for a country beyond the European continent. After their failed suicide attempt, Chaim and Siegmund must have devoted considerable time and money to the task. According to my father's 1943 statement, by August 1938 they had succeeded. Siegmund had a passport from the German government and, presumably armed with an affidavit from a family member in the United States guaranteeing that he would not become a financial burden on the American taxpayer, a treasured United States migration visa. According once more to my father's statement, on his way to the US Siegmund decided to remain in Britain and, later, to serve in the British Army – according to family folklore, in the same regiment as the famed Central European writer Arthur Koestler. When I was a schoolchild, we were asked to observe a minute's silence on November 11, the First World War's Armistice Day. I tried to conjure an image of Uncle Sigi as a soldier. I did not find it easy.

In January 1940 the Jewish community organisation in Austria, the *Israelitische Kultusgemeinde*, assessed how many Jews still in Vienna were likely candidates for emigration. Of the 54,000 remaining it considered that 24,000 were not because of age, illness or impoverishment. It is almost certain that Chaim Manne belonged to the latter category. Like many elderly Jews – at the time of the *Anschluss* he was in his mid-sixties – his concern had been the safety of his sons. For the Jews remaining in Vienna the walls were now closing in. The policies were the same as in the *Altreich* – the bans on free movement; the relinquishing of cars, radios and private telephones; the inadequate food rations; the concentration of the Jews in often squalid semi-ghettoes; the blocked bank accounts; the addition of Jewish identifiers, "Israel" and "Sarah", to their names; the J stamp in their passports; and the order of September 19, 1941, for a yellow Star of David to be sewn on their clothing. By the European autumn of 1941 most Viennese Jews had virtually no income or wealth and were living on charity, most importantly that provided by the American Joint Distribution Committee, known as The Joint. This money supported fourteen soup kitchens, eight old people's homes and regular cash payments to 30,000 people.

In October 1941, as we have seen, Jewish policy throughout the expanded Reich changed from enforced emigration to deportation to the East and, ultimately, murder. The first train of the new, general mass deportation left Vienna on October 15, three days earlier than Berlin. This train and each that followed carried almost exactly 1,000 Jews. (The Germans were nothing if not methodical, even "Prussian", as the stereotype goes.) Their destinations were either established ghettoes, like Lodz and Riga; or the showpiece concentration camp for "privileged" or the elderly or war veterans, Theresienstadt; or newly established killing sites like Sobibor and Maly Trostinec. Auschwitz-Birkenau came a little later.

The Viennese Jewish community's *Kultusgemeinde* – the rough equivalent of the Berlin Jews' *Reichsvereinigung* – had co-operated with the Gestapo in the enforced emigration policy, even issuing severe warnings to Jews not to try to leave Vienna unlawfully. Now, as a seemingly natural extension of this co-operation, the Jewish leadership of Vienna, like the Jewish leadership in Berlin and indeed throughout the Reich, worked closely with the Gestapo in compiling lists leading not to rescue through emigration but to ghettoisation or murder. Although they did not know where they were going or why, the Jews remaining in Vienna lived in deepest fear of a deportation order. The correspondence of the Secher family has been published. On October 15, 1941, one member wrote: "It's that P. [Poland] Action again. You can imagine our anxiety and fear every morning as we await the mail – and what a sigh of relief when it does not bring us that dreaded order." The Jewish remnant in Vienna was probably now too old, ill-used, fearful and beaten for any organised resistance. Nonetheless a Jewish force of police irregulars, *Ordners*, was created to ensure full co-operation with the deportation orders.

Jews on the lists were ordered to assemble at a local school on *Castellezgasse 35*. They were required to surrender the keys to their apartments and their ration cards. The apartments of the deportees were ransacked and remaining valuable possessions removed. As the open trucks drove them to the Aspang railway station, onlookers often jeered. The trains were loaded from midday to four in the afternoon and departed at seven in the evening. By October 1942, the month the mass deportation program ended, a leader of the *Kultusgemeinde*, Dr Josef Loewenherz, reported proudly to his German superiors that 32,721 Viennese Jews had been successfully deported to the East. But to what end? For almost everyone in Vienna, even at this time, a settled policy of systematic and cold-blooded extermination was still beyond belief, unthinkable.

In September 1941 the Germans began the construction of a concentration camp on the grounds of a Soviet *kolkhoz*, or collective farm, "Karl Marx", near the Belorussian village of Maly Trostinec, 12 kilometres south-east of Minsk. According to the order of the chief of the

GRANDPARENTS

SD and the Security Police, Reinhard Heydrich, the principal purpose of the deportations to Maly Trostinec was death. From May 1942, trains bearing Jews from Vienna, Hamburg, Cologne, Konigsberg and also Theresienstadt arrived at the Minsk goods' railway station or, later, at a makeshift station closer to Maly Trostinec. On arrival, they were required to leave their suitcases, money and other valuables, for which they were given receipts. A very small number were selected for work at the concentration camp. The rest were told that they would be settled on estates around Minsk. These Jews were loaded onto trucks and driven to killing sites, one in the Blagovshchina forest. Here, after the removal of any secreted valuables, they were marched to trenches. As they were killed, music from gramophones and loudspeakers was broadcast to drown out the screams. Almost all the Maly Trostinec victims were shot, although in June 1942 four gas vans were introduced as an auxiliary means of killing. In total, according to the historian Christian Gerlach, 60,000 killings took place at Maly Trostinec. In total, 9,486 Viennese Jews were transported to Maly Trostinec. Of these, there were nine survivors.

The first transport from Vienna to Minsk left on May 6, 1942, and arrived on May 11 – once more, as in Berlin, in regular third-class passenger carriages, but then from the village of Volkovysk in cattle cars. Eighty-one were selected for work in the Maly Trostinec concentration camp. The remainder were driven to a killing site, stripped to their underwear, ordered to lie face-down in the mass grave that had been prepared for them and shot in the back of the neck. My paternal grandfather, Chaim Manne – a man who had done no ill to any man or woman – was one of them, murdered because he was a Jew. He was shot in Maly Trostinec in the same week as my maternal grandfather, Otto Meyer, was asphyxiated by carbon monoxide gas in Chelmno.

[2.]

Father

HAVING TRAVELLED TO PRAGUE ON MARCH 9, 1938, for an international trade exhibition three days before the *Anschluss*, and most likely having learned from his parents or brother about the vicious pogrom that followed, my father decided not to return to Vienna. I cannot recall him ever speaking to me of what he felt about the loss of family and home. In Prague, on March 24, he applied to the United States for a passport. Although he was born in New York and had spent his first six years there, he was eventually informed that he had lost all claim to US citizenship when his own father and family left the United States permanently in 1910. Unlike his brother, Sigi, who was not born in the United States and who was granted but did not use an American migrant visa, my father appears not to have sought entry to the US as a migrant or refugee.

Henry Manne spent six weeks in Czechoslovakia, travelled to London, and then, on April 29, 1938, left for South Africa on the SS *Cape Town Castle*. I have learned, from an *Age* article he wrote on December 15, 1945, "JOHANNESBURG – City of Gold", that he was disturbed by the way the indigenous peoples were treated by the whites.

> The natives, as the negro aborigines are called in South Africa, are segregated in four townships at the outskirts of the city or in mining compounds. They are not permitted to move around the city after 8 p.m. without a special permit from their employer.

They are despised by the Europeans and grossly neglected by the Government ... The natives are kept behind barbed wire in the compounds.

While in South Africa my father was obliged by the immigration authorities there to present at the German Consulate in Johannesburg and surrender his Austrian passport. He received its replacement, a German passport, on October 11, 1938. There are photos of this new passport in the "Henry Manne" file that the Department of Immigration created following my father's application for a permit to enter Australia. It was embossed with an eagle and a swastika. A large, red "J" (Jew) was stamped on its first page. (Oddly, this was originally a requirement of the government of Switzerland.) Henry knew how the Jews were being treated by the Nazis. By this time, it is almost certain that he had learned from his brother about his mother's suicide and the fearful loneliness of his father. Being required to accept a passport from Nazi Germany must have been a sickening experience.

My father applied for an Australian migration visa from Johannesburg on February 4, 1939. On paper he was eminently qualified. He was single, thus with no dependents, relatively young at thirty-five, and in good health. The policy of the Department of the Interior was that non-British migrants without nomination from an Australian citizen should be able to bring with them at least 200 pounds. In his application, my father let the department know that he was able to bring with him 1200 pounds, a considerable sum. The department wanted to ensure that non-British migrants would not compete with Australians for jobs. In his application my father nominated "Furniture Manufacturing and Interior Decorator" as his "proposed occupation in Australia". Most likely, he would not steal jobs but create them. Within the department and the government, and indeed within the nation, there was a deep prejudice against Polish or Eastern European Jews and a clear preference for Jews from Germany and Austria. Although his family's roots were in the Polish part of the Habsburg Empire (as my mother, a true Berlin *yekke*, observed scathingly more than once), my father came from Vienna and thus from the German cultural sphere. And although he had left school at the age of fourteen, he was not only fluent in English and German, but was also (if it mattered, and it probably didn't) a truly cultivated man. My father's application for permission to enter Australia was successful. He appears to have been a beneficiary of the recent Australian government decision to offer entry to 15,000 refugees over the next three years, although even without that policy decision his application would probably have been accepted. In August 1939 Henry Manne set sail from Cape Town for Australia aboard the SS *Troja*, as an Austrian refugee with a German passport who had been granted permission to settle in Australia. He arrived in Melbourne on September 7, four days after Australia joined Britain in its declaration of war on Germany, still as an Austrian refugee but soon with the additional legal status of "enemy alien".

Although my father was single when he reached Australia, he married almost immediately – not once but twice. His first marriage, on December 3, 1939, was to Ruth, a young German Jew from Berlin, whose maiden surname I do not know. Within a year they separated. I have no idea why. On March 1, 1944, Henry was granted an absolute divorce by an Australian court. Three days later he married my mother, Kate Rosalie Marie Meyer, a 37-year-old Jewish refugee, also from Berlin. Neither I nor my elder sister, who was born almost exactly nine months after the marriage of our parents, were told about the divorce and we only learned about it from one of the mischievous children of family friends. Divorce in 1950s Australia was still both rare and shameful.

In late 1939 or early 1940, at much the same time as his marriage to Ruth, my father established what he described in correspondence with the Department of the Interior as "a substantial furniture manufacturing business" at 114–18 Toorak Road, South Yarra. In early 1942, not long after the entry of the United States to the Pacific War against Japan following Pearl Harbor, my father was obliged to surrender his factory premises in Toorak Road to the Commonwealth government for use by the US Army. Curiously, I first learned about the existence of this business in the Department of the Interior's "Henry Manne" file.

I have no recollection of my parents ever talking about it. My father was now conscripted to wartime labour service, employed for two years or more as "a process worker" doing "shift work" in what he called a "highly important chemical factory" established by the US corporation Monsanto, in the inner-western working-class suburb of Braybrook. The Monsanto plant produced sulphanilamide, an antibacterial drug widely used in the pre-antibiotic age to treat infections.

My father first applied to the secretary of the Department of the Interior for "naturalisation" on May 20, 1942. He argued that because of the insistence of "the South African Immigration Authorities" he had been obliged to surrender his Austrian passport and to take a German one, but that because of a November 1941 decree of the German government that had "de-naturalised" and confiscated the property of all Jewish refugees, he was "stateless". As a consequence, he argued, "I should now be regarded as having reverted to my nationality by birth, that is U.S. citizenship, for the purpose of Aliens Registration". His application was supported by a two-page memorandum (in which I learned many things about his early history I had previously not known). In it he described the family's suicide attempt in Vienna and his brother's decision to remain in Britain while on his way to the United States. The memorandum continued:

> My relatives in Poland, one of whom was a captain in the Polish Army, fled first from Cracow to Lwow (East Poland) and nothing is known to me about their fate, if they are still alive or murdered by the Nazi beasts. The same applies to my father.

On May 26, 1942, the secretary of the Department of the Interior passed my father's application to the director-general of the Security Service. The Security Service was in no rush to rule on it. Almost a full year later, on May 13, 1943, an assistant inquiry officer in the Security Service, A. Fry, used the rubber stamp: "Security Service object to the grant of this application on the grounds" and then, entirely unmoved by the memorandum, wrote in his own hand that "there is nothing to warrant such a privilege being granted in war time". On June 25, 1943, an official of the Department of the Interior informed my father that after "careful consideration" the minister had "decided to withhold the grant of a Certificate of Naturalisation in your favour". The five pounds he had forwarded with his application would "be refunded in due course".

I know that my father felt genuine gratitude to the country that had offered him a home. However, I also have learned that being categorised as an "enemy alien" rankled. In part because of the plethora of restrictions it imposed: not to leave the police district where you lived; to report to the local police once a week (later, once a month); not to travel interstate or overseas without permission; not to change address without approval; not to hold any meetings or demonstrations; not to publish anything "in an enemy alien language"; not to own a wireless, motor car, motor boat or camera; not to possess firearms, ammunition or "cipher code or means of secret writing"; not to own a freehold or a long-lease property. Et cetera. (Anyone interested in this subject can read the crucial documents in Noel W. Lamidey's *Aliens Control in Australia: 1939–46*.) And in part it rankled because it made no sense. As my father wanted the authorities to understand, there was no group who had greater reason to feel hatred for Nazi Germany and its allies than Jewish refugees from Germany or occupied Austria, or to feel a truer and more sincere allegiance to the British Empire and its dominions that had been at war against Nazi Germany since September 1939. It was because of the pointless restrictions imposed on Jewish refugees, but even more because of the absurdity of regarding Jewish refugees from Greater Germany as enemy aliens, that my father first began to write.

As soon as he began writing articles for newspapers – remarkably enough, after one year in South Africa before arriving in Australia and having left New York at the age of six – my father meticulously cut out with a razor blade all his articles and letters-to-the-editor, almost always making sure that the name of the newspaper or magazine and the date of publication were included. He then placed these pieces as well as the transcripts of his several ABC radio broadcasts in a stout, three-inch-high brown cardboard box. Although over the years I browsed the contents occasionally and only read all the articles carefully in the past few years, the box has always been one of my most treasured possessions. It is because of the contents of that brown cardboard box that I am able not merely to imagine what my father must have thought and felt but, finally, to hear his adult voice and discover what he valued and what he feared.

The first cutting in the brown cardboard box was a long, angry and indignant letter-to-the-editor that *The Australian Jewish News* published on July 31, 1942, two months after my father's first naturalisation application. The context was the tension between the Jewish refugees, still regarded in law as "enemy aliens", and the organisation recognised by Canberra as the official body representing Jews, the Australian Jewish Welfare Society. (More information on this topic can be found in Michael Blakeney's excellent study *Australia and the Jewish Refugees*.) In 1939 the AJWS had warned the refugees from Germany and Austria: "[D]o not speak German in the streets and in the trams. Modulate your voices. Do not make yourself conspicuous anywhere by walking with a group of persons all of who [sic] are loudly speaking in a foreign language." In July 1942 it had criticised the "enemy alien" refugees for complaining about their treatment:

> There is no justification for the grossly exaggerated statements about the sorry state of the refugees. When the war is over and won then every privilege of naturalized Australians will readily be obtained by everyone who has earned the honour. Till then they must put up with some of the disadvantages and inconveniences which really do not amount to a fraction of those imposed on many Australians.

My father's letter, signed simply "Jewish Refugee", was in response to this statement:

> Some arguments of the A.J.W.S. are so excellent that they may be used by Anti-Semites against us! What a disgrace for Jews when they say: "... they (the refugees) must put up with some

disadvantages and inconveniences which really do not amount to a fraction of those imposed on many Australians." How untrue! We share all the restrictions imposed on Australians and many more.

The AJWS did not seem to understand that what the Jewish refugees were complaining about was that their "treatment" showed that they were considered to be "enemies" and even "an inferior people". Refugees had "even more cause to hate the Nazis than the average Australian citizen".

Nonetheless, "[s]cores of refugees had to close down their businesses or factories, hundreds had to leave their jobs". They were not able to visit public libraries or even to see their friends. Why? "We want to share duties as well as priviliges [sic] with Australians without discrimination. That's all we want ... What has this treatment to do with National Security? Nothing whatsoever," my father wrote. The Welfare Society clearly had no idea that most refugees were dissatisfied with the "humiliating conditions" imposed upon them. "We wish only that the A.J.W.S. should stop bothering about our affairs and stop interfering."

It is probable that after writing this letter-to-the-editor, my father was invited by *The Australian Jewish News* to write an article expanding on its theme. The article that followed, the second in the brown paper box, was so long that it was published over three editions of the *AJN*, on August 14 (where it was the lead article on the front page), and then August 21 and 28, 1942. We have arrived at "a situation never before known in the history of modern times", the article announced. "It is quite indifferent what nationality a Jew has. He can only be an enemy of Hitler's Government and the Axis because their defeat is his only hope of survival." Anyone who did not understand this was either "an ignoramus" or an "anti-Semitic ... fifth columnist". More interestingly, the article argued without ambiguity of any kind that Hitler's policy was the extermination of the Jews. "Hundreds of thousands" of European Jews had been sent to "concentration camps in Germany and Poland and to ghettos to starve, to perish, to be tortured and murdered". And: "[N]ever in his career did Hitler compromise on the Jewish question. For 20 years *his ambition was to destroy the Jews and he predicted their extermination by the end of this war*" [my emphasis]. The sub-editor at the *AJN* grasped the meaning of what was being said with the section heading: "HITLER'S AIM COMPLETE EXTERMINATION".

Today everyone knows that complete extermination of European Jewry was indeed the policy of the Nazi state. Since mid-1942, the Jewish bearers of this frightful message, Shmuel Zygielbojm, Dr Ignacy Schwarzbart and Dr Gerhart Riegner, had been struggling to convince Western governments and peoples and even Jewish leaders, in large part unsuccessfully, that the attempted extermination of the entire Jewish population of Europe, a crime still without a name, was taking place. In the summer of 1943 Jan Karski, an eyewitness to the conditions inside the Warsaw Ghetto and a staging camp for one of the extermination camps, Belzec, met with the United States Supreme Court judge Felix Frankfurter. In what later became a famous exchange, Karski told Frankfurter of the horrors he had seen and explained their meaning. Frankfurter admitted that he was not convinced. When challenged by the ambassador of the Polish government-in-exile, he replied: "I did not say he was lying. I said I could not believe him. There is a difference." In 1964, Hannah Arendt, the great political theorist who had escaped from Nazi Germany in 1933, told her German television interviewer that neither she nor her husband, the military historian Heinrich Blücher, had truly grasped until 1945 when Allied troops arrived at the German concentration camps, Nazi Germany's attempted extermination of the Jews of Europe. In his study of this question, *The Terrible Secret: Suppression of the Truth About Hitler's Final Solution*, Walter Laqueur quotes a comment from a Protestant theologian, W.A. Visser 't Hooft, who tried to explain his own and others' difficulty in accepting the evidence of those who understood what was happening to the Jews of Europe. "[P]eople could find no place in their consciousness for such an unimaginable horror ... [T]hey did not have the imagination, together with the courage, to face it."

I was astonished when I first read my father's article of August 1942. Somehow, he did have the imagination and the courage to face what was happening to his family and to his people. It was probably because of his unusually early recognition of the exterminatory ambition of the Nazis' Jewish policy that the editor of *The Australian Jewish News* prefaced the publication of my father's article of August 1942 with an apology to his readers.

> We publish below an article by a Jewish refugee from Hitlerism, which though provocative contains many painful truths – painful for some members of the community. The theses are those with which we concur. If the expression is a little strong, just indignation arising out of obvious reasons, as well as a sub-conscious feeling of aloneness – a veritable "orphan of the storm" feeling – are its foundations, with which we fully sympathise.

Ten months later, on June 10, 1943, shortly after my father had been informed that his naturalisation application had been turned down, he wrote another letter-to-the-editor, this time to *The Jewish Herald*, and this time signed Henry Manne. The context was a debate taking place at the University of Melbourne concerning the possibility of employing racial quotas for entry to certain faculties. The question of "numerus clausus", as it was called – one of the causes championed by the Austrian Nazi Party – was acutely sensitive for any Austrian Jew. Jewish refugees, my father argued, were "grateful for the lucky fate of having been able to emigrate from the shambles of Europe to these shores and wish only to become full citizens to share the responsibilities and priviliges [sic] of all other Australians". (He still had not learned how to spell "privileges".) He was, however, especially interested in R.T.J. Galbally's claim about alien refugees who "owe no allegiance to our flag" and who "doubtless cherish the memories of their native soil and will, at the earliest opportunity, make every endeavour to return whence they came". In response my father wrote for the first and only time, so far as I am aware, about the meaning of what he had lost.

> We (and all human beings) cherish more than anything else our family, our friends, our brethren. And can it be assumed that Mr Galbally and his sympathisers do not know what happened to our brethren in Europe? Can we but curse the soil which bred scores of thousands of murderers of our people? And does he expect us to return to a country where we are sure to meet a murderer of our brethren or the murderer of our mother, our father, our sister or our brother any day, and any hour? To return to a soil whose dwellers are more alien and hostile to us than anyone else upon this world? No – I cannot imagine any sensible human being wishing to return to the country of the murderers of his people.

I never heard my father speak like that about his loss of family and home. I wish I had.

In September 1942 the Labor government's attorney-general, Dr Evatt, appointed what was called the Aliens Classification and Advisory Committee, under the chairmanship of Arthur Calwell. In its Interim Report of March 1943, the committee argued for the creation of a new legal category, "refugee alien". It accepted the view:

> ... strongly urged upon us, that it is both unjust and unwise to label as an "enemy alien" a person of enemy origin whose hatred and opposition to an enemy Government arises from bitter personal experience of persecution and oppression, actual or threatened, designed to and resulting in his expulsion from the nation of which he was formerly a subject ... We point out that under the conceptions which are firmly established in this community such people as these have certain rights as human beings.

In a largely bloodless report this was the sole paragraph showing civic passion. After what the secretary of the Aliens Classification and Advisory Committee described as "a long and protracted struggle", eventually "the views of the Committee prevailed". On November 22, 1943, under the new policy of the Labor government, my father, alongside some 6,000 others, was given the new legal status of "refugee alien". He applied once more for naturalisation. An official of the Ministry of the Interior advised him to answer the question of previous nationality not as a German but as stateless. This time the application was successful. He received his certificate of naturalisation on August 15, 1944.

By this time my father seems truly to have felt he had found a home in Australia. His greatest love was music. A short (undated) newspaper article in the brown cardboard box reported the existence of The Recorded Music Society, a small group of enthusiasts who met most Thursdays "in the rooms of the British Music Society" in Collins Street, Melbourne. The sixth meeting was devoted to the English composers Butterworth, Bliss and Elgar. Shortly there would be a concert of 2,000 years of music, from the Greeks to Palestrina. "Mr Henry Manne is the driving force behind the society, and it is from his magnificent library of 2,100 records that most of the recordings are drawn." On December 15, 1944, *The Australian Jewish News* reported another record recital for a women's Zionist group organised by Henry Manne on "Highlights from the Vienna Opera". "Selma Kurz – records of which are completely unknown in this country were so much applauded that Mr. Manne had to play an encore." Earlier that year my father had argued (under a pseudonym he used) the case for a national theatre in each state of Australia. It concluded with these words: "If we want to further an Australian culture, we must insist upon a Commonwealth-wide movement to make the theatre a force in our social life, and one that will become a rich influence in our development as a civilised nation." (K.H. Munter, "Case for National Theatres", *The Herald*, July 25, 1944.) K.H. Munter was a pseudonym, the maiden name of my mother's mother. The "we" reveals how confident he already was that he was an Australian, or what would be called in my childhood a New Australian.

In February 1944, at a time when he was still a process worker at the Monsanto factory at Braybrook, despite the fact that English was very much his second language, despite the fact that he had left school at the age of fourteen, despite the fact that so far as I know he did not publish one word in Vienna, my father began writing for newspapers and magazines. Over the next three years he wrote more than one hundred articles. He wrote regularly, fortnightly or even weekly for *The Age Literary Supplement*, the upmarket section of the paper that appeared on Saturday. His were frequently the *Supplement*'s leading articles, published on its front page. Almost always they concerned the history, culture, economy and current geopolitical significance of a region in Eastern Europe, the Balkans or Western Europe, and very occasionally in Asia or the Pacific – whichever was in the news because of the progress of the war or as points of tension in the early post-war world. He also wrote regularly for the weekend literary section of *The Age*'s rival newspaper in Melbourne, *The Argus*, and for the magazine connected with it, *The Australasian*. These articles usually concerned music, painting and sculpture, literature, furniture or architecture. He also had a great interest in significant raw materials, oil, gold and timber. My father also wrote occasionally in *The Australian Jewish News*, including two substantial pieces on the Jewish contribution to music and painting. Sometimes his angle of interest was unusual. He wrote on Tolstoy as a dramatist. On Zionism, he wrote about not Theodor Herzl but Baron Hirsch, the Jewish philanthropist who devoted a considerable part of his fortune to the search for a national home for the Jews but not in Palestine. Occasionally he wrote for Melbourne's afternoon paper, *The Herald*. And perhaps his most important pieces were two treatises on contemporary furniture for *Australian Home Beautiful*.

Most of these articles were lengthy – between 1,500 and 3,000 words or even longer. There were periods when he was extraordinarily prolific. In July 1944, still a factory worker, he published six articles – on Umbria, Prussia, Eastern Poland and Latvia for *The Age Literary Supplement*; on the birth of opera in Florence for *The Argus*; and the article arguing the case for Australian national theatres for *The Herald*. On his wedding day, March 4, 1944, not one but two of his articles were published, on General Franco's "totalitarian" Spain for *The Age* and on Nicolai Rimsky-Korsakov for *The Argus*. He also delivered between 1944 and 1946 several broadcasts for the ABC – on furniture, Jewish music, the strategic importance of oil and the progress of the wars in the Balkans and the Pacific. In the second half of 1946 the number of articles fell away. I assume that he was busy establishing his second furniture factory, in Lygon Street, North Carlton. After February 1947 he did not publish another word.

My father died when I was ten – or, as I would have said at the time, ten and a half. I was too young to have any understanding of what in German is called his *Weltanschauung*, his worldview. Apart from his argument about the absurdity of treating Jewish refugees as enemy aliens, he wrote only a very small number of what might be called opinion pieces – his case for publicly subsidised national theatres and his heartfelt advocacy of truly contemporary furniture. Nonetheless, throughout his geopolitical regional portraits for *The Age* and his cultural pieces for *The Argus* and *The Australasian*, various comments helped me understand his picture of the political world. Unless otherwise specified, the quotes in the following section come from my father's writings for *The Age* (mostly the *Literary Supplement*), *The Argus*, *The Australasian* and *The Australian Jewish News* between 1944 and 1947.

Most fundamental in his writing, not surprisingly, was his hatred of the Nazi regime that had brought such destruction to humanity. He wrote with uncharacteristic emotion in an article called "West of the Vistula", which was the land of his Cracow family. On this soil there had been many previous "pathetic scenes of misery and agony, until the Nazi monsters succeeded in bringing their sadistic barbarity to its unsurpassable climax by slaughtering millions of harmless human beings of all sexes and ages, eternity's silent witnesses of the Germans' evil instincts and utter depravity".

One of his heroes was the great German writer Thomas Mann, whose eyes had only opened gradually to the nature of the age, progressing from a typically apolitical Wilhelmine German conservatism to become one of the world's most important anti-Nazi voices. In a wonderful article about Mann, my father quoted with complete approval the "bitter words" that Mann addressed in a broadcast to "his former countrymen": "The world shudders at the sight of Germany … Germany stands today as the abomination of mankind and the epitome of evil ... Do not regard yourselves primarily as Germans, but as men and women returned to humanity."

My father regarded the Nazi regime as heir to the tradition of the Prussian landed nobility, the Junkers, the "remnant of feudal Europe ... the prototype of the military aristocracy". The province of Pomerania had "given its grenadiers to the Prussian Army." "[I]ts contribution to Germany's artistic and spiritual achievements were absolutely nil." The greatest tragedy in German history was the Kingdom of Prussia's military victory in 1867 over the Austrian Empire: "With the Hohenzollern's victory over the Habsburgs, German ultra-nationalism of the Prussian type conquered the cosmopolitan spirit of Austria. Thus the way was prepared for the supreme tragedy of Europe." On the basis of this military victory in 1867, "Bismarck realised his great idea ... a strongly unified German empire, as the stepping stone in the German dream to dominate the whole world."

In part, my father accepted the Marxist materialist interpretation of Nazism as the regime that served the interests of the Prussian landed classes and the steel and armaments industries of the Ruhr: "The steel magnates, of course, supported a cause which was bound to start an armaments race ... These abettors of the Nazi murder gang are largely responsible for the great catastrophe inflicted consciously upon humanity." (He was, after all, a subscriber of the Left Book Club.) But he was also aware of the similarity between the peculiar atmosphere in which Nazism took hold and the previous outbursts of religious fervour that a later historian, Norman Cohn, would call *The Pursuit of the Millennium.* In his article on Westphalia, my father pointed out that the "mass madness" of the Anabaptists "shows a distinct analogy to the hysteria of the present German generation which enabled Nazism to establish itself". And he was also open to the interpretation of Nazism as a profound perversion of spirit. "As Hitler often said to his friends – 'Whoever wants to understand National Socialist Germany must know Wagner.' Hence the musician's morbid philosophy explains more than hundreds of volumes on the German soul." My father understood and loathed Wagner's anti-Semitism. His article on the Jewish contribution to music began with a discussion of his notorious and influential 1850 pamphlet, *Judaism and Music*, in which, "disregarding all historical facts and all forms of decency and justice, Wagner contended that the Jews are not a people, but a group of parasites and middle men". Nonetheless, my father loved Wagner's music and played it loudly on his gramophone, a reliable source of quarrels between him and my mother. It is interesting to me that an article written in 1946, "You Will Remember Vienna", showed that my father had maintained his love for the city – its coffee houses, its parks, its Sunday mountain retreats and, above all, its theatres. "The Viennese ... still read first the repertoire of theatres in their morning papers, just as the Australian reads first the racing news!" He wondered whether the city would be able to retain its character without its 180,000 pre-war Jewish population. But he obviously blamed the Germans, not the Viennese, for the outburst of vile anti-Semitism unleashed by the *Anschluss* that had led to his mother's suicide.

My father was not only convinced by mid-1942 that the Germans were attempting to exterminate the Jews of Europe, he was also aware of the two most recent twentieth-century historical antecedents of what would now be termed genocide. In an article "by a Special Correspondent" on the situation in the Middle East, he described in some detail the "wholesale murder" by the Ottoman Turks of 1 million Armenians. And in an article on South West Africa, he wrote about the "abominable atrocities" the German army committed against the Herero people, with "a large number ... including women and children ... driven into the desert, where they perished for want of food and water". Unsurprisingly, my father was also sensitive to the plight of refugees in history. While "fate has often taken a savage revenge on persecutors of minority victims", England had shown a famous generosity to people in search of asylum. As he argued, "[T]he growth of British democracy – which led Europe in liberal thought – made England a by-word as a refuge for the homeless and oppressed." He recognised, however, that the world had a "short memory" for the "misery" experienced by refugees and, in a striking phrase that most likely reflected his own recent experience as an enemy alien, that it is not long before "suffering people become a nuisance only".

(My father's concern for refugees was passed to me and to his grandson, David Manne, who with principle and dedication has devoted his professional life to legal work on behalf of refugees.)

Because of my own political history, I was curious to learn about my father's attitude to the Soviet Union and the communist movement. During the war it was overwhelmingly positive. Karl Marx was described as "the spiritual father of the Soviet Union, a personality whose doctrines have borne and are bearing more influence on current world history than any political event in the last century". With the creation of the communist state, after the October 1917 revolution, "much suffering, a humiliating peace with Germany, famine and years of effort were to follow, but the torch had been lit". Wartime Russia was described as "our great ally" and "unconquerable", and its armies as "avalanches crushing everything beneath them". Quite mistakenly, my father believed that Latvians would "welcome the advancing Red Army and their pro-Soviet government returning from exile in Russia" and that Tito's Partisans were "democratic" and his conception of Yugoslavia was "based on the principle of the Atlantic Charter" (ABC broadcast, c.January 1945). There was no mention of the crimes of Stalin during the collectivisation of agriculture and the Great Terror.

As the first signs of the Cold War emerged, my father's judgements about the Soviet Union and communism shifted. He was critical of both Tito's claim to Trieste and the Soviet Union's claims on Tripolitania. He was pleased that in Austria's first post-war election, only two communist candidates were successful. Clearly my father could not be described as an anti-communist. But as soon as cracks within the wartime alliance appeared, he proved to be an Anglo-American Atlantic Charter man.

My father had what might be called a Western bias, a kind of premonitory pre-NATO world-picture. Because of its liberalism, he argued, "Holland is a great country." The Danes are "the most democratic people of Europe". France's "La Marseillaise" was "not only the beloved national anthem of the French people but ... also a hymn of all liberty loving workers of the world". If there was any possibility for Germany to overcome its militaristic and authoritarian historical legacy it lay with the "democratic and liberal tendencies" of the Rhineland in the west of Germany. My father argued that "[t]he greatness of England is based on a national characteristic of tolerance and foresightedness combined with a practical understanding of economic factors throughout the centuries". And he quoted with evident approval an argument of Thomas Mann's that prefigured the thought that would hold the Anglo-American and Western European alliance together throughout the Cold War: "I am not afraid to state openly that the Americanisation of the world, in a certain fundamental moral sense, would be a good fortune for mankind." My father evidently had great faith in the country of his birth. He was also, however, guilty of the extremely common wartime political bias identified by George Orwell in his essay "Notes on Nationalism". He condemned certain actions of his enemy "nation" (the Axis) while praising the almost identical actions of his own "nation" (the Grand Alliance). Of Germany's bombardment of Warsaw from the air, he wrote. "[T]ens of thousands of innocent civilians [have been] mercilessly slaughtered." However, like almost everyone on the Allied side during the war, he supported without reservation the mass bombing of both Germany and Japan. "[L]and bases nearer to Japanese soil ... will give us the chance to subject the industrial heart of Japan and her lifelines of communications to an intensive and continuous bombing on a scale equal to the terrific attacks on Germany's industrial regions" (broadcast on ABC, 3LO, January 23, 1945).

In May 1946 my father made a clumsy mistake, submitting two articles on a new gold rush in South Africa, one to *The Age* and one, under the pseudonym K.H. Munter, to *The Argus*. The articles were different but there was some overlap – not in lines or paragraphs but in some seminal facts and in the interpretation of the place of gold in the history of South Africa. This overlap was quite unusual: in the hundred or so articles published in the previous two years there had been nothing remotely like this. The editor of *The Argus* magazine, Bruce Kneale, wrote to my father, describing the situation as "most unsatisfactory" and claiming, incorrectly, that the articles were "practically identical". As a consequence, he wrote, "I shall be obliged ... if you will refrain in future from bringing, or sending in further articles to me, as I shall only be compelled to reject them." There was not a word of thanks for the many articles of his *The Argus* and *The Australasian* had published over the past two years. Six days later my father received a similar letter from the editor of *The Australasian Post*. I do not know whether he replied to either letter. What I do know is that this was the one and only time he placed the original typescripts sent to *The Age* and *The Argus* in the brown cardboard box. Perhaps he hoped that someone, maybe even his son, would one day read them and see that he had been treated unfairly. While I was still a young boy my father spoke to me about this incident. He seemed amused. I suspect now, however, that this was feigned. My father was a proud man.

In the following few months he wrote a few rather desultory articles for *The Age Literary Supplement*, but my guess is that his hopes were elsewhere, focused on the new furniture business he was re-establishing in North Carlton. Nonetheless I am certain that the articles he stored so carefully mattered to him greatly. As they should have. These articles reveal the breadth of his interests. He could write confidently about European history, politics, music, literature, the fine arts, architecture and, of course, furniture. They also reveal his energy. Between early 1944 and mid-1946, his more than 100 newspaper and magazine articles and his several radio broadcasts amounted to more than 250,000 words. In the first few months, he combined his journalism with work in the Monsanto chemicals factory. I have no idea how he managed. Factual accuracy mattered to him greatly. As a small child I remember a newly-arrived-immigrant dispute between my mother and father on the spelling of "playwright". My mother thought it was "playwrite". My father knew the correct spelling. After the disagreement was swiftly resolved by consulting my father's huge US *Webster's Dictionary*, my mother told me how much she admired my father's scrupulousness. This was a lesson I never forgot.

In his journalism he revealed not only mastery of detail but also the capacity for broad historical sweep. Here is a passage from his article "Opera Was Invented in Florence":

The development of opera reflects the various political and cultural changes of European society. Baroque, with its stage effects, the Da Capo aria, the Golden Age of Bel Canto were the artistic expression of absolute monarchy. The liberal spirit of the Age of Reason and the French Revolution was represented by Gluck's reformed classic operas, by the appearance of folk operas, and the revolutionary operas of Mozart and Beethoven. The political reaction after the Congress of Vienna created the grand opera of Rossini, Donizetti and Meyerbeer, showing the splendour of the stage and artistic devices, while the intrinsic value of the music was small.

The revolutions of 1848 and the rise of nationalism were expressed by the vigorous dramatic works of Verdi and Wagner. Naturalist tendencies brought forth Bizet's *Carmen* and later created the Italian "verismo" with Leoncavallo's *Pagliacci*, Mascagni's *Cavalleria* and Puccini. Impressionism was shown by Mussorgsky's *Boris Goudonov* and Debussy's *Pelleas and Melisande*. Psychology was put into Strauss's *Salome* and *Electra* and into Stravinsky's ballets. The wave of realism which followed the last war introduced jazz into Krenek's *Jonny Plays Up* and Gershwin's *Porgy and Bess*. The light genre from Lecocq, Offenbach, Johann Strauss and Sullivan down to Lehar, Kalman and Abraham was constantly influenced by contemporary society.

Although my father had grasped by mid-1942 the contemporary tragedy of European Jewry, unprecedented in history, I am surprised by how infrequently in his journalism the subject was touched upon – perhaps four or five brief mentions in over 250,000 words. We have already seen his description of Nazi barbarity in his article "West of the Vistula". In February 1945, K.H. Munter wrote: "The unfortunate Jews, constituting about a fifth of the population [of Cracow], were sent to death in concentration camps." In March 1946, Henry Manne wrote:

> [T]he 180,000 Jews then living in Vienna were one of the driving forces against Nazi products. Only time will tell how the

disappearance of all but a few thousand Jewish citizens, who trickled back from the concentration camps and from hiding places, will affect the commercial, artistic and social life of Vienna.

There was little more about the fate of his people than this. I am not sure why he wrote so little. Perhaps he feared the indifference or scepticism of his readership. Perhaps he was concerned that discussion of the Jewish catastrophe would look like special pleading. Or perhaps when he started writing for a general public in February 1944, he recognised that nothing except the victory of the Grand Alliance could now be done to save the Jewish remnant in Europe.

I am certain that this brown cardboard box affected my life. In my mind it represented my father's intellectual labour and evidence of the kind of scholarly life he might have lived if circumstances had been different. When I examined the contents of the box carefully for the first time a few years ago, I discovered that in late 1965 I had placed one item in it: a letter of congratulation on my matriculation results from John Levi, the rabbi at Temple Beth Israel. What that gesture meant, I suppose, is that I intended to continue what my father had been able, for a short time in his disrupted life, to begin.

[3.]

Childhood and Adolescence

MY MOTHER, KATE ROSALIE MARIE MEYER, married my father, Henry Manne, on March 4, 1944, three days after his divorce from Ruth became absolute. Nine months later my sister was born. On October 31, 1947, it was my turn. There were no more children, unsurprisingly, as my mother was now one month short of forty. Kate's middle-class Berlin family was comfortable enough to have employed a nanny, Paulschen – to whom, as my mother once confided, she felt closer than to her mother. Unlike my father, Kate did finish school and completed some kind of tertiary diploma in domestic science. For a brief time she was a communist and for another brief time a Zionist. More permanently, her politics were moderate but left-wing. One of our family's stories concerned the time she refused to allow my father – a small-businessman at the time, after all – to vote for Robert Menzies. Another of my mother's favourite stories was how she and fellow students had torn down the pro-Hindenburg posters before the German presidential election of 1925. General Hindenburg was a military hero and the candidate of conservative Germany.

Like my father, Kate was the beneficiary of the Menzies government's decision to take 15,000 refugees. (In his autobiography, Wilfred Burchett, the Australian communist journalist, writes about assisting Jews to escape to Australia from Nazi Germany. It is therefore remotely possible that my mother was one of those Jews Burchett helped, something that niggled when I was writing, decades later, about Burchett's enthusiasm for the blood-drenched regimes of Stalin, Kim Il-Sung and Mao.) Kate's journey to Australia was uneventful, except for the potentially disastrous matter of losing her papers temporarily while in Amsterdam. She arrived in Perth in September, 1939. Sometime after, she had a terrible accident at her place of work, spilling a pot of boiling oil on her upper leg. This landed her in hospital for some months and left a very large scar. How she managed to survive the pain and the loneliness of this time I do not know. All I know is that after her recovery she decided to travel to Melbourne, and that there she met and married my father. I am almost certain that she did not learn then or later what exactly had happened to her parents, although of course she knew that both had died at the hands of the Nazis. Her younger brother, Hans, my mother's only surviving close relation, joined Kate from Sweden in December 1946. Hans was a simple and good man, who worked in a delicatessen in the Prahran market. Despite much encouragement from my mother, Uncle Hans never married. Relations between them were sibling-tense. I still recall an uncharacteristic explosion after my mother criticised the way he was cutting my fingernails. Hans loved me dearly and I believe he knew I loved him. One of our joint pleasures was walking together with me standing on his feet. In some ways he understood me better than did my father. Henry tried to interest me in the rather dismal Victorian soccer competition and in barracking for Hakoah, the Jewish team. Hans was, by contrast, responsible for perhaps the most consequential decision I took before the age of five – unconditional (and, as it turned out, lifelong) support for the Geelong Football Club. In the early 1950s Geelong was the Victorian Football League's most powerful team, and my uncle suggested supporting them as he wanted me to be happy. Alas – in the fifty-five years between 1952 and 2006 they were premiers only once. Then again, after 2007 his hope for me was rather belatedly fulfilled. Uncle Hans died of cancer in 1974. His cancer was the principal reason I returned to Melbourne from London at that time. In his last days I did some shopping for him, and I have never forgotten his anguish and my shame when I once forgot to buy him butter. When

I first heard a line of Bob Dylan's "Po' Boy", "My uncle ... did a lot of nice things for me and I won't forget him", I almost wept.

My parents first lived in St Kilda, the suburb of choice for many German and Austrian Jews. (Polish Jews generally settled first in Carlton.) When I was four we moved to East Ivanhoe, where there were almost no other Jews. By this time my father had established a furniture factory, or really an old-fashioned Viennese-style workshop, in Lygon Street, North Carlton. Here, skilled European craftsmen built custom furniture that my father designed, mostly for Jewish or European clients. For some time, the business must have been doing well, or at least well enough for him to purchase a block of land on The Boulevard in East Ivanhoe, where young professional or business families had settled or were settling, and to have provided the plan for a rather splendid and, for the time, quite unusual two-storey, flat-roofed house.

This house was filled with furniture of his design in what he called the Modern International Style, which turned its back on the fashion of both the nineteenth and early twentieth centuries – dark-stained period furniture, with its "imitation of all styles of bygone ages" and tacked-on ornamentation – and its early-twentieth-century successor – harsh, purist functionalism. The furniture he designed for his clients and for his family was the kind he had championed in articles for *Australian Home Beautiful* and in an ABC broadcast – functionalism softened by gracious and elegant "slightly rounded forms"; unstained hardwoods (in his new country, "Tasmanian Oak, Queensland Maple and Silver Ash"); light, easily moved armchairs upholstered with the kind of "strong and vivid colours" found in the paintings of Van Gogh; comfortable dining room chairs with curved backs, cane and seats 15.5 inches from the floor (he was nothing if not precise); dining room tables that could be extended or folded away; nests of tables; built-in wardrobes at least 22 inches deep; and beds that doubled as couches (for his children; not for Henry and Kate). It is one of my life's deepest disappointments that I no longer own any of this furniture. My father also designed for his new home a beautiful curving wood banister for the staircase. (I was always nervous about bringing friends home, a feeling validated when one of them ran his metal-wheeled Dinky car up and down the banister, leaving indentations.) Of all the rooms, I remember most clearly the spacious upstairs room where my father designed his clients' furniture and where his substantial book and record libraries and a large wooden gramophone were found. Every Saturday afternoon during the football season, I was allowed to occupy this room alone to listen to the broadcasts of the Geelong games (on the local station, 3GL) and record in an exercise book our players' kicks, marks, goals and behinds. It was my first scholarly activity where both head and heart were fully engaged. I remember too in the early days the rush for pots and pans to catch the rainwater before it leaked onto the carpets or the Persian rugs. For a builder in the early 1950s, flat roofs were still, evidently, quite a challenge.

In his ABC furniture broadcast of November 1944, my father argued:

> [A] friendly surrounding will impart pleasure and comfort to its owner and make his life more happy and joyful. So let us insist on better designed and thought-out furniture for our New World. To waste our limited means and resources on shoddy out-of-date furniture of a hideous appearance would be a most deplorable national calamity in the cultural field. Let us develop the furnishing of our homes into an art concerned with the pursuit of happiness and beauty.

I will never know what my parents said to each other about the monstrous crimes that had been committed against their own parents and their people. I assume they decided not to speak to their children about the events that became known as the Holocaust, a decision which in my case had almost the opposite effect to the one apparently intended. What impresses me most, but also somewhat puzzles me, is how they managed to create together a moment of happiness in their own New World in Australia. Together they designed, furnished and decorated a home. At this home there were regular family gatherings. Although neither of my parents were observant, we celebrated Passover with Uncle Sigie and his family, our standing joke being the reliable lateness of their arrival. Uncle Hans was at our home much more frequently, arriving on his motorised bicycle. There were also frequent parties with their almost universally European but not necessarily Jewish friends, which included, if my memory does not fail me, one of the local Monsanto executives, from the chemical plant where my father had been a wartime process worker.

My father unsurprisingly remained an avid collector of records – he must have been one of the best customers of John Clements' city record store, buying classical music and opera, of course, but also Broadway musical comedies – *Showboat, Oklahoma!, South Pacific, Carousel, Annie Get Your Gun* – during the genre's golden age. He was no music snob. Even while his business absorbed so much of his energy, he took me and my sister to an opera season – Verdi's *Il Trovatore*, Bizet's *Carmen*, Rossini's *The Barber of Seville* and one of the great Mozart operas, from memory *The Marriage of Figaro* – but also several musical comedy films. Our home overflowed with books. My father was a voracious reader of serious non-fiction, my mother of novels and dramas. Each year she bought and read an annual collection: *The Best American Plays*. Each month or week magazines came in the post – *Time, Life, National Geographic, Woman's Day, The Women's Weekly* and no doubt many others. Each day it was newspapers – *The Age, The Argus*, perhaps (I cannot remember) *The Herald*. My contribution was *The Sporting Globe*, which I collected at the newsagency on Saturday evenings during the football season to read all about the match I had just attentively listened to.

My mother was an avid gardener – her favourite flower was the forget-me-not, her favourite bush the nondescript but sweet-scented native boronia. She was also an excellent cook. During these years we always had the finest meats, breads, ham (yes, ham), salami, sausage, cheese, (Melitta) filter coffee, the tastiest biscuits, dry and sweet, and the most delicious chocolates, peppermints, plums and dried and cured orange peel. There were arguments between my mother and father – I recall him pleading: "*Ich will meine Ruhe*", "I want my peace" – but I believe that in these years, despite everything, my parents were happy. Certainly they lived life to the full. Although they were truly grateful that Australia had offered them refuge, the pattern of their lives was shaped by a magical place they called not Germany (of course) nor Austria, not even Europe, but "The Continent".

In the mid-1950s, things fell apart. My father's business had begun to fail. The kind of individually designed and crafted furniture that was common in interwar Vienna was probably too expensive as good-quality mass-manufactured furniture – such as Fler, the brainchild of two other Austrian Jewish refugees, Fred Lowen and Ernest Rodeck – came onto the market. The failure of my father's business was both very painful and, at least so it seemed to me, interminable. I still recall the name of one client who refused to pay his bill. The way he was spoken about, he seemed destined to share an afterlife in the circle of Hell reserved for other wicked wrongdoers like Adolf Hitler. (On the off-chance that one of his children reads this book, I'll keep the name to myself.) My father then briefly tried his hand at a delicatessen with the help of Uncle Hans. Even after my inspired suggestion – hot dogs! – it, too, failed. My father took out something called "a second mortgage" on our East Ivanhoe house, a financial expedient I did not understand but gathered had been most unwise. His blood pressure was high and, as I also learned, he did not take his medication with sufficient regularity.

In early April 1958, my father suffered a major stroke or brain haemorrhage. I last saw him lying on the floor in our living room propped up against an armchair. My sister and I were sent to the garage. I still remember Uncle Sigie speaking to me about my father's death in a strange manner I had never before experienced, half sobbing, half (almost) laughing. (There was something very odd about their relationship. After his brother's death, Sigie took my father's name and became known, even to his wife and sons, as Henry.) At this time in my childhood, I had watched at a friend's home a popular television program called *Zorro*. Before justly dispatching his victims, Zorro made a flamboyant Z in the ground with his sword – *swish, swish, swish*. Shortly before my father's stroke I had made an equally flamboyant Z with a play sword on our East Ivanhoe drive. As a result, I secretly believed that I was responsible for his death. And as a ten-year-old, I had certainly not read Sigmund Freud on the Oedipus complex. In our home, after his death, I noticed on my father's bedside table a well-thumbed paperback on the recently discovered Dead Sea Scrolls. He was interested in world history to the end.

At the time my father's business was collapsing, my mother's health was deteriorating very seriously. Among many symptoms, she found walking increasingly difficult. Uncle Hans had given me a Five-Year Diary on my eleventh birthday. I began making short entries (only, alas, for a few weeks). On November 16, 1958, I wrote "Mum at hospital"; on November 17, "write a card to Mum"; on November 18, "Mum back morrow"; on November 19, "Mistake. Mum back to-morrow"; on November 20, "Mum home ... thin but better. Glad to be home"; on November 21, "Mum had diheria [*sic*]"; on November 24, "Mum sleepy. Wait till housekeeper comes first day"; on November 25, "Mum's birthday. Give pair stockings"; on December 5, "Mum falls. Call Frances and Betty" [Frances and Betty were neighbours]; on December 14, "Stay and make chicken dinner". The diary soon peters out until a final single entry on March 26, 1960. "Sorry I neglected you diary. We have shifted to Camb. Not as nice as I [Ivanhoe] but OK ... Having Barmitzvah lesson. I'm alright at it too. Mum is no better but no worse (THANK GOD)".

I was, in certain ways at least, a strange child. One evening after my bath I bent down and severely burned my bottom on a gas-fuelled radiator. For several days I hid the burns from my mother. I knew she would be upset but was not in the slightest afraid that she would be angry. I cannot recall any incident in my entire childhood where she was. I tried to conceal my burned bottom from my mother because I was ashamed. I have no idea why. One day I was walking idly along the path at the top of what was known as The Cutting on Lower Heidelberg Road. I thoughtlessly kicked some white stones onto the road below. To my horror, I thought I saw one of them smash a windscreen. I ran home in panic and went straight to bed, waiting for the doorknock of the police. This was the first occasion I experienced what psychologists call dissociation, the feeling that the mind was floating above the body.

There was a second occasion. Because of its proximity, I was enrolled in an Orthodox Jewish Sunday School in Kew, where I was, I believed, the only student who had no idea what was going on. On one parents' day my father decided not to turn up. The class teacher asked where he was. I told him that unfortunately he was very busy that day, at his work, designing furniture. When my father arrived to pick me up, to my horror, while I waited in the car, he began talking at some length to my teacher. I was certain that my lie would be exposed. As soon as we were home, once again I went to bed feigning illness, and once again my mind left my body. Neither my mother nor my father was strict with me. (The only time I can recall coming even close to being smacked was when, stupidly but not maliciously, I imitated something I had seen in a cartoon, leaving some tacks in my father's slippers.) And yet, for some reason I do not understand, from a very early age I grasped the difference between shame and guilt, if not yet the words, and knew that I was somewhat irrationally and excessively prone to both.

In 1959, after the death of my father, our family moved to Riversdale Road in Camberwell, needing to sell East Ivanhoe because of our perilous financial situation. Our income now came from an invalid pension from the commonwealth government and, later, a so-called restitution payment from West Germany. (My university mentor, Frank Knopfelmacher, with uncharacteristic high-mindedness, once argued that no Jew should take money from Germany. I thought that this was an easy opinion for someone on a tenured university senior lectureship to hold.) Eventually there was a diagnosis of my mother's illness: multiple sclerosis. Except for visits to hospital, the last time she left home, in her wheelchair, was for my Bar Mitzvah, in late October or early November 1960. Her legs were by then completely paralysed and she suffered permanent pain. My small bedroom was next to hers. For seven years, from 1959 to 1965, I was her night-time and sometimes day-time nurse, answering her calls, helping her onto and off the toilet arrangement and chamber pot in her bedroom via a smooth, varnished plank, regularly bathing and bandaging an ulcer on her foot that would not heal. Luckily, I loved her dearly, trusted her entirely and admired immensely her capacity to ward off despair. For some reason, what I best remember of these years are her shrieks of laughter while we watched the proto-feminist television comedy *I Love Lucy*. She was an endearingly eccentric television watcher, convinced for example that she could tell who was a redhead, despite the fact that we owned a black-and-white set, and (to my great frustration) believed that one of the game shows using a wheel of fortune was rigged. It was in the closeness of relations with my mother, both before and during her years of illness, that I learned the meaning of fidelity to another and of unconditional love.

In 2018, after the publication of my book of essays *On Borrowed Time*, I was a guest on Jon Faine's ABC radio program. One of the listeners recalled the kindness I had shown my mother in one of her hospital visits a half-century earlier. In all my life there has been no compliment that has pleased me more. I knew with complete certainty that I would remain with my mother for as long as she lived, no matter what. For an eighteen-year-old boy this could be a frightening thought. In late 1965, after my matriculation exams, my mother encouraged me to take a fortnight's hitch-hiking holiday with friends. It was the longest I had ever been away from her. While I was away my mother fell gravely ill and was admitted to hospital. Before I managed to return to Melbourne she died. I believe that she felt that she had done her duty to both her children. My sister had just turned twenty-one and I had just finished my final school exams. Once more – this time more rationally – I believed I was responsible for the death of a parent.

*

From an early age I was a keen political observer, fascinated by small, apparently insignificant events that seemed to reveal relations of power, the complexity of ethnic identity and the significance of myth and tradition.

In one of my first days at Ivanhoe East Primary School – in a grade called "the bubs" – an announcement concerning the death of King

George VI interrupted the morning broadcast of "Kindergarten Playtime". My teacher wept. I found the fact that the death of an old man who lived a very long way away was important enough to bring my teacher to tears something of serious interest. How had it come to be that the loss of a king could mean so much to one of his subjects? (I have on one earlier occasion written about this incident. Barry Jones pointed out that, because of the timing, it was unlikely that this was the first time my teacher had learned of King George's death. He was right. The teacher in question also read my account and told my nephew David that she was weeping because of a private matter concerning her love life. Of course, what matters here is not what precisely took place but what I imagined had happened and the curiosity this excited.) Like so many Australian children, my class welcomed the new Queen in 1954, standing for a long time on the pavement and waving as she went by. As a seasoned six-and-a-half-year-old this did not greatly interest me. More than two years earlier I had witnessed the sentimental sway of the monarchy and recognised the power of myth and symbol.

In one of my early grades at Ivanhoe East the teacher used to choose the pupil with the straightest back. Although we regarded the contest as fairly conducted, it seems more likely that our teacher rewarded all of us eventually. One day my back was adjudged the straightest. I reported this small victory to my mother, neither nonchalantly nor with any great pride. What struck me forcibly, and why it has stuck in my memory, was my mother's disproportionate delight that I deconstructed in the following way. In Europe, as I already was aware, the Jews had been looked down upon, frequently because of their supposed unattractive appearance or even physical deformity. One of the things that would never have occurred in anti-Semitic Europe, according to my mother's view, was that a Jewish child, among gentiles, could win a class contest for the straightest back. I think I already knew that Australia was not like Europe. In my early years I had not experienced even one instance of anti-Semitic behaviour. I realised, however, that my mother was not so sure. Her excessive delight at her son being chosen as the child with the straightest back was therefore, for me, evidence of both the kind of anti-Semitism my mother had come to expect growing up in Germany and the kind of anti-Semitism she was worried I might experience but that I already was confident I would not.

Although I had no experience of anti-Semitism, I also knew that I did not truly belong in the overwhelmingly Anglo-Scottish-Irish society of Australia in the early 1950s, the days before mass European migration changed Australia's ethnic balance forever. On one occasion I was at the birthday party of a school friend. The birthday boy's mother called us to come inside to get away from "the mozzies". I was the only one there who had no idea what a mozzie was. On another occasion I was staying with my best friend, John S. I took a bath and went under the water, and my very curly black hair was temporarily straight. John was amazed. Without a hint of malice or condescension, he said words to the effect: "You look like us!" As far as possible I tried to keep a distance between the world of my family and the world of my friends. I have already told the story of the Dinky toy and the wooden banister. A more excruciating case concerned John S. I was allowed to invite him to attend the circus with me and my family. Recently, perhaps even for the occasion, my mother had purchased for me a smart gabardine coat. European boys might wear gabardine coats; Australian boys did not. I was a stubborn child and absolutely refused to wear it. My father warned that if I persisted, I would not be going to the circus. To my horror, even though I was not allowed to go, they still took John. I was mortified – not that I was missing the circus but that John would be with my family unsupervised, without me to act as a cultural barrier and, if necessary, a cultural translator, explaining the ways of European Jews to John and the ways of Presbyterian Australian boys to my parents. The circus fiasco passed without incident.

John's mother, Frances, played a significant part in my early political education. Frances treated me extremely well, as a kind of honorary Scottish Presbyterian Australian, trying to teach me the Highland fling and inviting me to their regular, joyful gatherings of Highland dancing, where John played the piano accordion.

Frances took me with her family on a visit to a friend's sheep farm in the Western District. One evening, after the children had been put to bed, I overheard a hushed conversation between the adults about the conclusive evidence pointing to the imminent end of the world. That night I learned of a new kind of politics founded upon something I would later call apocalyptic and millennial thinking. Frances was also a British-Australian patriot. She invited me to come with John to see films showing the valour of the British imperial forces in the Second World War – *The Bridge on the River Kwai* and *The High and the Mighty*. I still recognise and am moved by their courage and am grateful for those invitations (although the jungle warfare in *The Bridge* terrified me). Between a Scottish Presbyterian Australian adult and a child of German and Austrian refugee parents there was not a sliver of difference concerning the justness of the war against Nazi Germany and Imperial Japan. Frances was also a woman of strong ethno-religious prejudices. On the way home from one of the patriotic films we saw what appeared to be a knife fight between Italian migrants. Frances explained to me that this was what one might expect from the foolish government decision to bring Italians to Australia. Italians were not, however, her gravest concern. One day when I was visiting John, their television announced that its next offering would be the film that featured the song "It's a Great Day for the Irish". Frances rose in horror from her armchair and rushed to turn the television off before her sitting room was sullied by one word or frame in praise of Irish Catholics.

This was not the only time I learned about one of the deep divides in Australian society – the hostility between Protestants and Catholics that the Catholics and academic scholars called sectarianism. One day after classes were over, insults were thrown and a fight almost broke out between my school friends and a group of boys from the local Catholic primary school. I was astonished. Only then did I learn that the overwhelming number of my school friends were not just Christians but Protestants. I was informed that Catholics ate human flesh and drank human blood, a garbled, slanderous reference to the sacrament of communion that even at the time I thought unlikely.

This was the only occasion I witnessed an outburst of sectarian hostility. It helped me understand earlier Australian political history.

I also became aware when still very young of the more durable social divide: class privilege and disadvantage. When I travelled from Ivanhoe to the city, I glimpsed through the train window the inner-suburban backyards of the working class whose squalor astonished me. More importantly, at the beginning of one year a Collingwood boy, Billy Mac, whose family had made good, enrolled at our school. So distinctive was he from the other children – in speech and demeanour – that he might have come to East Ivanhoe from another planet. Billy Mac's arrival suddenly allowed me to see the middle-class-ness of my school and neighbourhood. I learned that although Billy Mac was small, he had a reputation for settling disagreements with his fists swiftly and effectively. To my shame, it was for this reason – to avoid any possibility of conflict – that I decided to befriend him. Of the other great social divide in early 1950s Australia – between Indigenous and non-Indigenous Australians – I learned almost nothing and saw with my own eyes nothing whatsoever. My only distinct memory is of a class in Grade 3, where the teacher wrote on the blackboard: "Segregation or Assimilation?". This remained in my memory not because of the issue itself – as if eight-year-olds could sensibly discuss the fundamental policy question of the Paul Hasluck era – but because of the intellectual thrill and conceptual challenge posed by the opposition of two abstract words both never before encountered.

In October 1956, around my ninth birthday, I learned my first lesson about Soviet communism, a subject that would shape my political identity until the end of the Cold War in 1989. That lesson did not come principally from the sensational "blood in the water" newspaper stories I read, about the fight that broke out between the members of the Soviet and Hungarian water polo teams at the time of the Soviet Union's brutal suppression of the Hungarian Revolution. It came rather from a small, seemingly insignificant incident that I witnessed on home ground. The Boulevard was adjacent to the public Ivanhoe golf links (where John and I spent many pleasurable hours spying, retrieving and then selling golf balls players routinely lost in the long grass, with proceeds going to a milkshake and some lollies at the club house). One day a small busload of East German long-distance runners trained on the links. I regarded athletes of this calibre as very important people. When the training session was over, I entered the bus and asked if I might have their autographs. The first runner signed with a grin. He passed the autograph book to a second, who burst into laughter before signing. The same thing happened, time and again, until all the athletes had signed.

When I got home, I told my mother about this strange behaviour. She asked to see the autograph book. The first signature read: JOSEF STALIN. My mother explained that Stalin was the former Soviet leader who had died three years earlier. Until then I knew nothing about Stalin, let alone the fact that earlier in 1956 the new Soviet leader, Nikita Khrushchev, had changed the course of history with the secret speech he delivered on the crimes of Stalin to the Twentieth Congress of the Soviet Communist Party, that had been broadcast throughout Eastern Europe by channels of the CIA. Clearly, the athletes' laughter reflected the tremendous release of tension in the new political landscape inside the Soviet bloc created by Khrushchev's speech. One year earlier, the Ivanhoe golf links incident would have been inconceivable. Of course, I understood nothing of this. But what I did grasp was that if the mere act of writing down the name of a former, once revered and feared political leader was enough to cause a busload of distinguished young men to roar with laughter, there was something of genuine political interest here that was worth understanding.

There is one last childhood incident of future political significance for me that occurred shortly after our family had moved to Camberwell. The local council must have learned about the problems we faced with a single mother crippled by multiple sclerosis and two school-age children. One day, and for some period after, a doctor arrived to look after my mother and her medical needs without payment from my family. This took place perhaps fifteen years before Gough Whitlam's Medibank (the predecessor of Medicare). My parents had once separately both been rescued by Australia. Now my mother was reliant not only on a commonwealth government invalid pension – the restitution payment from the government of West Germany was still in the future – but also on a council-supported doctor. I did not take this government support for granted. I felt a little embarrassed about the additional problem we had now caused our generous hosts, the Australian people. More importantly, the arrival of the council doctor inoculated me forever against generalised hostility towards the welfare state, or what during the 1980s and beyond the neo-liberal movement would call the nanny state. This was a simple, perhaps even primitive, political thought, but nonetheless it has remained with me throughout my life.

On the questions that most interested me during my childhood and adolescence I was forced to think for myself. My father was too busy and died too early to discuss politics or history with me. My mother was not an intellectual, nor was Uncle Hans. Like most Jewish children of that era, I was a supporter of Israel. For a while there was a "blue box" in our East Ivanhoe home that collected money for the new Jewish state. But neither of my parents was a strong Zionist. Following my first meeting I refused to return to the junior Boy Scouts – the Cubs. The collective wolf chanting terrified me as greatly as jungle warfare. I did join the Israeli Labour Party's Zionist youth movement, Habonim, but left soon after. There was another brief period, around the time of my Bar Mitzvah, when I tried to find something in religion, travelling by tram to the liberal Jewish Temple Beth Israel synagogue in St Kilda, sometimes accompanied by David Nadel, later a Monash Maoist and deputy to Albert Langer. I did not find what I was looking for. On one occasion I asked the rabbi, John Levi, whether Jews believed in an afterlife, in Heaven, Purgatory and Hell. His answer was infuriatingly vague. I recognise now that Judaism is primarily a religion of community, not of individual belief and faith. As an adolescent I was shallowly attached to the Liberal Jewish community, centred around Temple Beth Israel, where I taught Jewish history at Sunday School and was president of its youth club, whose principal responsibility was organising dances. I took from this experience two important emotions that have remained with me throughout my life – a love of teaching and a fear of convening events where no one turns up – but learned little about the question that already haunted me and would never leave me – the decision taken by the German state to remove the Jewish people from the face of the Earth.

And what of sex? I know from my diary that I was interested in girls by the age of ten. The little I understood of relations between male and female came from a book called *Perfect Marriage* that I discovered in my father's library. During the middle years at Camberwell High School, I dated one or two girls but in the most innocent of ways; even holding hands took courage. Once, I took a girl from a Latvian family, Dana, to a dance but forgot to walk her to her front door from the car that was giving several of us a lift home. As I recognised that Latvians were not kindly disposed to Jews, I thought they were now certain to despise me. Until I discovered that Dana had arrived safely at her front door, I was once more racked by guilt. The only serious girlfriend, in my final year of high school, was a lovely young Presbyterian, Jan MacDonald. Very shortly after we matriculated, she was able to reveal her love for our young history teacher, Denis Grundy, whom she married and with whom she had four children. On the hitch-hiking holiday I took after the matriculation exams, I caught sight of the two friends I went with in the act of making love. I experienced mild envy. I left high school as a virgin. My rather sensitive and artistic closest circle of school friends included Ric Benson, later a doctoral scholar of French literature, rather famous high school teacher and vice-principal of University High School, and Alexander Soldatow, not yet at all the flamboyant, gay novelist that as Sasha Soldatow he would later become. We did not discuss sex.

To my genuine surprise, I gained excellent results in my matriculation exams. At the end of primary school I had competed for a scholarship to Scotch College but had failed. Shortly before the matric exams I spoke on the phone to a former Camberwell High School friend, Geoff L, who had moved to one of the elite private schools, Trinity College. He said it was a great pity I hadn't made it to a private school as I might then have been able to achieve really good exam results. I believed my best subject was English literature but here the Exhibition (top of the state) went to Mark Weinberg, now a Victorian Supreme Court judge. I did, however, share the Exhibition in Renaissance and Reformation history with David Fitzpatrick, later a distinguished historian of Ireland; won the Exhibition in British history outright; and was also awarded a General Exhibition. I received a phone call from the dean of law at the University of Melbourne, Professor Zelman Cowen, whose two sons I had taught at the Sunday School. Zelman had noticed that in my application for Melbourne University I had put down arts but not law. He encouraged me to do a combined arts/law degree. I told him that my overwhelming interest was the study of history. He argued that all the best historians in the British tradition had also studied law. I replied that my favourite historian – Sir Lewis Namier, a Polish Jew who revolutionised our understanding of eighteenth-century British political history – had not. Zelman gave up. Often, now, when I visit the splendid home of a barrister of my generation, I recall that conversation with a twinge of pain.

I shall try to sketch my political point of view before going to university. I was a supporter of Israel, the Jewish state, but didn't consider myself a Zionist. I had no intention of living in Israel, did not believe that young Jews had such an obligation and did not believe that I would encounter consequential anti-Semitism in Australia. I was interested in exploring and understanding at some depth the ideas of both left and right. During my early adolescence I resolved, on several occasions, to read in the summer holidays the books at the extreme ends of the political spectrum, Karl Marx's *Das Kapital* and Adolf Hitler's *Mein Kampf*. Each time my resolution failed, as the pleasures of friends, novels, continental films, jazz records, the beach and the local golf links all beckoned. On the issues of the day – capital punishment, the White Australia policy, censorship of literature and film, a better deal for the Aborigines, conscription for service in Vietnam, higher taxation and the expansion of the welfare state – my politics were standard left. At our school I led the struggle for a student representative council. One of the supporters was Terry

Counihan, the son of the communist artist Noel. I wrote the case for an SRC, which our aged principal, Roy Andrews, summarily dismissed as "half-baked". At this time, I would have described myself as a democratic socialist but was not attracted to the idea of communist revolution and did not believe that a better world was being built in the Soviet Union and Maoist China. Nor was I an anti-communist. I remember scoffing inwardly when I saw a young Christian female student borrow the anti-communist classic *The God That Failed* from our small school library.

By this time there were two dispositions that I can now see were responsible for my future political engagements. One was a conviction about the significance of reasoned argument. As a child I often listened to federal parliamentary debates on my crystal set, which were broadcast on the ABC. I was first convinced of one side, and then quickly of the other. I had enormous admiration for the rhetorical skills of certain parliamentarians and can still recall a magnificent speech on the future of the Great Barrier Reef delivered by Kim Beazley Senior. In one of my British history classes in early high school we read about the struggle over the Corn Laws between the protectionists and free traders. One of the free traders, we learned, presented a powerful, persuasive, watertight argument in the parliament. The Tory prime minister, the defender of protectionism, turned to a younger minister in his government: "You must answer this for I cannot." This, I thought, is how politics should be. I frequently took the tram into the city to listen to the speakers on the Yarra Bank – including both Australian communists and Eastern European anti-communists – to see who could persuade me. And at school, as a young teenager, I invited our English teacher, Mr Robertson, to debate the merits of a C.S. Lewis trilogy we had been required to read, which I believed to be thinly disguised Christian propaganda. My rather foolishly optimistic conviction about debate – the idea that the clash of opinion would result in the triumph of reason – has stayed with me throughout my life.

The second disposition was a belief in the capacity of history to answer the questions I most wanted to understand. In early high school most history lessons were dull – kings and queens, common fields and enclosures. On one occasion, however, in third form, a relief teacher – as it happened, Pippa Waten, the wife of Judah, one of Australia's most dogmatic communists – explained to us how history moved through stages – slave societies, feudalism, capitalism and then socialism – each stage before socialism representing the interests of a dominant class; each stage creating internal contradictions that allowed the next stage to emerge through revolution. I was transfixed. What I hoped was that the study of history might be able to explain how the Nazi Party had come to power in Germany, one of the most cultivated European nations, and why it was then able, without significant opposition, to set about the extermination of the Jewish people. At the time I went on to university I believed that I lived in one of the quietest and most successful democracies. But I was also searching for an understanding of what had happened to my grandparents and to my people in the decade before I was born. As I can see now, it was this tension – between the calmness and civility of my country that I at least had experienced and the violence of the recent history of my family and people – that shaped my future political life.

[4.]

University

FOLLOWING MATRICULATION, I WAS OFFERED a generous scholarship from the newly established Monash University, which was trying to attract students with the best exam results. Even though I had no immediate financial prospects and little income, apart from the commonwealth scholarship given each year to thousands of university students, I rejected the offer without the slightest hesitation. In my final school years, I had often travelled by tram to the University of Melbourne, where unpaid ushers could watch the plays put on by the Melbourne Theatre Company, at the time housed on the university campus. Monash University was in outer-suburban, semi-sewered Clayton. Melbourne University was near the heart of the city, where I believed a university should be. Strangely enough, I was also drawn to Melbourne University's pseudo-Gothic architecture, its sandstone buildings, quadrangles, clock towers and spires. In my romantic conception, that was how a university should look. Even before I had read *The Idea of the University*, I was a Cardinal Newman true believer, thinking of the university as an unworldly community of scholars and their students. Despite everything that has happened to universities over the past half-century – if the racial, class and gender biases of mid-nineteenth-century England were removed from Newman's conception of the university – I still am.

Having established where I would study and for what kind of degree – arts and not arts/law – the next question was which subjects

I should take. When I now recall the seriousness surrounding that decision, I am somewhat embarrassed. At that time if arts students wanted to study not for a three-year pass degree but a four-year honours degree, they were asked to nominate the discipline or disciplines at the beginning of their first year. History was my first choice. I was uncertain as to whether I should combine it with English (literature) or philosophy. My crystal-spirited high-school history teacher, Denis Grundy, took me to see a friend of his in philosophy. On his advice I enrolled in a tutorial with Mary McCloskey, a senior and well-respected member of the department. In the first class we were asked how we knew that one of the green chairs in her office was green. I did not think that was a foolish question or one for which there was an easy answer. However, I had arrived at the university hoping to understand the dark aspects of human history, genocide and war, not how the greenness of Mary McCloskey's green chair could be established. This single tutorial decided my choice for a combined history and English honours degree.

When I arrived at Melbourne University in 1966 there were five political clubs – from right to left (roughly), the Democratic Labor Party, the Liberals, the Australian Labor Party, the Democratic Socialists and Labour. I had no interest in the DLP or the Liberal Club and was barely aware of their existence. However, as I was intensely interested in politics and wanted to seize the opportunity of becoming politically active for the first time in my life, I had to choose one of the three supposedly left-wing clubs. It was the history of these clubs that determined my choice.

The Labour (not "Labor", the ALP's idiosyncratic spelling) Club had been dominant at the university in the immediate post-war period. In turn, it was dominated by its many Communist Party members. By 1950, however, the communists had lost their hegemonic position inside the Labour Club and, more generally, most of their influence at the university. By the time I arrived at the university, the principal interest of the Labour Club was fierce but non-violent opposition to Australia's involvement – alongside those the club described as the imperialist Americans – in the Vietnam War. Principally because of the communist influence inside the Labour Club, in the early 1950s the ALP Club was formed. By 1960 it was the most influential club at the university. On Easter Sunday, 1962, the club's leader, Bill Thomas, a man who many thought had a genius for politics, died in a road accident. Following his death, a rather arcane three-year struggle for control of the ALP Club broke out. One side was led for a time by the political scientist James Jupp, the other by the university's most influential and intellectually formidable anti-communist academic, Frank Knopfelmacher. Eventually the Knopfelmacher forces prevailed, although without Knopfelmacher himself, who announced his support for B.A. Santamaria and the DLP. In mid-1968 I described the ALP Club I encountered in the following way:

> The ALP Club has passed into the hands of a group of Catholic intellectuals who are fiercely anti-communist and who are more interested in the persecutions of writers, intellectuals, students and Jews behind the Iron Curtain than in the Australian political scene. They have also been the most violent spokesmen for Australia's participation in the war in Vietnam. They have thus been branded as extreme right-wingers and have almost no real influence on campus anymore.

By the mid-1960s a political space had opened at the university for a club that was positioned between the militantly anti-American Labour Club and the militantly anti-communist ALP Club. In 1964 that space was filled by the Democratic Socialists, the club I joined not long after arriving at the university and on whose committee I served. The Democratic Socialists was a rather lacklustre club with a small membership, primarily arranging talks on the conventional left-wing issues of the day – the censorship of books and films, education reform, Aboriginal advancement, the expansion of the welfare state and opposition to conscription and Australia's participation in America's Vietnam War. In the second half of the 1960s, the centre of gravity in student politics at Melbourne University was moving rapidly to the left. In 1967 the Labour Club led the campaign on campus for civil aid to be sent to the National Liberation Front (NLF, popularly known as the Viet Cong), whose soldiers were at war with the forces defending the South Vietnamese regime – including, of course, Australians, some of whom were conscripts. The right in Australia described the leaders of the Labour Club as traitors, in the words of the ancient *British Treason Act*, for "providing aid and comfort to the enemy". In late 1968 and early 1969 the Labour Club was outflanked on the left by a new political movement calling itself by the name of the radical movement in the United States, Students for a Democratic Society (SDS), and campaigning for civil disobedience and a university-wide strike against conscription and the Vietnam War. The Democratic Socialists were by now irrelevant. In a talk on student politics, I claimed that if "Whitlam showed his face on campus the reception would be cool if not hostile. Students generally, I believe, do not trust him or regard him as in the least radical ... The Whitlamite-prone Democratic Socialists have gone into a permanent grave." In September 1968 I joined the Labour Club and was immediately elected to its committee.

*

In truth, I had not been a particularly conscientious Democratic Socialist committee member. My political energy was expended and my political appetite satisfied in different ways. Although we did not realise it, in the second half of the 1960s Melbourne University offered interested students the possibility of a quite unusual and entirely extra-curricular political education. If any current students read this book, I hope it will help them understand what universities in Australia once were, what they no longer are, and what they might be again in a world of exclusionary populist nationalism, uncontrollable pandemics and, above all, catastrophic and irreversible climate change.

The university I encountered in 1966 was what I hoped for: a genuine community of scholar-teachers and students, open to anyone who wished to join. It is fair to say that most of the university's teachers and students had little interest in belonging to this community, except perhaps at times of high political tension, when meetings of

2,000 academics and students were possible. However, very many did feel a part of the community. Such members had long nicknamed Melbourne University The Shop, a sardonic reference to the way the ideal of the university as a place of learning was under permanent threat from the forces of commercialism and credentialism. If unresisted, this might succeed in transforming their university into nothing more than the tertiary training college for the nation's future professional classes – doctors, lawyers, architects, engineers, veterinarians, pharmacists, accountants, schoolteachers and so on. In his first *Farrago* editorial of 1969, Henry Rosenbloom warned freshers against wasting "countless hours talking in the Caf", "working for such ephemeral trivialities as *Farrago*", joining one of the "petty political clubs" and attending "too many lunchtime meetings". Remember, he mock-warned: "You have come to this University to get a Degree."

As this suggested, the university community had an informal meeting place, the cafeteria in the Union Building, known by all as the Caf. In the Caf, circles of students had their long lunches or their long morning or afternoon teas. These circles might be formed on the basis of membership of one or other political club, common political convictions, common courses or subjects, a shared interest in theatre, photography or journalism and so on, or on nothing more than chance friendships and sexual attractions. The circles were porous and they overlapped. Tutors often ate with their students. Sometimes so did older academics. Frank Knopfelmacher was frequently there, half teaching, half recruiting; Vincent Buckley less often but invariably surrounded by admirers. Although not welcomed, in the late afternoons students drank in Jimmy Watson's wine bar on Lygon Street. In the afternoons or evenings, staff and students drank together and talked in the local pubs: Naughtons on Royal Parade or Peter Poynton's on Grattan Street. Late at night some played pool at Johnny's Green Room on Faraday Street.

When I think back I am astonished by the number of undergraduate friendships retained or made – from school days, Ric Benson, Denis Grundy, Jan MacDonald (Grundy); some of the most lively fellow arts students, Susan Friedlander (later Hearst), Margaret Harrison (later Gaita), Michael Liffman, Cathy Lowy, Tony Barta, Jenny Doull, Janet McCalman and Ann Tregear (my first partner and the daughter of one of the most unbending members of the Australian Communist Party); the sons of Bundist families, Arnold and Harry Zable and Henry Rosenbloom; the director of plays on campus, Elijah Moshinsky (on his way to Covent Garden via Oxford), and one of his most talented actors, Jan Fordham (later Friedel); the rather eccentric history student who preferred Haydn to Bach and Trollope to Dickens, David Fitzpatrick; the engineer and sometime president of the SRC, Bruce Hartnett; the law students, Robert Richter, Jeremy Ruskin and Ben Lewin (a filmmaker, not a lawyer); and in my later undergraduate years, those Catholic apprentice intellectuals from the ALP Club, Terry Tobin and Michael Crennan, later both senior barristers, and Paddy Morgan, later editor of B.A. Santamaria's articles and correspondence. One became my closest male friend, the philosopher Raimond Gaita, author of *Good and Evil* and *Romulus, My Father*. While most of my friends were moderate social democrats, they ranged, rather promiscuously, from the rigid Maoism of David Fitzpatrick at one end of the ideological spectrum to the volcanic anti-communism of Paddy Morgan, with whom I later fell out dramatically, at the other. When I now meet any of them by chance, even after several decades, most greet me not as an acquaintance but as a friend.

The community was served by the student newspaper *Farrago*, which appeared each week during term. Both academics and undergraduates wrote for *Farrago*. For many undergraduates who later became political commentators or politically engaged academics, it was their first opportunity to publish, often at length. The editors of *Farrago* were under constant scrutiny. During my undergraduate years, on the grounds of his cultural uncouthness, the right made a serious attempt to dislodge Pete Steedman, who had moved from Monash University's *Lot's Wife* to *Farrago*. *Farrago* maintained a very lively letters-to-the-editor page or pages. Editors frequently answered their critics. Sometimes they gave ground. When a maudlin and sentimental article on a conscientious objector was published in 1969, both the editor and the article's author acknowledged the lapse of taste and judgement and apologised. During my undergraduate years (1966–69) *Farrago* published articles from students across the political spectrum, from Paddy Morgan and Gerard Henderson on the right; Raimond Gaita and Arnold Zable on the centre-left; to Douglas Kirsner and Michael Hamel-Green on the left. Perhaps most impressive was the capacity for extended arguments in *Farrago* over months and even years.

In the second half of the 1960s the conjoint issues of the Vietnam War and conscription for service in that war dominated. This lent to the debates a great urgency. The right argued that the communist guerrilla forces in the south, the NLF, were controlled by Hanoi and that if Vietnam "fell" to the communists, Australia's security would come under direct and immediate threat, with between 2 and 3 million South Vietnamese anti-communists murdered. The left replied that Australia was complicit in a United States–led policy of genocide in Vietnam and that the NLF were independent and indigenous. What was happening in South Vietnam was a civil war. Two members of the small anti-communist but anti-war centre-left, Raimond Gaita and Arnold Zable, reminded the left of communism's long history of murderous brutality, and the right of the extraordinary human cost of an unjust war. Such *Farrago* articles were almost always passionate and sometimes of high intellectual quality. No one seemed to have noticed the absence of female voices.

Another issue affected indirectly by the debate over the war in Vietnam was the nature of the university. In 1968 and 1969 two orthodox Marxists in the Labour Club, Stuart Macintyre and Kelvin Rowley, defended the idea of the university as a community of scholars and students and as the site of analysis and political education. Two SDS leaders, Michael Hamel-Green and Harry van Moorst, sought to show why the university must become a focus of revolutionary action. Their campaign eventually drew in the entire university community. For many years political issues had been debated at lunchtime meetings attended by hundreds of staff and students.

At the conclusion of these meetings motions were put and votes were taken. Although none of this was legally binding, it was generally accepted that these votes should determine future courses of action. In May 1965, a general meeting was asked to decide whether the Melbourne University community should protest over the almost unprecedented action of Sydney University's professorial board in rejecting the near-unanimous decision of a university committee to appoint Frank Knopfelmacher as senior lecturer in political philosophy. According to the *Farrago* report: "The meeting was attended by only about six hundred people despite a very wide advertising campaign." *Only* 600! In March 1969 a meeting of a similar kind and size was held to consider the SDS call for a university strike over conscription and the Vietnam War. This meeting directly raised the question of the nature of the university. It was here that my first political intervention took place.

*

In my first two years at Melbourne University my political identity was that of a conventional democratic socialist with a particular interest in the historical roots of anti-Semitism and the Holocaust. One of the first articles I published was a review of Norman Cohn's fascinating *Warrant for Genocide* – a study of a supposedly secret document, *The Protocols of the Elders of Zion*, that had been forged in the late nineteenth century by a member of the Czarist secret service. *The Protocols* outlined the conspiratorial plans of Jewish tribal leaders, the Elders of Zion, for world control. It played a significant part in forming the *Weltanschauung* of Adolf Hitler and the Nazi inner circle and provided the warrant for the attempted genocide. Another article I published was a study of the anti-Semitism of the early medieval Christian Crusaders who committed mass slaughter of European Jewish communities on their way to the attempted liberation of the Christian Holy Lands from occupation by Muslim (supposed) infidels. As I concluded: "The version of the Jews as filthy, plotting and money grabbing has, of course, found its way into our century. It has a longer heritage than many anti-Semites would imagine."

UNIVERSITY

In 1967 the Holocaust was as close in time as 9/11 is to us today. In June, a war broke out between Israel and the surrounding Arab states. At that time Israel's military capacity was unknown. Many Jewish students believed that the Arab armies might succeed where the *Einsatzgruppen* and the Nazi SS had failed. Hundreds of us attended an evening meeting in a hall on Albert Park Lake. Apart from a small circle of Monash Labour Club rebels that included my childhood friend David Nadel, whose misjudgement angered me but whose courage I privately admired, the atmosphere was one of genuine fear and of heightened patriotism – or perhaps, in George Orwell's terminology, of transferred nationalism. I fully shared this emotion, the like of which I have never felt before or since. A thick fog hung over the lake that evening. It somehow seemed appropriate. I rang Uncle Hans to tell him that I had decided to fly to Israel at once to help in whatever way I could. He listened quietly, probably somewhat alarmed. As the fog lifted next morning, so in small part had my resolve. And before I had made any firm plans, the war was over. I will never know whether I would have volunteered for service if Israel had been under threat. More than half a century later, Israel still controls the territories on the West Bank of the Jordan River and, indirectly, Gaza that it captured in what became known as the Six-Day War. As I write these words, the disastrous consequences are playing out – the vicious murder of 1,200 Israelis by the dominant Palestinian group in Gaza, Hamas, that has been answered by the Israeli Defense Force's destruction of Gaza with such astonishing cruelty that I feel profoundly ashamed, as a Jew, about the behaviour of the Israeli government and the level of support offered for its actions by the majority of the people of Israel and most Jewish leaders throughout the Diaspora.

I was strongly opposed to Australia's participation in the Vietnam War. I recall seeing a propaganda anti-war film produced by Wilfred Burchett that greatly moved me. Even though I was a member of the Democratic Socialists I was allowed to sit in on the Labour Club's tense and tightly packed meeting in the small Raymond Priestley Room – besieged by a large and angry student crowd outside the locked doors – that discussed the question of providing non-military aid to the NLF. After this meeting, I wrote a letter-to-the-editor (never sent). "Dear Sir," it began. "Are the members of the Monash and Melbourne Labour Clubs who propose aid to the National Liberation Front traitors?" I tried to show that they were not by drawing a distinction between the war with Japan in the 1940s and the Vietnam War in the present. In the case of Japan, Australia's security was at risk. In the case of Vietnam – "a virtually unwinnable war because of considerable civilian South Vietnamese support for the National Liberation Front" – we were fighting to strengthen our "defence pact" with the United States and to entangle the US forces in South-East Asia. For its part, I argued, the United States was involved in Vietnam not because its own security was at risk but out of what I called its global "balance of power strategy".

In 1968 my political identity shifted, rather awkwardly, first leftwards and then rightwards. As is apparent in a paper I wrote in mid-1968 on "student power", I was caught up in the leftward movement of political opinion that affected all the Western democracies. Student power, I argued, was not new. It had been a critical factor in the 1848 revolutions in Europe and in both the nationalist and communist revolutions in twentieth-century China. Student power moved through two stages: first a concentration on particular issues where "inhumanity and injustice" existed; second a general analysis that demonstrated the need not for reform but for revolutionary change. I argued that at some time students come to understand that "their society is totally corrupt and must be transformed". Eventually that moment would arrive in Australia. The paper advocated humanist not technocratic education; participatory not parliamentary democracy; and the rejection of the materialist and consumerist society for one based upon "meaningful manual and intellectual work". Thoughts such as these led me to dismiss the now near-extinct Democratic Socialist Club witheringly in a single word, as "Whitlamite", and not only to become a member of the Labour Club but to agree to serve on its committee.

*

If the tidal wave of 1968 and the idea of student power pulled me to the left, at almost the same time what I learned about the communist movement pulled me with greater force to the right. I learned this lesson from two of the most complex and talented academics at Melbourne University: Vincent Buckley and Frank Knopfelmacher.

Before my studies began in 1966, Denis Grundy had spoken to me of Vin Buckley. Denis thought he was probably the most profound thinker at the university. Buckley was the son of a poor Irish Catholic family from Romsey in the Kilmore district of Central Victoria. By 1966 he had just turned forty but was already an accomplished and admired principally religious poet, having published *The World's Flesh* and *Masters in Israel* and being about to publish *Arcady and Other Places*. Vin Buckley was also one of the early champions of Australian literature, via his *Essays in Poetry: Mainly Australian*. During the 1950s, one of Buckley's deepest passions was his intellectual co-leadership of the Catholic community, "the Apostolate", which sought to infuse the university, and then whatever professional or familial life the Catholic students chose, with the spirit of Christianity, in a process Buckley and the Apostolate called "incarnation". Buckley withdrew from the Apostolate in the early 1960s. He believed that for him it had already lasted too long. It was my impression that by the time I came to know him in 1967, the once bright religious flame within him was flickering or had even already quite blown out.

Vincent Buckley was a profoundly political person. In 1950 he was one of the founders of the ALP Club. During the 1950s he was associated with the mildly left-wing *Catholic Worker*. Anti-communism, however, gradually became a fundamental and settled feature of Buckley's political identity. He drew away from *The Catholic Worker*, increasingly a paper for progressivist university Catholics that one of its political enemies rechristened *The Catholic Senior Lecturer*, and became a member of the editorial committee of *Prospect*, an intellectual magazine associated with the Apostolate that filled the political and theological space between B.A. Santamaria's politically and theologically conservative "Movement" and the liberal anti-anti-communist *Catholic Worker*.

In 1967 I made my way into one of Buckley's second-year English literature tutorials. I was amused to discover that in our group of fifteen or so students, one was named Coleridge and another Wordsworth. (Coleridge became the Brisbane archbishop; I have no idea about what became of Wordsworth.) Occasionally Buckley would leave the class for a few minutes for no apparent reason. I wondered whether the poetry we were discussing had overwhelmed him. Later I learned that he was checking on a race result in which he had an interest.

For some reason I best recall the class where we discussed W.B. Yeats. Vin Buckley read us the lines:

> A barricade of stone and wood;
> Some fourteen days of civil war;
> Last night they trundled down the road
> That dead young soldier in his blood:

I recall how we discussed at length the power of Yeats' "trundled". I was not always convinced by Buckley's firm teacherly judgements. He was disturbed, even disapproving, of Yeats' final line in the wonderful poem "The Circus Animals' Desertion", about feeling abandoned in old age, with nothing to call upon but "the foul rag and bone shop of the heart". I loved the line, as I think I told him, and love it still. I never doubted Buckley's seriousness as a teacher. After a couple of tutorials, he asked me to stay behind. He told me that he was worried that something was not working. I was immensely impressed that he cared enough and was honest enough to discuss the atmosphere in a tutorial with one of his students. What most affected me in Vin was the coming together of thought and feeling in the making of a judgement. Sometimes his judgements stung. I still recall his comment on an essay I wrote about Charles Dickens' *Dombey and Son*. It was all very well, he wrote in his elegant and neat hand, but what I had failed to notice was Dickens' "exuberance". I was stricken because I realised that he was absolutely right.

At the end of 1967 I left the English department. At the time the department was divided between old-fashioned scholars, Ian Maxwell and Keith Macartney; poets and litterateurs, Chris Wallace-Crabbe, Robin Grove, Evan Jones, Peter Steele and of course Vincent Buckley. The running, however, was now made by the followers of F.R. Leavis that Professor Sam Goldberg had brought with him from Sydney, the lecturers Maggie and Jock Tomlinson, and the team of tutors who lacked Goldberg's penetrating intelligence but made up for it with the desire to enforce an orthodoxy. I was invited to give a talk about my withdrawal from the discipline. I complained about the coded language we were required by the Leavisites to use – "organic", "human possibilities", "energies" and so on. I also complained about the way the Leavisites followed their master by accepting a predetermined list of the great and not-so-great writers: "I became more and more aware that a certain judgement had been made on every poet … [T]he activity of discovering the relative value of Pope and Goldsmith is more important than the ability of confidently asserting that Pope is greater than Goldsmith."

In my final second-year honours exam, I chose to write an essay on Kingsley Amis' *Lucky Jim*. It was my way of saying goodbye to the English department. But not to Vincent Buckley, who became a good, if never altogether equal, friend for many years. It was not long before I learned more than I wished about Vin's rather terrifying darker side, most obvious when he drank but also close to the surface when he was sober.

A small incident in 1968 involving Buckley had a profound effect on me. At that time, while I regarded Nazism as evil, my views on communism were unformed and unstable. As president of the undergraduate History Society, I planned a forum on the Soviet Union. One of those I invited was the ex-Stalinist but still orthodox communist Judah Waten (whose wife had introduced me to Marxist historical materialism in Form 3). Another was Vincent Buckley. When I told him that I had invited Waten, Buckley reacted with visceral anger. He told me he would not share a platform with such a man. I was shaken. So perhaps it was not only Nazism that incarnated political evil in our century. Because of my respect for the Buckley sensibility I had encountered in the tutorial room, his tone on this occasion precipitated an inner rebellion against the standard anti-anti-communism of the mainstream Melbourne University liberal left. Vin Buckley's anger changed the trajectory of my political thought and thus my identity. Even more important was one of Buckley's political friends, Frank Knopfelmacher.

*

Frank Knopfelmacher was a Czech Jew from an upper-middle-class family of mainly professionals. In November 1939, at the age of sixteen, he managed to escape to Palestine. Almost all his family were subsequently murdered by the Nazis. For a brief time in Palestine, Knopfelmacher became a rather ill-disciplined member of the Communist Party, from which he was expelled for his refusal to obey the order not to speak German. Knopfelmacher joined a Czechoslovak division of the British Army. It was now that his political identity – as an anti-communist social democrat – was shaped, by his encounter with Arthur Koestler's great political novel about the 1930s show trials in Stalin's Soviet Union, *Darkness at Noon*, and by George Orwell's free-wheeling revolutionary socialist but anti-communist "As I Please" column in Aneurin Bevan and Jennie Lee's newspaper, *Tribune*.

Offered a choice between Czechoslovakia and Palestine at the end of the war, Knopfelmacher chose Czechoslovakia. The eyewitness observation of the slow destruction of the democratic system by the communists, completed in the so-called coup of February 1948, provided him, as he later wrote, with an indispensable political education "under laboratory conditions". In late 1948 Knopfelmacher (with his Czech wife, Jarmila) managed to bribe his way out of Czechoslovakia and make his way to Britain via Paris. By 1955 he had completed a first-class honours degree in philosophy and psychology and a doctorate in psychology, both at Bristol University. In that year Knopfelmacher was appointed to a lectureship in the psychology department at Melbourne University. He regarded the department as dominated by communists – claiming that he had been pressured to teach the nonsensical theories of Stalin's biologist, Trofim Lysenko – and saw the professor of psychology, Oscar Oeser, whom he loathed, as a pro-communist fellow traveller. He believed that his most important work was the education of the members of the Melbourne University ALP Club, like Bill Thomas, in order to create a future political elite.

Frank Knopfelmacher was at the centre of two of the greatest university controversies of the 1960s – the 1961 anti-communist campaign at the University of Melbourne that sought to prove the existence of a communist conspiracy to take control of the social studies department, and the 1965 counter-campaign at the University of Sydney, led by two Communist Party members, that successfully prevented his appointment as senior lecturer in the philosophy department. At the mid-point between these controversies Knopfelmacher's worldview was outlined with greatest clarity in an extraordinary, nearly 10,000-word article titled "Man Who Can Bear Very Much Reality", published over two issues and four entire pages of *Farrago* in April and May 1963. It was based on an interview conducted by Nigel Jackson, who claimed that Knopfelmacher lacked "spiritual wisdom", and was on his way to becoming a David Irving–inspired Holocaust denialist. Knopfelmacher told Jackson that in the present century, the world was at war. It was being fought between the forces of totalitarianism and the defenders of an open society. The totalitarians wished to create a "perfect society" which, because of the collapse of religion, filled a psychological need for large numbers of those belonging to the class of the intelligentsia. Thus far there had been only two totalitarian state forms – Nazism and communism. As the ambition to create the secular paradise was "delusional", to disguise recognition of failure from themselves, totalitarians became "ferocious", and capable of committing history's greatest crimes. In the case of the Nazis it was the murder of 6 million Jews, and in the case of the communists the starvation of 6 million Ukrainian peasants. Nazism had been defeated. At present communism, or what Knopfelmacher called "the Sino-Soviet bloc", controlled one-third of the world. The present struggle for the world was between the Sino-Soviet bloc and Western liberal democracy. Knopfelmacher acknowledged the existence of the ideological split between the Soviet Union and China but, as he argued elsewhere, the split was essentially over how best to slit the throats of their liberal-democratic enemies. The regions where communism had the best chance of gaining ground were Latin America and South-East Asia. For this geographical reason, Australia was under threat. Knopfelmacher acknowledged that in Australia the Communist Party was now "ludicrously small", with no more than 4,000 members. However, it still had the capacity to exert its influence in societies' "opinion-making machines". One such site of opinion formation was the university.

In order to awaken the nation from its slumber – "its present state of gross military unpreparedness, ignorance of South-East Asia, and general moral apathy and decay" – future political elites needed to be educated and armed for the struggle to defend Australia from the external communist threat with the most formidable weapon of all, "analytic intelligence". The education presently available to students at the University of Melbourne was "still very defective". To overcome this deficiency Knopfelmacher saw it as his duty to fill the gap. It was for this reason that he was devoted to educating the students at Melbourne University and retaining his influence within the university's ALP Club. What was needed were young Australians who understood what the great German sociologist Max Weber had called "the demands of the day". Bill Thomas was one such. Perhaps when we became acquainted, he came to think of me as another. Knopfelmacher conveyed this worldview, time and again, principally through his lunchtime lectures and, even more significantly, in the scores of informal tutorials he conducted in the Caf for any students willing to listen. It persuaded many of us – including, by late 1968, me.

It is difficult to convey both the extent to which the figure of Frank Knopfelmacher dominated political discussion at Melbourne University in the '60s, and the hatred and mockery shown towards him by left-wing students. At a meeting of August 11, 1967, where students overwhelmingly voted (576–121) in favour of the motion: "That every Australian has the democratic right to send aid to the NLF", *Farrago* reported – "Knopfels – interjecting about his usual concerns 'the Monash sewer' etc. and making a peculiar pumping action with his right arm while speaking, that was much commented upon." On March 22, 1968, Michael Helmer was allowed to publish in *Farrago* this unrestrained abuse:

> [T]he fears of Knopfelmania bounce round their heads and paralyse their mouths so they cannot speak out against his perverted tirades, his "çommo baiting". O mr Knopfelmacher, your frustrations and prejudices have no limits! Your barb-wired face is gnarled by hate and fear. You empty empty man. You despicable husk of a once beautiful child!

It was Rai Gaita – no supporter of either Knopfelmacher's "political standpoint" or some of his "methods" – who captured most accurately the dynamic of the poisonous relationship that had developed between Knopfelmacher and the Melbourne University student left, and what he called "the systematic degradation of a leading intellectual on the campus".

> How many times when Knopfelmacher gives a public lecture do people go along not to listen but to laugh? How many times does some imbecile from the Labour Club stand up and abuse Knopfelmacher, and then, as he becomes shaken, urge him to one hysterical outburst after another? Then when the farce is over, and an intelligent man has been made to seem like an hysterical, paranoid fool, how many of the crowd that degraded him go off grinning smugly to one another?

Like many politically engaged students I was intensely interested in the attempt in Czechoslovakia to democratise a formerly hardline communist regime. On May 10, 1968, *Farrago* reported a lunchtime Knopfelmacher talk on developments there. "The recent revolution in Czechoslovakia", he argued, "was an exciting experiment for socialists and the nearest thing yet to democratic socialism in Europe." On August 2, in a *Farrago* interview, Knopfelmacher provided an intelligent and complex analysis of the balance of forces both inside and outside Czechoslovakia. Finally, he made a prediction:

What would happen if there was a Soviet intervention is that the Russians would pass through a period of extreme unpopularity in the west, which they would ride out ... We are facing the sad fact that the Russians are willing to impose their will with force on their colonies ...

Three weeks later the Soviet-led troops of the Warsaw Pact invaded Czechoslovakia. As far as I knew, Knopfelmacher was the only Australian academic who had predicted this. I was mightily impressed.

At almost the same time as I joined the Labour Club and was elected to its committee (September 1968) I began talking to Knopfelmacher in the Caf and to the members of the ALP Club I had disparaged a few months earlier. At one of my first meetings with Knopfelmacher, discussion concerned a letter-to-the-editor about a Soviet matter that had been published in one of the Melbourne newspapers. The author was Alexander (later Sasha) Soldatow. Knopfelmacher began explaining to the circle of listeners that Soldatow was self-evidently a KGB plant. As it happened, Soldatow was not a KGB asset but a close schoolfriend of mine, whose vaguely pro-Soviet feelings could best be explained by his difficult relations with his mother, an anti-communist "White Russian". I pointed this out. Knopfelmacher was entirely uninterested and, without taking breath, continued to mount his Soldatow-as-a-KGB-asset case. I learned from this a lesson that served me well over the next quarter-century of our friendship. On macro-matters, like Czechoslovakia, Knopfelmacher was almost always worth listening to; on micro-matters, like Soldatow, he had an infuriating capacity to overrate his intuition and to repel inconvenient evidence. On such micro-matters he was best ignored.

Knopfelmacher was a truly gifted teacher. One habit was to tell his students – for the most part outside his psychology classes – what to read. In late 1968 and 1969 he provided me with a short essential-reading list that I devoured. On the deepest questions of the age, Hannah Arendt's *The Origins of Totalitarianism*. On the historical precursors of totalitarianism, Norman Cohn's *The Pursuit of the Millennium* and J.L. Talmon's *The Origins of Totalitarian Democracy*. On the Holocaust, Hannah Arendt's *Eichmann in Jerusalem*. On the Stalin show trials, Arthur Koestler's *Darkness at Noon*. On the Comintern, Franz Borkenau's *World Communism* and the two-volume Koestler autobiography, *Arrow in the Blue* and *The Invisible Writing*. And as the most perceptive political observer of the 1930s and '40s, George Orwell – his classics, of course, *Animal Farm* and *Nineteen Eighty-Four*, but even more his collected political essays. If Knopfelmacher had one lesson to teach it was the essential similarity of the ideology of Nazism and Bolshevism, and the equal, inseparable evil of the crimes of Hitler and Stalin, who now dwelt for Knopfelmacher in the lowest circle of Dante's Hell.

As a teacher, Knopfelmacher had a great capacity for aphorism. In the discussion occasioned by totalitarian theory about whether there was a significant difference between Nazism and Soviet communism, Knopfelmacher argued: "There is only one important difference. Nazism is defeated; communism is not." There was a discussion occasioned by the claim of a historian that only 4 million Jews had been murdered in the Holocaust, not 6 million. In answer to the question posed by exasperated moralists – "What is the difference between 4 and 6 million?" – Knopfelmacher answered: "Two million", which for me, at least, went deep. Even though he was a fierce intellectual combatant who took no prisoners and was frequently unjust and cruel, he had a quality I think of as refined moral taste. Knopfelmacher loathed false heroics. As Buckley recalls: "He was delighted when I said that *The Good Soldier Schweik* was the best commentary ever written on war." For anyone using the Holocaust for political purposes, he felt and expressed profound contempt. In later years, he joked darkly, "There's no business like Shoah business." And he was often just funny. One ferociously hot day in late February or early March, Knopfelmacher began his lunchtime talk: "This is an historic day. It is the first time since Palestine in 1943 that I have delivered a lecture in shorts."

If my politics had shifted to the left, from the Democratic Socialists to the Labour Club, in the last months of 1968 they shifted to the right, at least according to the conventional labelling of the day. At that time anti-communism was viewed with suspicion on the left, or worse: as an ideological neighbour of fascism. In late 1968 I published a piece called "The Three Faces of Anti-Communism" in *Melbourne University Magazine.* For Anglo imperialists – like Eric Butler of the Australian League of Rights or Sir Wilfred Kent Hughes – anti-communism was associated with the British Empire, white supremacy and sometimes anti-Semitism. For Roman Catholics – like Archbishop Daniel Mannix or B.A. Santamaria – anti-communism was associated with their anti-modernist rejection of materialism and atheism. While for Jews – like Knopfelmacher – anti-communism was the expression of anti-totalitarianism. As I put it in the essay: "In his recent book, *Intellectuals and Politics,* he uses the symbol of the concentration camp for both Nazism and *all* communist systems." Decoded, what I was saying was that one type of anti-communism – the white supremacists – was contemptible; another type – the orthodox Catholics – reactionary; while yet another – Jewish anti-totalitarianism – was kosher, an understandable, rational response to the darkest episodes in recent European history. My political identity – that had always been grounded in reflection on the meaning of the Holocaust – was shifting. The theory of totalitarianism claimed that Hitler's Nazism and Stalin's communism were not at the opposite ends of the old nineteenth-century left–right political spectrum, but at the same end of a new twentieth-century political spectrum that placed totalitarianism at one end and the liberal-democratic open society at the other. This is how I was now beginning to see things.

Knopfelmacher saw where I was headed. In October 1968 he invited me to come to his apartment in East Melbourne to interview an avowedly anti-communist Czech medical student who had fled his homeland following the Soviet invasion. After the publication of the interview, a member of the Labour Club, Martin Munz, called me a fascist. This stung. In early 1969, as a kind of joke, members of the Labour Club put up a Stalin poster in the Union Building. I had read enough to know by now that Stalin was the murderer of tens of millions. The humour escaped me. No one would have pinned up a poster of Hitler, even as a lark. I resigned from the Labour Club committee. To my considerable surprise, Paddy Morgan of the ALP Club, confronted me angrily in the *Farrago* office. Apparently, I realised, he had interpreted my membership of the Labour Club's committee as a stealthy political advance for the forces of anti-communism. By resigning I had let down a team of which I did not consider myself a member.

*

In the first months of 1969, Students for a Democratic Society (SDS) became the principal left-wing force on campus. In June, the Labour Club held an AGM where only thirty-four attended. There were thoughts about closing down. SDS sought a new form of politics – participatory democracy and a non-violent "people's revolution". Their most eloquent and impassioned leader was Michael Hamel-Green. He argued in one of his several *Farrago* essays that we lived in "society whose representatives have killed, burned, or orphaned over a million Vietnamese children". Worst of all were the "bourgeois intellectuals" who "poison action at its very birth". And of such despicable intellectuals "the most ludicrous … are the 'radicals' found in Labour Clubs all over the country, who buzz continuously with radical *ideas*, but sneer at the slightest *actions* that call the government's aura of legitimacy into question". The political temperature at the university was rising. In March 1969, SDS mounted a campaign for a university strike in defence of anti–Vietnam War protestors, like the five Melbourne University SDS members who faced short prison sentences for refusing to pay fines for distributing anti-conscription literature outside Melbourne's General Post Office. The question of the strike was placed before a large and rowdy meeting of students in the Public Lecture Theatre on March 19. The meeting voted in favour of a demonstration but rejected a strike. I delivered an anti-strike speech, which according to *Farrago*'s editor, Henry Rosenbloom, "was received with unanimous and prolonged applause, and almost certainly decided the issue". This was the first time in my life that I felt I had some real political influence.

Inside that issue of *Farrago* I set out my case. I argued that I placed the highest value on the idea of the university, a unique institution defined by freedom of thought within its walls that was respected by the state. If the university acted like a "corporation" with a political ambition and an apparent single point of view, it was betraying its institutional essence – as the place where values and ideas, no matter how popular or unpopular, contended. It was also endangering its future. If a university became a political actor challenging the state, was it not almost certain that the state would fight back, by withdrawing the privilege it accorded to the university, of untrammelled freedom of thought?

Some months later, at a meeting of the National Union of Australian University Students, it was proposed that "non-compliers of the *National Service Act*" – that is, those defying conscription – should be offered sanctuary and support on university campuses across Australia. As this was an obvious invitation to the police to move onto the campuses – something that according to the idea or perhaps the mythology of the university they should not and even could not do – I was also opposed. A similar motion to shut the university for one day was brought before a very large Melbourne University audience in Wilson Hall on May 1, 1970. The motion was narrowly defeated: 889 votes in favour, 946 votes against.

My defence of the traditional idea of the university and opposition to plans to turn the university into a political actor and radicalise the student body was my first political intervention of any consequence. Some months later, Knopfelmacher claimed that the successful opposition to the SDS campaign for a university strike was a key moment in the politics of Melbourne University. Whether that was true – and if it was, whether that was for better or for worse – I do not know. Having waded into the revolutionary student Rubicon up to my ankles in 1968, by 1969 I had turned back.

An independent member of the student left, Peter d'Abbs, queried the case I had made about the vulnerability of the university and challenged a "reformist" like me to provide a more general "critique" or "theory" of Australian society. In the next issue of *Farrago* I accepted the challenge. D'Abbs claimed that the university was not in danger from a conservative government because "a technologically advanced society" like Australia needed "technologically trained people to keep it going". It might be true, I replied, that technologically advanced societies did need their "engineers, doctors and lawyers" but it was not at all obvious that they needed "philosophers and historians" or that the technologically trained experts needed what the university offered – "extraordinary freedom of speech and access to a wide range of intellectual opinion".

D'Abbs had characterised my general view of Australian society as "a basically good social system with certain bad features", and I accepted this characterisation. What was wrong with Australian society, I argued, was not the exploitation of workers by capitalists, as many student revolutionaries claimed. "Is that vision of the enormous car park outside the factory illusion or reality?" Australia was a remarkably "egalitarian" society where doctors drank with fitters-and-turners and their sons surfed together. What was wrong was the way a "mediocre middle class" excluded minorities like homosexuals or intellectuals and closed its eyes to "the truly impoverished". I invited my contemporaries to turn their minds from the presiding fantasy of the revolutionary worker–student alliance to concrete questions: "[T]he paltry indignity of the pension, the plight of the man unemployed through sickness, the tragic position of the young widow or divorcee with her numerous children, or the family whose poverty is too great to enable them medical benefits."

What was needed was increased taxation and "an overhaul of the social service system". This was not a society that needed, in d'Abbs' words, to be "smashed to pieces". For the left, my political position was all too plain. Articles and letters in *Farrago* now claimed that I was "an apologist for Australian capitalism". I had "drifted away" from the Labour Club "spectacularly ... to the extreme right". I was now "closer to Paddy Morgan or Gerald [*sic*] Henderson than to the cross-section of Labour Club thinking".

One extremely minor incident at this time was not forgotten. By 1969 Gerard Henderson and I were indeed on the same side on certain issues – most importantly against the campaigns of the Monash Labour Club and the SDS at Melbourne University to turn the universities into revolutionary political actors. In 1969 I was a co-editor of *Melbourne University Magazine*. Henderson submitted an article. I favoured its publication. Neither of my co-editors, Cathy Lowy and Michael Liffman, agreed. As it would have been bad form to tell Henderson of our disagreement, all he knew was that an article he had submitted to a magazine of which I was a co-editor was rejected. I was astonished to discover some forty years later that Henderson had never forgiven me for this imagined slight.

*

I recall seeing Raimond Gaita outside the Union Building, sitting alongside Michael Hamel-Green (before he moved to SDS) selling copies of *Threshold*, a magazine on phenomenology, a contemporary movement in European philosophy. Sales did not appear to be brisk. I also recall seeing him speak at a lunchtime meeting on existentialism with the philosopher Max Charlesworth and the prominent student gadfly Patrick McCaughey. In Gaita's talk there was an analytic depth, a radical intelligence, but most of all a purity of spirit that shone through and astonished me. I suppose that I decided then to do my best to strike up a friendship. In my last two years as an undergraduate, Rai became my closest friend. Although we rarely, if ever, talked about our pasts, we were probably drawn together by our difficult childhoods and adolescences. I had lost my father at the age of ten and then nursed my mother. Rai had been abandoned by his desperately troubled mother, who at a young age took her own life. And he had witnessed the torment of grief this caused his father, a man of the sternest and finest principle. Rai and I were both on the left, but we both believed it was vital that the left recognise and acknowledge the astonishing crimes of Stalin, Mao and Ho Chi Minh fully and unflinchingly. In one of his *Farrago* articles in July 1970, Rai made this clear:

> After at least twenty years of committed political writing we still propose class-based violence as a solution. As though we weren't sick of it. Marxists urge us to look at the face of history, but even

the simplest man knows that that face is blood-stained. That socialism had something to do with the celebration of liberty and justice is something that one finds difficult to remember. Perhaps that is why these words, along with wisdom and beauty, sound strange to us now.

By 1970, Rai was further to the left than I was. Somehow, though, he managed to be friends with the most bitter political enemies among the academics at Melbourne University, the two principal protagonists in the Social Studies Affair of 1961: Geoff Sharp and Frank Knopfelmacher. Rai was never close to the Catholic student intellectuals in the ALP Club. However, he once confessed to me how astonished he was to find that one of their favourite authors – George Orwell – was indeed so interesting.

As friends, Rai and I had a lot of fun. He remained in many ways a country boy, with a love of Elvis Presley and Citroën cars. He also lived a rather chaotic life, on one occasion missing part of a fourth-year exam by sleeping in. But we were also serious, often talking until two or three o'clock in the morning about questions being discussed on campus, especially those concerning Vietnam. I learned from him in these discussions the power of a non-utilitarian ethics that was developing in his mind and that would be fully expressed in his most important philosophical work, *Good and Evil: An Absolute Conception*. By then, almost everything he wrote expanded on a line of Socrates: "It is better to suffer evil than to do it." According to my memory, our conversations often reached this stalemate. Neither Rai nor I was a pacifist. Both of us regarded the war waged by the Allies against the Axis as paradigmatically just. Rai, however, would argue that it was impermissible to take the life of an innocent human being. And I would argue that since the advent of air power, under his stipulation every war, including that between the Allies and the Axis, was necessarily unjust. So he would try to convince me that in certain circumstances we could not morally do that which politically we must. Thus began a lifelong friendship.

By the time I left Melbourne for Oxford, my political outlook was beginning to take form. I was a non-revolutionary democratic socialist, most strongly influenced by the writings of George Orwell, the subject of my fourth-year honours thesis, but with little interest, alas, in the discipline of economics. My undergraduate studies occurred in the era historians, even Marxist historians, subsequently called capitalism's golden age. It seemed to many of us that, within the West, full employment and gradually increasing prosperity would be around forever. On the darkest chapters of twentieth-century European history, I was most influenced by the theory of totalitarianism. Hannah Arendt's *The Origins of Totalitarianism*, especially her chapter on the meaning of the concentration camp, was by far the most important source. The final pages of another of Arendt's books, *Eichmann in Jerusalem*, regarding the nature of the crime of genocide Nazi Germany had committed against European Jewry – the cold-blooded decision to remove one people in its entirety from the face of the Earth – stayed with me. In brief, in my words, this is what Arendt said the judge in this case should have told Eichmann: "Just as you did not wish to share the Earth with the Jews so does humankind not wish to share the Earth with you. For this reason, you will be hanged." Because of the essential similarity in totalitarian theory between Nazi Germany and the Soviet Union, I was also a strong anti-communist, with a special interest in and some knowledge of the era of Stalin, having read Knopfelmacher's recommendations and having reviewed Robert Conquest's classic, *The Great Terror*, in *Farrago*.

Regarding the war in Vietnam that dominated our political discussions, I believed that the National Liberation Front was under the control of the North Vietnamese leadership and that once the North took control of the South there would be much killing and persecution of the communists' political enemies. However, I was not convinced that the war in Vietnam was winnable; or that the terrible human cost of America's overwhelming high-tech arsenal, including napalm, unleashed on Vietnamese villagers under NLF control was justified; or that an American victory in Vietnam was required for the United States to win (as I hoped it would) the larger Cold War contest between the United States and the Soviet Union that was the central question of post-war international relations. In the months between my matriculation exams and the beginning of the next year's university semester, between 500,000 and 1 million left-leaning Indonesian peasants had been murdered on the orders of the Indonesian army and with the support of local anti-communist organisations. However, throughout my undergraduate years, these murders, which the American and Australian governments had aided through their military assistance and their public silence, were never discussed. If they had been, my political position would have been more complicated and nuanced. Oddly enough, even though I was due to enter the Australian armed forces once my studies were complete – my birthdate had come up in the conscription lottery – I gave this prospect little thought as I did not believe that I would ever be called upon to fight. I knew of only two Melbourne University students who had been required to serve in Vietnam after being conscripted. Before setting off to Oxford in mid-1970 I marched with Rai Gaita and some other university friends in the large anti–Vietnam War Moratorium in Melbourne and gravitated to the banner (probably of a Trotskyist grouplet) which read "Neither Washington Nor Hanoi".

I was a strong believer in the traditional idea of the university as a community of scholar-teachers and students and wanted to live my life within its walls. I was also a believer in classical nineteenth-century liberalism – freedom of speech, freedom of assembly, representative parliamentary democracy and the rule of law – all of which I thought to be entirely compatible with what was then called the mixed economy of nationalised public instrumentalities and free enterprise in agriculture, manufacturing, mining and retail. I was an Australian patriot who felt gratitude for the country that had given homes to my parents, whose own parents' lives had been lost, one way or another, in the Holocaust. Because of my parents' and my people's history, I was naturally sympathetic to refugees. I was interested in the well-being of the Indigenous Australians but was largely ignorant of both settler history and anthropology. Although I was now entirely without religious faith, my belonging to the Jewish people was the most fundamental aspect of my political identity.

Although second-wave feminism had barely reached Australia by the time I left for England, I had been unnerved by various incidents of terrible male behaviour I had witnessed. At the meeting I spoke to when I decided to abandon the study of English, Professor Sam Goldberg spoke after me. He said that English would not be a truly serious university subject until the majority of those who studied it were men. Among the predominantly female audience, no matter what they might have felt, there was no sign of public disapproval or dissent. This did astonish me. I was present at Naughtons pub one night when a friend began auctioning his current girlfriend. I was privately disgusted but, to my shame, just walked away. At the end of my fourth year, I applied for a Shell scholarship. The scholarship was for two years' study at either Oxford or Cambridge, and offered full costs of travel and an unusually healthy stipend. This was probably the last time when postgraduate study at Oxford or Cambridge seemed more natural for Australian students than study in the United States at Harvard or Yale. In preparing for this chapter, I came upon the "Shell Postgraduate Arts Scholarship" advertisement. It advised that the scholarship was "open to male students who will have successfully completed a full-time honours course". No one, including me, noticed how extraordinary a stipulation this was. I belonged to the last student cohort untouched by the second-wave feminist revolution.

I must not have taken the application for the Shell scholarship too seriously. The application form asked which sports I played. I answered "pool". One member of the judging panel asked if this was a form of swimming. When I won the scholarship, on the recommendation of Melbourne's professor of history, John Poynter, I chose to study at Oxford University's Magdalen College, for no better reason than the beauty of its spires, clock towers and quadrangles.

[5.]

From Oxford to Bundoora

AS THE TRAIN WAS DRAWING INTO OXFORD STATION, I caught glimpses of the towers and domes I had long imagined. As I had nowhere to stay, I knocked on the door of a bed-sitter not far from (male-only) Magdalen College. The woman who answered and showed me to a room asked me how long I intended to stay. "Two years," I replied. She looked at me as if I were mad. The usual length of stay in a bed-sitter of this kind was two days.

It was not too late in the day to take my first look at Magdalen, so I left my bag there and set off. I passed through the entrance to the college without introducing myself to the man sitting inside the small office. As I strolled across the lawn in the first quadrangle, to my considerable surprise I was brought to the ground in a rugby tackle. "What exactly do you think you are doing walking on the grass? Did you not read the signs instructing visitors to walk on the paths?" I was rather shaken. I apologised and explained that I came from Australia, where people were in general permitted, even at universities, to walk on grass. I was visiting Magdalen because my postgraduate studies were due to begin there in a few days. The porter looked stricken. It was his turn to apologise. "Oh, sir, I am so sorry. I had no idea. Had I known, sir, that you were a member of the college ..." And so on. Thus did I learn that I was now a temporary member of a hierarchical society based on class. Because I was a student at Magdalen and my tackler a porter, I was his superior – despite the fact that I had just arrived at a place where he had probably served loyally for decades. For an inferior to rugby tackle a superior was an outrage and perhaps even dangerous. I had never been more pleased that my parents had found refuge not in Britain but in Australia. The porter led me to his office. Having verified my claim to be a student, he told me that a room was awaiting me in a building outside the college walls. I went at once to the bed-sitter to pick up my suitcase. My stay there had lasted not two years or two days but two hours.

Finding Magdalen College had been straightforward. Finding the university was not. I believed that all universities had something like the Union Building and the Caf, where members of the university community met. I believed that this university community would hold meetings where contentious issues were debated and where decisions about political action were taken. I believed that at Oxford there would be several political clubs – from communist to conservative – giving shape to political life and debate. I believed there would be lunchtime lectures like those in the Old Arts Building at Melbourne. I believed there would be an Oxford student newspaper, an equivalent to *Farrago*. Perhaps I wasn't looking hard enough, but my search for the Oxford University political community failed. Insofar as community existed at Oxford, it appeared to be situated in the colleges and not the university. In the colleges, however, the students who seemed to matter were the undergraduates, not the postgraduates. The undergraduates at Magdalen were given rooms in the college. The postgraduates' rooms were in a decrepit building on a laneway outside the college's imposing wall. The Magdalen undergraduates seemed to me like bright children from wealthy families who talked a lot with great confidence and comically exaggerated Eton accents. Even living in one of the postgraduate rooms in the gloomy building beyond the wall felt like time had gone backwards. As soon as I could I found rooms in a fine sandstone Georgian building in the centre of Oxford, unhappily on the floor above a thriving dental practice where it was impossible during the day to get away from the shrill whining of the drill. I was joined here by Ann Tregear, my first serious partner from my Melbourne University days.

My new friends at Oxford were other outsiders. One was a conservative Jew from a Yiddish community in Montreal who was studying the Old Tory opponents of Winston Churchill's foreign policy. In our lunchbreak at the splendid Bodleian Library, we composed a counterfactual history of twentieth-century Europe, beginning with the accidental death of Adolf Hitler in 1932. Another was a very middle-class Englishman from the north who was studying for a Bachelor of Civil Law. Inadvertently, he taught me another lesson about class when he introduced me to a friend of his who pretended to be an accountant or some-such but was actually a train-driver – a far more interesting occupation, I would have thought, but definitely on a lower rung of the class hierarchy.

Before long I abandoned hope of finding the Oxford political community – where, as a non-citizen, I would anyhow have been an observer and not a participant – and settled down, in reality for the first time in my life, to serious study. As the Shell scholarship was for two years, I enrolled not for a doctorate, for which I was probably unprepared, but for the prestigious and demanding B.Phil, the Bachelor of Philosophy. Typical of Oxford, the name of the degree made no sense. It was a postgraduate degree and had no necessary connection with philosophy. The degree consisted of four subjects, each assessed at the end of the second year in a three-hour examination (where one was required to wear an academic gown) and a thesis of 40–50,000 words. I started with politics but after one term changed to international relations. This meant that I had one term for each subject and the summer holiday plus one free term for the thesis. The subjects I chose were the history of international relations in the nineteenth century (with A.J.P. Taylor), the history of international relations in the twentieth century (Wilfred Knapp), the international communist movement (Richard Kindersley), and a micro-study of the making of the Treaty of Versailles (A.J. Nicholls). One of my tutors, Knapp, was very close to British intelligence. After graduation, when the other international relations B.Phil student in my year told him he was disillusioned with his work in journalism, within a week he received a job offer from either MI5 or MI6. The terms lasted eight weeks. Each week the candidate for the degree was required to write an essay on a topic selected by the tutor of 3–4,000 words. The more conscientious tutors read the essay in advance of the weekly tutorial, thus leaving the full hour for discussion. The less conscientious asked the student to read the essay before a briefer discussion.

It was – or, more accurately, ought to have been – a privilege to study with A.J.P. Taylor, a man of the left but also a foreign policy realist and almost certainly, because of television appearances, the most famous historian in Britain. Taylor was the author of a revisionist (and wrong-headed) account of the origins of the Second World War, a sparkling biography of the most consequential figure in the history of nineteenth-century Europe, Otto von Bismarck, and a diplomatic history of Europe between the 1848 revolutions and the outbreak of war in 1914 that he called *The Struggle for Mastery in Europe*, one of the most brilliant works of history I have ever read. My first class with Taylor was rather terrifying. When I arrived back from a short holiday, I found in my pigeonhole at Magdalen the following note:

Dear Manne,

Write an account of how the problem of Germany was handled by the great powers at the 1815 Congress of Vienna. Do not make it too ~~wrong~~ long.

AJP Taylor

I had four days to write on a complex subject that I knew nothing about.

I met each week with Taylor in the late afternoon in his room in the breathtakingly graceful and handsome so-called New Building at Magdalen, built 200 years earlier. After a couple of classes Taylor relaxed. Perhaps too greatly. On one occasion – when I was reading my essay on (from memory) European international relations during the unification of Italy and Germany – I arrived at the conclusion that Taylor had fallen asleep. I decided nonetheless to read on in case I was mistaken. The moment I finished Taylor awoke, snapped to attention and told me his views. What I now remember from these tutorials are some of the judgements ("Bismarck was a genuinely great statesman. Metternich was a lightweight, a mere dilettante"), the depth of his knowledge and the ease of his recall of the smallest historical detail.

The topic I chose for my thesis was the negotiations between the United Kingdom and the Soviet Union between the disintegration of Czechoslovakia in mid-March 1939 and the announcement of the Nazi–Soviet Non-Aggression Pact in late August, on the eve of the German invasion of Poland and the consequent Anglo-French declaration of war. There were two reasons for my choice. The negotiations had become a standard item in the left-wing version of the origins of the Second World War. According to this version, Britain had refused military alliance with Russia, leaving Stalin no alternative to the ideologically embarrassing non-aggression pact with Nazi Germany. I was interested in finding out whether this version was true. This was now possible because, to my good fortune, the 1939 Cabinet minutes and the Foreign Office records had only months earlier become available, following the British government's decision to reduce the fifty-year government archival rule to thirty years. For four weeks or so, I travelled every weekday by train from Oxford to Kew Gardens, where the Public Records Office was found. I discovered that on the question of the Soviet alliance, there had been deep divisions within Neville Chamberlain's Cabinet. Those opposed to the alliance were led by Chamberlain, and those in favour by the foreign secretary, Lord Halifax. On May 15, 1939, after a lengthy discussion in the Foreign Policy Committee of Cabinet, Halifax finally prevailed. From that time the Chamberlain government pursued a military alliance with the Soviet Union and, while trying to preserve the independence of the Baltic States, negotiated in good faith. In August, Britain had a military mission in Moscow led by Admiral Ernle-Erle-Drax, a name worthy of Gilbert and Sullivan and for that reason a gift to later Soviet apologists. On August 17, Moscow terminated the military discussions. One week later the Nazi–Soviet Non-Aggression Pact was announced.

My thesis supervisor was R.A.C. Parker, who appeared to me, in both demeanour and accent, an almost stereotypical upper-class Englishman. As I discovered later, some Oxford colleagues called him "Back-to-Back Parker", a snide reference to the working-class housing in Yorkshire where he grew up. Parker was a warm-hearted and generous teacher. It is one of my Oxford regrets that I did not get to know him better. I did not even realise that he was, at Manchester University, a protégé of my once favourite historian, Sir Lewis Namier. At the time of the supervision his books on the foreign policy of Chamberlain and Churchill and his short history of the Second World War, where his humane and democratic sensibility shone through, were still in the future. After reading the thesis Parker encouraged me to try to publish it as a short book, a suggestion I declined. The topic seemed to me too narrow. In trepidation I showed the thesis to A.J.P. Taylor, whose *Origins of the Second World War* had recounted the standard left-wing "perfidious Albion" version of Anglo–Soviet relations that the newly released records had shown to be mistaken. After reading the thesis, Taylor summoned me. "Thank you, Manne," he said. "Just as I always believed."

It is not easy to assess the impact of Oxford on my later political writing and thought. Although I followed British politics closely in the two outstanding newspapers, *The Times* and *The Guardian*, it was entirely as an observer. During my time in Britain, I did not write so much as a letter-to-the-editor. Rai Gaita arrived in London on his way to Leeds shortly after I had completed the B.Phil. He remembers conversations where I told him that I was determined to return to Australia and become politically involved in one way or another. Nothing that I observed or read in these years altered my political identity as an anti-communist democratic socialist.

I did learn how to write without procrastination. With the expectation of substantial weekly essays during term there was no alternative. I also became familiar with archival historical research and the special kind of "Eureka" moment experienced when among the many apparently dreary papers something that overturns conventional wisdom is discovered. There was, however, something lacking in my writing at Oxford, in total some 150,000 words in eighteen months. The political works that have affected me most deeply are those driven by a moral intelligence capable of finding a language equal to the enormity of the evil that is analysed – on Stalinism, Aleksandr Solzhenitsyn's *The Gulag Archipelago*; on Nazism, Primo Levi's *If This Is a Man*. But I was also drawn to political writing of cool, analytic intelligence, like Hannah Arendt's *Eichmann in Jerusalem*, Walter Bagehot's *The English Constitution* or Alexis de Tocqueville's *The Old Regime and the French Revolution*. I came to the study of twentieth-century history because I hoped to understand the sources of its political evil, the burden of our times – totalitarianism, genocide and war. Were it not for that desire I would have followed Zelman Cowen's advice. Yet in the essays and the thesis I wrote at Oxford, the tone I adopted was morally neutral and on occasion imitative of A.J.P. Taylor's "powers will be powers" foreign policy realism. I had not yet found my voice.

In the summer of 1972, I moved from Oxford to London. I considered researching and writing a doctorate on Anglo-Soviet diplomatic relations from 1939 to 1945, incorporating the work already done. Shell was willing to fund me for one more year. I felt, however, too tired to contemplate researching and writing three-quarters of a doctoral thesis in twelve months. Instead, I applied for a job as a junior history master at one of Britain's best public schools, Dulwich College, just one rung below Eton and Harrow and the possessor of some of eighteenth-century Europe's finest paintings. The principal history master, E.N. ("Taffy") Williams, the author of *The Ancien Régime in Europe*, part of a Penguin historical series, was possibly the most unworldly man I have ever encountered. One of his colleagues told me that Taffy was unacquainted with the notes and coins of contemporary British money, leaving all those kind of transactions to his wife. I did not find this difficult to believe. Williams appointed me as a history master (teaching up to "A levels") exclusively on the basis of my Oxford degree, without worrying about my lack of teaching experience or my near-total ignorance of the complicated British education system. From time to time I have a nightmare where

I encounter the best "A level" student I taught, who informs me in a menacing way that he had not been prepared for even one question on the exam. Nor did I feel socially comfortable at Dulwich. On one occasion, a senior teacher asked me to explain the meaning of a phrase I had used in a student report – "from here on in" – that he regarded as an uncouth "Australian-ism". On another, a different teacher, having observed me wearing a multicoloured outfit and playing tennis remarkably poorly, informed me in an irritable tone that at Dulwich there was a strict tennis dress code – white shirt, white shorts, white sandshoes, white socks.

Having separated from Ann Tregear at the end of Oxford, I lived in London alone. In theory, my domestic circumstance seemed wonderful. For a reasonable rent I had to myself the entire second floor of one of the handsome houses on Thurloe Square in South Kensington, overlooking the magnificent Victoria and Albert Museum. In practice, I was more uncomfortable than at any time in my life. The owner of the house, Lady Campbell, was an aged member of Britain's high aristocracy, who lived on the ground and first floor and who had fallen on very hard times. When I moved in, Lady Campbell told me that her house was centrally heated. Unfortunately, she could only afford to heat her house by coal once or twice a month. For the winter of 1972–73, when I was at home, I huddled by an electric radiator dressed in my overcoat. I greatly enjoyed conversation with Lady Campbell. As a little girl, she told me, she had visited the court of Czar Nicholas II.

She was, however, a terrible snob, mocking the Queen Mother as a class upstart – a "mere Bowes-Lyon" (whatever that meant). She was also unexpectedly kind. On one occasion I forgot to turn off my bath, flooding her first floor. As we mopped up together, she was both excited by the drama and altogether forgiving. The principal problem of her domestic arrangements was the couple who lived in the basement flat. In return for the risibly small Edwardian rent of 3 guineas per week that she charged, she believed them to be Edwardian-style servants. Almost every day and night she knocked tirelessly with a shoe on the iron staircase banister leading down to their flat demanding the service she thought they owed her.

They generally ignored her banging. On one occasion I observed the young woman eventually emerge from the basement flat and scream in a London cockney, "Who do you think you are?" To which Lady Campbell answered, simply and truly: "A princess."

When I learned that Uncle Hans, whom I loved, had cancer, I left London almost at once. I was uneasy about my job at Dulwich College. Thurloe Square was both cold and, because of the drama of the basement flat, nerve-racking. For the first time ever I was lonely. And I had never intended to make my life in England. My home was Australia.

*

In 1974 I tutored in German history at the University of Melbourne. The lecturer was John Foster, a delightful man who will probably be best remembered for his charming and whimsical AIDS memoir, *Take Me to Paris, Johnny*. I realised at once that teaching would not be a job for me but a vocation. During that year one of my students was a beautiful young woman, Anne D. In our first tutorial she arrived wearing a motorcycle helmet and an elegant antique coat she had bought at an op shop. I quickly understood that Anne was a forensic and unusually sensitive writer. In the first essay of hers I read I was struck by her empathetic description of the anguish of the chain-smoking and brow-beaten Austrian chancellor in his negotiations with Hitler on the eve of the *Anschluss*. I learned that Anne was also a first-rate eventing equestrian rider, which involved dressage, show jumping and cross-country galloping over obstacles at speed. Anne had so little money that she was obliged to carry her saddle on public transport to a paddock on the outskirts of Melbourne where her beloved horse, Joe, was agisted. I was almost as impressed with what I learned about her as a rider as I was with what I already knew about her as an apprentice historian and writer. I did not realise that during that year Anne's mother experienced a recurrence of a psychotic illness, schizophrenia. Anne gave up a lucrative scholarship at a university college to look after her. She did this for the next two and a half years, and searched for good psychiatric care, while finishing her honours degree. Although Anne was already anti-communist, she was also a member of the anti–nuclear weapons environmental left and wore a "Right to Choose" badge that we argued amicably about. It was some years before we married. However, meeting her in 1974 was without doubt my life's greatest good fortune.

While I was teaching with John Foster I applied unsuccessfully for a lectureship at the University of Melbourne. The professor of history, Greg Dening, advised me to think about trying for a job at a teachers' college. This suggestion so outraged Frank Knopfelmacher – who had checked up on the progress of my Oxford studies when he visited there while I was a student – that he decided to take my future in hand.

Even though Knopfelmacher later fell out badly with Hugo Wolfsohn, as eventually he did with almost everyone, at the time they were friends. On Knopfelmacher's recommendation, Wolfsohn appointed me in late 1974 to a lectureship in the department of politics at La Trobe University. I doubt that Wolfsohn had read a word I had written. I was not asked to submit a formal application. I was not interviewed. I did not have a doctorate. I had published just one academic article. I was twenty-seven years old. And yet I had been appointed to a position from which, because of academic tenure, I would not be able to be removed – short of criminality or madness – for the remainder of my working life. The reign of the God Professor was already almost over but, at least in the person of Hugo, not yet entirely dead.

I arrived at La Trobe at the beginning of 1975, a decade after its establishment. In the areas of the humanities and the social sciences it had already attracted many outstanding academics. The husband-and-wife team of Allan Martin, the biographer of Henry Parkes and Robert Menzies, and Jean Martin, the pioneering sociologist of Australian migration, had left a year or so before I arrived. One of the most prominent members of the "Australian School" of philosophical materialism, Jack Smart, was still at La Trobe as a reader in philosophy. Younger members of his department included Peter Singer and Frank Jackson, both about to embark on distinguished careers. Greg

Dening had already moved from La Trobe to Melbourne, but other members of the Clifford Geertz–influenced La Trobe ethnographic school of history, Inga Clendinnen and Rhys Isaac, remained. Rhys was soon to be awarded a Pulitzer Prize for his study of eighteenth-century colonial Virginia. Inga eventually moved, because of ill health, from her studies of the Aztecs to two celebrated popular histories, *Reading the Holocaust* and *Dancing with Strangers*, and a wonderful memoir, *Tiger's Eye*. A distinctly non-ethnographic colleague of theirs, John Hirst, was by now a senior lecturer. With his trilogy, *Convict Society and Its Enemies*, *The Strange Birth of Colonial Democracy* and *The Sentimental Nation*, he established himself as Australia's pre-eminent nineteenth-century political historian. John became one of my most valued La Trobe friends. Inexplicably, in 2016 he took his own life.

John was a liberal empiricist. The gloomy and renowned Icelandic scholar Jóhann Árnason was, by contrast, a wide-ranging and sophisticated Marxist social theorist, a member of the department of sociology. One of its professors was Claudio Véliz, a charming, elegant and snobbish economic historian who had been driven into exile by the actions of revolutionary students at the University of Chile during the brief period of the Allende government. Once a moderate left-winger, by 1975 Claudio was a staunch conservative, as was a lecturer in the department, John Carroll, the author of two brilliant early books, *Break-out from the Crystal Palace* and *Puritan, Paranoid, Remissive*. Irreconcilably different political visions finally pulled us apart in the mid-1990s. Before then, for almost two decades, he was my closest La Trobe friend. Of all the scholars of the humanities at La Trobe at the time of my arrival, however, perhaps the most distinguished was Dale Trendall, the world authority on the southern Italian vases in the time of Ancient Greece. How he had been convinced to make his way to the paddocks of Bundoora was something I never learned.

According to Leo Tolstoy, "All happy families are alike; every unhappy family is unhappy in its own way." The same is true of university departments. When I arrived at La Trobe, I quickly discovered not only that the department of politics was seriously unhappy, but also that the reason was the strange personality of Hugo Wolfsohn. Hugo was a German Jew who had escaped from Nazi Germany to Italy as a young man, had been interned as an enemy alien in 1940 in wartime Britain and had then been transported on the HMS *Dunera* to Australia and the detention camps in Hay and Tatura. Although he hardly published anything, Hugo was appointed the foundation professor of politics at La Trobe – almost certainly because of glowing references from his University of Melbourne colleagues. Once I got to know him, I wondered whether his colleagues had an additional, secret reason for their recommendation. The prospect of departmental life without Hugo would undoubtedly have been alluring.

At La Trobe, Hugo regarded the department of politics as a small community – or a *Gemeinschaft*, as he might have put it – over which he enjoyed unchallengeable authority. My first vision of the department was of a human caravan, made up of its members, on the walkway that led to the staff club. Perhaps they had been summoned to greet their recently appointed colleague. One of Hugo's peculiarities was the expectation that, whenever possible, members of his department, especially junior members, would take their lunch together and with him. Because of this, I became friendly with Hugo's curious choices of departmental tutors. Another recently appointed lecturer, John Chiddick, was less accommodating of these lunches, and after some months, refused to attend. Unhappily for Hugo, he had recently appointed not only Chiddick but another similarly conservative young English political theorist, Michael James. Their presence seemed to have upset the departmental equilibrium; shortly after my arrival they led a rebellion. The issue was whether minutes would be taken at departmental meetings. For some months the department was in turmoil over this grave matter. Hugo was supported by a reader in the department, Joan Rydon, best known as the accumulator of information about commonwealth parliamentarians, and by Gerard Henderson, a tutor who was still working on his doctorate on B.A. Santamaria and the Australian Roman Catholic bishops. I sided with the rebels, drinking regularly with the departmental Englishmen – the two theorists and a Yorkshire-born Sovietologist, John Miller – at a pub in Fairfield we re-christened The Whingeing Pom. John Chiddick was openly gay, and because of this – as several of us discovered – Hugo had conducted a merciless campaign of persecution. At one of our drinking sessions, John argued that Hugo was worse than Hitler. I told him I thought the claim somewhat excessive. The days of drinking at The Whingeing Pom were over. For many months, John and I did not speak to each other. Later we again became friends.

Eventually, in 1979, the students in the department of politics, led by Theo Theophanous, a future minister in three Victorian Labor governments, staged their own rebellion, forming a politics society and demanding the right to elect two student representatives to participate in departmental meetings. The majority of the staff supported the suggestion. Hugo and Joan were bitterly opposed. On this occasion I do not have to rely upon memory. *Rabelais*, the student newspaper, recorded what happened as the vote for the student representatives was taken.

> At the conclusion of the voting ... those students still left were treated to scenes of which the Marx Brothers would be proud. Professors Wolfsohn and Rydon entered the room and attempted to disrupt the meeting. The tirade centred around the supposed illegality of the elections and the illegality of the Politics Society ... To report the tantrum in full would be impossible.

The following issue reported that most of the staff had condemned Hugo and Joan's intervention. Even though the vice-chancellor, John Scott, publicly criticised *Rabelais*' entirely credible report as "a mixture of fact, fiction, rumour and innuendos", it was clear by now that the *ancien régime* had fallen. In a remark often (incorrectly) attributed to Henry Kissinger, academic disputes were so bitter precisely because so little was at stake. But even Kissinger would have been surprised by the prolonged pettiness of this one. When one of Europe's most brilliant intellectuals, Ágnes Heller, in exile from Kadar's communist

Hungary, took a position in sociology at La Trobe in 1977, her immediate characterisation of Hugo was brutal – as La Trobe's version of the bitter, reactionary conspirator Dudu from Thomas Mann's *Joseph and His Brothers*.

I once more or less concurred with this judgement. I now regard it as harsh. Hugo was a tormented man who had lost home and family as a teenager and never regained his balance. When he fought student politicians, he thought he was fighting student Maoists from a decade earlier. More importantly, psychologically speaking, when he thought he was fighting student Maoists, he imagined he was fighting Nazis. He was at his scintillating best only at the lectern or in conversation. In February 1982 Hugo Wolfsohn decided to undergo heart bypass surgery. Although for years they had not spoken, Frank Knopfelmacher tried to warn him through an intermediary not to proceed because of the danger. Hugo died on the operating table. For the next thirty-five years, the collective life of the department of politics was happy, and from one point of view rather boring, resembling all other untroubled academic departments.

The first subjects I taught at La Trobe were Nazism in Theory and Practice (with Hugo, although I did most of the work) and International Communism – a study of the Comintern, the Stalinisation of Eastern Europe and the subsequent splits in the communist movement. In the late 1960s and early 1970s La Trobe had a well-deserved reputation as a radical campus. By 1975, in general all was quiet on the northern front. Small groups of revolutionaries, however, still existed – most importantly the Maoists and a splinter group of Trotskyists, known as the Spartacists. Such groups denounced the mainstream so-called Independent Left as traitors to the revolution. Even more enthusiastically, they denounced each other. In 1975 several Maoists and Spartacists enrolled in my subject, no doubt believing that I was a supporter of the international communist movement. They were soon disillusioned. Most wandered off.

It is customary to look back fondly on the days of the La Trobe revolutionaries. Because of an incident that occurred within months of my arrival – when one of my students almost killed another – this is a nostalgia I do not share. This incident was comprehensively reported in the pages of *Rabelais*. Liberal Party students had invited the premier of Victoria, Dick Hamer, to deliver a lecture. A group of Maoists, who called themselves the Prisoner Action Group, broke into the room where Hamer was dining and tried to force him to eat porridge. A smaller group of Spartacists also broke in and raised "Down with Imperialism" placards. The Maoists were enraged by their impertinence. They launched a furious attack, punching and kicking the defenceless Spartacists, who were all badly beaten. One of my students, who led the fighting, threw another of my students, a Spartacist, Andrew Georgiou, through a plate-glass window. He was taken to hospital with a punctured lung. The Maoists threatened the editors of *Rabelais* that if their names were published reprisals would follow. To their honour, the editors published their names. One of the more violent Maoists of that era studied with me a few years later. Following one tutorial, he asked me whether I regarded Malcolm Fraser's creation of a "razor gang" to oversee minor budget cuts as sufficient grounds for a political assassination. I stared at him in disbelief. One of the Maoists at the Hamer lunch later became a leading and affable trade unionist; another a principled defender of multiculturalism. For his part, Andrew Georgiou recovered to become (aptly) a professor at Macquarie University's Centre for Health Systems and Safety Research.

I now began to lecture and tutor first-year students on the political history of Europe. For the most part this was a pleasurable experience. I can vividly recall the enthusiasm shown by a young woman of working-class Greek background for Walter Bagehot's *The English Constitution*. Some of the students I taught in their first year were genuinely brilliant. I will never forget the moment when one, Shaun Kenaelly, strolled down after a lecture and corrected me on a detail concerning Queen Anne and the succession to the British Crown in the confusing period between the Stuarts and the Hanoverians. Some, however, had scraped through their final high-school year and could barely read or write. I would be lying if I did not admit that the experience of teaching some of these first-year students was rather a shock.

Whatever position one might take in the discussions about the nature of the university – and mine was still shaped by a democratised and feminised version of Cardinal Newman – a common assumption was the prior existence of basic literacy, or so it seemed to me.

Nineteen eighty-three turned out to be a very poor year in our four first-year politics subjects. Almost half of those enrolled either dropped out of their classes or failed. Something in me cracked. With another teacher of first-year politics – one of the whingeing poms, Michael James – I decided to co-write an article on the problems facing the newer universities in the post-Whitlam era of expansion. Part of our argument was statistical. We discovered in the university records that between 1975 and 1983 the failure and dropout rate in the six most popular humanities and social sciences subjects had increased from a quarter to a third. Part of our argument was anecdotal. We reproduced five not untypical passages from essays or exam scripts to illustrate for the general public the kind of conceptual confusion we believed was commonly encountered among some students, not only at La Trobe but also, we assumed, at other newer universities. One read: "Germany was on the spot where she was face to face with a new original problem, a strike, which involved herself and fellow countries, and so it was a great political strain upon her shoulders." And another: "Socially Chinese society is divided according to capital accumulated per individual as all population is equally subject to the Monarch." Our conclusion was that as numbers entering universities were increasing, it was vital that governments acknowledge the existence of a problem and that secondary schools, especially government-funded ones, accept their responsibility for preparing students for university. The article was accepted by a magazine called *Australian Society*. We sent an advance copy to the education editor of *The Age*. On February 23, 1984, it published a front-page article with the headline: "Decline in Students' Literacy Is Alarming, Say Academics". In *The Age*, weeks of controversy raged. Most memorable for me was an article headlined, "Standards Are Oppressions".

At La Trobe, all hell broke loose. On the day *The Age*'s report was published, the vice-chancellor, Professor John Scott, issued a statement entitled "La Trobe Is Proud!" Although conceding our right to express our personal opinions, it was his "duty as Vice-Chancellor to comment when such viewpoints are *not* in accord with university policy". Several La Trobe academics published letters of condemnation in *The Age*. A strident article was published in *Australian Society*'s April issue, entitled "How to Fail at Education Statistics". It was written by the dean of social sciences, Ron Wild, the deputy dean, "Kit" Carson, and a lecturer in sociology with a specialty in social statistics, David de Vaus (later a great dean). Its tone is captured in its concluding remarks:

> Manne and James have attacked a progressive education policy on the basis of their own narrow, conservative and elitist values and have attempted to support this position with misleading statistics and erroneous interpretations... We hope that Manne and James' lectures to Politics 1 students are more adequately prepared and argued.

By contrast, the responses of the minister for Education, Senator Susan Ryan, and a left-wing student in *Rabelais* were positively civil. The only support I can recall (apart from that of friends) came from La Trobe University's dean of education, Brian Crittenden, and, surprisingly enough for those who have followed the subsequent development of our relations, from a member of the staff of John Howard, at the time the deputy leader of the Opposition: my old La Trobe colleague Gerard Henderson.

Looking back, I am struck by how politically naive I was in thinking that an article of this kind could be published without some form of institutional backlash. I also think that we made mistakes in our article. One was to describe La Trobe as a "lower status" university. The phrase was meant only to recognise an undeniable reality. Like all the newer universities, La Trobe had not yet been able to attract many students who scored the highest marks in Year 12. As a consequence, it was certain, in the age of rapid university expansion, to experience far more severely than Melbourne or Monash or their interstate equivalents the problems associated with poor-quality secondary schooling. We had not intended even remotely to demean our academic colleagues, or indeed ourselves. We also should have known that for a political historian and a political theorist to enter the minefield of statistical analysis was unwise. In their criticism of our competence with statistics, our many critics were often probably right. In their angry and abusive dismissal of the concerns we identified – poor-quality secondary schooling and the problem of high levels of first-year student failure and dropout – they were almost certainly wrong.

The most venomous critic of our *Australian Society* article was our dean, Ron Wild. Ten weeks after the publication of our article, because of his many personal insults – which included a doctored quote and questions about the quality of my teaching – I sent him a letter resigning from the Social Sciences Board of Studies. I promised that I would return to the board when his term of office expired. That came sooner than imagined. In 1986 Wild published a textbook, of which large parts, it transpired, appeared to be plagiarised. One of the problems our article had raised was that of plagiarism – among first-year students, but not professors. Wild offered his resignation and accepted a teaching post in Port Hedland. I would like to be able to say this unexpected turn of events afforded me no secret pleasure.

Academics choose a life at university to research and write as well as to teach. Regarding this aspect of my life at La Trobe I still feel extremely fortunate. Currently, young lecturers are under permanent pressure to produce peer-reviewed publications, if possible in leading academic journals, for which they are awarded points. Effectively, they are discouraged from spending time on writing and research which will not contribute to their score. Somewhat contradictorily, they are also encouraged to write for newspapers or in online publications like *The Conversation*, to boost their university's public profile. When I arrived at La Trobe the system was entirely different. There were no metrics of any kind. It was perfectly possible to spend thirty pleasant years as a tenured academic without publishing anything. In social sciences at La Trobe the only evidence of publication was an annual list distributed to all staff. After Ágnes

Heller arrived, a considerable portion of that list was filled by her diligently documented new books and articles and the translations of her previous works. The only rewards for publication were intercollegial pride and, far more importantly, eventual promotion up the academic ladder – lecturer, senior lecturer, reader or associate professor and then, bingo, professor! (The only academic I knew who declined the final prize was John Hirst. As great an enigma in his life as in his death, he explained to his friends that he didn't feel like a professor.) There was no reason not to spend considerable time writing magazine articles or books aimed at the general public, but, oddly enough, publication in newspapers was considered a somewhat downmarket activity. As the university in Australia had not yet been corporatised, concern about the university's profile was in its infancy. Branding or logos at this time were unthinkable.

In retrospect, I see that during my first years at La Trobe my publications took two quite separate tracks. On the first track were articles in well-regarded academic journals concerning my "specialty": British foreign policy before the outbreak of the Second World War, the subject to which my existential interest in the causes and consequences of Nazism had, according to scholarly convention, by now shrunk. I was never, however, quite able to forget a passage about an academic article written by the antihero of Kingsley Amis' *Lucky Jim*: "It was a perfect title, in that it crystallized the article's niggling mindlessness, its funereal parade of yawn-enforcing facts, the pseudo-light it threw on non-problems." I did not regard my academic journal publications like this. I knew that a small number of academic articles in scholarly journals, although not mine, had revolutionised a field of study. But I could not help myself from seeing the similarities between my own productions – "Some British Light on the Nazi–Soviet Pact" or "The Foreign Office and the Failure of Anglo-Soviet Rapprochement" – and Lucky Jim's, "The Economic Influence of the Developments in Shipbuilding Techniques, 1450 to 1485".

On the second track, I began writing regularly for *Quadrant*, Australia's anti-communist "small magazine": longish articles on the foreign policy books of George Kennan (Mr X) and Henry Kissinger, for example, or the memoir of Richard Nixon. At first, I did not regard this writing as nearly as significant as my work on British foreign policy. However, I did notice that people actually read the articles and that they appeared in print within weeks of completion rather than within years, as was the case with my academic work. Even more importantly, I was able to write on subjects that arose from present political passion rather than longstanding historical curiosity. Between 1975 and 1979, as I shall explain in greater detail in the next chapter, I took a great interest in the catastrophe occurring in Pol Pot's Cambodia. It was because I wrote in *Quadrant* that I was able to publish a critique of the blindness of the extreme left to the crimes of the Khmer Rouge.

Shortly after arriving at La Trobe, I knocked on Professor Claudio Véliz's door to ask why, in his opinion, the socialist government of Salvador Allende had been destroyed in a bloody coup and replaced by the dictatorship of General Pinochet. Claudio told me he had been a friend of Allende and his family, but that due to economic mismanagement and other matters, the army had been provoked into action by the anger of society – in particular, by groups of conservative women, who had thrown grains of wheat at the generals to show that they thought them to be chickens. (It occurred to me that if the army had indeed been intimidated by this, the women were almost certainly right in their assessment.) It was not long before I was invited by Claudio to attend something called the Seminar on the Sociology of Culture.

Everything about the seminar sat oddly with the culture of the 1970s Australian university. Attendance was by invitation only. Discussions took place under Chatham House rules: anything learned at the seminar might be published or broadcast, but never the name of the person who had provided the information. The seminar met regularly at lunchtime on Wednesday in Claudio's office. Sandwiches were served by a gracious woman who appeared to be Claudio's private secretary, and whom we all addressed as Mrs Mitchell. Regular attendees at the seminar, apart from Claudio, were John Carroll; John Hirst; Dale Kent, a Renaissance historian and author, decades later, of an extraordinarily honest and self-lacerating memoir, *The Most I Could Be* (and the only regular female participant in the early days); the dean of education, Brian Crittenden; a senior lecturer in art history, Bob Gaston; the curator of art at La Trobe, John Waterhouse; the professor of accounting, Michael Lawriwsky; very occasionally Ágnes Heller; somewhat later, the professor of applied mathematics, Ed Smith; and somewhat later still, the linguist Kate Burridge. Almost every week a guest from business, politics, the public service or the arts was invited. The purpose was nothing other than conversation. Understandably, there was some ill feeling about the group among our colleagues, because of its exclusivity and its supposed conservatism. The former charge was obviously true; the latter only partially so. Some in the seminar were genuine conservatives. Some were merely independent spirits or mavericks or eccentrics. It was among this group that I found, for some considerable time, my closest university friends.

There were very many interesting lunches. Three memories abide. In the mid-1980s, Hugh Morgan, the head of Western Mining, attended. He announced his intention to use his personal influence and some small change from his company's financial resources to transform Australia's political culture. Over the next years, Western Mining donated money to what were then called "New Right" think-tanks, like the reinvigorated Institute of Public Affairs or the recently created Centre for Independent Studies. At the same time, Morgan's speechwriter, Ray Evans, launched with John Stone, the former Treasury secretary, a series of conservative "societies" – the H.R. Nicholls, the Samuel Griffith, the Bennelong and the Lavoisier – whose purpose was to influence public policy in the areas of industrial relations, constitutional law, Indigenous affairs and climate change respectively. A less alarming memory is of a lunch with Sir Zelman Cowen following his retirement as Australia's governor-general. Zelman told us a story about his very elderly aunt, who had migrated to England from Russia and retained a strongly Jewish manner and a heavy Yiddish accent. Zelman's aunt had been hospitalised after hitting her head on her bath, which had temporarily put her in a coma. The attending doctors wondered whether her mental capacities had been affected. When she eventually emerged from the coma, her only clear memory was that her nephew was the governor-general of Australia. The doctors now believed they had their answer: she had, perhaps temporarily, lost her mind. As Zelman told this story, tears of laughter welled up in his eyes.

My favourite memory, however, came at the conclusion of a visit from Barry Jones, at the time the Hawke government's minister for science. Despite all his subsequent achievements, Jones was still most famous for the astonishing memory for facts he had revealed as the champion of champions of an early Australian television program, *Pick a Box*. As Barry left Claudio's office, he turned and exclaimed in his characteristically booming voice, "Thank you, Sergio."

Claudio's Wednesday lunches were accompanied by a series of invitation-only evening meetings on the Bundoora campus, called *conversazioni*. Someone remarked that it was at these occasions that several members of the Melbourne Establishment met each other for the first time. For a man who had settled in Australia in the early 1970s, this was, I suppose, a remarkable achievement. The *conversazioni* were formal occasions. A lecture was delivered. Dinner was taken, followed by discussion. No matter how uninteresting, each lecture was then published in a glossy brochure with a painting by one of the European Old Masters on the cover. The style of the lectures can be gleaned from some of the authors and titles: George Pell, "Catholicism in Australia"; Geoffrey Blainey, "Bill of Rights: Bill of Wrongs?"; Ronald Conway, "On the Need for Religion in a Secular Society"; Sir Claus Moser, "Running an Opera House"; the Earl of Harewood, "Opera and Elitism". The lecture I remember most vividly was delivered by Richard Searby, the chair of Rupert Murdoch's News Corporation, who argued that Ned Kelly was a serious criminal who had little to recommend him. Although I attended dutifully, privately I found the *conversazioni* somewhat comical. Decades later, in *Quadrant*, Claudio recalled that in all the events associated with the Seminar on the Sociology of Culture I never once wore a tie. He was right to consider this revealing.

In 1988 a super-*conversazione* was held at La Trobe on the future of the university. One of the speakers was John Silber, the ruthless, much hated but extremely effective president of Boston University. Silber was so impressed by Claudio that he managed to convince him to become the head of his university's elite "Professors Program". This had unforeseen consequences. Claudio had expected that he would retain his office at La Trobe. John Carroll, at that time the head of sociology, could not oblige and had no wish to. Claudio had left boxes of his glossy brochures in his office. John had to get rid of them. Claudio was furious. Relations between him and John broke down. I sided with John.

In the first years I spent at La Trobe I was uncertain about my future, and on two occasions was tempted by the possibility of escape. The first occurred around 1980, when Owen Harries – who became famous as the editor of the US foreign-policy magazine *The National Interest*, which published Francis Fukuyama's "The End of History?" – recommended me for a position on the staff of Prime Minister Malcolm Fraser. My application was rejected. If it had been accepted, I would have gone to Canberra and my life taken an altogether different course. In 1983 I applied for another political position, as a member of staff of the leader of the Opposition, Andrew Peacock. This time my application was successful. Thankfully, after trying my hand at writing a speech not one word of which I believed, I decided against it. Nineteen eighty-three was one of the happiest years of my life. Anne and I had recently married. We were deliriously in love. Our first child, Kate, had just been born. I could not bear the thought of being separated from Anne and Kate in order to write speeches concerning things I did not care about for a politician I did not much admire. My discontent at La Trobe at this time had nothing to do with feelings of political marginality at a left-wing university. It was due rather to a determination to try to play a more active political role in the life of the nation, the main reason I had returned from England to Australia.

Part II
Cold War

[6.]

Cambodia

WITHIN FOUR MONTHS OF MY COMMENCEMENT at La Trobe on January 1, 1975, the three Indochina communist parties had taken power in South Vietnam, Cambodia and Laos. The Vietnam War was over. Anti-communist publicists and intellectuals had long predicted – frequently with pseudo-precision as to numbers – that if these parties were successful, "bloodbaths" would inevitably follow. Although there was an immediate flood of millions of refugees from the three new communist states, it was only in Cambodia that the "bloodbath" prediction came true.

During the Cambodian civil war from 1970 to 1975 the capital, Phnom Penh, had swollen to between 2 and 3 million inhabitants. Some had fled from the vicious fighting between the pro-American forces of Marshal Lon Nol and the Khmer Rouge. Some had taken shelter from the saturation bombing campaigns that the United States' B52 aircraft rained down upon the peasant villages of eastern Cambodia where North Vietnamese troops were believed to be found. Some had escaped the terrifying rigours of new life in the "liberated" towns or villages under Khmer Rouge control.

On April 17, 1975, when the victorious Khmer Rouge entered Phnom Penh, the entire city was emptied of its inhabitants – immediately and without exception. Even pregnant women close to giving birth, even patients from hospitals – with their drips attached or on their trolley beds, some close to death – were ordered at gunpoint by Khmer Rouge soldiers, often teenagers, to join the slow march on the choked highways out of Phnom Penh in scorching 38-degree heat. What this evacuation also meant was that many members of families – parents and children, wives and husbands, brothers and sisters – who happened to be separated on April 17 never saw each other again. The Khmer Rouge ordered all non-Cambodians in Phnom Penh – including all remaining foreign correspondents – to gather in the grounds of the French Embassy. Three weeks or so later they were trucked to the Thai border. Because of this delay, eyewitness reports of the forced march out of Phnom Penh appeared in newspapers throughout the world. Among the best accounts were those of the *New York Times* correspondent Sydney Schanberg, published in the United States but widely syndicated beyond. (Schanberg is now best known as the author of *The Killing Fields* – the story of his relations with his Cambodian offsider, Dith Pran, and of Pran's experience of life under the Khmer Rouge – that in turn inspired the film that, more than anything else, brought the nightmare of the Khmer Rouge regime to the attention of the world.) Schanberg's vivid, lengthy and hair-raising reports of the forced march out of Phnom Penh and several other similar reports, like Jon Swain's in *The Guardian*, appeared in early May 1975. By now incontrovertible evidence of the astonishing cruelty of the Khmer Rouge was universally available. How could anyone give the benefit of the doubt to a regime that announced its victory to the world with a callous act of this magnitude and in such plain sight?

For the next three and a half years a small number of ideological fellow travellers or diplomats from kindly disposed governments were allowed entry into Cambodia. Both could be relied upon to report favourably on the Khmer Rouge regime. For an understanding of what was happening in the country that in late 1975 called itself Democratic Kampuchea, one source was the often bizarre and bombastic broadcasts of Radio Phnom Penh monitored and translated by the BBC. These, of course, required expert interpretation. "Each day passes in a holiday atmosphere", the Khmer Rouge's Radio Phnom Penh informed the world on March 24, 1976, "everywhere there resounds songs and cries of joy". Even more important were the eyewitness accounts of the thousands of refugees who escaped into Thailand. Even though a larger number of those fleeing from the Khmer Rouge regime made their way into Vietnam, their account of life in Democratic Kampuchea was generally suppressed until the Vietnamese regime's invasion that began on Christmas Day 1978. In the years between the evacuation of Phnom Penh and the Vietnamese invasion, the most useful journalism on Democratic Kampuchea appeared in the *Far Eastern Economic Review*, which covered the Khmer Rouge regime in detail and without any ideological bias. In 1977 two books primarily based on refugee witness were published: John Barron and Anthony Paul's *Murder of a Gentle Land* and François Ponchaud's *Cambodge, L'Année Zero*, the work of the French Catholic scholar who had spent the past ten years in Cambodia, that appeared in English translation the following year as *Cambodia Year Zero*.

I followed developments in Cambodia, including the monitored Radio Phnom Penh broadcasts, as closely as possible and in October 1977 published a review of the two books in *Quadrant*. I argued that while both were valuable, Ponchaud's was far better, avoiding altogether "the occasional lapses into vulgarity or triviality" that marred Barron and Paul. Already the reality of life under the Khmer Rouge, I argued, was in danger of being lost in a rather typical Cold War spat among the political intelligentsia:

> "[T]he left" in Australia either ignore the Cambodian refugees' stories entirely, or dismiss the stories as media fabrications ... [T]he "right" in general seem merely to *use* the stories of the suffering in Cambodia as debating points in their argument with the "left."

In my judgement, by 1977 the evidence of the criminal character of the Khmer Rouge regime was overwhelming and undeniable. Already Democratic Kampuchea had taken its place alongside Stalin's Soviet Union with its 20 million victims (according to Robert

Conquest's calculation), and the even greater number of Chinese who were either starved to death in Mao Zedong's Great Leap Forward or murdered in his Cultural Revolution.

As it happens, as the true character of the Khmer Rouge regime was emerging, the three volumes of Aleksandr Solzhenitsyn's magnificent *Gulag Archipelago* were published in English translation. I read each volume as soon as it appeared, volume two in one sitting on a flight from London to Melbourne. The *Gulag*'s unrelieved intensity of feeling; its volcanic sarcasm (a tone unusual in great literature) that captured the "yawning gap" between the moral claims of Soviet communism and its real-world consequences; the vast canvas of suffering Solzhenitsyn had painted; and his unmistakably sincere pity for the millions of Soviet communism's victims – affected me as nothing about the era of Stalin (and also Lenin) ever had before – or indeed has ever since. The books affected me so deeply, I now have little doubt, because of the soul-shock I experienced as a child when I learned about the Holocaust. In my political imaginary, when his leadership of the Khmer Rouge regime as secretary general of the Cambodian Communist Party was finally revealed, Pol Pot joined Hitler, Stalin and Mao as one of humankind's greatest evildoers. In my argument with those left-wing intellectuals who defended the Khmer Rouge, for the first time in my writing I was no longer able to contain my anger.

The evacuation of Phnom Penh and indeed of all other Cambodian cities and towns, we knew by now, had proven to be a human catastrophe. Some 20,000 patients, for example, were driven out of Phnom Penh's hospitals, if necessary at gunpoint. As Sydney Schanberg reported: "They went – limping, crawling on crutches, carried on relatives' backs, wheeled on their hospital beds." Women gave birth by the roadside. Civil servants of the Lon Nol government, soldiers of the Lon Nol army, Buddhist notables – were all summarily executed by Khmer Rouge cadres, often teenagers in black shirts and pants. From time to time, the people on the choked roads, while trudging out of Phnom Penh, came upon rotting corpses. Everyone from the evacuated towns and cities had been ordered to settle in the countryside. Radio Phnom Penh announced on March 11, 1976, that Kampuchea had already been transformed into "one huge worksite". Many of those without connection to rural Cambodia – like the mercantile Chinese – settled down wherever they were accepted or eventually landed. (There is a truly astonishing work of concentrated empathetic imagination about one Chinese Cambodian family that survived the killing fields, written by a daughter who was born shortly after the fall of the regime: Alice Pung's *Her Father's Daughter*.) In the early months of the revolution, many "intellectuals" – as those with an education or even just a pair of glasses were called – were taken from the rural labour brigades and executed. Despite the promise of absolute equality, rural Cambodia divided into two classes – the old inhabitants, the "base" people, and the arrivals, the "new" people. The new people were ordered to construct huts from whatever local materials they could find and then set to harsh physical work, sometimes ploughing formerly uncultivated ground in teams and by hand, in place of oxen, no matter their age, health or previous experience of manual labour.

Radio Phnom Penh informed these people that they were participating in the most advanced revolution in human history, surpassing those of Russia and even the Khmer Rouge's principal ally, China. The people worked for ten or twelve hours each day and sometimes, in moonlight or with braziers, even longer, for nine days out of ten. Families were no longer allowed to take their meals together. Everyone was required to eat communally. Rice was a luxury. People mostly ate something described to Ponchaud as "a black gruel out of rice, green bananas and red or white maize". As a consequence of the forced labour and the food, vast numbers of people were starving, and illness was everywhere. Pol Pot admitted on Chinese radio in late 1977 that 80 per cent of Cambodians were suffering from malaria. Dysentery, typhoid, cholera and beri-beri were also common. Although in Democratic Kampuchea money had been abolished, a black market existed where antibiotics or vitamins could be exchanged for rice. Illness, Ponchaud learned, was "virtually equivalent to a death sentence".

For the first two years or so, the authority under which everyone lived was called "Angka" (the Organisation) or "Angka Loeu" (the Organisation on High). Angka was surrounded by an aura of mystery and was treated as a kind of impersonal divinity. (Only in late 1977 was the rule of the Kampuchea Communist Party under the leadership of Pol Pot revealed with an ideology he described, at least in Beijing, as "Marxism-Leninism and Mao-Tse-tung thought".) Under Angka even the smallest infractions – avoiding work, grumbling, asking unwanted questions, making love, fossicking for food, eating with family – could be capital offences. Children acted as Angka's spies. In Democratic Kampuchea, unlike Vietnam, re-education camps were uncommon. The phrase "Angka wants to see you" was understood to be a death sentence. Offenders summoned by Angka were led away, perhaps tortured, and then executed. If anyone seeking to escape from Democratic Kampuchea was captured, they too were executed, or first tortured and then executed. No one was yet sure of the death toll in Democratic Kampuchea on the eve of the Vietnamese invasion, but it was most likely at least 1.5 million of the April 1975 population of fewer than 8 million.

In general, in the years before the Vietnamese invasion, the revolution taking place in Democratic Kampuchea was defended by the anti–Vietnam War left, with a small number of intellectuals devoting their lives to championing the Khmer Rouge regime. In France, Serge Thion and the authors of *Phnom Penh Libérée*, Jérôme and Jocelyne Steinbach; in the United Kingdom, Malcolm Caldwell from the School of Oriental and African Studies at the University of London and in the journal he founded the *Journey of Contemporary Asia*; and in the United States, most famously of all, Noam Chomsky with Edward Herman, but also George Hildebrand and Gareth Porter, authors of *Cambodia: Starvation and Revolution* (1976) and co-directors of the Indochina Resource Center. Australia played a surprisingly important role in the early muscular and enthusiastic defence of the Khmer Rouge regime. At Monash University, a former US foreign affairs officer and a historian of Cambodia, David Chandler, extended to the Khmer Rouge regime the benefit of whatever doubt still existed and quietly cheered on the younger Pol Pot enthusiasts to his left. As Chandler explained in an April 1977 article in *Commonweal*: "Surely, as a friend of mine has written, we Americans with our squalid record in Cambodia should be 'cautiously optimistic' about the new regime, 'or else shut up'".

Among Chandler's students, by far the most energetic supporter of Democratic Kampuchea was the young postgraduate Ben Kiernan. Kiernan would later become the most authoritative and prolific historian of what he came to regard as the genocidal and totalitarian Pol Pot regime. However, he began his academic career with several pro-Khmer Rouge articles. With his Cambodian partner, Chantou Boua, and the New Zealand couple Shane Tarr and Chou Meng Tarr, together with several Cambodians studying in Australia, Kiernan was also one of the key figures in the so-called Committee of Patriotic Cambodians, which from April 1977 published a roughly produced magazine called *News from Kampuchea*. To help explain my growing anger in what was the first political controversy in which I engaged, there is no better starting point than an analysis of *News from Kampuchea*.

The most interesting article published in the first two issues was the Tarrs' unselfconsciously revealing essay, "Our Experiences During the Liberation of Phnom Penh", a repudiation of the accounts of the evacuation by Sydney Schanberg and Jon Swain. The Tarrs took part in the slow march out of Phnom Penh. They had seen inside the hospitals that were in a dreadful state and were convinced they had been emptied because they were "unhygienic". Without evidence, they were certain that the patients must have been sent somewhere better. The Tarrs had not encountered any dead bodies apart from fifteen rotting corpses of Lon Nol soldiers opposite the Pepsi-Cola factory. They did assist in a roadside birth but, astonishingly, thought that what happened shone a positive light on the Khmer Rouge. The father begged the Tarrs to take their newborn baby as he knew that he and his wife would not be able to care for it. They agreed to assist and then "handed over responsibility" to a female Khmer Rouge cadre, who assured them that "Angkar would cope with the child". The Tarrs discussed the problem of the Cambodian bourgeoisie with Khmer Rouge soldiers and were told that most were "Chinese merchants" who "contributed absolutely nothing to Kampuchea". The Tarrs had heard the rumours about the looting of Khmer Rouge soldiers, their seizure at gunpoint of jewellery, radios and watches. Once more without evidence, they did not think this kind of robbery was "the general rule", except perhaps for the removal of motor cars, which was justifiable.

The Tarrs had trouble convincing the Khmer Rouge that Chou Meng should be allowed to leave Cambodia with her husband. Eventually they succeeded. On the truck ride out of Phnom Penh, Chou Meng informed members of the Khmer Rouge that in her opinion several of their fellow travellers most likely "worked for the CIA or other spy organisations". She appeared surprised, even discommoded, that those she fingered were allowed to leave Cambodia "unpunished". The New Zealand military attaché in Bangkok met the Tarrs at the Thai–Cambodian border. On hearing his voice, Chou Meng realised that she was "trapped in the West", at least for the present. The Tarrs were convinced that for the first time in centuries, Cambodia was master of its destiny.

This was indeed the central theme of *News from Kampuchea*. The first issue promised accurate information to counter "the worldwide campaign against Kampuchea in the right-wing Western press". It offered its readers "ninety minutes of cassette tapes featuring revolutionary songs in Khmer, including the Kampuchean National Anthem". The second issue took up the fight against the "notorious anti-communists" John Barron and Anthony Paul and François Ponchaud. Both *Murder of a Gentle Land* and *Cambodia, Year Zero* of necessity relied on refugee testimony for their understanding of what was happening inside the Khmer Rouge regime. The editorial in the second issue, one of whose authors was Ben Kiernan, claimed that "nearly all" the refugees on whom Barron and Paul and Ponchaud relied were "members of the old bourgeoisie" and indeed that "most of them are from the Chinese merchant class" who left "because the revolution did not allow them to go on exploiting the poor people of Kampuchea". The editorial pointed out that the small number of working-class refugees who had reached Australia claimed that "work in Australia is 'harder' than in revolutionary Kampuchea". The second issue also published a prediction by a Kampuchean leader: "Fifteen years from now, we consider we will have earned ourselves one of the highest living standards in Asia." This was supported by an article from a Radio Phnom Penh broadcast: "Constant Improvement in the Living Conditions of the Peasants of Kampuchea." At this time, through illness due to overwork and starvation rations, very large numbers of Cambodians were dying like flies, as many of those who had escaped from Democratic Kampuchea now put it.

And so it went. In issue three, *News from Kampuchea* published a *Der Spiegel* interview with the foreign minister of Democratic Kampuchea, Ieng Sary, who told of plans to create an economy of a kind "that has never yet occurred in history", one that placed "agriculture as the base". It also re-published a defamatory article from *The Sydney Morning Herald* that claimed that some recent Vietnamese refugees arrived in Broome with servants and gold bars, and a celebratory article from Radio Phnom Penh, of purest propaganda, that reported how the women of Kampuchea embraced the anniversary of the Kampuchean army's creation "with overflowing joy".

There was a particular and pressing reason why I became involved in the question of the Khmer Rouge regime's character. In recent years two books, Nicholas Bethell's *The Last Secret* (1974) and Nikolai Tolstoy's *Victims of Yalta* (1977), had been published on one of the most scandalous Allied actions at the end of the Second World War. Both recorded in great detail the British and American agreement to repatriate – involuntarily if necessary – the 3 million or so Soviet subjects who had fallen under their control. Some, like the soldiers of the Vlasov Army, had fought with the Germans. Others had not. That turned out not to matter greatly. Members of both groups of repatriates were either executed as soon as they were handed over to Stalin's secret police, the NKVD, or sentenced to a virtual death in one of the Arctic or Siberian labour camps of the Gulag Archipelago.

By 1977 several newspaper reports revealed that the Thai army was forcibly handing Cambodian refugees to the Khmer Rouge. Enough was known by now about their near-certain fate. There were even some eyewitness accounts of their murder soon after they crossed the border. I composed a letter-to-the-editor about this humanitarian issue, criss-crossing Melbourne to gather the signatures of several prominent people. With a man I had not previously known, Laurie Crozier (the brother of one of the most radical and well-connected Western Cold Warriors, Brian Crozier), a lobby group called the Committee for Cambodian Refugees emerged, whose membership never exceeded two. More letters-to-the-editor followed. On my way back from a research trip to London, I stopped off at Bangkok and, with papers from the local United Nations High Commissioner for Refugees office, visited a refugee camp on the Thai–Cambodian border, Aranyaprathet. Dozens of refugees with a smattering of English handed me pieces of paper with their details, begging for help. I said I would do everything I could to help their cases for settlement in Australia, which even at the time I knew would come to nothing. Nonetheless I regarded those pieces of paper as precious and held on to them. My strongest memory of the Aranyaprathet camp is of a Cambodian mother of Chinese ethnicity, who invited me into the small hut she and her husband had been allocated where, out of nothing and in the most desperate of circumstances, she had managed miraculously to fashion for the family a place of domestic order and harmony, a home.

In late 1977 I learned that the Australian Council for Overseas Aid (ACFOA) was holding a major conference on human rights in Asia the following January, in Hobart. My academic specialty was not Cambodia in the 1970s but British foreign policy in the 1930s. However, I knew that the conference would be dominated by academics of the left and either Christian or secular humanitarian aid agencies, none of whom had shown any interest in investigating the hair-raising stories of what was happening in Cambodia under the Khmer Rouge. At the end of the Vietnam War, anti-anticommunism was almost universal on the left. Nonetheless I thought that a conference on human rights in Asia in 1978 without discussion of Cambodia would be a travesty, the equivalent of a conference on human rights in Europe in 1938 where Hitler, Mussolini and the threat of Franco were discussed without mentioning what had happened in Stalin's Soviet Union at the time of the state-induced famine in Ukraine and its 5 or 6 million dead, or the post-1936 Stalin-Yezhov Great Terror, during which hundreds of thousands were executed and millions transported to a Siberian or Arctic labour camp. The history of interwar Europe – from Sarajevo to Yalta – here and elsewhere, influenced the way I interpreted contemporary Cold War politics.

The organisers of the ACFOA conference turned my offer of a paper into a debate with Ben Kiernan, who was still a Monash University PhD candidate. According to Kiernan, Western media reports about the death toll in Democratic Kampuchea – 500,000 or even 1 million – were "wildly speculative" and considered "absurd" by "responsible journalists" in Bangkok. (As we now know, by the end of 1977 the excess death toll was probably already more than a million.) Kiernan claimed that some of the evidence used to blacken the reputation of the Khmer Rouge had been produced for anti-communist propaganda purposes and was fake. *The Sydney Morning Herald* had published photos, supposedly of a Khmer Rouge execution, a forced slave labour brigade and a forced wedding, unaware that five days earlier their authenticity had been questioned by the conservative *Bangkok Post*. An article in *Time* magazine had even suggested that there existed a Khmer Rouge "extermination order ... [to] kill anyone with an education". According to Kiernan, this was ridiculous. If this were true (as we now know it was) "[w]hy, then, did the Khmer Rouge grant permission to return home to over 500 Cambodians living abroad", most of whom were "well educated"? In a *Melbourne Journal of Politics* article Kiernan named five Cambodians who had been studying in Australia, all of whom had returned to Cambodia. As Kiernan subsequently discovered, all five had been murdered.

The debate about what was happening in Cambodia was never purely academic but rather, as it turned out, a matter of life and death. Kiernan quoted the view of Ith Sarin, a Cambodian primary school inspector who had spent nine months among the resistance fighters in the remote countryside. The first rule of the Khmer Rouge was, he said, "Love, respect and serve the people." As we now know, Khmer Rouge cadres executed on a whim. Their second rule was, "Do not touch the people's possessions, not even a tiny chilli or a cup of rice." In fact, as the last Western journalists in Cambodia observed, as soon as the Khmer Rouge entered Phnom Penh their cadres looted everything they could get their hands on. Kiernan believed that the Khmer Rouge were achieving great things. Agriculture was progressing wonderfully well with three or even four rice crops per year. "A new society" was under construction, with "neither rich nor poor".

The case I made at Hobart could hardly have been more different. There was nothing original about it. It was simply a distillation of Barron and Paul and, even more, Ponchaud, paying attention to the bombast of Radio Phnom Penh, and a willingness to draw comparisons with the historic crimes of Stalin and the contemporary crimes of Mao. These were my concluding words:

> The central motifs ... of the refugees' accounts of lives in the new villages are of continual gnawing hunger, the murderous overwork, and the ravages of diseases against which the exhausted body has no resistance. Spiritually the dominant motifs are a crippling and permanent fear, and an overwhelming feeling of powerlessness, of their being (and their family's being) in the eyes of "Angka" literally worthless ... If one is interested in the question of human rights in Asia, Cambodia is the place to look. The people of Cambodia have come to understand what it is like to be stripped bare of all rights and of anything familiar – custom, religion, home, even meagre possessions – which might offer the individual protection against the Regime and History. Even if in the future the regime manages to provide the people with adequate shelter, food and medicine, the psychological and spiritual scars may take generations to heal. No trust between rulers and ruled seems possible. Nor can the crude simplicities of

their ideology – a mish-mash of populism and Marxist slogans – replace (although it can extirpate) the Khmer religion, Buddhism. For it is not only true that ends cannot justify means, it is also (and more importantly) true that means determine ends. Cambodia – people and rulers – will live for a long time to be haunted by the terrible crimes of the last two and a half years.

My talk was met by a stony silence. The conference organisers had chosen as chair of the session Derek Roebuck, who had recently co-authored with Wilfred Burchett *The Whores of War*, a book on the civil wars between communist and non-communist forces in southern Africa. During my talk, Nonie Sharp, one of the editors of *Arena*, the Marxist journal, tiptoed out. As she later explained, there were other talks being delivered simultaneously that she hoped would be of greater interest. A young international relations academic, Richard Tanter, asked me how I justified the use of fake photographs for anti-Khmer Rouge propaganda purposes. I replied that I had no inside knowledge that would allow me to conclude whether the photographs were fake but that nothing I said relied on them. Ben Kiernan's partner, Boua Chanthou, was called on by the chair. She declared something like: "Mr Manne, you will not be welcome in Democratic Kampuchea." The audience applauded. The chair said something like: "That seems like the best way for this session to end."

The next morning, a conference attendee told me that my talk had not gone down well. The fact that I had spoken about Cambodia and not Democratic Kampuchea, the regime's self-description, was regarded as both scandalous and revealing. I was finished with the ACFOA conference. For the one and only time in my life I visited a casino – Hobart's was Australia's first – to get as far away as I could from the smug and pious atmosphere of conventional anti-anticommunism that prevailed in the late 1970s on the left in Australia. My first roulette wager was successful. I used the money to hire a car and travel across beautiful Tasmania. Eighteen months later I received a letter from Eris Mary Smyth, a Catholic mother of eight, staunch trade unionist and supporter of women's causes:

I first heard your expose of the Cambodian situation at an ACFOA Conference in Hobart – where in the interests of even-handedness the organisers had also sponsored a pro "Pol Pot" speaker who concentrating on grammes [sic] and ounces tried to convince us that Cambodians were eating better than ever. The travesty of the Conference ... finished many of us – & especially me – with the objectivity of both "academic" and "church sponsored" overseas aid organisations. Your paper – and that of Mr James Dunn, who seemed much concerned with the fate of the East Timorese – were the only two not self seeking, self serving or self promoting.

On December 25, 1978, Vietnam invaded Cambodia with 150,000 no doubt battle-hardened troops. By the end of January 1979, the Khmer Rouge regime was defeated. Pol Pot retreated to the jungles on the Thai border where, on a far smaller scale, his blood-soaked method of rule continued. Phnom Penh was in the hands of a pro-Vietnamese Cambodian government led by Heng Samrin and Hun Sen, Khmer Rouge defectors favoured by Hanoi. Wilfred Burchett, the pro-communist journalist and preferred Hanoi publicist, at one time a supporter of the Khmer Rouge, led Vietnam's anti–Khmer Rouge propaganda campaign in the English-speaking world. In March 1979 he wrote:

> I have come to the reluctant conclusion that even the worst of the "horror" stories were understatements of a generalized type of medieval barbarity that has reigned in Cambodia since "liberation" on April 17, 1975. *In over forty years of reporting, starting with the anti-Jewish pogroms in Nazi Germany in November 1938, I have never heard more horrifying fact-based denunciations of a government's genocidal activities against its own people and its ethnic minorities* [Burchett's emphasis].

The same month, Burchett published in *The Guardian* his calculation of the number of people who had been killed by Pol Pot.

He arrived at the startling conclusion that of the 7 or 8 million Cambodians alive on April 17, 1975, only slightly more than 5 million had survived. If Burchett's claim was accurate or even plausible, it was now clear to almost everyone that something truly astonishing had taken place: the Pol Pot regime had killed between 25 and 30 per cent of its own people in three years and eight months. History records nothing comparable. In a famous review of Ponchaud that appeared in *The New York Review of Books* in 1977, the French leftist Jean Lacouture coined a phrase to capture what the Khmer Rouge were doing – "auto-genocide".

In *Quadrant* in October 1979, I published an analysis of the genocide denialist campaign. This was the first significant political article I had ever written. The campaigners argued that supporters of America's failed war in Indochina needed to invent a communist bloodbath to provide some retrospective justification for the catastrophic damage the US and its allies had visited upon Vietnam and, more broadly, Indochina. If the idea of the communist bloodbath was indeed a fabrication of the US government and its captive media, I argued, was it not puzzling that Cambodia rather than Vietnam was the country chosen? After all, it was Vietnam where most of the fighting and the destruction had taken place. Insofar as it was admitted at all, the violence that occurred after the April 17 Khmer Rouge victory was treated by the genocide denialists as small in scale, limited in time and unsanctioned by the Party Centre. Even if this were true – and evidence of the refugees overwhelmingly suggested that it wasn't – undisciplined Khmer Rouge cadres killing their own people to avenge the actions of the Americans and Lon Nol made no sense. In addition, the Pol Pot genocide denialists time and again claimed individual pieces of evidence were fabrications. Photos published in *The Washington Post* and *The Sydney Morning Herald* were treated as fake. There were indeed occasional errors made by the genocide affirmationists, but the denialists treated such errors not as evidence of sloppiness but as lending weight to the proposition that no mass Khmer Rouge killing had ever taken place.

Barron and Paul's *Murder of a Gentle Land* had in general been dismissed contemptuously by the genocide denialist campaigners for no other reason than it had been published by the "notorious anti-communists" at *Reader's Digest*. In 1982 Susan Sontag, the brilliant, non-conforming US intellectual, created pandemonium on the left when she suggested that someone who had relied solely on the *Reader's Digest* in the twenty years between 1950 and 1970 would have a better understanding of the realities of communism than someone who relied solely on *The Nation* or *The New Statesman*. The sneering treatment of Barron and Paul was a perfect example. In turn, François Ponchaud had been dismissed in part on the false basis that he had interviewed only wealthy and literate Cambodian refugees. As he had written, for him the most important witnesses were the hundreds of illiterate peasants, workers and fishermen he interviewed. Even more significantly, his portrait of Cambodia under the Khmer Rouge was dismissed on the "methodological" ground that refugee testimony itself was notoriously both unreliable and unverifiable. Was it not the case that refugees told their interviewers, like Ponchaud, what they thought they wanted to hear? How could the accuracy of the conclusions Ponchaud had drawn from his interviews be independently assessed? In response, I argued that as the Khmer Rouge had sealed Cambodia's borders, the only solid evidence about what was happening came from refugees. If refugee testimony was to be dismissed, the case against the Khmer Rouge had to be regarded as not proven. Catch 22. In the English edition of *Cambodia, Year Zero*, with Gareth Porter and Noam Chomsky in mind, Ponchaud pointed out:

> After an investigation of this kind, it is surprising to see that "experts" who have spoken to few if any of the Khmer refugees should reject their very significant place in any study of modern Cambodia. These experts would rather base their arguments on reasoning: if something seems impossible to their personal logic, then it doesn't exist. Their only sources for evaluation are deliberately chosen official statements. Where is that critical approach which they accuse others of not having?

Hanoi's successful invasion of Cambodia and the accompanying cogent and well-evidenced argument, pioneered by Wilfred Burchett, that described the Khmer Rouge regime as arguably the most bloody in world history, placed the relatively small number of pro–Khmer Rouge intellectuals, academics and journalists in an awkward situation. The Cambodian genocide denialists had supported with great intensity and moral indignation both the guerrilla fighters in the south – the Viet Cong – and the North Vietnamese regime. How could they now condemn Hanoi's invasion of Cambodia? One way of extricating themselves from this dilemma was almost comical, although it did not seem so to me at the time. Dr Gavan McCormack was a colleague of mine in the history department at La Trobe whom I had never met. In a lengthy article in *Arena* and then in *The Journal of Contemporary Asia*, he argued both that the 1975–77 exposé of the Khmer Rouge was a right-wing, anti-communist fabrication *and* that the 1978–79 account of the Khmer Rouge mounted by Hanoi that compared Pol Pot to Hitler was, by contrast, almost certainly true. "Till some time in my view," McCormack argued, "the evidence remained ambiguous and inconclusive. Since then, however, and in particular since the fall of the Pol Pot government early in 1979, a great deal of new evidence has accumulated which is of a very damning kind indeed, which points to the conclusions of the Barron and Paul and Ponchaud books being close to the truth." He summarised his present understanding with these words:

> The Western media and intelligence worked hard on Kampuchea. But, and here is the tragic irony, it becomes increasingly likely that the most malicious fantasies of the propagandists, conceived with little or no regard for the truth, may actually be close to the truth.

In the following issue of *Arena* I answered McCormack. Thousands of refugees who had fled to Thailand spoke in almost identical language "of executions, starvation, disease and political terrorisation". Why were they not believed? Why had intellectuals of the left muddied "the waters concerning one of the greatest human tragedies of this century"? And in conclusion:

> I cannot disguise my anger about this whole issue. How can you bring yourself to believe that those (including yourself) who were so wrong about the Kampuchean revolution were right to be wrong and that others – like Ponchaud, Barron/Paul, Shawcross, Lacouture and Milton Osborne – were wrong in being right? ... And how can you – I am sorry to indulge yet again in what you think of as fatuous moralising – not feel ashamed of the role you and those you support have played in this whole appalling episode?

At this point the leader of the most serious student revolutionary movement in Australian history, Albert Langer, a Maoist and a supporter of Pol Pot, joined the debate. "From an opposite perspective, I must agree with some points Robert Manne makes against Gavan McCormack." I was entitled, he argued, "to be angry at such a partial and ambiguous confession from someone who is supposed to be admitting to having publicly defended a regime of mass murderers". McCormack's suggestion that "by sheer coincidence" the "malicious fantasies" of right-wing propagandists were "close to the truth" was "patently absurd". How did the malicious propagandists manage to fantasise the truth? "By ESP?"

The most common response of the genocide denialists and their supporters, following the successful Vietnamese invasion and occupation of Cambodia, was to admit error, try to explain why the error had been made and then "move on" with self-confidence, unabashed. The best example here was Kiernan, who made the transition from defender of the Khmer Rouge regime to defender of the Vietnamese invasion with considerable aplomb in several pieces published in 1979. The editors of his article in the *Bulletin of Concerned Asian Scholars* asked Kiernan to explain why he had "changed his mind" about the Khmer Rouge. Kiernan answered intelligently, even breezily. He now could see that the extreme violence of the Khmer Rouge was not entirely caused by rage at US bombing – although of course, he added, that had helped. The ultra-nationalism of the Khmer Rouge and of Pol Pot in particular was not progressive, as he had once believed, but xenophobic and racist. Until the Vietnamese invasion, there had not been sufficient testimony from the Cambodian refugees of the lower classes. Kiernan could still not admit that Ponchaud had interviewed hundreds of peasants, workers and fishermen.

Kiernan regretted that his eyes were not opened to the true nature of the Khmer Rouge regime until "early 1978". Early 1978? Had he already forgotten his unambiguous defence of the Khmer Rouge regime in our Hobart debate in early 1978? Nor could Kiernan admit that it was the Vietnamese decision to invade Cambodia that had rather suddenly opened his eyes and the eyes of other genocide denialists to the true character of the Khmer Rouge regime. On May 2, 1980, Kiernan published a major article in *New Statesman* on the Khmer Rouge's Tuol Sleng torture prison. He had by now parted company with the world's most famous and intellectually talented leftist, Noam Chomsky, who had not renounced what Kiernan believed was his defence of the Khmer Rouge. "There is", Kiernan wrote in the *New Statesman*, "a left-wing argument ... still held, apparently by Noam Chomsky – which suggests that, although Pol Pot made numerous brutal errors, the conception of something especially outlandish about his regime is a chimera bred up by the Western (and Vietnamese) mass-media."

With co-author Edward Herman, in June 1977 in *The Nation*, Noam Chomsky had written "Distortions at Fourth Hand", the most influential attack on those who claimed that the Khmer Rouge were already responsible for the death by execution, starvation and disease of more than a million Cambodians. In my October 1979 analysis of left-wing intellectuals and Pol Pot I offered a critique of "Distortions". I was unaware that around that time Chomsky and Herman would publish the two-volume *After the Cataclysm: The Political Economy of Human Rights*, whose second volume contained a 160-page chapter on Western media and Cambodia under the Khmer Rouge. Even though the Pol Pot regime had collapsed by the time of publication, and the eyes of most of the Western left-wing intelligentsia had been opened, rather suddenly, to its genocidal and totalitarian character in a process I called "the epistemology of the tank", Chomsky and Herman (hereafter Chomsky) conceded nothing, if anything digging in even deeper. In the 1930s, Sidney and Beatrice Webb published a massive volume entitled *Soviet Communism: A New Civilisation?* In the reprint, the question mark was removed from the title. This work became notorious because it was thought to exemplify a kind of intellectual blindness or folly. Chomsky's chapter on Cambodia deserves a similar notoriety.

Chomsky was not a communist fellow traveller. Nor was he driven to write in support of anarchism, the form of state he favoured. He was, rather, a perfect example of a type of intellectual Orwell identified in his taxonomy in "Notes on Nationalism": the "negative nationalist". A great part of what Chomsky has written is an attack on American imperialism. In the second volume of *After the Cataclysm* concerning Indochina, what Chomsky analysed was not the character of the communist governments of Vietnam, Laos and Cambodia but rather the manner in which these governments were portrayed by the Western – or really the American – mass media. "[O]ur primary concern here", Chomsky pointed out "is not to establish the facts with regard to postwar Indochina but rather to investigate their refraction through the prism of Western ideology, a very different task."

Chomsky did not commit himself to a particular account of the Khmer Rouge regime. His chapter was peppered with qualifiers: "the limited evidence currently available suggests"; "it would seem not unlikely"; "we suspect"; it is "plausible" and so on. According to "the facts", the Khmer Rouge could be building a socialist paradise or a totalitarian hell. Which one of these possibilities would eventually turn out to be closer to the truth did not greatly matter. In either case, Chomsky thought he could show through textual criticism that the portrait the American media – "a propaganda agency for the state" – was presenting of Vietnam, Laos and Cambodia was systematic "brain-washing" of a more effective kind than the rather crude version of transparent media control occurring under totalitarian regimes.

Rather than picking up sticks and travelling to Cambodia to talk to former subjects of the Khmer Rouge, Chomsky was content to sit at his desk in Boston, from where, with his very big brain, he could reveal through his exhaustive analysis of the mass media how US imperialism duped the American people in the case of Cambodia and elsewhere.

One half of Chomsky's method was to demolish the evidence in the books and articles revealing the astonishing cruelty and violence of the Khmer Rouge, most importantly *Cambodia, Year Zero* – whose "evidence about Cambodia begins to crumble when one begins to look at it closely" – and to show how Ponchaud came to be presented to the American public by the American media, via simplifications and distortions. The other half of his method was to highlight the evidence in the books and articles that appeared to praise the Khmer Rouge and absolve them of any serious fault, and to reveal how evidence of this kind was scandalously neglected. It was obvious that the most important evidence for the case against the Khmer Rouge came from the refugees. Time and again, Chomsky reminded us that refugee evidence could not be taken "on trust". Chomsky dismissed Barron and Paul in two words: *Reader's Digest*! Although he was aware that Ponchaud's book had some merit, nonetheless in the end it too could not be trusted. Ponchaud was accused of "fakery" and "anti-communist bias", of being "untrustworthy" and of playing "fast and loose with numbers", of being "highly unreliable with quotations" and, in the end, of having written a book that "cannot be taken very seriously". Ponchaud was also accused, in his criticism of Chomsky, of displaying "petty deceit". "Work of this calibre would be dismissed out of hand if it were critical of the United States," Chomsky claimed. The United States had suffered a humiliating defeat in Vietnam. Much was therefore now at stake. The portrait of a genocidal and totalitarian state in communist Cambodia, confected by the almost wholly subservient mass media, was one means of restoring the reputation and self-confidence of imperial America.

So there it was, as I saw it. One response of those who had denied that a terrible tragedy was taking place in Cambodia was to claim those who were right about the Khmer Rouge were wrong in having been right, and those who were wrong were right in having been wrong. Another was to reverse judgement about the Khmer Rouge almost overnight, following the Vietnamese invasion of Cambodia, and consign one's earlier writings and opinions down the memory hole. Yet another was to argue that even if the Khmer Rouge regime turned out to be both genocidal and totalitarian, in leading the gullible American public to believe that the Khmer Rouge regime was both genocidal and totalitarian, the mass media had revealed once more its "awesome" capacity as a "system of indoctrination and thought control" in service to the imperial state.

My October 1979 *Quadrant* article on Pol Pot and the intellectuals ended with these words:

> Nor are the "lessons" of these controversies – that there is no regime too base to be defended; that there is no evidence that will shake the faith of its defenders; that refugees are more reliable guides to twentieth-century politics than professors – in any way surprising for someone with even a passing knowledge of the history of the relationship between intellectuals and totalitarian movements in our century ... What may be learnt ... from the debate concerning Cambodia is that during the 1970s liberal anticommunism was so completely defeated in Western universities and intellectual circles that one could no longer hope that arguments couched in its language would be listened to seriously. Nor, sad to say, is it possible to expect that the political self-confidence of the former supporters of Pol Pot will be in the slightest deflated by the fact that concerning their estimation of him and his odious regime they were wholly, shamefully and ludicrously wrong. Pol Pot has passed; Noam Chomsky, I fear, persisteth.

For the next decade, liberal anti-communism was the political movement to which I belonged.

Not everything I was involved with over Cambodia concerned intellectual combat. Father Jeffries Foale, an Adelaide Redemptorist priest, read one of the letters-to-the-editor I wrote as president of the two-man Committee for Cambodian Refugees. He asked whether I might create a Victorian branch of the Indo-China Refugee Association he had established in South Australia. I accepted the invitation. In the years between 1976 and 1980 I was president of the Victorian branch of ICRA. Most of our committee members were leaders of the Vietnamese, Cambodian and Lao refugee communities, although there were also some young, left-leaning Catholics from the Jesuit Refugee Service and an extremely energetic member of an inter-country adoption lobby group, Paula Kelly. Because there was some tension between the three principal national groups, especially the Vietnamese and the Cambodians, and between all of them and the refugees of Chinese ethnicity, a certain delicacy was needed that I had to learn on the job. We were, for example, required to call ourselves the grammatically awkward Indo-China Refugee Association rather than the Indo-Chinese Refugee Association because of the (usually mild) anti-Chinese prejudice of some of the ethnic Vietnamese, Cambodians and Laos. I also realised that I had to be careful not to speak too openly about the situation in Cambodia because of the fear our Cambodian committee members felt for their families. I admired and enjoyed the company of many of our members – like the elegant and gentle Dr Dan, the former South Vietnamese ambassador to France, and the politically savvy Sino-Cambodian Hong Lim, who eventually made his way to the Legislative Council in Victoria, and Ung Huot, a Cambodian postgraduate student at the University of Melbourne who had come to Australia under the Colombo Plan.

As is well known, between April and December 1975 the Whitlam government resisted the idea of re-settling substantial numbers of South Vietnamese. This included those who had worked closely with Australian forces and whose lives were in danger following the victory of the North in late April 1975, or those refugees from communism who fled on often unseaworthy boats or across the land border into Thailand after the victory of the communist parties in all three Indochinese states. According to Clyde Cameron, one of the government's left-wing Cabinet ministers, Whitlam described the Vietnamese refugees to him as "yellow Balts" – that is to say, conservative anti-communists who would never support Labor. (The Whitlam government's lack of generosity towards the refugees from Indochina was one of the main reasons why I was not disturbed by the events of November 11, 1975.) It is not well known, however, that in 1976, in its first year of office, the Fraser government settled fewer refugees from Indochina than its predecessor had in 1975. My role in ICRA, as I saw it, was to address dozens of community meetings and to produce a newsletter bringing facts about the refugee crisis in the growing archipelago of camps throughout South-East Asia to the attention of the general public and arguing that their resettlement was our country's responsibility. I believed this in general because as fellow human beings they desperately needed our help, and in particular because they felt threatened or had fled following the victories of the communist parties and armies we had unsuccessfully opposed with force of arms.

There were some amusing moments. On several occasions I visited the migrant hostel in Springvale which was the first home for many of the refugees from Indochina. Here, incidentally, they were treated generously, even the small number who had arrived in Darwin by boat. It was my habit at the time to wear a fawn-check woollen scarf in winter. Unfortunately, the scarf resembled the "krama" scarf that was part of the Khmer Rouge uniform. I was told that some of the Cambodian refugees in Springvale thought I was a supporter of the Khmer Rouge and mistook me for Ben Kiernan. Because of those young, left-leaning Jesuits who were part of ICRA, I learned that members of Bob Santamaria's National Civic Council were trying to undermine our influence with the refugees at Springvale.

Our demands on the government were modest. Early in 1978, ICRA suggested something like an additional intake of 2,000 refugees from Indochina in the following year. Shortly after, on May 28, the minister for Immigration, Michael McKellar, announced that Australia had decided to resettle 9,000 refugees from Indochina in the 1978/79 financial year. I remember feeling rather foolish. My principal concern was now for the Cambodian refugees in the

Thai camps. By the end of 1979 Australia had resettled approximately 25,000 Vietnamese refugees, but only 1,000 Cambodians. There remained work to do.

On November 30, 1979, shortly before my retirement from ICRA, which was now more concerned with resettlement than with lobbying for greater numbers of refugees, I wrote the following letter to Vivien Thwaites, my partner at the time. It captures several of the issues we dealt with over the years:

> Mr MacKellar ... came to our [ICRA] office for no apparent reason ... At one point today he gave as a reason for not taking Cambodian refugees to Australia the idea that four years of the Khmer Rouge they'd been brutalised! ... AB's parents both died under the Khmer Rouge from starvation, as did one of his brothers but all the other brothers and sisters are – miraculously enough – still alive. Their misery is of course far from over. They managed to get to Thailand after the Vietnamese invasion of Cambodia by the middle of this year but were then forced back into Cambodia by the Thai Army (along with 60,000 others). One of them has now walked to Vietnam, simply in order to be able to keep up contact with AB. [AB is] of course desperate and deeply angry ... All the old unease he used to feel with me (because he didn't want to accept what he knew I thought about Cambodia) has now fallen away ... We are going to work together to try and prepare a submission concerning *all* the relatives of Cambodians here who are at present in the Thai camps. MacKellar, under pressure, more or less promised to take it very seriously if we could produce such a submission. The meeting with MacKellar was punctuated by a phone call telling him that a boat of 150 refugees (who it turns out had been saved from drowning by a British tanker near Singapore) were on their way to Darwin. He looked – as I always thought he would – puzzled and forlorn.

*

In the 1990s there were two echoes of my involvement with Cambodia. In January 1995 I wrote a column in *The Age* on Noam Chomsky and Cambodia to coincide with his visit. Chomsky was seriously displeased. The column was published on January 25. A front-page article about his contemptuous response appeared on the following day. Chomsky called his 1977 *Nation* review of Ponchaud "very positive" and described me as a "conscious liar" and a "Stalinist commissar". Obviously still seething, immediately after returning to Boston, on January 31, he sent a 3,000-word letter-to-the-editor of *The Age*. According to this letter, written with a rather frightening, incandescent rage, I was also a faithful servant of the United States who felt "an enthusiasm for huge atrocities when carried out by the right hands". Chomsky wrote all this despite knowing nothing at all about me. When I later read Bruce Sharp's analysis of Chomsky's record on Cambodia, I discovered I was at least in large company. For criticising Chomsky over Cambodia, David Horowitz was, like me, a "Stalinist", Alan Dershowitz of Harvard a "clown", the *New York Times* columnist Anthony Lewis "a coward" and the author of *The Killing Fields*, Sydney Schanberg, "a person of utter depravity". Sharp also provides a convincing description of the character type of those who, like Chomsky, are incapable of admitting serious error or accepting non-trivial criticism: "You are either with me, or you are an enemy of everything that is good and decent."

Four or five years later I was having lunch in the staff cafe at La Trobe. The former Cambodian ICRA committee member Ung Huot approached me, beaming. We embraced.

"So what have you been up to?" I asked.

"Most recently I was the prime minister of Cambodia," he replied.

I must admit I later checked just in case Ung Huot was pulling my leg. He was not. In 1997 he had been chosen as prime minister by the Cambodian strong-man Hun Sen, and had served in that post until 1998.

*

Following the publication in late 1979 of the article I called "Pol Pot and the Intellectuals", I was a well-known younger member of the

Quadrant circle. In 1980 I was teaching a master's course at La Trobe on the concept and the consequences of totalitarianism. One student was Valerie Haye, who worked for Oxford University Press. We discussed the birth of a new kind of conservatism in Australia, one that took account of the failure of the United States and Australia in Vietnam; the impact of the Whitlam government and its removal; the growth of a university-trained youthful left-wing intelligentsia; and the emergence of multiculturalism in place of the post-war ambition of immigrant assimilation. Valerie commissioned me to edit a book called *The New Conservatism in Australia*, published in 1982. It included many of the most significant *Quadrant* voices, many still quite young and, to my current embarrassment, all men. In the end I decided not to have a chapter on neo-liberalism, or what in Australia we called economic rationalism, the new economic wave that – with the election of Margaret Thatcher in the United Kingdom (1979) and Ronald Reagan in the United States (1980) – had just begun to transform the political economy of the English-speaking world. As I explained:

> I was tempted to include a section on the tension between Keynesian and libertarian economics but quickly lost heart. *I must admit to having no competence in economics whatsoever*, and little sympathy for some of the social consequences apparently acceptable to the more doctrinaire enthusiasts of monetarism and the unshackled Free Market [my emphasis].

The italicised words were used against me for the following forty years by enemies on the right – many of whose self-delusions about competence in economics consisted of nothing more than the ability to regurgitate the message of the neo-liberal economists in the most simplified form.

[7.]

Wilfred Burchett

RICHARD KRYGIER WAS THE WARM-HEARTED and good-humoured behind-the-scenes organiser of the Australian Association of Cultural Freedom (AACF), the local branch of the worldwide "liberal" anti-communist organisation, the Congress for Cultural Freedom. Richard was a Polish socialist who had survived the Holocaust by fleeing eastwards with his wife, Roma. From the safety of Tokyo, Shanghai and, later, Sydney, he had watched with disgust and alarm the communist takeover of his homeland made possible by the occupying Soviet Army and its ruthless political apparatus. Richard was the linkman between Sydney and Paris, where the congress was based and from where the local branches received some funds. In 1967 the then American leftist Christopher Lasch, later of *Culture of Narcissism* fame, had discovered that the congress was conceived of and funded by the CIA, under the cover of the Ford Foundation. Not long after, the Australian Maoist Humphrey McQueen came upon some of the details of the money flow and correspondence between Paris and Sydney in the AACF papers deposited in the National Library of Australia.

The AACF was split between supporters who were outraged by the clandestine CIA connection and those who were, at least in the end, unfussed. The unfussed believed that the Cold War struggle for the future of the world – between communism and liberal democracy, or between the Soviet Union and the United States and their satellites or allies – overrode the principled or perhaps high-minded and hypocritical scruples of the outraged. Richard, who knew all about the CIA connection of the congress, was of course one of the unfussed, as were several of the association's most prominent members: the philosopher David Armstrong; the journalist and Liberal Party politician Peter Coleman; and my teacher, the social theorist and provocateur Frank Knopfelmacher. Although these events preceded by almost two decades my involvement (as co-editor and then editor of *Quadrant*) in the internal politics of the association, which was by then almost non-existent, I was retrospectively but very firmly in the camp of the unfussed.

In August 1984, Richard Krygier alerted me to an article published in *Australian Society*, the magazine where the piece I had co-authored on the declining standards of the university had recently appeared. The article was entitled: "An Australian Dreyfus? A Re-examination of the Strange Case Against Wilfred Burchett, Journalist". Its author was my Cambodian antagonist and La Trobe colleague Dr Gavan McCormack. Richard asked if I might be willing to reply. I agreed at once. I did not wish to devote my intellectual energies to *Lucky Jim*–style refereed articles in academic journals that only a handful of fellow scholars read.

Alfred Dreyfus was a Jewish captain in the French army who was found guilty of spying for the Germans, stripped of his rank in the public square and imprisoned for years under atrocious conditions on Devil's Island. In the popular imagination, the key moment in the affair was the 1898 publication of a stirring piece by the great French novelist Émile Zola called "J'Accuse". After publication, Zola was forced to flee his country. The Dreyfus Affair deepened the division of France into the camps of left and right, a division that lasted for several decades. Eventually it was discovered beyond all doubt that Dreyfus had been the victim of a conservative anti-Semitic conspiracy and he was pardoned. As a boy I was greatly affected by the story and especially the scene in a film about the affair where Dreyfus' badges of rank were torn from his army jacket and his sword snapped in two. As an academic, I was amused beyond measure on discovering that the pardoned Dreyfus had said later, of an altogether different political case, the French equivalent of "no smoke without fire".

Wilfred Burchett (Australia's Dreyfus, according to McCormack) was an Australian journalist of talent and courage, who I believed had supported the cause of communism with propaganda disguised as reportage since the end of the Second World War. This was no straightforward feat, following the ideological split between the Soviet Union and China of the early 1960s. After the publication of his ferociously anti-American book *Cold War in Germany* and its sequel, *Peoples' Democracies*, a glorification of the Stalinisation of Eastern and Central Europe, Burchett travelled to Maoist China and, with breathless enthusiasm, wrote *China's Feet Unbound*. Soon, alongside the British communist Alan Winnington, he went with the Chinese army to cover the peace talks at Panmunjom, where he worked for China and against the United Nations forces – led by the United States and including an Australian contingent – who were defending South Korea following North Korea's June 1950 invasion.

In the words of the ancient English treason law, Burchett now provided "aid and comfort" to Australia's enemies at time of war. The aid and comfort he provided was in part propaganda. Burchett argued, in scores of articles and broadcasts, that the American forces in Korea were engaged in "germ warfare", dropping bombs of deadly, plague-infested insects on North Korean villages in hundreds of air raids – something not only monstrous but also novel in the history of human combat. He claimed that the United Nations forces were driving their North Korean and Chinese prisoners of war into "concentration and extermination camps" no less evil than the Nazi camps, where millions of their victims had perished.

At the site of the peace talks, Panmunjom, Burchett made no secret of his employment by the Chinese. His support for the communist side in the Korean War, however, went beyond propaganda. Once the captured American pilots were released, considerable evidence emerged of Burchett's involvement in the process whereby, after physical and mental torture, false confessions to germ warfare were collected, edited and published or broadcast on Chinese radio and shown in films of the scripted evidence the captured pilots presented before the International Scientific Commission. The ISC was created by the Chinese after they had rejected investigation by the Red Cross or the World Health Organization. It is difficult to communicate to a generation for whom the Cold War is the distant past what many Australians thought about someone working openly for the enemy during the Korean War. The closest contemporary analogy might be an Australian Muslim journalist joining the forces of the Islamic State in Iraq and Syria, helping in the transmission of its chilling messages to the world and writing the scripts recited by captured Americans and Europeans.

At the end of the Korean War, the Menzies government considered laying charges of treason against Burchett. For several reasons – some technical matters of law, some based on the kind of evidence available – this course of action was rejected. The only legal penalty Burchett suffered was the Australian government's refusal to replace his passport after his British one was lost or stolen in 1955. (His Korean War collaborator, Alan Winnington, was also refused a new passport by the British government.) Even without an Australian passport, though, Burchett was able to travel the world, eventually to both the United Kingdom and the United States, principally with a diplomatic "laissez-passer" provided by the North Vietnamese. Before he was finally issued with an Australian passport by the Whitlam government in December 1972, he was even able to travel to Australia and leave again, as he did in 1970 with the support of a left-leaning businessman, Gordon Barton.

In his *Australian Society* article, Gavan McCormack not only suggested an equivalence between the injustices suffered by Dreyfus and Burchett, he argued that from several points of view Burchett's treatment had been worse. While Dreyfus was tried and sentenced – albeit on false charges – Burchett's efforts "to get a forum in which to argue his case were in vain". And while Dreyfus' case lasted twelve years, "Burchett's, begun in the early 1950s, remains unsettled now". "Above all", while "Dreyfus found French supporters who cared enough about the issues to explore the record and write passionately in his defence ... Burchett's friends in Australia have been few." McCormack concluded:

Successive Australian governments in the 1950s and 1960s subjected [Burchett] to various punishments, especially deprivation of citizenship, without ever spelling out what he was supposed to have done. [T]hough never tried, Wilfred Burchett was, and is, widely believed to have been a traitor ... If Australia has a Dreyfus, it is Wilfred Burchett.

McCormack explained that in the 1974 defamation action Burchett had brought against Senator Jack Kane of the Democratic Labor Party, the jury agreed that Burchett had indeed been defamed. However, he lost the case because of what McCormack described as a technicality. The jury found that the short article in an obscure DLP magazine claiming that Burchett had been recruited by the KGB in 1957 was a fair report of proceedings in the Australian parliament and therefore covered by privilege. Although Burchett appealed successfully against that verdict, the judges refused to order a retrial, because Senator Kane would not be able to reassemble his witnesses and because counsel for Burchett had not challenged in court the part of the trial that formed the basis of the appeal. Costs of $60,000 were awarded against Burchett, far beyond his capacity to pay. He was once again an exile, not as a passport-less suspected traitor this time, but as a debtor.

Most of McCormack's article was concerned with picking supposed holes in the evidence of the many witnesses from across the world that Senator Kane had assembled. According to McCormack, one of the captured American pilots who had confessed to germ warfare, Walker Mahurin, had changed his Burchett story fundamentally between 1962 and 1974. Another captured pilot and germ warfare confessor, Paul Kniss, claimed that in his prison cell he had picked up the list of typed questions Burchett had provided for his interrogator. This seemed to be the "smoking gun" regarding Burchett's role in the germ warfare confessions. However, McCormack asked, was it not "curious" that his "charge was not made until 22 years after the event?" Most importantly, the Soviet defector who had been involved in Burchett's recruitment to the KGB, Yuri Krotkov, not only had "a very dirty mind" but had also supposedly withdrawn the "more or less trivial charges" he had outlined. All this impressive-looking evidentiary detail was of a kind readers of McCormack's article could not possibly independently assess. But the sting of his article was, as they say, in the tail:

> Burchett was a journalist inspired by an uncommon moral passion. When all the false, garbled, and malicious stories of his activities in Korea are discounted, what remains is the portrait of an honest man who tried to tell the truth, who was almost alone in seeing the war primarily from the viewpoint of the suffering Korean people rather than that of great powers or his own or any other government, and who, by helping to crack the censorship and the lies other journalists propagated when they were told to by "responsible military headquarters" may well have helped shorten the war. In time he will be recognised as one of the greatest journalists of his time, and as an outstanding Australian.

Were it not for this concluding paragraph, perhaps even this final sentence, I doubt that I would have accepted Richard Krygier's commission.

I am not sure what kind of essay Krygier and the *Quadrant* editor, Peter Coleman, expected me to write, but they certainly supported my suggestion of a lengthy re-examination of Burchett's career. McCormack had offered a challenge that we all believed needed to be answered. If Burchett was a moral hero, a political martyr, a great journalist and an outstanding Australian, as McCormack argued, his political enemies – the anti-communists, sometimes now called the Cold Warriors – deserved contempt and condemnation. I think everyone involved in the Burchett debate recognised that the evaluation of his career served as a proxy for a much larger question: how we should judge the performance of the three (not two) camps of the Australian intelligentsia that had taken shape during the long years of the Cold War: the communists and their fellow travellers, the supporters of Burchett; the anti-communists, the enemies of Burchett; and the often ignored or underestimated camp of the anti-anticommunists, which had grown in both numbers and self-confidence following the American and Australian defeat in Vietnam, whose political animus in Australia was directed primarily against the anti-communist camp and *Quadrant*.

As mentioned earlier, as an undergraduate I was at first favourably disposed towards Burchett, greatly affected by one of his films on the war in Vietnam that depicted the Americans as ruthless imperialists and the Viet Cong as a patriotic peasant guerrilla force entirely independent of Hanoi. A decade or so later, by the time of the 1978–79 Vietnamese invasion of Pol Pot's Kampuchea, an invasion Burchett enthusiastically supported, I had come to regard him as a skilful and mendacious propagandist for the communist cause. My essay, "Pol Pot and the Intellectuals", began with a passage from Burchett arguing that in three years under the Khmer Rouge, 2 to 3 million of 7 or 8 million Cambodians had been killed. I then commented: "Burchett, whose career as a publicist for communist movements had stretched over several decades, was, if nothing else, a professional ... [I]n these reports (for the first time possibly in his career) *the truth concerning communist atrocities was expedient.*"

Because of the role Burchett had played during the Vietnam War as an unofficial envoy of Hanoi – in Paris during the peace talks and even in Washington, where he took breakfast with Henry Kissinger – I had come to regard him as by far the most consequential communist in the history of Australia.

The sources on Wilfred Burchett were abundant. Of his thirty books, two were most important to me: *Peoples' Democracies* (1951) and *China: The Quality of Life* (1974). In his book on the Sovietisation of Eastern Europe, Burchett summarised the risible stories about the plots between the Anglo-American imperialists and Marshall Tito of Yugoslavia. In *China: The Quality of Life*, written with Rewi Alley, the authors spoke favourably of the Great Leap Forward, where, as we now know, between 30 and 40 million Chinese starved to death, "as an epoch-making success, the full dimensions of which are only dimly realised in the outside world". They wrote even more favourably of the Maoist political culture following the Cultural Revolution, which threw China into years of vicious, bloody turmoil. China had created a new and a finer "human nature", and a world without crime or mental illness. Burchett and Alley also offered highest praise for the swift and effective communist repression of the ancient culture in Tibet. As they were informed: "All our people have seen the difference between a Dalai Lama and Chairman Mao. No force can turn our people back to the old times."

There were also three archival collections that illuminated some of the chapters of Burchett's political career. In the National Archives of Australia, ASIO's files on Burchett had been opened (of course with some redactions), apparently at his family's request. Under the thirty-year rule, when I began research the released records ended in December 1953. The greatest surprise in the archive was a request to the Menzies government from US commander-in-chief in Korea, General Mark Clark, that he hoped would be treated by Canberra as a matter of "greatest urgency". Via an intermediary in the US press corps, the Americans had learned that Burchett was willing to re-defect to the West, as it were, and to provide military intelligence – but only if the Australian government promised not to try him for his activities in Korea. The Menzies government refused to go along with what the Americans called their "exfiltration" plan. Instead, it began to collect evidence and take legal counsel for a possible Burchett treason trial.

The second archive of value were the papers of Denis Warner, the retired anti-communist Australian journalist who had been collecting evidence on the activities of his former friend, but who had been effectively silenced during Burchett's lifetime by a threatened defamation action neither pursued nor withdrawn, known in the legal trade as a "stop writ". I travelled to Warner's rather grand home on the Mornington Peninsula to pick up some boxes of the Burchett material Warner had continued to collect. I regarded some of his views as far-fetched – for example, his opinion that Burchett had personally invented the germ warfare accusation based on a story by one of Burchett's favourite authors, Jack London. Warner had clearly been bruised by his long struggle with Burchett. He advised me not to mention his assistance, advice I blithely ignored.

In the Warner boxes there was some fascinating material. He had collected the transcripts of Burchett's articles for the New China News Agency. These included his description of one of the communists' prisoner-of-war camps as looking "like a holiday resort in Switzerland", where the prisoners were offered a meat ration "several times higher than the ration in England" and lazed around during the days, "swimming, fishing, sports, reading, writing". By contrast, Burchett described their UN equivalents at the time of the prisoner-of-war repatriations as "American concentration and extermination camps" where "the torture-rooms, the gas-chambers, the steam-heat rooms, the branding irons and the tattooers' needles and the gallows were kept busy".

Most importantly, among the Denis Warner papers was the 180-page transcript of the testimony of Paul Kniss, one of the germ warfare pilot confessors. Kniss' account of Burchett's intimate involvement in the creation of his false confession was based not on a rusty 22-year-old memory, as McCormack claimed, but on the detailed account he had given six weeks after his release. Kniss told his American interrogators that he had been interviewed by Burchett shortly after his plane was shot down in early June 1952. He denied any involvement in germ warfare. After several weeks of profound anxiety and an illness he thought was dysentery, his interrogation recommenced. Eventually, on July 7 or 8, in a state of exhaustion and bewilderment, Kniss was broken. He agreed to confess to germ warfare. Eventually a twenty-page confession emerged. According to Kniss, Burchett "told me he personally edited" the confession. "He showed me stacks of so-called evidence he had this high (indicating) from others. I learned later that O'Neal [another captured pilot and germ warfare confessor] had seen him the same day I had seen him." Next day, Kniss was once more interrogated by a Chinese officer with an interpreter:

> When he left the room, he left a piece of paper that he had been working on – had been reading off of. I picked that up and it was

typewritten, again, and written in just about these words: Suggest that the interrogator ask Kniss the following questions ... and on the bottom W.G. Burchett, and signed.

There was a reason the evidence of Burchett's pivotal involvement in the extraction of false confessions had such a profound effect on me. In my view, the finest novel ever written about Stalinism was Arthur Koestler's *Darkness at Noon*. Its locale is a prison cell and its subject the extraction of a false confession. This is why I wrote in my *Quadrant* essay:

> False confessions to fantastic crimes, extorted by protracted processes of mental and physical torture, were of course a standard feature of the international Stalinist culture ... Since [Burchett] had arrived in Korea he had passed rapidly through a series of doors that had brought him to the inner sanctum of the world of totalitarianism, the interrogation cell.

In 1969, the Soviet defector Yuri Krotkov had given evidence about Burchett to a congressional committee. Krotkov, a playwright, was also what was called a "co-opted KGB" worker involved in "honey pot" operations whose aim was to compromise significant foreigners with sexual encounters. Krotkov's evidence went like this: He and Burchett had struck up a thin friendship in the Soviet sector of Germany shortly after the end of the Second World War. In 1956, Burchett, who was in Moscow, phoned Krotkov. When they met, Burchett told Krotkov that he was a secret member of the Communist Party of Australia (CPA). He explained that since 1950 he had been supported financially by both the Chinese and the North Vietnamese communist governments. He wanted to establish himself in Moscow but needed money. Krotkov discovered that the KGB were interested and willing. When Burchett returned to Moscow the following year, after a little bureaucratic confusion, with Krotkov's assistance a connection was established between Burchett and a senior KGB officer, Victor Kartsev. Krotkov learned that Burchett had been provided with a handsome flat. Kartsev told Krotkov that relations with Burchett were progressing favourably and that he was under the control of the KGB officer in charge of work with foreign correspondents. Krotkov and Burchett lost contact. Sometime later, however, they bumped into each other at a petrol station. Burchett told Krotkov that he found Kartsev's manner and his anti-Semitism offensive.

In his "Australian Dreyfus" article, McCormack claimed that Krotkov's evidence was false, and his accusations "trivial and absurd". But on the basis of irrefutable evidence – principally Burchett's letters home – I was able to establish the accuracy of many of Krotkov's claims about his 1956 conversation with Burchett in the third archive I worked on, the Burchett papers deposited in the State Library of Victoria. In court in 1974, Burchett was asked whether in the early 1950s he was paid by the Chinese government. "Certainly not"; he had "no relations whatever with the Communist Party of China". In April 1951, Burchett had written home that he was "relieved of all financial cares" and provided with all his needs, including food and travel costs, by the Chinese government. In court, he was asked whether he had been involved, as Krotkov claimed, in work with the Pathet Lao, the Laotian communist party. "Nonsense," Burchett replied. But in letters to his father in December 1955 and again in January 1957, Burchett had written about political expeditions into Laos, the second involving the formation of a new government that included the Pathet Lao leader, a splendid development which, he confided, he "did help along a little". Krotkov claimed that the KGB had provided Burchett with an expensive flat. According to McCormack: "In fact, Burchett lived in an old apartment block (known locally as 'Stalin's folly')." But on June 4, 1957, Burchett wrote to his father: "We have a very nice apartment of five rooms, wonderfully located in a modern skyscraper and looking out over the whole of Moscow, particularly the river which flows at our doorstep and the Kremlin."

In the mid-1980s, Krotkov's 1969 Washington testimony was the only evidence about Burchett's employment by the KGB. Burchett understood the significance of Krotkov's story. His posthumously published autobiography, *Memoirs of a Rebel Journalist*, includes a sarcastically titled chapter, "How I Joined the KGB", a politically cunning attempt to characterise Krotkov's witness as risible McCarthyism. I think Burchett knew that if Krotkov was believed, his carefully crafted reputation as an independent journalist was finished, which was why he sued Senator Jack Kane. In the *Quadrant* essay I concluded:

> Krotkov as a witness in Washington was not only truthful as far as can be judged; he also revealed a remarkable memory for fine detail of fact and tone. There is every reason to accept his story of how he helped recruit Burchett in 1956–7 for the KGB.

In his "Australian Dreyfus" article, McCormack alerted readers to his 1983 book, *Cold War, Hot War: An Australian Perspective on the Korean War*. His version of the history of the Korean War, delivered in measured and muffled academic prose, astonished me. McCormack suggested that the Korean War did not begin with the North Korean invasion of the South. June 1950 was merely a "moment of drastic escalation of the war, not its origin". He described what was taking place in Korea by 1950 as a "revolutionary civil war" in which North Korea under Kim Il-Sung and the influence of the Soviet Union stood for progress and South Korea under Syngman Rhee and the influence of anti-communist America stood for reaction.

The evidence that the Americans had deployed germ warfare in Korea – most likely in a manner McCormack characterised as "partly experimental and partly designed to sow panic and confusion among the enemy, rather than seriously to annihilate him" – had, in his opinion, "to be treated with absolute seriousness. The case closed for thirty years has to be reopened." Because of his revisionist interpretation of the Korean War, that restored the version provided at the time of Stalin, and because of his enthusiasm for the social revolution of Kim Il-Sung's North Korea, I described McCormack's version of North Asian history as "neo-Stalinist", a description he and his supporters, unsurprisingly, resented.

Burchett's Korean War reportage, based as we now know on daily briefings from Chinese army sources, was self-evidently, remorselessly, almost comically biased. In his voluminous books and newspaper articles Burchett wrote not one sentence of praise for the United States and not one sentence of criticism of the Chinese and North Koreans. Nonetheless, his publications were described by McCormack as the journalism of "an honest man who tried to tell the truth ... primarily from the viewpoint of the suffering Korean people rather than that of the great powers or his own *or any other government*" [my emphasis]. I called this description one of "unusual preposterousness and gall". I argued that "to describe Burchett as an objective and honest reporter of the Korean War (as Dr McCormack does) is the equivalent of calling Julius Streicher a commentator on German Jewish affairs *or Horatio Bottomley a student of Wilhelmine foreign policy*". Especially because these italicised words were almost always omitted, this much-quoted shortened sentence caused me even greater trouble than my description of McCormack's interpretation of the Korean War as neo-Stalinist. Even though I had praised Burchett for his support of German Jewish emigration on the eve of the Second World War and had pointed out that Burchett had complained about the anti-Semitism of his first KGB handler, Victor Kartsev, nonsensically, in article after article, I was supposed to have claimed that Burchett was an anti-Semite.

*

On July 31, 1985, one day before the August edition of *Quadrant* was published, *The Sydney Morning Herald* carried a detailed report on the Burchett essay across the top of its front page. The title the *SMH* chose, "Burchett, Paid KGB Agent and Author of Fake Confessions?", accurately located two of the issues that would dominate the Burchett debate, although the description of Burchett as "the author" of the false confessions went beyond the evidence of my essay. However, "the editor" would have been too weak. And the question mark was, of course, important. The next day, *The Age* carried an equally detailed page-six report that concentrated on the third issue of the debate — the question of treason.

In the first five months, from the end of July 1985 to the beginning of January 1986, the Burchett debate following my article took place principally in newspapers and magazines – *The Sydney Morning Herald*, *The Age*, *The Australian*, the Melbourne *Herald*, *The Bulletin*, *News Weekly*, *Australian Society*, *Quadrant* and the *Australian Left Review*. The chief protagonists on one side were Gavan McCormack and Ben Kiernan, supported by members of the CPA, including Laurie Aarons, the former general secretary, and Joseph Waters, the publisher of some of Burchett's early books. On the other side, apart from myself, there were B.A. Santamaria, Frank Knopfelmacher and Anthony McAdam. Much of this early debate took place in letters-to-the-editor – I collected thirty by January 1986 but undoubtedly there were more. God alone knows what the interested public made of all this. The debate must have seemed like a fierce game of intellectual doubles table tennis with, on one side of the net, *Drs* McCormack and Kiernan, and on the other, *Messrs* Manne and McAdam.

For those of us who were involved, however, nerves were on edge because we believed that the stakes were high. According to McCormack, the atmosphere resembled "the hysteria of seventeenth-century Salem or 1950s Washington". His "faith in the power of reasoned argument", he revealed, was "sadly diminished". According to Knopfelmacher, the lionisation of Burchett served a "deeper purpose ... [it was] an attempt to destroy the legitimacy of empirico-rational discourse as such". McCormack claimed that the case against Burchett had collapsed before the nation's eyes. He also believed the opposite: that while my "rehash" of the case against Burchett had been given "vast coverage", his "sober analysis" had been "ignored".

In all this, there was only one unpredictable development. The filmmaker Edwin Morrisby had worked with Burchett. In 1969, in the car park of the Phnom Penh airport, he had seen Vietnamese communists handing Burchett an envelope of travellers' cheques that Burchett had opened in front of him. Those Morrisby saw were each worth US$100. "*Un cadeau de vos amis de Starigrad*" (a gift from your Starigrad friends), they had "smirked". Morrisby thought Starigrad was, most likely, Moscow. Morrisby's article was published first in the October 1985 issue of *Quadrant* and then in *The Weekend Australian*. By now, however, the newspapers were growing weary. *The Age* pulled the plug on this extended combat by letters-to-the-editor in late October 1985. Kiernan had what the editor of *Australian Society*, in seeming exasperation, called "the last word" in January 1986. (The importance of having the last word is one of the illusions public intellectuals don't seem to be able to shake off, myself included.)

Out of public view things were happening. McCormack and I were invited to debate the Burchett issue on an ABC television evening program. Following the debate, in the ABC foyer McCormack loudly informed me, "I will sue you!" Unsurprisingly, the debate was never broadcast. According to McCormack, he had been censored: "A national television program in which a critical voice, mine, might also have been heard was canned." The reason for canning the encounter, however, was almost certainly because the pre-recorded debate had quickly descended into an incomprehensible shouting match over distant events and unknown persons. The writ never arrived. McCormack, however, successfully rallied the State Library of Victoria against me. On August 26, I received a letter from the acting state librarian:

> [T]he publication of extracts from Wilfred Burchett's letters has caused considerable distress to Mr. Winston Burchett ... who, jointly with the Library, has control over their publication ... Your future use of material from our collections must depend on assurances that you will abide by the conditions which we, and our donors, impose on the material.

A little over a fortnight later I received a letter from McCormack, marked "Confidential". The letter pointed to two passages in my *Quadrant* essay, one concerning my claim about McCormack's "neo-Stalinist" interpretation of Korean history and the other where I expressed my "anger at the doctoring of history". According to McCormack, these passages suggested that I believed he was a propagandist "favourable to dictatorship and mass murder" rather than "a scholar committed to truth and open-mindedness". These suggestions had damaged his reputation. As McCormack "assume[d]" these suggestions were "inadvertent" and that I had since come to realise that they were both "damaging and false" (on what basis he had made such an assumption was not clear), he expected an apology in *Quadrant* at the earliest opportunity. (One of the lessons I had already learned was never to threaten a defamation suit unless you intend to go ahead.) Because important issues about "the nature and values of the institution we serve" were involved, he had decided to "enclose a copy of this letter to the Vice Chancellor, with whom you may wish to discuss the principles involved, and also to the Deans and Heads of our respective departments". (How a letter marked "Confidential" could also be copied to five senior members of the university or how he justified to himself his flight to authority were also not made clear.)

I think McCormack to some degree succeeded in damaging my reputation at La Trobe. When in 1990 I was appointed sole editor of *Quadrant* – a thick magazine of ideas published ten times a year – John Hirst and other members of the Seminar on the Sociology of Culture requested that I be relieved of some of my teaching duties. The answer from the vice chancellor, John Scott, was a definitive "No!". Later I met Scott regarding a cause of which he approved. He expressed surprise and relief that I seemed to have shed my reactionary past and joined the party of progress or – better still perhaps, because he was a pious Protestant – was now on the side of the angels.

In 1986 a book on Wilfred Burchett, *Burchett: Reporting the Other Side of the World*, edited by Ben Kiernan was published. Although my *Quadrant* Burchett essay had provoked six months of public controversy, in this volume it was almost entirely ignored. The only aspect deemed worthy of comment was the KGB question where, over fewer than four pages, Kiernan summarily dismissed the Krotkov evidence. In Kiernan's volume, Gavan McCormack contributed almost fifty tightly packed pages and 214 footnotes on Burchett's record during the Korean War. I was worth one footnote, a reference to Burchett's reputation as a Don Juan. McCormack did not mention Burchett's Korean War journalism for the *New China News Agency*, the Chinese Communist Party's official English language voice. Nor did he outline the most important evidence about the role Burchett played in the production and distribution of the false germ warfare confessions, the 180-page transcript of Lieutenant Paul Kniss' interrogation.

McCormack's answer to my essay was published in 1986 by *Meanjin*. He informed readers that I had "defied the rules of the State Library of Victoria in such a way as to earn a severe rebuke", and dismissed the critical Kniss interrogation transcript that he had not read. He claimed that the Americans were almost certainly guilty of germ warfare, as charged. "[T]he credibility of the Burchett allegations of American use of germ warfare has risen steadily in recent years." He apparently believed that a secret committee of anti-communists existed who made collective decisions about how to prosecute the Burchett case. That Burchett was not a secret member of the CPA but "a lonely figure", driven by "a rough, bush-socialist, internationalist instinct" was, according to McCormack, "beyond the imagination of dogmatic, Cold War minds". And of course, he believed Yuri Krotkov, the self-confessed ex-KGB pimp, was a despicable person whose evidence about Burchett's recruitment to the KGB was both wicked and ridiculous. "The 'Burchett as KGB-man' case has been prosecuted with tremendous energy and lack of principle for thirty-five years; in 1986 it is evidently in tatters."

*

At the time of Burchett's death in Bulgaria in September 1983, no one could have predicted that within a few years, following the collapse of every Communist Party state in Eastern and Central Europe in 1989 and then the Soviet Union itself in 1991, parts of the archives of the communist movement would open. Documents discovered settled beyond reasonable doubt two questions at the centre of the Burchett debate.

The first was whether Burchett was an independent radical, as he claimed, or a secret member of the CPA. The scholar Peter Hruby worked for thirteen years in the Czechoslovak section of Radio Free Europe. In October 1996 he inspected files in the State

Central Archive of the Czech Republic. Several documents from the early 1950s, discussed in his book *Dangerous Dreamers*, proved that Burchett was a party member. For instance, on June 18, 1951, the leaders of the CPA, R. Dixon and L.L. Sharkey, wrote a letter supporting Burchett from their Sydney office: "Comrade Burchett has the trust of the Party … Since the entry into the Party he has been its member without interruption." Both Yuri Krotkov and Tibor Méray, the Hungarian journalist who had reported on the Korean War for the communist side, remembered Burchett confiding in them that he was a secret member of the Communist Party of Australia. On this question, Burchett had fooled most of the world – including Harrison Salisbury of *The New York Times*; his most prominent Australian supporters, John Pilger, Phillip Knightley, Ben Kiernan and Gavan McCormack; and his painfully naive biographer, Tom Heenan. There is another intriguing story. A senior member of the CPA, Mavis Robertson, told journalist Mark Aarons that in 1958 she presented Burchett in Moscow with his Australian party card. He threw it in the rubbish bin. While he remained a CPA member, as a friend of Zhou Enlai and Ho Chi Minh he was, it appears, far too grand a communist by now to submit, even theoretically, to the discipline of his provincial Australian comrades.

The second question was resolved following the brief opening of the most secret archives of the Communist Party of the Soviet Union (CPSU). In 2013 a Russian scholar working in La Trobe's politics department, Robert Horvath, sent me a document he had translated. Its origin was the collection of documents that the great Soviet dissident Vladimir Bukovsky had managed to photocopy while working for Boris Yeltsin, the first non-communist Russian leader since 1917. One of these documents concerned Wilfred Burchett, of whom Bukovsky had never heard. The initial author of the document concerning Burchett was Ivan Serov, the chairman of the KGB. On July 17, 1957, he wrote to the Central Committee of the CPSU. According to Serov, one of the KGB's agents "was placed close" to Burchett. Already the KGB had received "an array of interesting materials from him [Burchett] in written form". On the KGB's instructions, according to Serov, "Burchett is seeking opportunities to penetrate the American and West European press." Already, the KGB had provided Burchett with an apartment and "taken a decision to engage Burchett in collaboration with the organs of the KGB". As, however, the newspaper Burchett represented, the US *National Guardian*, could not afford to pay him, Serov requested a (very substantial) 20,000-rouble down payment to Burchett and a handsome monthly salary of 4,000 roubles. The Central Committee of the CPSU informed Serov on October 25, 1957, that, as requested, they would pay Burchett 20,000 roubles and a monthly salary of 3,000 roubles.

Not only, then, did Burchett become an agent of the KGB in 1957, but the accuracy of Krotkov's 1969 testimony to the US congressional committee was also confirmed. So how did the Burchettistas respond to this evidence? So far as I am aware, the historical heavyweight supporters of Burchett, Stuart Macintyre and Ben Kiernan, were silent. And what of Gavan McCormack? Having acknowledged that the Serov document was most likely not a forgery, my old sparring partner argued in *Arena Magazine* that of four possible outcomes of the KGB's financial offer, "the least likely" was that Burchett took the money.

*

The Wilfred Burchett essay of 1985 enhanced my reputation with the most influential Australian anti-communists – B.A. Santamaria, Frank Knopfelmacher and Peter Coleman, the editor of *Quadrant*. On the other hand, it also made me more hated by the progressive intelligentsia than at any time in my life. In a letter to me, Rai Gaita recalled vividly the atmosphere among even the most intelligent members of the non-communist left at the time, where the predominant ideological posture was anti-anticommunism. At a farewell lunch for Rai, who was returning to King's College London after a six-month teaching exchange, the University of Melbourne philosopher Tony Coady declared:

"Your friend Manne has called my friend Gavan McCormack a neo-Stalinist". We then had an argument that dominated and, of course spoilt, the lunch. I was struck by how often friends prefaced their hostility to you by saying "Your friend Manne". Referring to a reply in *Meanjin* to your article in *Quadrant* Graeme Marshall [another University of Melbourne philosopher] said "I see that your friend Manne has been bested". When I asked him whether he had read your article, he said that "*Quadrant* was the kind of magazine you asked to be given under the counter in a brown paper bag." The implication of the reiterated "your friend Manne" was something like: "We like you Rai. We know your heart is on the left. We've put up with your friendship with Manne for a long time. It's now time for you to decide. Are you with him or with us?"

In answer to Coady and Marshall and all other members of the anti-anticommunist intelligentsia, this is what I would now say. It is true that Wilfred Burchett helped some Jews get out of Germany in the months between *Kristallnacht* and the outbreak of war in September 1939. It is also true that his report on the impact of the atomic bombing of Hiroshima in August 1945 was of civilisational significance, although he was severely compromised by his later support for Mao against Khrushchev on the morality of using nuclear weapons if the cause of communism was advanced. It cannot be denied that he backed the winning side in the Vietnam War, but he did so for more than a decade not with honest reportage but with cleverly crafted propaganda. While Burchett supported the Khmer Rouge regime of Pol Pot in its early years, following the Vietnamese invasion of Christmas Day 1978 he became, almost overnight, one of its most influential and ferocious enemies.

Beyond this, his record was dark. In the late 1940s and very early 1950s Burchett celebrated the Stalinisation of Eastern and Central Europe, and even the judicial murder of leading communists following show trials. Shortly thereafter, during the Korean War, while working under close Chinese communist supervision, Burchett produced an endless stream of propaganda about the peace talks; helped prepare, edit and then film or broadcast the fake germ warfare confessions of physically and mentally tortured US pilots; and visited the communist-run POW camps, which he likened to Swiss luxury holiday resorts, where thousands of captured soldiers defending the South, including his Australian countrymen, were held and severely mistreated. In 1956 Burchett had cheered on the Soviet Union's brutal and bloody crushing of the 1956 Hungarian Revolution. In the late 1950s he turned a blind eye to the tens of millions of Chinese peasants who starved to death during the Great Leap Forward, and then failed to notice the madness and cruelty of the Maoist Cultural Revolution while offering the Chinese communist regime high praise for its attempted destruction of the ancient civilisation of Tibet. During these years Burchett lied about his membership of the Communist Party of Australia, posing as an independent radical. From 1957 until the mid-1960s Burchett worked from a splendid riverside apartment in Moscow for the blood-stained Soviet secret intelligence service, the KGB, as a generously salaried agent of influence.

There are several causes I supported or opposed in the '80s that I now regret – but not the case I mounted against Wilfred Burchett.

[8.]

The Petrov Affair

SHORTLY AFTER THE PUBLICATION of my Wilfred Burchett essay, Sam Lipski, a first-rate, Knopfelmacher-educated, Jewish-Australian journalist, asked me if I would be the historical adviser for the television miniseries he had proposed to Kerry Packer. As a high school student, Sam had been fascinated by the dramatic defections of two members of the Soviet Embassy in Canberra – Vladimir and Evdokia Petrov – and their political consequences. I was too young to remember anything about the Petrov Affair. However, shortly after I returned from Britain in 1974, Henry Rosenbloom, a university friend now working for a minister in the Whitlam government, had given me a copy of John Stubbs and Nicholas Whitlam's new Petrov book, *Nest of Traitors.* Henry was convinced that Stubbs and Whitlam provided at least a partial explanation of the failure of the ALP in every federal election between 1954 and 1969, and compelling evidence about the wickedness of the forces of conservatism in Australia. Perhaps Henry believed I was badly in need of some education concerning recent Australian political history.

In April 1954, the head of Soviet political intelligence in Australia, the MVD (later KGB) officer Vladimir Petrov, had defected in Sydney, followed by the more spectacular defection in Darwin of his wife, Evdokia Petrova, also an MVD intelligence officer. *Nest of Traitors* retold the version of the Petrov Affair as a political conspiracy that had held sway on the left – and in both the Communist Party of Australia and the Australian Labor Party – for twenty years. According to this version, the defections – and the explosive political consequences – were the result of a conspiracy between Robert Menzies, Liberal Party prime minister; Colonel Charles Spry, director of the domestic intelligence service, ASIO; and B.A. Santamaria, leader of the secretive, Roman Catholic, anti-communist organisation known as The Movement. The purpose of the conspiracy was, supposedly, to manipulate the timing of the defections to ensure the Menzies government was returned in the May 1954 federal election. The left believed the conspiracy had succeeded: the Liberal–Country Party Coalition government narrowly won an election that, without the Petrov defections, it was certain to lose, thus robbing the most brilliant Australian politician of the era, Dr Herbert Vere Evatt – the former High Court judge, occasional historical scholar and the Labor leader – of the final prize of his stellar career, the prime ministership of Australia. Even worse, the theory went, Dr Evatt – or, as he was known, "the Doc" – bravely attempted to unmask the anti-communist Menzies-Spry-Santamaria conspiracy at the Royal Commission on Espionage before wrongfully being tossed out. As he continued to mount his case in public, this interpretation of the Petrov defections continued, the anti-Evatt Movement members within the federal ALP caucus turned against him, thus revealing their loyalty to B.A. Santamaria and their disloyalty to Doc Evatt and the Australian Labor Party. In early October 1954, Evatt had no choice but to expose the insidious danger represented by these Santamaria forces within Labor. After six months, the ALP was split and a new reactionary, anti-working-class party formed, calling itself first the Anti-Communist Labor Party and then the Democratic Labor Party. By delivering its preferences to the Liberal–Country Party Coalition, the DLP kept Labor out of office for a generation. In considerable part because of the conviction on the left about a political conspiracy involving conservative forces and Australia's domestic intelligence agency, relations between the ALP Left and ASIO were poisonous.

This conspiratorial interpretation of the Petrov Affair seemed to me quite improbable, even fantastical. For this reason, in the book I edited in the early 1980s, *The New Conservatism in Australia*, I commissioned what turned out to be a carefully argued chapter debunking Labor's Petrov myth by the arch-conservative University of New South Wales political historian J.B. Paul. It is unlikely that Paul convinced anyone not already convinced. When Sam Lipski invited me in 1984 to become the historical researcher for the mini-series he proposed, the Menzies-Spry-Santamaria Petrov conspiracy theory was still alive, and was seen as a precursor to the more recent and even more shameful chapter, the conservative "coup d'état" of November 11, 1975: the governor-general's dismissal of the Whitlam government at a time when it held a comfortable majority in the House of Representatives.

I did not feel about the Petrov Affair what I felt about the career of Wilfred Burchett. The Burchett question turned on some of the critical events of twentieth-century history – the record of communism in the Soviet Union, Eastern Europe, China and Cambodia and the wars between the communist and non-communist forces in Korea and Vietnam that served as proxies for the larger Cold War conflict between the Soviet Union and the United States – that is to say, between democratic capitalism and communism. With these questions I was not only historically curious but also fully politically and morally engaged. The attempt to portray Burchett as Australia's Dreyfus and a Cold War martyr angered me. The Petrov Affair seemed, on the other hand, principally a question of Australian domestic politics. For me, at least, the stakes were much lower. If in my research I had discovered evidence of a political conspiracy between Menzies, Spry and Santamaria or anyone else I would have been surprised, but would not have hesitated in bringing it to the attention of the mini-series' writers, Cliff Green and, later, Mac Gudgeon.

Sam's proposal got up. I had been lucky that when I began research at Oxford the British government had just moved from a fifty- to a thirty-year rule for its archives. I was now lucky again. Shortly before I began research on the Petrov Affair, under contract to Kerry Packer's production company, PBL, the Hawke government decided to open almost all ASIO and royal commission records concerning the

Petrov defections. Within the cultural sphere of the United Kingdom and its former dominions, the comprehensive early release of security or intelligence service archives was highly unusual, perhaps even unprecedented. (It was commonly claimed, only half in jest, that in the United Kingdom the Napoleonic War records of its secret service were still under wraps.) When I began the research in the Australian National Archives in Canberra, I was not sure whether the Hawke government had decided on the release in the hope of proving or disproving the conspiracy theory. What I was sure about, however, was that the fascinating story I began to discover was quite unlike that dreamed of by either the left or the right. In fact it was far more suspenseful and entertaining.

After a few weeks in the National Archives I decided that I would be able to provide Cliff Green, best known for his screenplay for Peter Weir's *Picnic at Hanging Rock*, with an accurate but also original account of the Petrov defections and their explosive political aftermath. I was also convinced that there was a book about the affair demanding to be written. Because of Robert Maxwell's real or supposed past as an Israeli spy, his Oxford-based academic press, Pergamon, was interested in stories of espionage. Its Australian manager, Jerry Mayer, was keen on the book I proposed. A second contract was signed.

What became clear from the archival evidence was that the timing of the defection was not determined by ASIO on behalf of the Menzies government, but by Vladimir Petrov himself. At any moment between the beginning of ASIO's interest in the possibility of Petrov's defection in 1953 – called "Operation Cabin 12" – and its realisation on April 4, 1954, ASIO would have accepted the defection with enthusiasm and relief. In late 1953 the possibility of defection seemed close. The ASIO records showed that a safe house was rented for a month in preparation. They also told much more about the roles of the two doctors ASIO had employed to reel Petrov in – the highly conventional Anglo-Australian eye doctor H.C. Beckett, whom Petrov needed to see, and the part-time paid ASIO agent and flamboyant, Polish and far less respectable Michael Bialoguski. Dr Bialoguski was a talented musician, his medical practice included abortion and, most significantly for ASIO, he moved in left-wing circles, including among the members of the Russian Social Club in Sydney occasionally frequented by Petrov.

In convincing Petrov that he should defect, Dr Bialoguski was far more important than Dr Beckett. Bialoguski befriended Petrov, who, as an intelligence officer with the task of cultivating and recruiting Australians as agents, was permitted by his government to move around Sydney freely. He began to talk to Petrov about the possibility of a future in Australia together, perhaps as the proprietors of a chicken farm they visited, Dream Acres, or a cafe where they often met, The Adria. Petrov's work as the head of political intelligence in Australia had been severely criticised by Moscow Centre as unenterprising and incompetent. Even more dangerously, in the politically uncertain time following the death of Stalin in March 1953, when Stalin's MVD chief, Lavrentiy Beria, was arrested and then six months later executed, both Petrov and his wife were accused of forming a "Beria ring" within the Soviet Embassy in Canberra.

Despite Bialoguski's best efforts, the records showed that Petrov dithered. It was not until February 1954 that he was willing to meet with former policeman Ron Richards, the senior ASIO officer Colonel Spry entrusted with the Petrov operation. Richards met Petrov, by now a bundle of nerves, on a dozen occasions in Sydney and Canberra. Spry decided not only to promise Petrov 5,000 pounds if he should defect and a further 5,000 if he brought with him valuable documents, but also to have Richards actually show him the banknotes of the first instalment. I was able to read Richards' reports of these meetings and listen to his Minifon wire recordings (tapes were still in the future) of their tense conversations. In one, in a car in Canberra, Petrov's beloved dog, Jack, could sometimes be heard barking in the back seat. Historians are strange people; hearing the long-dead dramatis personae of their studies (or their dogs) speaking (or barking) is thrilling.

ASIO's records showed that Prime Minister Menzies knew almost nothing of all this. In August 1953, Spry mentioned to him the remote possibility of the defection of a Soviet intelligence officer sometime in the future. In February 1954 Spry first mentioned Petrov's name to Menzies in what the ASIO record called a "preliminary briefing". Petrov decided to defect on April 4, the day his MVD successor, Yuri Kovalenok, arrived from Moscow. Until Petrov entered an ASIO car in Sydney and was driven to a safe house, neither Spry nor Richards was certain that they had their man. After I'd read these records carefully and listened to several recorded conversations, it became obvious that Dr Evatt's belief in an ASIO–Menzies conspiracy was false. Conservative forces had not saved up the defection until the eve of the 1954 election to help the Liberal–Country Party Coalition win an unwinnable election. The idea was a consolatory fantasy.

The ASIO archive concerning "Operation Cabin 12" also shattered the right's rather romantic version of the Petrov defection, which, before beginning the research, I had shared. Petrov did not emerge from these records as an anti-communist idealist who had "chosen freedom". In Bialoguski's lengthy and rather salacious reports to ASIO headquarters – which I later learned had amused Spry and Richards but shocked ASIO's director of counterespionage, the Moral Rearmament poet Michael Thwaites – what became clear is that Petrov spent his evenings in Sydney not so much recruiting spies as carousing with Bialoguski, chasing prostitutes and drinking himself into a stupor. ASIO even became aware that Petrov and Bialoguski were using Vladimir's diplomatic status to purchase large quantities of duty-free Bells Whisky – with Petrova (Mrs Petrov) cooking the books – and reselling it to Sydney nightspots for a tidy profit. The Petrov that emerged from the ASIO records was a simple man of peasant stock who had managed to survive the savage and bloody purges of the 1930s and beyond, which included the Soviet intelligence and security services, who had been promoted well beyond his competence, and for whom freedom meant wine and women rather than democracy and the rule of law.

The defection of Evdokia Petrova on April 19–20 was far more dramatic than that of her husband. According to the popular version of the events, Australians believed they had witnessed a frightened, weeping woman forced by two scowling Slavic thugs onto a plane bound for Moscow. A desperate and angry anti-communist immigrant crowd swarmed onto the Mascot tarmac but could not save her from the imprisonment and possible death that awaited her at home. In her struggle, Petrova lost one of her shoes. This lost red shoe soon became famous. Once the plane landed in Darwin, all passengers were asked to disembark for refuelling. Petrova's guards were instantly tackled and disarmed by several burly Northern Territory policemen and soldiers. Separated from her escorts, so the popular story continued, Petrova applied for and was granted political asylum and was soon romantically reunited with her husband. The newsreel of Petrova's abduction at Mascot was shown in cinemas across the nation, and the photo of her rescue at Darwin dominated the next day's newspapers. The mainstream values of Australia in the 1950s – political freedom and married love – had triumphed over totalitarian communist thuggery.

The story of Evdokia Petrova's defection that I discovered in the archive bore almost no relation to the version that entered Australian folklore. At Mascot, Petrova had indeed been very frightened, but not of her guards or her likely fate in Moscow. She believed that the anti-communist Eastern European refugee crowd hated her and intended her harm. One of the witnesses to the events at Mascot was the fiery anti-communist Liberal Party backbencher Bill Wentworth. Wentworth rang the Lodge in Canberra, where Menzies was hosting a pre-election dinner party for his Cabinet. Unless Petrova was saved, Wentworth told Defence Minister Philip McBride, who picked up the phone, Menzies could say goodbye to his re-election prospects. An impromptu Cabinet meeting was convened. Menzies then rang Spry. An MI5 offer of asylum for Petrova had been planned for Singapore. A second defection of a Soviet intelligence officer on Australian soil was thought to be more than diplomatic relations between Moscow and Canberra could bear. But the threat of an election loss trumped a minor diplomatic setback. Menzies asked Spry if the offer of asylum could be made in Darwin. Spry immediately got to work. Learning from the plane's captain that Petrova's guards were armed, in breach of Australian civil aviation regulation, he instructed the deputy administrator in Darwin, R.S. Leydin, to arrange for a greeting party of policemen and soldiers to disarm Petrova's guards as soon as they set foot in Darwin.

This, at least, went according to plan. However, when Leydin offered Petrova asylum, in a conversation she insisted should be in the presence of her guards, she refused the offer. Leydin had almost given up when, on parting, Petrova winked at him. Leydin took what he thought to be a hint and tried once more. Petrova was now willing to speak without her guards. At first she appeared to be frozen in an agony of indecision. Was her husband alive? A telephone line from the safe house in Sydney proved that he was. Could she be kidnapped by the Australian government rather than apply for asylum? Leydin, aghast, told her that was not possible. Eventually Leydin succeeded; Petrova did apply for political asylum. However, rather than the reunion of a loving married couple, when Petrova was reunited with Petrov, she accused him of placing her family in deadly peril. This was the first of many months of flaming rows, all recorded with objectivity and compassion by their ASIO safe-house companions.

What happened next would help determine the shape of Australian politics over the next two decades. Despite gaining more votes than the Coalition, the ALP lost the May 29 election. According to a Gallup poll (the only such poll that then existed in Australia), the Petrov defections had no influence on the popularity of the parties. The Menzies government had convened the Royal Commission on Espionage before the May election, probably to present Evatt with a fait accompli should he become prime minister. Following the election, it was revealed at the commission that two of the documents Petrov had brought with him involved members of Evatt's staff. Document H – a guide to the political views, religious affiliations and personal habits of the Canberra press gallery – had been written in 1951 for a Soviet intelligence officer by the journalist who had become Evatt's young press secretary, Fergan O'Sullivan. Document J was a rollicking history of Australian politics and history that included a single page on Dr Evatt. According to both Petrov and Petrova, it had been written inside the Soviet Embassy in 1953 by the Australian communist Rupert Lockwood, for Pakhomov's replacement, Antonov. Document J named three members of Evatt's staff – O'Sullivan, Allan Dalziel and Albert Grundeman – as sources of information. Dr Evatt already appeared to have been psychologically destabilised by the election loss. He now came to a terrifying conclusion: Documents H and J were part of the Menzies-Spry-Santamaria conspiracy designed to destroy his prime ministerial prospects. O'Sullivan was a Catholic Action/Santamaria plant. The page in Document J citing O'Sullivan, Dalziel and Grundeman as sources was a Menzies/Spry–inspired forgery. Dr Evatt likened Documents H and J to the "Zinoviev letter" believed to lie behind the British Labour Party's 1924 election defeat, and even to the Reichstag Fire of 1933, used by Hitler to lay the foundations for his dictatorship.

Dr Evatt summarily dismissed Fergan O'Sullivan. He then appeared at the royal commission as counsel for Dalziel and Grundeman, even though they were accused of nothing. The editor of *Quadrant*, Peter Coleman, gave me the three thick volumes containing the transcript of evidence presented to the royal commission. For three weeks Dr Evatt dominated its proceedings. Having "realised" that Document J was a forgery, Evatt now searched in a frenzy for the evidence he needed. He suggested that the pencilled lettering was not in Lockwood's hand and that the typewriter used was not Lockwood's. But this forgery theory was refuted by handwriting and typing experts. Evatt also claimed that certain staple marks on Document J revealed that the supposedly incriminating page had been inserted.

Evatt did not appear to have noticed that his forgery and ring-in theories were contradictory. Furthermore, they flew in the face of rather convincing evidence: before Evatt arrived at the commission, Lockwood had admitted to the document's authorship in a Communist Party pamphlet entitled, "What Is in Document J?" Most deeply of all, Dr Evatt's conspiracy claim made no sense. If Documents H and J had been written to destroy his election prospects, why had they not been leaked to the press during the election campaign or presented to the royal commission until the election was over? As Menzies remarked, he did not mind being regarded as a rogue but he did object to being treated as a fool. The transcript of the royal commission proceedings over the three weeks of Evatt's appearance was evidence of a once formidable legal and political mind that had altogether lost its bearings. As I later wrote:

> [Evatt] now came to see with a terrifying certainty the connections between apparently unconnected persons and events. Progressively from this moment, Dr Evatt, a man whose life had been devoted to Justice, Reason and Scholarship, abandoned himself to the darkest suspicions concerning real and imagined enemies and to an absolute faith in his own intuition.

As part of my research, in early 1986 I visited the Evatt Collection at Flinders University in Adelaide. I was surprised to discover that Evatt had become a magnet for all manner of Petrov miscellanea, like the memoirs of Bialoguski's estranged and mistreated wife, Patricia, and of the woman from the Russian Social Club who pretended she was a spy, Lydia Mokras. Even more revealingly, the Evatt Collection contained scores of wild, disordered and sectarian anti-Menzies-Spry-Santamaria theorising from someone who called himself "Phil's Friend". This was, I was able to discover, the former deputy director of ASIO R.F.B. Wake, whom Colonel Spry had dismissed for erratic behaviour. I also found the letter Evatt had written to the Soviet Union's foreign minister, Vyacheslav Molotov, in which he pleaded for evidence from the MVD to prove that the Petrov documents were ASIO forgeries: "In order to expose what I believe to be a crime against humanity, I request an immediate intervention from Your Excellency."

This letter helped seal Evatt's and even Labor's political fate. On October 19, 1955, Dr Evatt initiated a parliamentary debate on the report of the Royal Commission on Espionage. He referred to his Molotov letter, to the dismay of many ALP parliamentarians and the delight of Robert Menzies. Many regard Menzies' reply as one of his greatest parliamentary performances. (Happily, as ASIO had recorded both speeches I was able to listen to them.) Almost immediately

Menzies called an early election, where the second preferences of the DLP went to the government, and where, as a consequence, Menzies' Liberal–Country Party Coalition won seventy-five seats and Evatt's Labor Party forty-nine. This was, as I argued, not a mere election victory but the beginning of the Menzies era.

In May 1985, when I was some six months into my research and had paid a brief visit to the National Archives, Sir Charles Spry, quite unusually, agreed to an interview. We got on so well that we spoke three times. The transcript of the second interview amounted to more than 15,000 words. In the introduction to *The Petrov Affair*, I wrote that the conversations with Spry were "among the most enjoyable of my life", a description that Knopfelmacher thought was a political mistake. I had never met anyone who so embodied the virtues and some of the shortcomings of the old-fashioned Anglo-Australian character. The interviews with Spry breathed life into the documents I had begun reading.

Spry told me that he had never met Menzies when he was appointed director-general of ASIO in 1950. In fact at that time, he thought of him as a "puffed up, conceited damn politician". He came, however, to regard Menzies as one of the four most impressive people he had known. Spry explained that he had not alerted Menzies to the likelihood of the Petrov defection until February 1954 because of a lesson from his military superior, General Blamey, during the 1941 Greek campaign. Blamey had crossed out everything in a report Spry had written. "If you want to get on in the army, never make a forecast to any politician because if you are wrong, he'll hold it against you to your dying day." Spry thought Menzies had come to trust him because of the way he had handled Petrova's Darwin defection. Menzies went to bed on 19 April facing a potential political disaster. "He woke up in the morning and it was all fixed." According to Spry, Menzies never told him what to do. They became close friends. When Spry was in Canberra, they often met and had a drink or two. Spry admired Menzies' intellect and loved his way with words. On Spry's retirement, Menzies told him that had he remained a soldier, he would have appointed him chief of the Australian army. I sensed his regret.

One of the principal reasons for the regret was Dr Evatt. Spry still clearly loathed him. He described Evatt as "malevolent" and "vindictive" and a "megalomaniac". He told me of a meeting where Evatt had chastised and humiliated the former head of the Commonwealth Investigation Service, "the poor dear old Longfield Lloyd", in front of his colleagues. "[I]n the army you have a code of loyalty," Spry said, "and this [was] a terrible thing to see." Following the defections, Evatt phoned Spry, who explained that he had been instructed to pass all Petrov enquiries to the prime minister. "So, there is a bit of silence, then bang on the telephone. And that is the last time I ever spoke to Dr Evatt." Spry recalled "old Bert [Evatt]" on the sidelines at the commission the day after he was thrown out, "tugging the coat tails of [Ted] Hill saying, 'Ask him this, ask him that.'" When I asked Spry what he thought of Hill, later the leader of the Maoist breakaway Communist Party, he said that if Australia had become a communist country, Hill would most likely have become Australia's Beria or Stalin.

Spry told me his relations with the next leader of the Labor Party, Arthur Calwell, were good. Calwell had told Spry that the members of the ALP could scarcely believe their ears when Evatt had referred in the parliament to his correspondence with Molotov. When I asked Spry how he would explain Evatt's strange behaviour at the royal commission, he said that he thought Evatt was "going mad". He thought that Evatt was a large part of the reason relations between the ALP and ASIO had been so poisonous. Spry also told me that if Labor under Evatt had won the election, ASIO would have hidden the Petrovs from the government.

At the time I interviewed Spry in May 1985, I was still uncertain about the character of Vladimir Petrov and the reasons for his defection. Spry described Petrov as "pickled" in alcohol, and as someone who had been tempted by "la dolce vita" he had experienced with Bialoguski. He thought Petrov had defected in part because his work as an intelligence officer had come under such criticism in Moscow, in part because he was terrified of being killed or sent to Siberia on return to the Soviet Union in the anticipated anti-Beria purge, and in part perhaps because his marriage was so rocky. It was Spry's idea to show Petrov the banknotes on offer should he defect.

Spry told me that he was "never more relieved [than] when I got a ring from Sydney" telling him that "the old bugger had defected". He was amused and not alarmed by Petrov's post-defection drink-induced antics, running riot on the Gold Coast on one occasion and knocking on the door of the wrong flat. Vladimir is hardly a difficult name to pronounce or remember, but throughout the three interviews Spry called him either "Peter" or "Jack". Such was the way in pre-multicultural Anglo Australia. Perhaps most memorably for me, however, was the affection and the pity Spry had obviously felt for Petrov. Spry described Petrov as "a warm, friendly fellow". He told me of Petrov's uncanny way with animals and birds. He could "attract around him" possums and cats. "[I]n one of the safe houses he had birds sitting on his hands." In Spry's last visit to see Petrov after his stroke, Petrov was barely able to speak but for a long time held onto Spry's hand. The former director-general of ASIO remained loyal until the end, many years after Petrov had been squeezed dry of all the intelligence he had – or, more likely, had been willing to divulge.

Evdokia Petrova was a capable and intelligent "tough cookie", Spry said, but it was her sexuality that seemed to have made the greatest impression. Spry either knew or believed – I was not sure which – that she had slept with many members of the Soviet intelligence service, "including the top generals and some of the cleverest fellows in the MVD". Another Soviet intelligence defector told Spry that her nickname in the MVD was Matahari. Some years after the defection, the Petrovs were invited to dine with a celebrated Soviet intelligence defector, Anatoliy Golitsyn. The sexual charge between Evdokia and Anatoli was palpable. Spry thought that the hostility she experienced at her work in the Soviet Embassy – ostensibly as an accountant and secretary, in reality as an intelligence officer responsible for encoding and decoding messages to and from Moscow – could in part be explained by the envy of the wives of the embassy staff. Above all, Spry remembered Petrova's "mischievous sense of fun". She was "full of laughter" and then "would wink at you". That wink again.

Spry was insistent on the high intelligence value of the defections. The Petrovs were interrogated for months by both ASIO and MI5. The only other intelligence service allowed to interrogate them came from Sweden, where the Petrovs had been placed during part of the war. The CIA was provided with information gathered during the interrogations by MI5. The Petrovs provided Western intelligence with a detailed understanding of the present structure and methods of the MVD, including their cypher system. They were also able to identify 535 MVD intelligence officers. One of the Soviet intelligence officers working in Australia was Philip Kislytsin. He was flown back to Moscow on the same plane Petrova had been on. As Spry explained, Kislytsin had rejected the asylum offered to him by the British in Singapore. "If it hadn't been for the mistress, I think we might have got him." Once home, Kislytsin was never heard of again. The Petrov defections, Spry told me, became ASIO's entry card to Western intelligence. They "opened every door to us". On his post-Petrov visit to the United States, the CIA and its director, Allen Dulles, welcomed Spry as "a long-lost brother". One of the famed heads of the CIA, James Angleton, once told Spry: "You see more and get more information from us, Charles, than we give to anybody." Less happily, the head of MI6 later informed Spry that all the Petrovs' intelligence had been sent to Moscow Centre by George Blake, a Soviet spy working for him. "He was ashamed to tell me that they had a traitor in their organisation."

Australia was a potentially fruitful field for Soviet espionage, Spry explained to me, not because of our own intelligence but because of the information we received from both the British and the Americans. ASIO had been created by the Chifley government in 1949 after serious leakages from the Department of External Affairs between 1945 and 1948 had been discovered. Until they were satisfied that Australia had created a professional domestic intelligence service, the British and the Americans sent the most sensitive information either not at all or only to trusted Australians, like Spry, on an "eyes only" basis. Two members of the Department of External Affairs – Ian Milner, who had founded the department of political science at the University of Melbourne, and Jim Hill (the brother of Ted) – were known by the Americans and the British to be the sources of the leaks. Walter Clayton, at that time the head of the Australian Communist Party's internal security force, was known to be the link between Milner and Hill and the Soviet intelligence officers in Canberra. In reality, with regard to Soviet espionage inside Australia, the Petrovs confirmed what ASIO already knew about Milner, Hill and Clayton. However, Spry told me that neither he nor Richards believed that Petrov had told his interrogators everything he knew or had done while the head of Soviet intelligence in Australia.

Spry knew for certain that Ian Milner had provided Moscow Centre with one particular post-war British defence assessment. Spry told me: "I know what [Milner] sent ... *I have seen the documents* ... There is no more important document we would have had in Australia, military-wise ... *I can't tell you in detail*" [my emphases]. In letting me know that there was something of great significance he could not tell me – the only occasion this happened during the three interviews – Spry was speaking about what was still the most closely guarded secret among Western intelligence services: the breaking of the Soviet code during the Second World War in a program known as Venona. Spry wanted me to understand how he had come to see documents Milner had passed to Clayton, who had then passed them to Petrov's Soviet intelligence predecessor. Although he could not tell me directly, he suggested I read one of Chapman Pincher's books, where the Venona breakthrough was discussed. That was how I was able to outline Venona, although not by name, in my book. In *The Spy Catchers: The Official History of ASIO*, David Horner writes: "Manne's study, based on ASIO documents, provides a highly detailed account of the defection – one that is confirmed by a re-examination of the documents, *including those not released at the time he researched his book*" [my emphasis]. I assume it is to my knowledge of Venona that this refers.

At the end of the third interview, Spry took me for lunch at his club. He introduced me to the legendary founder of ASIS, Alfred Deakin Brookes. For a moment, I was in the bosom of the old

Anglo-Australian Establishment. Not long after, Spry invited Anne and me to lunch. He cooked two delicious curries for the occasion. Also there were his son, Ian, and Ian's wife, Helen. In my memory at least, Ian wore a knitted cardigan. He looked like a country vicar from an Anthony Trollope novel.

*

The PBL miniseries on the Petrov Affair was scripted and filmed in 1985 and 1986. As early as June 1985 Cliff Green showed me his initial treatment. There was still a lot of work to be done. A new writer, Mac Gudgeon, was brought in. Regardless, after the filming was complete, insiders knew that the miniseries had not worked. The screening was long delayed. When it was finally shown in May 1987, it crashed. On May 27 in *The Age*, Barbara Hooks expressed the general sentiment. The miniseries had "all the lure of a long-winded night at the Politburo ... *Petrov* founders and finally subsides under the weight of its own worthiness." In 1988 a television series about the troubles of Labor, called *The True Believers*, scripted in part by Bob Ellis, resurrected the Evatt myth about the Menzies-Spry-Santamaria conspiracy, based on the version of the Petrov Affair found in *Nest of Traitors*.

Although I was responsible for the history that sank the series, I was not much involved during the filming. Except for one incident. Evdokia Petrova was now Anna Allyson, living in the almost deathly quiet Melbourne suburb of Bentleigh, and working as a typist-secretary for a tractor company. Claiming, reasonably but in fact falsely, that the miniseries was based upon the Petrovs' book, *Empire of Fear*, which had been ghostwritten by Michael Thwaites, she asked for payment. I was invited to a dinner with her where this matter was discussed. As she was leaving the dinner, Anna Allyson winked at me. It was that wink, on the Darwin tarmac on April 19, 1954, that had drawn Leydin into one final attempt to convince Evdokia Petrova to stay in Australia. It was therefore that wink that had perhaps saved the Menzies government from the tongue-lashing it might have received from Dr Evatt – in this highly possible counterfactual version of events, Evdokia Petrova's champion – for allowing Petrova to be strong-armed against her will back to Moscow and to almost certain death. The wink had perhaps altered the course of Australian political history. And all she had probably meant by it was "best wishes" and "goodbye".

The manuscript of my book, *The Petrov Affair: Politics and Espionage*, was finished by early October 1986. I sent it to Sir Charles Spry, who read it quickly and, to my relief, approved. Spry suggested only one change. At the time Richards was trying to convince Petrov to defect he offered 5,000 pounds and an additional 5,000 if he brought with him important documents: "If your information is of extreme value and you have something to support it – you may have a report or something like that – then, as I told you before, it could be 10,000 pounds." During the royal commission, the offer of the additional 5,000 pounds was never revealed. Indeed, as I pointed out in a footnote in *The Petrov Affair*, the additional money appeared to have been deliberately concealed from the royal commissioners:

> The Commissioners were handed the minifon tapes which should have included the entire March 26 discussion. However if they relied on the file of minifon transcripts they would not have read of the money talk of March 26. The transcription of that conversation is incomplete.

Not one reviewer – and they came primarily from the left – appeared to notice this potentially quite damning criticism of ASIO. The reason ASIO misled the royal commission and thus the political nation was easy to understand. As I wrote: "[I]n the conspiracy atmosphere of September, a belated admission of even an entirely innocent bonus-payment-offer to Petrov in exchange for documents would have presented ASIO's enemies with a quite devastating weapon." Nonetheless, it was a serious matter. In the manuscript I showed Spry, I wrote that on the question of the possible bonus payment Richards "lied" to the royal commissioners. Spry asked whether I might soften the expression. In the book it reads: "Richards, at least in his public evidence, clearly misled the Commissioners." Spry might have been defending Richards' reputation but, as the director-general of ASIO, he was also defending his own. The fact that I remember this thirty-five years later shows that it still niggles at my conscience.

The Petrov Affair was published in mid-March 1987. On March 19 I heard on the radio news and read in the Melbourne *Sun* – "Canberra to Probe Book on Petrov" – that the Labor government was conducting an investigation. A spokesman for the attorney-general pointed out that that there were twenty-one "direct quotes" attributed to Sir Charles Spry and that, while most of the material on the Petrov case was no longer confidential, there were "still 12 ASIO papers classified top secret". "[W]e will be looking to see if there is any breach of confidentiality" and "if anything in the book refers to them". I rang Spry. We were both aware of the almost exquisite irony: a government of the party that had come close to abolishing ASIO was now investigating the greatest super-hawk in ASIO's history on all matters concerning Australian security, to see whether he had breached confidentiality by providing information on a matter (undoubtedly Venona) still regarded as top secret. I was alarmed; Spry was amused. He assured me that nothing would come of the investigation. Nothing did. In my chapter on "The Case" there were several endnotes referring to Chapman Pincher's *Too Secret, Too Long*, published in 1984. Of course, I owed my understanding of the Venona program to Spry.

The first substantial review of *The Petrov Affair* was published by *The Sydney Morning Herald* and written by the former Labor senator James McClelland. McClelland admitted that if he had come across *The Petrov Affair* in a bookshop, he would have tossed it aside. Its author's "credentials", as a regular *Quadrant* contributor, were "impeccably far right". This is how things were in Australian political culture in the final years of the Cold War. McClelland described the book as "the first comprehensive history of the defection of Petrov and his wife"; recommended it as "a rattling good spy story" and "a great entertainment"; and concluded that its demolition of Labor's long-held Petrov–Evatt myth was unanswerable. The lengthy review was given the banner headline at the top of the book review page:

"The Petrov Conspiracy Theory Is Killed Stone Dead". I could not have wished for a better opening review.

Unsurprisingly, *The Petrov Affair* was welcomed by the right. On the left, McClelland set the tone. *The Petrov Affair* ran the gauntlet of Australia's best-informed foreign policy and defence intelligentsia of the left – Richard Hall in *The Age*, Max Teichmann in *The Times on Sunday*, Brian Toohey in *Australian Book Review*, Graeme Duncan in the *Australian Journal of Politics and History* and Kelvin Rowley in the *Far Eastern Economic Review*. It survived more or less unscathed. When there was a new edition in 2005, the Maoist historian Humphrey McQueen, who, as we shall see, had attacked me quite viciously over Manning Clark, and who was the author of *Gallipoli to Petrov*, conceded that "Manne's mastery of so much archival material in the three years following its 1984 declassification appeared miraculous and his account was more coherent and polished than any subsequent academic volumes on 'the nest of traitors'."

Not yet liberated from Australian intellectuals' cultural cringe, I was particularly chuffed by the positive notices in Washington and London – a brief comment in the *Times Literary Supplement* ("rich and intensely interesting") and from the prominent espionage authority Nigel West in *Intelligence Quarterly*, who approved of the book but drew my attention to a blooper: George Blake escaped from "Wormwood Scrubs" not "Wentworth Scrubs" as, to my considerable embarrassment, I had claimed.

There were criticisms I had to think about. Several reviewers pointed to the absence of context – Australian political history and culture during the early years of the Cold War. This was true. I had researched *The Petrov Affair* in fifteen months and written it in nine. An accurate sketch of the Cold War in Australia between 1945 and 1954 would have taken at least an additional year. Having finished with Petrov, I thought about writing a general history of the Australian Cold War. Had I done so, it would not have pleased those critics, primarily from the left, who called for context. Others thought that I had failed to recognise the suffering of those whose names appeared in Petrov's document, who were required to give evidence at the royal commission. The commissioners were, if anything, vulnerable to the opposite criticism – namely that they were too forbearing. When he defected, Petrov claimed that there was an undercover agent still employed inside the Department of External Affairs, Ric Throssell. After hearing his evidence, the commissioners cleared him of all suspicion.

There was one criticism with which I strongly agreed. The aged Australian diplomat and man of affairs Sir Walter Crocker thought the book was "excellent". "Who is Manne?" he inquired. However, "it is a detail but an important detail and a defect from the book as a work of art – he fails to say how the various *dramatis personae* ended up – e.g. Wake, Mme Ollier, the sinister evil Dr Bialoguski etc. etc." One reviewer called the prose at times "florid"; another called it "bland". Except for Anne, Crocker was the only early reader of *The Petrov Affair* who recognised that I had tried to write with artistry.

What then? Lengthy extracts of *The Petrov Affair* were published in several metropolitan broadsheet newspapers: I could obviously write for general audiences. For a few weeks *The Petrov Affair* appeared on some bestseller lists. In 1988, a serious institution in the United States, co-founded by the legendary Clare Boothe Luce, the National Intelligence Study Center (of which I had not previously heard) judged it to be the best book on espionage to be published in 1987 by a non-American author. "[I]t is an outstanding contribution to both scholarly research and popular understanding ... This award reflects high credit on Dr. [*sic*] Manne." However, although *The Petrov Affair* was thought to be worthy of a prestigious American award, in Australia it did not make any "book of the year" shortlist. I noticed that one of the Melbourne judges for *The Age*'s non-fiction prize was Margaret Whitlam, mother of the co-author of *Nest of Traitors*. The literary world was dominated by the left. At least, after the reasonable success of *The Petrov Affair*, my political enemies could no longer sneer at the uncredentialed Mr Manne.

In his review of *The Petrov Affair*, Professor Harry Gelber of the University of Tasmania wrote, "It is not often that a scholar can claim to have settled an issue of such political and historical controversy.

Manne can plausibly make such a claim." Unfortunately, this was not true. The Petrov defection conspiracy myth was resurrected in a major biography, Peter Crockett's *Evatt: A Life*, which is more than half convinced that Document J was, as Evatt fantasised, a wicked forgery. It also appeared in Frank Cain's unofficial history of ASIO, where he argues that Petrov was either a petty clerk pretending to be a member of the KGB or a false defector and that the documents he supposedly brought with him were forged by ASIO. According to David Horner's *The Spy Catchers*, while Jenny Hocking's biography *Gough Whitlam* was published in 2008, it "repeats many of the claims about the defection that had been refuted by Manne in 1987". My favourite example of the capacity of myth to withstand history occurred in a 2017 article by the old-fashioned, principled conservative Stephen Charles QC. Charles was the lawyer who represented and defended ASIO against almost the entire Canberra press gallery at the 1984 royal commission investigating the expulsion of Valery Ivanov of the KGB for his attempted recruitment, as an agent of influence, of the former Labor Party secretary David Combe. According to Charles:

> In 1954, Robert Menzies ... was facing an election and on the brink of defeat. ASIO then secured the defection of Vladimir Petrov ... and his wife. Petrov made startling allegations of a spy ring operating in Australia, including in the office of the Leader of the Opposition, Dr HV Evatt. The furore which followed resulted in a narrow Liberal Party victory. The Labor Party was enraged.

Sometimes I wonder, why bother writing history?

★

Sir Charles Spry died in late May 1994. I was asked by *The Age* and *The Sydney Morning Herald* to write the obituary. I tried to capture his sense of fun. Spry told me and others that his school reports all said more or less: "This boy would do much better if he worked." And that when he was asked what he had done to deserve his first military posting, he answered, "Nothing." Although it was as the director-general of ASIO that he would, rightly, be remembered, "Charles Spry was an altogether different figure from the harsh caricature painted by his political enemies. He was a bon vivant, a man of learning and penetrating wit, of unfailing humour, courtesy and charm, utterly without pomposity or self-pity." The obituary struck a chord with the biographer of Robert Menzies, Allan Martin. Spry had answered Martin's request for an interview with an invitation to lunch:

> [W]e had a hot three course meal which he had cooked himself. He was the soul of courtesy to me, without for a moment neglecting the needs of his invalid wife, to whose care he was obviously wholly devoted. It was difficult to see in him the sinister ogre depicted by the long line of paranoic writers on ASIO.

I attended Spry's funeral. At one moment some of the mourners walked out. There was obviously something amiss – connected, it was rumoured, to a deep rift between Spry and his son, Ian. Details of Spry's will were reported in *The Age* in October 1994, five months after his death. He had assets of $582,000, most of which was the estimated value of his Toorak home. Like Robert Menzies, Spry belonged to a conservative generation that did not profit from a lifetime of public service. He wrote in his will about the question of a biography:

> I leave to my daughter Caroline the decision as to whether a biography should be written referring to myself. Robert Manne would be my first choice, if agreeable ... I have no views as to whether such a biography should be written.

This was curious. Why had Spry left the decision about the will not to first-born son Ian but to daughter Caroline? Shortly after Spry's death, I was approached by a solicitor who claimed to be acting on behalf not of Caroline but of Spry's family. He told me that Spry had named me as his first choice if a biography was indeed to be written. However, he warned me off very firmly. The family did not want me to write the biography. He was unable to tell me why. Although I did not want to write it, I regarded the solicitor's warning as both improper and strange, a family (supposedly) working against their father's clear intentions.

A year or so later, *The Age* reported that "in the early to middle months of 1994" a barrister had formally complained to the Victorian Bar Council that Ian Spry was harassing and stalking her. After a protracted, year-long process the Bar Council had failed to reach any resolution, and the barrister had taken her complaint to the police. Recently the police had entered Ian Spry's offices and removed some spray paint to see whether it was the kind used for laneway graffiti. ("Ian Spry Named As 'Stalking' Barrister", *The Age*, August 30, 1995; "How the Bar Deals With Its Own", *The Age*, September 2, 1995.) As I knew the woman involved, and even better her former husband, Andrew Campbell – a right-wing political associate of Ian Spry – I thought it likely that her accusation was true. It was also likely that shortly before his death Charles Spry had received intelligence about the Bar Council complaint against his son – he had, after all, been director-general of ASIO for nineteen years. This might explain both the apparent walkout at the funeral of Ian and his friends, and the direction in Spry's will that Caroline, not Ian, should decide whether a biography should be commissioned and approach me first if she believed it should. The police eventually abandoned the investigation without charges being laid.

Around September 1995, I attended a large, supposedly private, dinner that the Sydney neo-liberal think-tank the Centre for Independent Studies had arranged for the visiting pro-Thatcher Peruvian novelist Mario Vargas Llosa. At my table we discussed *The Age*'s recent front-page story about the police investigation into a senior Melbourne lawyer charged with stalking a fellow female barrister. All other diners were appalled by the article. I told them I believed the alleged victim, Diane Phelan, whom I knew, and defended *The Age*'s editor, Alan Kohler, who had decided to name the lawyer under investigation. On March 24, 1996, I received an upsetting letter on Lauriston Girls' School letterhead from a teacher there, Helen Spry. Someone at the dinner had informed Ian or Helen that I had "very publicly" (at a private dinner!) defended Kohler because I believed Diane:

> I cannot tell you how distressed and betrayed we felt ... I understand only too well just how effective Diane's charm and apparent sincerity is in manipulating people ... For five years I have had to endure a prolonged and vicious attack on me, my family and my marriage ... I shall never understand your actions. They seem completely at odds with the man of integrity I thought Robert Manne to be.

Two years later, according to a High Court document, the marriage of Ian and Helen fell into "difficulty". In 2003 Helen won a divorce. Before this, Ian Spry had apparently sought to deprive his wife of more than $2 million by placing money into four trusts for their daughters. This case eventually reached the High Court. Ian lost (4–1) and was ordered to pay all legal costs. He abused the judges who found against him with withering contempt, and, in the case of Mary Gaudron, also with undisguised sexism. Sir Charles Spry was probably fortunate to have died when he did.

*

In 1987 Rupert Murdoch had offered Eric Beecher – the whiz-kid who had edited *The Sydney Morning Herald* before the age of thirty-five – the position of editor-in-chief of his newly acquired Melbourne *Herald and Weekly Times* (as foredoomed a journalistic mismatch as it is possible to imagine). As a result of *The Petrov Affair*, Eric offered me a weekly column in the Melbourne *Herald*, which I accepted. This changed the trajectory of my life. I continued writing public affairs commentary in regular columns for several newspapers until December 2004 and, from 2005, for publisher Morry Schwartz's new magazine, *The Monthly*, becoming therefore for more than thirty years a minor player in Australian domestic politics. More immediately, the *Herald* column was probably in part responsible for the invitation in 1988 to edit Australia's most important liberal-conservative Cold War magazine, *Quadrant*.

[9.]

The 1980s – My Conservative Decade

NOT LONG AFTER I RETURNED FROM ENGLAND in 1974, something happened that I am not able to understand let alone explain. One morning I came out of sleep with a psychic pain so absolute – overwhelming is too weak a word – that I knew with certainty that if it continued or even returned for more than a few moments, I would not be able to continue living. On two occasions before this, as described earlier, I had experienced the rather common state that psychologists call dissociation, the feeling that my mind was floating above my body. This had occurred in moments of excessive guilt: when I believed that a lie I had told a teacher had been discovered, and when I kicked a pebble from a height that I thought had smashed the windscreen of a passing car. But this pain was entirely different. I somehow recognised that the content of the pain was alone-ness.

In a few moments the pain lifted and vanished in the way dreams do. Nothing like it has ever returned. This moment of radical aloneness fell in the period between the time I lived in Oxford with Ann Tregear and the time I was with Vivien Thwaites, a scholar of fine arts, on my return. Even though neither relationship worked out, I still remember the years with warmth, and with hope that such feelings are reciprocated. During this time of my life, I also was unhappy and felt I was a wretched, rather loathsome being. (Some of my political enemies will no doubt think this a reasonable assessment.) I identified totally with the miserable character played by Elliott Gould in

The Touch, one of Ingmar Bergman's lesser, poorer films. I felt that the resemblance was uncanny. The best way, perhaps the only way, I can call up this unflattering self-assessment that ambushed me from time to time during the 1970s is to watch the film. Eventually this feeling also passed.

I found my soulmate in Anne, the beautiful young woman I had taught at Melbourne University in a course on German history in 1974. Sometime later we became lovers, and we married in 1982. We have loved each other and been in love for the past nearly fifty years. I have learned from Anne the meaning of care. But not only that. After all these years we still enjoy coffee and conversation every morning, usually for longer than an hour, talking about everything, often weeping with laughter. Anne has read every word I have written; I have read every word of hers. I have learned to rely on her penetrating intelligence, her moral and intellectual courage, and her judgement. Often she has understood things years before I saw them or was willing to. I joke that when she publishes a memoir of childhood and adolescence, as she must, she should call it *The Girl Who Saw Too Much*. If there were a God, I would send exquisite offerings of thanks.

In August 1980, at the age of thirty-two, I attended a lecture at a La Trobe University conference on the sociology of culture delivered by the University of Pennsylvania sociologist Philip Rieff. The lecture almost changed my life. Rieff had been invited by John Carroll, whose book on the trajectory of the contemporary Western upper middle class, *Puritan, Paranoid, Remissive*, Rieff admired. Rieff was the author of a fine book on Freud, *The Triumph of the Therapeutic*, although he was probably more famous among the intelligentsia because of the story of his marriage to Susan Sontag. According to this story, Sontag attended a Rieff lecture while still a student and was entranced. They spoke all night. Within a fortnight they were married. It is hard to think of a more unlikely couple.

By the time he arrived at La Trobe, Rieff was an archconservative. The lecture he delivered was uninhibitedly rude. As he began, he informed his audience: "I don't believe in reading manuscripts [of lectures]. I think it is a cruel and unusual punishment to which you have been subjected for a number of days by *academics innocent in their brutality* [my emphasis]." Some of these innocent brutes, as Rieff must have known, were in the audience. His lecture was highly mannered. "Jesuit probabilism, using canon law, as you know better than I ..." Many members of the audience who apparently understood Jesuit probabilism better than Rieff were undergraduate or postgraduate students, many from working-class suburbs. For his fellow sociologists he was contemptuous in a familiar kind of way. (Knopfelmacher often spoke like this.) They were members of "the semi-skilled intelligentsia", "arrogant frauds" who "in America nowadays usually become chairmen of sociology departments". In fairness to Rieff (and to myself) he was high-spirited throughout and on occasion very funny. At a dinner party, he told us, someone suggested that he visit the Great Barrier Reef. "But madam, I am the barrier Rieff!!" He was deft enough to omit "great" from his accurate self-description.

The theme of his lecture was what mattered to me. According to Rieff, all cultures when in good health rested on "interdicts", absolute commands that demanded "obedience" to "sacred authority" and forbade certain kinds of behaviour. Rieff's exposition moved effortlessly across centuries of Western theory and culture, from St Augustine to Sigmund Freud, from Dante to Duchamp. As a student of Freud, he argued that most of the interdicts contemporary Western culture sought to overturn and to disobey seemed to concern sex. Rieff showed a slide of a painting by an Italian old master, Antonio Bellucci, where a daughter offers her breast, with milk for an infant, to her father, who is in prison and starving. She looks away, in shame. Rieff informed his audience that in the West today the response to this act, at once an act of charity and a terrible violation of the "sacred order", was a shrug of the shoulders and a puzzled: "Why not?" Rieff offered a powerful reading of Roman Polanski's *Chinatown*, which ends with the result of incest, John Huston's character embracing his daughter, who is also his granddaughter. The intellectual trajectory of contemporary Western culture, according to Rieff, was captured in the slogan: "It is forbidden to forbid"; its political trajectory in the idea that "there is nothing worth dying for", which itself is an idea not worth dying for; and its high culture in "Étant Donnés", a painting by Marcel Duchamp of "a mutilated female body ... a violation, an obvious, gross, crude violation with the clitoris showing". Rieff ended his lecture with these words:

> Let's have the next furtive, criminally taken slide of this image ... This is the genitalia of this horrible, horrible masterpiece that is, in fact, the key work in one of the great museums in the world to which thousands pay reverential visits, to peek in. I think it describes the condition of a remissive culture run brilliantly amok.

The lecture was genuinely powerful. It was not difficult to understand why Rieff had captivated the young Susan Sontag. One member of the audience was Ágnes Heller, a more important thinker than Rieff and a much nicer human being. I spotted her on a public phone after the lecture speaking in Hungarian, in anger and what looked like anguish, most likely to her husband, Ferenc Fehér. Shortly after the lecture I took Rieff and his wife, a rather frozen Protestant member of the American judiciary, to a day at the Flemington races. I inquired whether I might spend some time at the University of Pennsylvania studying with him. Later, from Philadelphia, he wrote back politely – like a chairman of a sociology department – pointing to the bureaucratic difficulties. What, I now wonder, had I hoped to learn? What was I thinking?

When I was an undergraduate, there were two visual images of the cultural revolution we call "the '60s" that stayed with me and that illustrate my ambivalence about that revolution. One was Julie Christie in the movie *Darling*, striding with a confidence and joy that seemed both new and wonderful. In politics, that stride was called feminism. The other was a couple making love in the sunshine on a Melbourne University lawn, towards which a whooping crowd swarmed, reminding me of the way primary schoolkids used to run to form a circle around a fistfight that had broken out. At the time

I attended the Rieff lecture I was troubled by the arrival of something that seemed to me entirely new in the history of the West – values-free sexual libertinism. Instinctively I agreed with the argument advanced by Freud in his late, gloomy master essay, *Civilization and Its Discontents*, which sought to answer a difficult question: If Western Man (Freud seemed little concerned with women on this matter) might have found the happiness he sought in a condition of unlimited sexual freedom, towards which he was strongly drawn by his polyamorously perverse nature, how did he find himself trapped in a society that tried, from earliest childhood, to force him into a narrow sexual life limited to standard "genital relations" with one lifelong female partner? Freud's answer was that unless the energy that might have been exhausted in the pursuit of happiness in sexual freedom was directed elsewhere, the triumphs of civilisation – "scientific, artistic or ideological" – would not have come into being. Civilisation was thus built on sexual repression and sublimation. Freud argued with his characteristic mordant humour:

> Present-day civilisation makes it plain that it will only permit sexual relationships on the basis of a solitary, indissoluble bond between one man and one woman, and that it does not like sexuality as a source of pleasure in its own right and is only prepared to tolerate it because there is so far no substitute for it as a means of propagating the human race.

For a brief time I was attracted to the ridiculous idea that sex should be practised exclusively for the purpose of bringing children into the world. What was I thinking?

The corner of this vast issue that I wrote about in the newspapers from time to time, and later in *Quadrant*, was the apparent abandonment of the censorship of pornography during the 1980s and '90s. The distinction I drew was between Eros and Porn. I was all in favour of D.H. Lawrence's celebration of sexuality in *Lady Chatterley's Lover*. Indeed, Lawrence was responsible for the best description of porn, the dirt it did on sex and life. I also would have regarded the joyous sexual high jinks in Henry Miller's Parisian novels as erotica, not porn. However, in the argument over censorship, Eros versus Porn was the wrong distinction to make. What I always argued against was the violent misogyny that, according to the best studies I read, was coming to dominate the market. I was open to both the case made by feminists, which centred on objectification and misogyny, and the case advanced by conservatives, which centred on spiritual damage and moral anarchy. The superb radio broadcaster Terry Lane argued that he opposed censorship. I told him, on air, that I did not believe him. Was he in favour of allowing a film showing the sexual abuse of children to be screened? Silence. Peter Craven took up this argument: such films were wrong not because of their subject matter but because, in their production, children were abused. Was he then, I asked, in favour of films showing the sexual abuse of children produced through some technical means of simulation where no real children were involved? Silence.

I went to Sydney to see John Howard, at the time leader of the Opposition. He told me that political discussion of pornography was very difficult because of the grubbiness of the topic, which I took to mean the male-to-male smirking when the subject was raised. At the time I entered the censorship debate, masturbation – at least for boomers and earlier generations, the principal purpose of pornography – was undiscussed and undiscussable, except in comedy. One of the favourite lines of the wonderful television show *The Gillies Report* was the papal warning, delivered with characteristic exuberance by Max Gillies: "Stop it or you'll go blind." Men pretended that pornography did not affect them; it only affected frustrated dirty old men in raincoats. This was, in general, dishonest. I was opposed to pornography because it widened the divide in males against which civilisation fought: between sex and love, and even between sex and care for another human being. This happened not only with violent pornography.

As it has turned out, it was a losing battle. When I was arguing for censorship of certain kinds of material – porn involving children, or where violence was involved – the market was growing. When the internet arrived, the market exploded. Almost all young males and very large numbers of females, in the West at least, now view pornography as a matter of course. Many studies show that it has affected sexual relations, with men coercing their female partners into varieties of what is for them unpleasant sex, or worse. As I was writing these words, an article by Billie Eilish, a brilliant young singer/songwriter, arrived via *The Guardian*. Eilish wrote that she had watched "a lot of porn" from the age of eleven and had become addicted. Some involved abuse and violence: "I think it really destroyed my brain and I feel incredibly devastated that I was exposed to so much porn … The first few times I, you know, had sex I was not saying no to things that were not good."

The argument that there is no hope of controlling pornography in the age of the internet is obviously false. If paedophile pornography can be criminalised and at least to some extent suppressed, so could violent pornography. What will be the social effect of the general circulation of this kind of pornography, even to children? As Zhou Enlai was once famously supposed to have said of the French Revolution, it is too early to tell. Has civilisation overthrown one form of discontent only to enthusiastically embrace another?

My moral conservatism had another dimension, best captured in one argument with Peter Singer, who was by the 1980s possibly the Western world's best-known and most-admired moral philosopher, and a near-contemporary of mine at Melbourne University. Singer justly became famous for his book on animal liberation, which has done immense good. This was not where I disagreed with him. In 1979 he published a very successful book called *Practical Ethics* and in 1985, with Helga Kuhse, *Should the Baby Live?* In both books he advocated infanticide. Singer wrote that in its first twenty-eight days, any baby might lawfully be killed either by its parents or, if the parents were not alive, by society. While it was likely that all healthy babies would in present circumstances find adoptive parents, if circumstances changed, in Singer's philosophy perfectly healthy babies might be killed in their first month of life. As he wrote: "[Human babies] are not persons … the life of a newborn is of less value than the life of a pig, a dog or a chimpanzee." In practice, there was every likelihood that neither natural nor adoptive parents nor institutions supported by taxpayers would always be found to raise babies with disabilities. While infanticide was at least morally understandable if the disabilities were so severe that the baby would suffer constant severe pain or never reach a state of consciousness, Singer made it clear that babies meeting his criteria for justifiable killing included those afflicted by nothing more serious than Down syndrome or various physical or mental equivalents, where love of the baby for its parents or siblings was perfectly possible, and where the baby might grow up to be a beloved child and then adult with capacity for love and joy and wonder.

I did not disagree with Singer because I thought there was a logical weakness in his argument; I was disturbed and dismayed that an intelligent academic was widely admired among his peer group (and mine) after advocating the possible killing of mildly disabled babies who were not yet "persons" under the Peter Singer definition. Eventually, I am pleased to say, the culture came to understand the inhumanity of this strand of Singer's thought. The circle of civilisation that expanded to treat peoples of all genders, ethnicities and sexualities as full equals came to include those affected by disability. First in Germany and later in the United States, people with disabilities read Singer and were horrified to realise he thought of them as having been candidates for killing in their first twenty-eight days. One of the disability movements opposed to Singer called itself "Not Dead Yet".

Singer did not think infants reached personhood in their first two years. Some of these babies did not ever reach personhood. What might be done with these non-persons? Not surprisingly, Singer was frequently accused of supporting, at least in logic, something that resembled the Nazi regime's "euthanasia" program, codenamed T4, which resulted in the state murder of tens of thousands of institutionalised mental patients and those with physical disabilities. Many of the participants in T4 graduated to the Nazi extermination camps. T4 also pioneered methods of murder later used in the Holocaust, like the carbon dioxide–filled gas van (responsible, as I much later discovered, for the murder of my maternal grandfather). As three of his grandparents had been murdered by the Nazi regime, Singer was offended by the suggestion. It was true, of course, that no liberal-democratic state would replicate the Nazi "euthanasia" campaign. That was only conceivable under conditions of totalitarianism. It was also true that no liberal-democratic state would kill to improve the nation's genetic stock. Eugenics had been thoroughly discredited by what happened under Nazism.

However, I was surprised to discover that Singer did not understand, after years of controversy precisely on this point, that the Nazi euthanasia campaign was rooted in mainstream, pre-Nazi German medicine, jurisprudence and science. It was based on the conclusions of the famed nineteenth-century Darwinian "racial scientist" Ernst Haeckel, and in Karl Binding and Alfred Hoche's *The Destruction of Life Unworthy of Living* (1920), a work that was not anti-Semitic. In 1984 Singer had challenged the leader of the Right to Life movement in Australia, Margaret Tighe, to provide evidence about the influence of Haeckel, and of Binding and Hoche on Nazi ideology and the regime's secret euthanasia campaign. Singer told us he had consulted the index of William Shirer's outdated popular history of the Third Reich, and their names did not appear. I wrote in reply citing more recent studies. In *The Scientific Origins of National Socialism*, Daniel Gasman argued that Haeckel was "decisive" in the formation of Nazi ideology. And in his *Towards the Final Solution*, George Mosse claimed that Binding and Hoche provided the Nazi euthanasia campaign with one of its intellectual foundations. The question that disturbed me was this: according to Singer, babies in their first twenty-eight days might be killed because they were not yet persons. If societies came to accept Singer on this point, is it not implausible to believe that such societies would continue to prohibit the killing of children or adults with a mental disability after the twenty-eight days had passed? In liberal societies this would not occur in something resembling the Nazi "euthanasia" campaign but in a legally regulated involuntary euthanasia after mandatory consultations between physicians and the families of the mentally disabled.

The shadow of the Holocaust was cast over many of the discussions in which I became involved during the 1980s and early '90s. One concerned the British historian David Irving. There were three phases in Irving's career. In the first, he was a conventional right-wing archival historian whose first book, on the Allied bombing of Dresden, was in general well received. In the second phase, Irving argued in his notorious *Hitler's War* (1977) that although the Holocaust had occurred, Adolf Hitler did not give the orders, did not know what was happening, and when it was possible sought to spare the Jews. In the third phase, Irving became the world's most influential Holocaust denialist and political anti-Semite, who claimed that the gas chambers at Auschwitz-Birkenau never existed, and that the number of Jews killed during the Second World War – limited to 25,000, all in Auschwitz – had been wildly exaggerated for either sordid commercial gain or Israel's political advantage.

In 1983 I was involved in a debate with David Irving on Melbourne daytime television. Irving was offering 1,000 pounds to anyone who could prove that Hitler ordered or even knew about the Holocaust. I asked him who would be the judge. There was a ripple of laughter from the audience. I don't recall his answer. I reviewed his 1987 book, *Churchill's War*, in *Quadrant*. It portrayed Churchill as a drunkard and warmonger in the pay of a sinister Jewish cabal, called Focus, who refused a reasonable peace offer from Hitler in 1940 and who, as a result, was responsible for the destruction of the British Empire. It was hard to think of an instance where the moral distance between a biographer and their subject was greater. I called the review "Iago's History of Othello".

In February 1993 a journalist rang me about the Keating government's decision to refuse Irving a visa to visit Australia. I told him I was opposed to it: although Irving's views were sickening, banning someone from entering Australia because you do not like their views set a dangerous precedent. I changed my mind shortly after, in July 1993, having read the transcript of Irving's recent speech to his political supporters, in which he referred to the Jews as "our traditional enemies", claimed that the Holocaust was a "'blood lie' against the innocent German people", and a big business swindle by Jewish racketeers. Younger Australian journalists were frequently surprisingly ignorant of history and had picked up at university what I called "a half-baked and philosophically confused scepticism regarding the very idea of truth". During an earlier Irving visit, as I recalled, one journalist had responded to his portrait of Churchill by suggesting that it was all too easy "to criticise with the benefit of hindsight". More importantly, Irving was now infamous and certain to be given much publicity. His denialism would confuse the general public about the Holocaust. To debate him on the question of whether or not the Holocaust had happened was itself a considerable cultural victory for Irving. I argued that his kind of Holocaust denialism was the equivalent of arguing that there had been no First World War. Later, I added what was for me the most important consideration:

> I simply cannot see why people whose lives have been ruined in the Holocaust have to endure a nationwide tour by a man who argues that their families did not really perish and that they are only claiming that they did because of psychiatric disorder or for sordid financial gain.

There was a general right to freedom of speech. There should be no impediment to the publication of his books. However, there did not exist any general right to visit a country if political or moral damage was predictable.

Then there was Israel. Although, as we have seen, I considered volunteering in June 1967 if Israel's existence was threatened, I never believed that Jews in the Diaspora were under some politico-moral obligation to uproot and live in Israel, or even that it would be a good thing if the centre of Jewish civilisation was in Israel and the Diaspora gradually withered away. On my way to Oxford in 1970 I had visited Israel. One evening, on the busy commercial avenue in Tel Aviv, Dizengoff Street, an elderly woman approached me. Where was I from, she asked. I told her. Did I not realise I had a duty to live in Israel? I did not; I was an Australian. In 1976, I was one of the Jewish academics in Australia offered a free trip to Israel by an enterprise called Academics for Peace in the Middle East. Although of course I knew that its purpose was propaganda, I accepted. My views were unlikely to be influenced by anything that looked like special pleading; if anything, the reverse was true. I went because we would get the kind of access to Israeli politicians and opinion-makers impossible in any other circumstance.

The first Israeli who talked to us was the Defence minister, military hero Moshe Dayan. As he spoke the walls swayed alarmingly, not because of enemy artillery fire but because of my lingering jet-lag. Later we were addressed by Yitzhak Rabin, Abba Eban and the Eichmann chief prosecutor, Gideon Hausner. Most of the Israelis we met were Ashkenazi Jews from the cultural circle of the ruling Labour Party. Our bus tour, shared with a group of American academics, did travel to the Golan Heights but not the Arab-populated territories of the West Bank and the Gaza Strip. We visited the Holocaust museum, Yad Vashem. Our working-class bus driver told us we must never let anything like this ever happen again. These are the only words of the visit I still remember. The most significant event I observed was unplanned by the trip organisers – the ebullient crowds of Mizrahi Jewish Israelis, principally from the Middle East and North Africa, on their way to an election rally for the legendary Zionist Revisionist Menachem Begin, leader of Likud, the right-wing party that had been in permanent Opposition since the creation of Israel.

Almost exactly ten years after the Six-Day War, on June 20, 1977, Begin became the Israeli prime minister. His government began referring to the West Bank by its Biblical names, Judea and Samaria. This was a political disaster. It is one thing to leave territory thought of as the West Bank. It is quite a different matter to leave old Biblical lands you believe God had given to the Jews. The pace of state-supported Jewish settlements on these lands now accelerated. For decades some right-wing Israelis pretended to the world, and even to themselves perhaps, that they supported a two-state solution, with the Palestinians on the West Bank and in Gaza, and with Jews and a small percentage of Palestinian Arabs in Israel within pre-1967 borders. In recent times, for many Israelis, that pretence has been abandoned. The Jewish settlement of Judea and Samaria has involved a gradual or creeping annexation. Shortly after the Begin victory, Sam Lipski invited me to speak to young supporters of the *Australia/Israel Review*, which he edited. The talk I gave was not meant to be published but Sam took a recording and published it. I'm grateful that he did. The critical paragraph read:

> I think (and this will be the thing that most offends you), it will become increasingly difficult to deny the charge that has grown over the last few years that Israel resembles South Africa. Israel will increasingly appear to be an isolated and besieged white separatist colony whose political survival rests on the maintenance of armed might against her neighbours while holding down an irredentist and restless unenfranchised native population. I do not believe this is true. But I do believe it is going to be much harder to combat the idea that Israel is like South Africa ... It appears to me, then, that Begin's attitude [to the West Bank and Gaza] is obviously disastrous for Israel's future.

In the next few weeks I gave talks to Jewish groups along similar lines. At one, an elderly gentleman took me aside and explained, "Now is not the time to be saying such things." That time has never arrived.

Some problems in politics are appallingly simple. With settlements of Jews on the West Bank now exceeding 700,000 people, no Israeli government could survive the decision to hand the West Bank to the Palestinians. If Israel enfranchises the close to 3 million Palestinians of the West Bank, and allows the more than 2 million Palestinians of Gaza to be united as citizens of Israel with the enfranchised West Bank Palestinians, Israel will no longer be a Jewish state. If it fails to enfranchise the Palestinians, Israel will be required either to administer a permanent quasi-apartheid regime on the West Bank and in Gaza or to commit a great historic crime – the mass expulsion of Palestinians from the West Bank and Gaza.

★

Between 1976 and 1980, as discussed earlier, I was president of the Victorian branch of the Indochina Refugee Association, whose primary purpose was convincing the Fraser government to settle more Vietnamese, Cambodian and Lao refugees stranded in miserable camps in Thailand, Malaysia and Indonesia. In September 1979, Fraser announced that in the next year Australia would settle 9,000 Indochinese refugees. Shortly after, I resigned from ICRA; my lobbying work was done. During the 1980s, however, I wrote regularly about the politics of the Indochinese refugee settlement in particular, and Asian migration in general, in *Migration Action* in late 1978, in *Dyason House Papers* in 1984, in *Quadrant* in 1985 and in several columns in the Melbourne *Herald* between 1987 and 1990. I am therefore able to reconstruct what I believed with exact and sometimes embarrassing accuracy.

During the 1980s, Australia settled some 10,000 Indochinese refugees every year. I argued that in the history of Australia, this represented a genuine turning point – the first mass arrival of Asian migrants, not the carefully chosen professionals or businesspeople from Singapore or Hong Kong of the late 1960s and early '70s but a cross-section of Vietnamese society, including peasants, workers, fishermen and their families. In part, Fraser was motivated by domestic political considerations. From 1976, boats of Vietnamese refugees began arriving in Darwin with some regularity – some 400 refugees arrived in November 1977 alone. Although by later standards the number was small, the boat arrivals were greeted with suspicion, hostility and undisguised racism. In the *Migration Action* article, I quoted newspaper reports that claimed some refugees were arriving with gold bullion, and others threatening the cattle industry in northern Australia with exotic disease. The Labor spokesperson on immigration, Tony Mulvihill, thought the navy should tow the boats of refugees back "to South-East Asia". A popular Melbourne *Sun* journalist, Douglas Wilkie, reckoned that their arrival posed an existential test: were we willing to fight for the survival of a white civilisation in the Antipodes?

I argued in several articles that Fraser had discovered it was easier to settle thousands brought to Australia by the government by air than hundreds who arrived spontaneously by boat. There was also pressure from the US Carter administration. It would not look good to our great-power ally if France, the former colonial ruler in Indochina, or even Canada, which had not fought alongside the United States in the Vietnam War and was not proximate to South-East Asia, should prove more generous in the settlement of Indochinese refugees than Australia. There was also, I believed, in Fraser's decision a belatedly recognised question of honour. Our moral obligation to the people of South Vietnam now fleeing at risk of life from the communist regime imposed by Hanoi – with the "re-education" camps and the persecution of the propertied classes – did not end with the victory of the North Vietnamese Army in May 1975.

What I believed was genuinely remarkable about the settlement of Indochinese refugees during the Fraser years was the effective bipartisan support for a policy that marked the conspicuous end of white Australia. My favourite quote came from the Labor Party's former shadow minister for Immigration, Mick Young, who told parliament in 1984, "If ever the Australian Labor Party wanted to get down in the gutter and kick heads about immigration policy, the period from 1975 to 1982 was the golden opportunity for us to do it." The leader of the Opposition between 1977 and early 1983, Bill Hayden, told parliament that he had come under "a great deal of pressure, outside the Parliament, from narrowly based groups in the community, to take up a racist position. It was said it would be good for votes." I believed that Australia owed a great deal to the principled restraint of the Hayden Opposition. This was the era of what the historian of the Indochinese refugee settlement Nancy Viviani called "elite consensus".

In mid-March 1984, that consensus was broken in a talk given at Warrnambool by conservative Australia's most popular and accomplished historian, Geoffrey Blainey. At first Blainey said little more than that the pace of Asian migration was too fast, that the annual number of Asian migrants needed to be reduced, and that if it was not, longstanding general support for Australia's immigration program would be lost. A furious controversy was the result, with cheers from the cultural right, boos from the cultural left, and considerable interest from Australia's political class. Under severe personal attack from fellow academics, even from most of his colleagues in Melbourne's University's history department, Blainey dug in. In 1984 he published a book called *All for Australia*, which I was invited to review for *Quadrant* – perhaps because of the kind of middle position, between the left and the right, I had outlined in an article for the journal of the Australian Institute of International Affairs, *Dyason House Papers*.

My argument in the Blainey review was complicated. I made it clear that I did not agree with Blainey's claim that Asian migration was proceeding too quickly. Nor, to put it mildly, did I agree with his claims about a sinister cabal inside the Department of Immigration who were trying in secret to "Asianise" Australia. I also did not believe there was any evidence that Asian migrants – supported by policies and opinions of those from the wealthy suburbs – were colonising the suburbs of the old Australian working class. I was dismayed that among the fragments of anti-Asian immigration opinion Blainey reproduced as his evidence, one was a disordered, crudely racist letter about spitting on pavements and the acrid smell of goats being barbecued in backyards. I did, however, agree with his claim that something as significant as the transformation of Australia's migration policy and thus its ethnic composition could not be imposed upon society without free debate.

Blainey's colleagues had claimed that they had no intention of limiting his freedom of speech, but only rejected the way he had framed the question in racial terms. How one could conduct a debate about the level of Asian immigration to Australia in a non-racial framework was, I argued, far from clear. Most importantly, I was sympathetic to his defence of old Australia aimed at those members of the left who expressed contempt for their country's racist and deferentially Anglophile political culture – prior to its possible redemption following the arrival of the freshly minted ideology of multiculturalism. I was even moved (to my current embarrassment) by Blainey's long pre-Federation quotation from Sir Henry Parkes about the "crimson thread of kinship" that held British Australians of the separate colonies together. In conclusion, I argued, Blainey was aiming his fire at the wrong target. While the radical multicultural left might find little virtue in old Australia, there was no group who more deeply and instinctively cherished what I described as its gentle temper and political values – parliamentary democracy, freedom of speech, the rule of law, religious and ethnic tolerance – than the largest group of Asian immigrants, the refugees from the communist dictatorships of Indochina.

Three years later, Blainey appeared to have converted the Coalition to his view. In one of my early *Herald* columns (May 27, 1988), I argued that because of the growing hostility towards Asian immigration, discussed in a report written by the former ambassador to China Stephen FitzGerald, "[T]he opposition will be sorely tempted to capitalise on anti-Asian sentiment." The leader of the Opposition, John Howard, had recently "warned that bipartisanship in immigration policy was drawing to a close. It is impossible to know whether this signalled the beginning of a coalition drift towards the policy of Prof. Blainey. I, for one, hope not." In early August, it seemed that we had the answer. Returning from a visit to Britain and conversation with the Iron Lady, Margaret Thatcher, Howard announced that when the Coalition returned to power it would abandon multiculturalism and slow the pace of Asian migration. In my *Herald* column of August 5, 1988, I argued that "Howard had crossed the Rubicon" and that, as a consequence, "Australian politics will never be quite the same again." My ambivalence or uncertainty arose, on the one hand, because of my support for current levels of Asian migration, in particular the refugees from Indochina, but, on the other, because of my hostility to the radical version of multiculturalism that had replaced assimilation as the philosophy of migrant settlement.

My final position on multiculturalism, during the period of the Blainey debate, was explained in a talk I delivered in 1989:

> In Australia, multiculturalism has tended to divide into a conservative and a radical form. The multiculturalism of the Fraser government was concerned with explicit support for ethnic pluralism, as a means of maintaining social cohesion ... Multiculturalism, however, also developed a more radical wing ...

which sought to transform Australia from an Anglo-dominated racist colony into a new paradise where there would be no cultural cringe towards Britain and no foreign dependence upon the United States ... It was extremely insensitive to the culture and values of old Australians, treating Australia before the coming of the post-war migrants as a racist hell and cultural desert. As Max Harris has put it, before the coming of the migrants "Australia embodied the smelliest and shittiest end of the racist stick left in the Anglo-Saxon Celtic world".

In the short term, the radical form created a backlash, most importantly seen in the Pauline Hanson/One Nation phenomenon. In the long term, the conservative version prevailed. Multiculturalism was nothing more than pride in Australia's ethnic diversity.

On September 16, 1988, I argued in *The Herald* that after several weeks of attack by the government and the media because of his remarks on Asian migration, John Howard – "no Margaret Thatcher ... now gives the impression of someone who regrets a momentary rush of blood but can find no honourable means of retreat". The prime minister, Bob Hawke, was using the issue of Asian migration in a masterful manner to destabilise the Coalition, which stretched from John Stone on the right to Ian Macphee on the left, exactly the way Robert Menzies in the early 1950s had used the communist issue to destabilise the Labor Party, whose members stretched from Santamaria anti-communists on the right to Communist Party fellow travellers on the left. I argued that Howard's position on Asian migration was "the most serious blunder, thus far, of his political career". Eight months later, in May 1989, he was gone. "[T]hree distinctive sources of opposition to the Howard leadership [had] converged," I wrote in the column of May 12, 1989. "Pro-Elliott Dries, pro-Macphee Wets and alarmed backbench dead wood all padded up the parliamentary corridor to talk with the man for all seasons – Mr Peacock. The Howard leadership was over." His end came as no surprise. "Even admirers of John Howard must know in their hearts that their man was never quite cut from the cloth of political leadership." Ouch.

In several *Herald* columns published during 1988, the year of Australia's Bicentenary, I argued that the most fundamental division in Australia was no longer based on class, "capitalist and worker", but on the starkly different worldviews of "the intelligentsia" and those I called "ordinary people". On January 27, 1988, I reviewed *Manning Clark's History of Australia: The Musical.* Here we learned that "[o]ur foundation is a crime, built upon the sweat of the convicts and the Irish and the blood of the Aboriginals. Our federation is nothing but a pious fraud of the bourgeoisie – compounded of racism, capitalism and Anglophilia." While there was certainly "great energy from the performers and some fine music," I wrote, "its bleakness is so unremitting and its interpretation of our history so unbalanced that it leaves the audience bewildered and numb". On February 26, I wrote a scathing review of John Pilger's three-part television documentary on Australia, *The Last Dream.* According to Henry Reynolds, 20,000 Indigenous Australians had been killed by British settlers; that was "grave enough". However, by fudging the distinction between death by rifle or poison and death by disease (whose numbers are unknown and unknowable), Pilger had come up with the figure of 500,000 settler killings of Aboriginal people. According to Pilger, white Australia had always been "a place of social hardship and struggle". In reality, I argued:

> [F]or a considerable part of [its] 200 years Australia enjoyed the highest standard of living in the world. Compared with the history of paradise, the history of Australia is, no doubt, one of misery and grinding poverty. However, compared with almost every other country on earth, it is a tale of material opportunity and prosperity.

Towards the end of the series, Pilger argued that during the atomic tests at Maralinga, warning signs had been posted "in several languages – except Aboriginal":

> Now, even Pilger must be aware that tribal Aboriginals do not read and write a language known as "Aboriginal". Perhaps, it occurred to me, he was pulling our legs. Was it not possible that Pilger was

a master satirist, revealing by *Reductio Ad Absurdum*, the fatuousness of propaganda documentaries? The thought soon faded. John Pilger is as he appears, the Australian expatriate heir-apparent not to Barry Humphries but Wilfred Burchett.

For me, the most telling moment of Australia's Bicentenary year were the events that surrounded the arrival of the replica First Fleet vessel. As it glided majestically into Sydney Harbour, its mainsail displayed a prominent advertisement for Coca-Cola. On the eve of the collapse of communism throughout Eastern Europe, capitalism ruled, OK. However, because of the Bicentennial argument between the intelligentsia and ordinary people over the meaning of the arrival of the First Fleet, "Captain Phillip and his crew ... were never to set foot on land". If the pretend captain and crew could not land on Australian soil, why had the pretend ship set sail? Australians were watching "with numbness the terrible stories of demoralisation emerging from the Royal Commission into Aboriginal Deaths in Custody". Yet what value for Indigenous Australians would come from "European self-flagellation?"

> When historians look back on the Bicentenary, their most challenging task will be to explain the cultural pessimism which, during this year, took hold of the intellectual class and cast its shadow across our celebrations.

As we had learned, it was not possible to know what to feel if, on the same day, one both celebrated a birthday and attended a funeral.

*

By 1988, things were happening in Jewish politics that I found disturbing. The dominant figure in Australia, Isi Leibler, had been at the centre of the movement that finally convinced the Soviet leader, Mikhail Gorbachev, to allow the migration to Israel of Soviet Jews known as "refuseniks". I observed what was happening but was in no way involved, not even as a commentator. The Australian prime minister, Bob Hawke, had played a prominent role in the struggle. On May 17, 1988, a meeting in Melbourne attended by 1500 people was held to offer thanks. A Human Rights Award was presented to Hawke by the president of the World Jewish Congress, Edgar Bronfman. Fifteen prominent refuseniks were flown in from Israel for the occasion. In his speech, Hawke entered forbidden territory. No one, he told the audience, could doubt his commitment to Israel. Because of recent "tragic events" – the first Intifada, the uprising of the Palestinians living under occupation on the West Bank and in Gaza – he was even more convinced that:

> [T]he democratic, humanist principles on which Israel was built do not sit easily with the role of master of occupied territories and subject peoples. *The Palestinian in the occupied territories, as the Jew in the Soviet Union and the black in South Africa, has his aspirations to be fully free* [my emphasis] ... Is there not emerging the danger of Israel being blinded to the threat to its very soul and the vision of its founders? ... [T]he time bomb of demography is ticking ... [I]f Israel seeks to maintain its hegemony in the occupied territories, the Jews of Israel face the certain prospect of being a minority in their own land. They will face the stark choice of being a democratic State or a Jewish State – they will not be able to be both.

In the audience was the editor of the *Jewish Times*, Susan Bures. According to her: "One could almost feel a horrified shudder rippling through an audience which found this a morally offensive equivalence of the first order." Isi Leibler corralled his fifteen refuseniks to sign a letter to Hawke expressing their own shock. For his own part, Leibler wrote Hawke a private letter of such "explosive" aggression that, according to Leibler's biographer, Suzanne Rutland, their once very close relationship was over, forever. I agreed with Hawke's every word. Twenty years after the Six-Day War, ten years after the election of Menachem Begin, in my view a political blindness, really a madness, had taken over the Jewish world. Hawke called this "eyeless in Gaza".

At this time the Hawke government was preparing what was effectively a new *War Crimes Act*, whose purpose was to bring to trial those post-war migrants from Eastern Europe and the Balkans for whom evidence existed of involvement in the crimes of the Holocaust. The local inspiration for this new *War Crimes Act* was a series of radio broadcasts in 1986 on the ABC's intellectually serious Radio National, researched and presented by Mark Aarons. I did not know him at the time; the Cold War was not over, and he was on the left and I was on the right. (He is now a close and valued friend.) Outside Australia, the inspiration for these Holocaust war crimes trials and much of the research came from three US-based organisations, the Simon Wiesenthal Center, the Office of Special Investigations inside the US Justice department, and the World Jewish Congress. Leibler claimed that "the Jewish community in Australia was able to persuade the government to enact the necessary war crimes legislation". The Hawke government commissioned a retired public servant to review the evidence, Andrew Menzies, who recommended legislation and then some prosecutions. By early 1988, through three *Herald* columns, I was known to be opposed to the idea of holding Holocaust trials in Australia and was invited by the umbrella bodies of both the supporters and the opponents of the war crimes legislation – the Victorian branch of the Jewish Board of Deputies and the Captive Nations Council representing Ukrainians, Croats, Slovenians, Belarusians and all three Baltic peoples – to state my case. My talks were published in *The Australian Jewish News* of May 20, 1988, and in a booklet published by the Captive Nations Council.

As I made clear in a *Herald* column about Mark Aarons' book, *Sanctuary*, I did not doubt that he had found disturbing evidence about the wartime activities of some of the migrants from the Baltic States, East-Central Europe and the Balkans. Aarons had provided evidence of migrants "who seem to have been involved in terrible atrocities. While none of the key figures in this book could be regarded as a prominent Nazi official or even as a major war criminal, all seem to have shocking war records. To have placed this material on the public record alone makes Mark Aarons' book eminently worthwhile."

I was, however, opposed to holding Holocaust trials in Australia for a dozen reasons, none of which was by itself sufficient, but all of which, in combination, were in my opinion overwhelmingly so.

The war crimes legislation would necessarily be retrospective, concerned with crimes not imagined in Australian law between 1939 and 1945. Retrospective law would sit uneasily on the consciences of Australian lawyers, even those on the liberal left like Justice Michael Kirby. Indeed, although much of the impetus for these trials came from the United States, none could be heard in the United States, where retrospective law was unconstitutional. The trials were being held forty-five years after the event. Many of the potential witnesses were now dead. Defending counsel would not find it difficult to show the memories of those still alive to be unreliable. Many of the witnesses were living in communist countries. Would they be given permission to travel to Australia so their evidence could be tested in court? Much of the documentary evidence would be supplied by the KGB or the secret police of other communist countries. Could their evidence be regarded as reliable? Among their employees were skilful forgers. They could, I learned, even transfer fingerprints from one document to another. The trials would not educate the world about what had happened during the Holocaust, as many hoped. As Hannah Arendt outlined in *Eichmann in Jerusalem*, the Israeli court that tried Eichmann was used by the prosecution as a kind of history lesson to the world.

In Australian courts, by contrast, most of the evidence about the Holocaust would be regarded as irrelevant, as the historian advising the prosecution in Australia, Professor Konrad Kwiet, eventually discovered to his frustration. The cases brought to court were for all these reasons likely to collapse. In turn, acquittals would strengthen the propaganda efforts of Holocaust denialists. Before the trials began, many Australians would think the new war crimes legislation demonstrated the secret and disproportionate power of the Jews, in this case over Bob Hawke and his government. They were also likely to revive one of the oldest prejudices in the European world – Jewish vengefulness compared with Christian forgiveness, most famously captured in Shakespeare's *Merchant of Venice* with Shylock's "pound of flesh" and Portia's "quality of mercy". The whole nationalities of those on trial – the Ukrainians, Poles, Latvians, Estonians, Lithuanians, Croats – could be tarnished as sympathetic to Nazism. As a consequence, relations in Australia between the Jewish community and the communities of Eastern Europe and the Balkans were certain to suffer, even though as victims of totalitarianism they should be drawn together in sympathy and common understanding. Indeed, relations had already suffered.

Beyond all this, there was a very important reason I opposed the war crimes trials that I found difficult to express. I believed as deeply as I believed anything that the Holocaust should never be weaponised for political purposes. In a review of Claude Lanzmann's great documentary *Shoah*, I argued, "To his credit, Lanzmann seeks to extract from his subject no political advantage for any contemporary cause." I believed that at least some of those who supported the war crimes trials were doing so as a means of creating sympathy for Israel and drawing the world's attention away from Israeli oppression of the Palestinians on the West Bank and in Gaza. In sum: "It seems to me ... of vital importance", I argued, "to grasp that the law is not an instrument of politics, with which we can achieve whatever we desire."

The new war crimes legislation succeeded in parliament. A small Special Investigations Unit was established inside the attorney-general's department, led first by Robert Greenwood and then by Graham Blewitt. Of the three or four cases it hoped to prosecute, all collapsed for different reasons. In the one case that came to trial, the defendant, Ivan Polyukhovich, who had attempted suicide, was acquitted by the jury. At the same time, a court in Israel was hearing the case of John Demjanjuk, whom some elderly witnesses claimed was the monstrous Treblinka guard known as Ivan the Terrible. Principally based on their evidence, the Israeli court was satisfied that Demjanjuk was indeed Ivan the Terrible and sentenced him to the gallows.

Despite the torrent of abuse I experienced in 1989 for my opposition to the revised *War Crimes Act* from Isi Leibler's paid offsider, Professor W.D. Rubinstein – a complicated story I will outline in the next chapter – I followed closely and then wrote about the Demjanjuk case, the most important Israeli Holocaust trial since Eichmann's thirty years earlier. Before Demjanjuk was hanged for the crimes of Ivan the Terrible, during the brief period of Gorbachev's *glasnost*, evidence emerged from the Soviet archives that revealed that a certain Ivan Marchenko, who bore some physical resemblance to Demjanjuk, was in fact Ivan the Terrible. What seemed truly disgraceful was that the team inside the US Department of Justice, the Office of Special Investigations, which had worked closely with Australia's Special Investigations Unit, had apparently withheld from the Israeli court the evidence in its possession that revealed the true identity of Ivan the Terrible. This evidence was now presented to an Israeli court. It had no alternative but to acquit Demjanjuk in a vote of 5–0. In one of the fortnightly columns I was by now writing for *The Age*, I concluded:

> A combination of factors led to the near-fatal miscarriage of justice in the Demjanjuk case – faults of memory in the tormented survivors; emotional imbalance in the judges; vast gaps in the evidence; zeal and dishonesty in the investigative organs. Can these or other failings be avoided in future Nazi war crimes trials? Is it not time to bring this whole process to a close?

Not long after, Paul Keating shut down the Special Investigations Unit. I learned from the Rutland biography that Leibler regarded the Keating government's decision to abandon Nazi war crime trials in Australia as "abominable behaviour". He described many of the gentiles who opposed the legislation as anti-Semites, and the small number of Jews who, like me, opposed it, as "trembling Israelites".

*

Throughout the 1980s I was what would now be called a Cold Warrior. I believed that the most important international issue was the struggle between the United States and the Soviet Union, and that it was vital that the United States, the leader of the liberal democratic capitalist world, should not be defeated by the Soviet Union, the leader of the totalitarian communist world. I was an unambiguous defender of the Australian alliance with the United States. (The reward was a fully funded month in the United States, where I met some of the luminaries of the right – William Buckley, Irving Kristol and Gertrude Himmelfarb, Robert Conquest and Norman Podhoretz.) In Australia during the Cold War, I argued, the national interest had been pursued not with sycophancy but with realism and guile.

In recent years Australians have misunderstood this national tradition of dependency, upon "great and powerful friends" as Robert Menzies called them, for sycophancy of the "all the way with LBJ" slogan. In fact, considerable skill and cunning were required to try and induce Great Britain and the United States to defend our interests, especially as another tradition of the Australian state was the unwillingness to spend large sums on defence.

During the period of the Japanese threat, Australia had sought to draw the British navy into the defence of South-East Asia and during the period of the supposed communist threat from China, likewise the United States. On the left in Australia during the 1980s, at that time composed principally of the ALP Left and large parts of the intelligentsia – the Communist Party no longer counted – anti-American feeling was strong. In 1985 Bob Hawke was forced to back down after offering minor technical assistance to the United States over the testing on our soil of their so-called MX missile. In the same year, New Zealand had banned all US naval vessels from its ports because of the uncertainty as to which vessels were carrying nuclear weapons and the risk of an accident on one of their nuclear-armed or nuclear-powered ships while docked. This marked the effective withdrawal of New Zealand from the ANZUS Treaty. There was strong pressure from the Australian left to follow suit, in a process Frank Knopfelmacher christened "the New Zealandisation of Australia". I argued that "the Americans are hardly likely to deploy to our defence ships which the day before were banned from our ports".

Even more important was the general question of nuclear disarmament. In the early 1980s the Soviet Union deployed intermediate-range missiles, the SS-20s, which targeted Europe. In response, the United States and European NATO countries proposed the installation of intermediate-range nuclear weapons of their own, the Cruise and Pershing II missiles. The peace movement was furiously opposed, arguing that as a consequence of this vicious spiral, nuclear war between the Soviet Union and the United States threatened. At a conference organised by the Australian Institute of International Affairs in April 1986, where two leading thinkers on the left, Richard Tanter and Senator Jo Vallentine, were also present, I argued that there was nothing more terrible than the prospect of such a nuclear war: "If offered a choice between Soviet world hegemony and all-out war between the Soviet Union and the United States, no sane person would ... choose all-out nuclear war." People like me were thus committed to preparations for a war that we would never fight. Even though total nuclear disarmament would actually increase the danger of conventional war between the superpowers, there was no ambition more significant and daunting than superpower nuclear disarmament. How might it be achieved?

The left advocated unilateral action. In my view it was certain that the Soviet Union would exploit what it would interpret as weakness in its adversary if handed nuclear weapon superiority. The belief that "the Soviet Union is going to become a less ambitious or ruthless power if it perceives weakness in its major adversary ... runs against both the history of Imperial and Soviet Russia and against any coherent analysis of the mechanisms of the totalitarian state". A far more viable path to peace was bilateral nuclear disarmament agreements. Their success seemed, however, unlikely. Shortly after mid-1986, to the surprise of both left and right, disarmament talks between Reagan and Gorbachev began to make genuine progress, including before too long an agreement to remove all intermediate range nuclear weapons. "The original aim of NATO – the total removal of the SS 20s – has been achieved," I pointed out in a *Herald* column of December 3, 1987. "So far as the question of the Soviet nuclear escalation in Europe was concerned, the peace movement had [*sic*] proven to be profoundly wrong and its opponents essentially right." Even more astonishingly, under the leadership of Gorbachev, the apparently formidable, totalitarian Soviet state embarked, without any pressure from the United States – except its ever-increasing economic and technological superiority – upon a once unthinkable reform road.

The unravelling of the Soviet Union and the loss of its East-Central European empire were the most significant international developments while I was serving my apprenticeship as a so-called public intellectual with a weekly column in the Melbourne *Herald* in 1988–89. A column I wrote in March 1988 recognised that Gorbachev was a genuine reformer – at that time many anti-communists thought he was a Trojan Horse – but warned about the dangers he faced. It began – "Experience teaches us, Tocqueville once wrote, that generally speaking the most perilous moment for a bad government is the one when it seeks to mend its ways" – and ended with the famous Chinese curse: "May you live in interesting times." Already two Soviet republics, Armenia and Azerbaijan, were at each other's throats over a contested territory, Nagorno-Karabakh. In July, I wrote about the meeting of the Soviet Communist Party where Gorbachev outlined his plan for a radical restructure of Soviet politics and radical reduction of the party's power. The Communist Party survived Stalin's murderous purges. The question now was "whether it can maintain its power and privileges in the face of a quite different challenge – the reforming zeal of Mikhail Gorbachev".

It soon became clear to me that Gorbachev knew not what he had begun. Under his leadership the truth about the murder of millions during Stalin's rule became discussible inside the Soviet Union. "George Orwell understood best of all that the fundamental condition of totalitarian rule was the suppression of history. Under Mr Gorbachev, history is slowly being released from the iron grip of ideology" (September 1988). In the three Baltic States, Latvia, Estonia and Lithuania, which had experienced genuine nationhood between the First and Second World Wars, the return of history was of greatest political significance. Nationalism had come alive. "Mr Gorbachev is a great gambler. His Baltic strategy is one of his greatest" (November 1988). By early 1989 I had come to believe that Gorbachev was not a gambler but a bungler. "It is rather difficult for the ruling party in a single-party state to lose an election," I wrote in March 1989. "This week, however, the Communist Party of the Soviet Union came close to achieving the impossible." In Moscow, Boris Yeltsin, a disgraced former Politburo member, won 90 per cent of the vote. In almost half of the electoral regions where communists were unopposed, more than 50 per cent of electors crossed out the name of its candidates. In Ukraine, unexpectedly, five party bosses were thus defeated. "[A] slumbering national movement has begun to stir ... The West is presently besotted with Gorbachev. It has, in my opinion, mistaken his undoubted political audacity for sagacity ... He knows not what he does or what he risks."

Gorbachev did not grasp, or so it seemed, that the Communist Party of the Soviet Union lacked the most fundamental requirement of power: legitimacy. He did not understand that for seventy years its power had relied instead upon fear and the threat of armed force. By the beginning of 1990 the nationalist movements in the Baltic republics were demanding genuine independence. If Gorbachev accepted this demand, I argued in January 1990, he was endangering "the territorial integrity of the Soviet Union". However: "[I]f he prevents the Baltic peoples from getting what they want – by the deployment of armed force – he will undo at a stroke everything that he has hoped, since 1985, to achieve." Both courses were "unthinkable". Yet one or other had to be taken.

By this time Gorbachev had already lost the Soviet Union's empire in Eastern and Central Europe. Soviet control there had rested upon single communist party rule, behind which stood the threat of Soviet military intervention (Hungary in 1956; Czechoslovakia in 1968) or political manipulation (Poland in 1981). In Eastern and Central Europe, the legitimacy of single-party rule was even weaker than in the Soviet Union. By the beginning of 1989, I was convinced that "[t]he invasion threat has all but disappeared from the rational calculus of Central

European politics". Neither could ideological orthodoxy be enforced. Indeed, no one any longer knew what that orthodoxy was. Young Central Europeans read Adam Smith rather than Karl Marx; Hayek rather than Lenin (February 1989). The Hungarians and the Poles told the best jokes. *You pretend to pay us; we pretend to work. We live with Swedish taxes and Ethiopian wages. A coffin will arrive earlier than a flat. The Soviet Union is best described as Upper Volta with rockets. What has occurred is not socialism with a human face but totalitarianism with its teeth knocked out. Communism is the long and painful road between capitalism and capitalism.*

As I argued, at least tentatively, in June 1989, the trajectories of Asian and European communism were moving in opposite directions. In China, tanks crushed the students demonstrating in favour of democracy on Tiananmen Square. In Poland, on the same day, in the first free election for more than forty years, Solidarity humiliated the Communist Party, winning all but one of the seats for which it was allowed to stand candidates.

> This week's extraordinary election in Poland – an anti-communist plebiscite if ever there was one – is the consequence for Soviet-bloc politics of the radical decline of fear. Half-consciously, most observers seem to have believed ... that the collapse of the taste for state terror ... had also transformed post-Maoist China. As it has turned out, they were wrong ... Having been educated in the school of totalitarianism, Deng [Xiaoping] is a true believer in the efficacy of fear.

Gorbachev was clearly not. In East-Central Europe, by the end of 1989, he was rather a destabilising force – or, as I put it, "an empty vessel" into which "the youth of Central Europe ... pour their hopes for the future". One of the Soviet leaders, Valery Gerasimov, now joked that the Sinatra Doctrine had replaced the Brezhnev Doctrine. The Brezhnev Doctrine argued that military action was required if any of the Soviet satellites attempted to return to the bad old days of capitalism, meaningful elections and freedom of speech. Under the new

Sinatra Doctrine, the countries of Eastern and Central Europe were now free "to do it their way". Following the fall of the Berlin Wall, the instant "symbol for the dramatic collapse of communist power in Central Europe", one remaining old-style leader was Miloš Jakeš in Czechoslovakia. It was doubtful whether "he could, in present circumstances, survive a goodwill visit from Mr Gorbachev. What Stalin built in Central Europe, it has become Gorbachev's destiny to destroy. This alone makes him the most important leader of the decade."

Nineteen eighty-nine was the year of Tiananmen Square and the fall of the Berlin Wall. In my final *Herald* column, of January 19, 1990, I reminded readers of the sour words of the liberal Sir William Harcourt a century earlier: "We are all socialists now." I had recently heard a left-wing activist describe Nicolae Ceaușescu, the communist dictator of Romania, in language indistinguishable from Ronald Reagan's. Broadcaster Phillip Adams had admitted that "B.A. Santamaria and Frank Knopfelmacher had been right about communism all along!" So: We are all anti-communists now. I cannot suppress a wry smile.

Part III
Quadrant

[10.]

Editing *Quadrant* (1989–1992)

IN 1986, THE MUCH-LOVED RICHARD KRYGIER DIED. He had organised *Quadrant*'s affairs behind the scenes since its first issue in 1956. Management of the magazine now fell to a board of conservative business and academic notables, the Committee of Management, which included, as chair, Sir Noel Foley, the former head of the Commonwealth Bank; Richard Searby, the former chair of Rupert Murdoch's News Limited; Dame Leonie Kramer, the chancellor of the University of Sydney; David Armstrong, one of Sydney University's Challis professors, and one of the founders of the so-called "Australian School" of philosophical materialists; Heinz Arndt, the emeritus professor of economics at the Australian National University; and a handful of mining industry representatives, the most forceful and ideologically self-confident of whom was an old ALP Club acquaintance, Ray Evans, the author of a series of inflammatory speeches delivered by Hugh Morgan, the head of Western Mining, throughout the 1980s. It also included a close friend, Martin Krygier, Richard's son, and a friend of Martin's, Tom Gregory, a successful businessman, whom I came to know and deeply admire. The board was needed to oversee finances, appoint editors and raise money, something that had become especially important when the Literature Board of the Australia Council seized the opportunity of *Quadrant*'s turmoil, deepened in 1987 by the resignation of Peter Coleman, *Quadrant*'s off-and-on editor for some twenty years, to savagely reduce *Quadrant*'s annual grant.

Dr Roger Sandall, an anthropologist from Sydney University, was appointed *Quadrant* editor from the beginning of 1988. To judge by a sour article he wrote for *The Sydney Morning Herald* published on November 16, 1989, a year or so after his resignation, Sandall had a miserable time. As he put it, a year of editing *Quadrant* was six months too long. He was appalled by the physical surroundings, a shabby office in a shabby building in Sydney's business district. He appears to have felt amused contempt for the three "permed" women who rather miraculously somehow produced the magazine each month – one of whom, Robin Marsden, was the sweet-natured and gentle but also intelligent and loyal champion of "the *Quadrant* tradition". Sandall was angered by Robin's reverence for *Quadrant*'s principal authors. According to him, when Frank Knopfelmacher, for example, was on song he was very, very good, but when he was bad, he was horrid. Sandall sought new mainstream authors for *Quadrant*. His letters were either answered curtly or altogether ignored. He tried to introduce articles on science but claimed that he was criticised by reactionaries hostile to Charles Darwin and the Enlightenment. He thought *Quadrant* was too dour, and its writers too entitled; they needed to accept that their precious offerings could be improved by an editor's cuts.

During Sandall's time as editor, I genuinely tried to assist him, agreeing to become an unofficial associate and to write an occasional column on foreign affairs. I wrote only one short article for *Quadrant* in 1988 – "The Soviet Tilt" – which was critical of the Hawke government's policy of accommodation of the Soviet Union. As the Soviet Union was already undergoing the near-suicidal but genuinely radical Gorbachev reform program of *perestroika* and *glasnost*, it is an article I did not genuinely believe in at the time and shortly after came to regret.

In July 1988 Sandall wrote an editorial that attempted to put distance between the magazine that James McAuley had launched in 1956 and the one he now wished to edit. Sandall quoted the famous McAuley lines in his editorial for *Quadrant*'s first issue: "[O]ne huge glaring visage ... an enormous mask made of blood and lies ...

dominates the landscape." Such apocalyptic times had passed. Marxists were everywhere "scratching their heads". It was time for *Quadrant* to engage with the intellectual "mainstream" and, without abandoning its former *gravitas*, out of "compassion for its readers" (a curious way of putting it) to lighten up.

Not everyone was pleased with Sandall's vision of the new post–Cold War *Quadrant*. When Sandall issued an invitation for an August 18 meeting of the normally somnolent Editorial Advisory Board, to which I belonged (not to be confused with the Committee of Management), I wrote a letter with a suggested agenda that included consideration of "the general question of *Quadrant*'s identity. A useful way into this question might be a discussion of some of the issues in your editorial, and in particular the connection between *Quadrant*'s origins (roughly as a cultural-political journal born out of the Cold War) and its present and future role in Australia." One response to my letter was a long paper from Greg Sheridan that concluded with praise for the "splendid" job Sandall was doing. More significant, however, were the anti-Sandall forces, who were led by Paddy Morgan, an intelligent but politically explosive cultural critic who was once a student of Vin Buckley's and a member of the Melbourne University ALP Club, as we have seen, and now teaching at a Gippsland tertiary college.

Three days before the August 18 meeting, Paddy Morgan distributed what he called a "Statement", a withering critique of Sandall's *Quadrant*. He was "very worried about the direction – or lack of it – that *Quadrant* is taking". A press release under Sandall's name had described some contributors as "soliloquizing" and "introverted". Such talk, Morgan argued, "demoralises the magazine's supporters, and gives aid and comfort to its detractors". It was also wrong to describe the magazine in public as "humourless". "If you want more humour etc. you quietly go about commissioning it."

For Morgan, James McAuley's editorial in the original issue of *Quadrant* in 1956 was still entirely relevant. McAuley had warned about the dangers of "enlightenment doctrines" of all kinds, of which communism was only one example. In contrast, Sandall's recipe for the new *Quadrant* – "humour, relaxation and the absence of distemper" – did "not constitute a policy". According to Morgan, *Quadrant* had fallen into the hands of those "who have not written extensively for the magazine, nor gone out on a limb publicly on unpopular issues". He suggested that those truly "representing the *Quadrant* tradition", like "Robert Manne, Peter Shrubb and Robin Marsden", be appointed as associate editors. *Quadrant* was once "the Jewel in the Crown" of anti-totalitarian forces in Australia. It would be a "tragedy" if it should now "go down".

I thought that, on balance, Paddy was probably right. It was already clear that the Cold War was ending and on the overriding question of the Cold War on terms favourable to *Quadrant*'s worldview. While Sandall certainly wanted to edit a sophisticated and civilised magazine, the problem was that he had nothing in particular in the coming post–Cold War world that he wished the magazine to say or stand for. As the enemies of *Quadrant* circled, sensing weakness, I doubted that, under Sandall, it could survive. (In Britain, *Quadrant*'s classier elder sibling, *Encounter*, did not.) I thought, however, that Paddy Morgan's incendiary "Statement" was unfair, as Sandall had not been given enough time to find his way.

I also found myself in an awkward position. My offer of assistance to Sandall in the letter of July 19 – in which I had proposed the agenda for the August 18 meeting – was perfectly sincere. Nonetheless, in the days before the meeting of the Editorial Advisory Board, I had been drawn by Paddy into involvement in what I belatedly recognised, following Paddy's "Statement", as a campaign to remove Sandall as editor. I was also suspicious of Paddy's motives. He sent me the correspondence in which Sandall had suggested a politically significant edit of a long review Paddy had written about Tom Wolfe's *The Bonfire of the Vanities*. He was outraged by what he called, in a note to me, Sandall's "silly" editorial suggestions. As a long-time *Quadrant* insider, Paddy was the self-appointed flag-bearer of the James McAuley tradition. However it seemed to me that his ego had been wounded by Sandall's edit of his article. Not being able to see my way through all this, I decided not to attend the August 18 meeting. It is one of the moments in my political life of which I felt at the time – and still now feel, thirty-six years later – ashamed. I should have attended.

On February 11, 1989, in an article entitled "Bunfight Among Knights of the Right", John Lyons provided a detailed but snide report for *The Sydney Morning Herald* about what had taken place at the August 18, 1988, meeting. According to Lyons, Paddy Morgan and Tony McAdam, a Melbourne-based conservative who had written a regular column on the media for *Quadrant*, mounted a full-scale attack on Sandall's editorship. The meeting began with McAdam's claim that *Quadrant* had become "an academic wank", given to publishing, in McAdam's later words to Lyons, "quite nice, tame and probably quite boring critique pieces about *Jane Eyre*". Under Sandall, *Quadrant* had lost readers and advertising revenue. Most importantly, it had lost almost entirely the kind of political influence it had wielded during the Cold War. On the evening following the meeting, as Lyons had learned, Paddy phoned McAdam to congratulate him on the way he had handled "the dirty work". Apart from Morgan and McAdam, according to Lyons, the anti-Sandall side included Robin Marsden and the Islamophile poet Anne Fairbairn. Martin Krygier and David Armstrong defended Sandall. There was dispute about which side Sam Lipski and the Labor senator John Wheeldon supported. The meeting lasted for two hours. By its end, everyone, at least according to Lyons, recognised that *Quadrant* would never be the same again.

Shortly after this meeting Sandall rang me. I agreed to becoming soon an associate editor, reading articles, suggesting topics, involving myself in the daily life of the magazine – in the disputes between editors and contributors, and even in the finances. At the same time, Sandall sent a letter to all members of the Editorial Advisory Board. "After a lively meeting let's get down to business!" he declared. "Less academicism" was the order of the day. Sandall asked for suggestions about possible TV/radio, art and drama critics; new specialist columnists; and new "all-purpose" book reviewers. "*New* names please." Sandall turned to the words of Paul Johnson, the editor of the London *Spectator*, for inspiration. *Quadrant* should respond to the issues of interest to "the chattering classes". It should "exhibit the permanent virtues of good writing ... sober judgment, breadth of interests, and civilised manners". Most difficult of all, "it must have wit ... nothing too forced or vulgar, just a dry chuckle or two".

The "dry chuckle" of Sandall in 1988 was a very long distance from the "enormous mask made of blood and lies" of McAuley in 1956. It soon became clear to Sandall that his heart was no longer in the job. On October 12, he wrote to Sir Noel Foley submitting his resignation. As Sandall told John Lyons, he knew following the August 18 meeting that he was done with *Quadrant*. According to both Lyons and Sandall, a possible pluralist future for *Quadrant* had been defeated. A coup of sorts had taken place. The "old guard" had won.

That old guard, apparently, included me. By telephone, Sir Noel Foley offered me the editorship of *Quadrant*. I explained that, as someone without sufficient experience of editing a magazine (neither *Prospice* at Camberwell High School in 1965 nor *Melbourne University Magazine* in 1969 seemed enough), and as someone who lived and worked in Melbourne (with a family of four to support), I could not accept the offer. There were further talks involving Foley, David Armstrong, Peter Coleman, Tom Gregory and me. On November 21, I wrote to Foley accepting the offer of co-editorship of *Quadrant* with Peter Coleman: he in Sydney and me in Melbourne. I argued that the only way the idea of co-editorship could work was on the basis of complete equality:

> I do not believe any kind of association with Peter Coleman, other than that of full and equal co-editorship, would be viable ... As I have been friendly with Peter Coleman for many years and have always found myself in general philosophical agreement with him, I believe it is likely that we would get on well ... and be able to iron out amicably the differences between us that will arise.

There was only a very small detail in these negotiations that seemed off-key. Peter told me that he wanted our names to appear in the magazine in alphabetical order. C clearly preceded M. I told

Peter, truthfully, that I didn't give a damn. Privately, I chuckled (drily) and noted what I probably should have recognised as a warning. I enclosed with my letter of acceptance to Sir Noel Foley a few of my recent *Herald* columns. I made a point of including one that showed that I was a critic of what was now in Australia called "economic rationalism" (and elsewhere "neo-liberalism"). Nor was I someone able to celebrate capitalism as not only a more effective economic system than communism but also a superior civilisation, as was now becoming fashionable.

In March 1989, the first issue of *Quadrant* Peter and I co-edited appeared. We led with three short talks delivered by B.A. Santamaria, John Carroll and me at a dinner I had organised in honour of Frank Knopfelmacher on his retirement from Melbourne University, which, with his characteristically self-lacerating and deadly accurate wit, Knopfelmacher invariably henceforth referred to as his "funeral". Bob Santamaria spoke about Knopfelmacher as his twentieth-century European history teacher: "While I cannot aspire to play the role of Plato to Frank's Socrates, as one of the thinker's less distinguished pupils, I join in paying honour to him tonight." I began with Isaiah Berlin's evocation of another Ancient Greek, Antilochus: "The fox knows many things, but the hedgehog knows one big thing." Knopfelmacher was our hedgehog. The one big thing he knew, better than any intellectual in Australia, was the nature of Soviet communism. For his part, John Carroll thought Knopfelmacher embodied the intellectual virtue that Max Weber valued most: "A passion for unconditional sobriety" – a pretty neat summary, I quietly thought, of precisely the kind of intellectual Knopfelmacher was not.

This dinner, incidentally, had an unanticipated consequence. Gerard Henderson wrote a letter complaining bitterly about not having received an invitation: "As far as I am aware, I have not done anything to upset you. You have stayed at our house and I went out of my way to give your Petrov book a run in both *The Australian* and *The Wall Street Journal*." Thus was born, or perhaps reborn, a vicious hatred that has now lasted for almost sixty years. What I could not tell Gerard was that if Santamaria had known that we had invited

Henderson, it was most likely that he would not have agreed to speak. Santamaria regarded Henderson as a traitor because of the way, as he told me, Henderson had used privileged access to private papers to tarnish Santamaria's reputation. And, despite their sometimes-turbulent relations, Bob Santamaria meant a lot more to Knopfelmacher than Gerard Henderson.

I wrote the unsigned editorial for our first edition, which was an only slightly rephrased version of my explanation of what I saw as the role of *Quadrant* at the end of the Cold War in my November 21 letter to Sir Noel Foley. It represented a period in my thought of which I am not proud. Very few intellectuals in Australia, I argued, were any longer affected by what Jean-François Revel had called "the totalitarian temptation" – that is to say, by enthusiasm for the kind of grotesque and blood-drenched societies that had emerged under communism in the Soviet Union or China. Many were, however, now affected by what Edward Shils had called the "antinomian" temptation, the total rejection of centuries-old patterns of thought and established authority. While the Cold War conflict between communism and democratic capitalism had been decided in favour of the arguments of the right, the culture in the universities, churches and media had moved rapidly to the left.

> A variety of new radical ideologies – radical feminism, gay liberationism, anti-nuclearism, extreme environmentalism, multiculturalism, animal liberationism – have filled the political and spiritual vacuum left by the collapse of the Socialist faith ... In their collective lives, intellectuals now often seem more concerned with harassing those who have fallen into one of the three sinful categories of thought – racism, sexism, elitism – than with the pursuit of scholarship and truth.

This provided those who valued cultural freedom with their new challenge in the post–Cold War world.

In a letter in our May issue, Ian Marsh of the University of New South Wales took issue with this editorial. It was all very well to argue with the "extremism of some reform movement protagonists" of the left. But this took no heed of "another potential threat – this time from the right":

> This arises from those neo-liberal libertarians (often free market economists ...) who vaunt individualism, casting the will as the sole source of value and market transactions as its sole measure ... *Quadrant* needs to decide whether it is to be absorbed by the so-called "new right" or whether a concern for cultural freedom now dictates an enlarged perspective and a more discriminating, sometimes a more moderate, less feisty disposition.

As soon as I read this letter, I realised, almost with shock, that I agreed with every word. The *Quadrant* I hoped to edit at this moment would interrogate the two most powerful mindsets of the post–Cold War intelligentsia in the West: the antinomianism of the left, as argued in the editorial, and, as Ian Marsh contended, the neo-liberalism of the right. As I went on, I discovered that what I wanted to do was to liberate *Quadrant* (and myself) from the most characteristic disease of intellectual discourse in our era, the blindness of ideological self-certainty. Since the Dreyfus Affair, intellectuals in the West had divided into two broad camps of left and right. Within these camps, smaller tribes emerged. Each tribe developed its own rigid ideology. In his classic essay "Notes on Nationalism", George Orwell provided a brilliant taxonomy of both the principal tribes in mid-twentieth-century Britain and the ways in which tribal membership fashioned and distorted thought. Since reading Orwell as an undergraduate, this was how I interpreted the world of intellectual discourse and combat.

*

Before any of this could occur, my co-editorship was overwhelmed by the most unpleasant controversy of my life, at least thus far. Peter Coleman suggested that we should publish two of my *Herald* columns in each issue. For April, one of the columns I chose concerned the most recent development in the Hawke government's "war crimes" legislation. Not only were the war crimes that might be prosecuted limited in time to the Second World War, in a last-moment amendment they were also limited geographically to what one minister, Michael Tate, called the continent of Europe "left of the Urals". It was generally believed that this amendment had been introduced in case the war crimes legislation interfered with the emerging Japanese tourist trade.

As it happened, the passage of the amended war crimes legislation coincided with the death of Emperor Hirohito, the Japanese war leader, who was actively responsible for troops involved in the murder of vast numbers of Chinese – according to the recent estimate by Francis Pike in his *Hirohito's War*, 20 million – and for the executions and torture of large numbers of Australian prisoners of war, captured by the Japanese following the fall of Singapore. While preparing to prosecute a handful of obscure Eastern Europeans involved in Hitler's war against the Jews, the Hawke government was preparing to send to Tokyo a high-level delegation to mourn the death of this major war criminal. My brief column explored the paradoxical presence of moral absolutism in Europe and moral ultra-pragmatism in Asia. "Most Australians' direct experience of war crimes stems from the Burma Railway and not Auschwitz," I wrote. "Judgment has deserted a Government which thinks it can ask Australians to mourn Hirohito and, simultaneously, put some local East European SS guard on trial."

By now almost everyone in the Jewish community following the debate about the war crimes legislation was probably aware of the reasons for my opposition. My friend Sam Lipski had published in full the talk I had given to the Victorian branch of the Jewish Board of Deputies on April 17, 1988, for which I had received thanks from its president, Jeremy Rapke, for "taking part and making a most thought provoking and interesting contribution to the discussion … All who have spoken to me about the evening have commented favourably on your excellent address." In addition, many involved in the cultural politics of the Jewish community must have known of my engagement, in thought and in writing, with what I regarded as the unique evil of the Holocaust.

Recently I had led various discussions in the community on Claude Lanzmann's extraordinary film *Shoah*, and had written a column on it for *The Herald*, which the *Australia/Israel Review* had reprinted.

And yet *Quadrant* received the following extraordinary letter from Bill Rubinstein, a New York historian with an academic post at Deakin University in Melbourne, and a man for whom courtesy was an unknown human quality. Rubinstein's letter-to-the-editors began thus:

> In his column, "Left of the Urals" ... Robert Manne makes one of the most obscene false analogies ever to appear in *Quadrant*; indeed, one would have to turn to a racist journal of the neo-fascist extreme right to find a similar point in print ... The "minor European war criminals" whom Manne weeps over may well have murdered 500 Jewish (and other) women and children in cold blood ... Imperial Japan at its worst never engaged in genocide and never attempted to murder a whole people ... Indeed concerning the Nazi genocide of the Jews, it is well-known that Japan pointedly refused to kill any of the Jews living in its domains ... I simply despair for the future of a once-great magazine ... Might I ask Manne to explain what he means by the commercialization of the Holocaust ...? It is exceedingly strange that a man whose grand-parents were murdered by the Nazis should be so keen to see that their murderers get off scot-free, is it not? ... Richard Krygier must be turning in his grave.

There have been very many unpleasant things written about me over the years, but nothing can compare with Rubinstein's letter, which we published in *Quadrant* in June 1989.

There were two excellent letters in response. In July, Martin Krygier wrote:

> [I]t is poor logic to attack Manne's analogy on the grounds that Nazism was horribly worse than the Japanese participation in the War. That is tragically true. It does not follow that all individual Japanese soldiers behaved better than individual Nazis ...

> [Australia's] legal system ... dispenses *individual* rather than group or race justice. Manne obviously understands that; Rubinstein does not.

Martin also pointed out that he knew his father somewhat better than did Rubinstein:

> I don't know what his attitude to the war crimes legislation would have been ... I do know that, like me, he considered claims to exclusive moral rights over the Holocaust odious ... I find this sort of rhetorical bullying offensive at any time ... Particularly so when my father's name is spuriously invoked to dignify it.

In August, Mark Braham, an Orthodox Jew, argued that "it might come as a surprise to Professor Bill Rubinstein that the double standard of prosecuting war criminals in Australia while sending high-level mourners to Emperor Hirohito's funeral was first pointed out to me by a rabbi, a man of unusual piety, learning and, above all, honesty". He also provided Rubinstein with an answer to his ignorant or mendacious question about the commercialisation of the Holocaust. Recently, the United Kingdom's chief rabbi, Lord Immanuel Jakobovits, had written: "We might as well recognise at once that the Holocaust has now generated an entire industry, with handsome profits for writers, researchers, film-makers, monument-builders, museum-planners, conference-organisers and even politicians seeking to dramatise 'Never Again' slogans." Rabbi Jakobovits described all this money-making Holocaust activity as a "catastrophic perversion of the Jewish spirit".

I had been aware for a long time that my mentor and friend Frank Knopfelmacher, overcome by the tragedy of twentieth-century Europe – by the almost unprecedented evil of both Nazism and Stalinism – was gradually losing his mind. When in 1984 New Zealand banned US warships from its ports on the grounds that they might be carrying nuclear weapons, Knopfelmacher told me that Australia was finished and urged Rai Gaita to move his family to Britain. He was not joking. The gradual collapse of the Soviet Union following the arrival of Gorbachev afforded him no pleasure, as I thought it should. No one grasped the illegitimacy of the Soviet Union and its Eastern European satellite states as accurately as he. Needing a formidable enemy, Knopfelmacher turned to the group he believed now ran the show in the United States: neo-conservative, Zionist-inclined American Jews.

It was in this frame of mind that Knopfelmacher now sprang to my defence against Rubinstein with his own letter. He was happy we had published Rubinstein's letter because it provided "an example of the kind of verbal bullying and attempted terror with which the 'war-crimes' racket has been shielded against critical evaluation". Knopfelmacher argued that the consequence and purpose of the war crimes racket was ethnic destabilisation in Australia, targeting "Communist bloc ethnics and the rapidly diminishing holocaust survivors". He advocated refusing entry visas to "operatives" working for the Nazi-hunting outfit in the United States, the Simon Wiesenthal Center, and turning back at the border officials of the US Office of Special Investigations (such as Neal Sher, who was one of the speakers at the meeting of the Victorian Jewish Board of Deputies where I also spoke).

Knopfelmacher argued that the racket was engineered by the Likud government in Israel and powerful forces in both the United States and Australia. He hinted that some of the leading actors were Mossad agents: "Sudetenethnics attached as a fifth column to overseas fatherlands, and at the beck and call of their political directives". "Pollard" – an American Jew who had spied for Israel and was currently in prison – "was only the tip of an iceberg": "the transformation of the Jewish diaspora into a reservoir of political auxiliaries for a country other than the one in which they live and prosper, and from which they neither came and to which they do not intend to go is a historically attested road to strife and ruin."

With the publication of Knopfelmacher's letter – which I realised was pretty crazy – the shit, as they say, truly hit the fan. With friends like Knopfelmacher, as they also say, who needed enemies?

I had been listening to analyses of this kind for a long time in almost nightly telephone calls from Knopfelmacher. I quickly learned that publishing pieces like this in *Quadrant* was a luxury I could not afford.

It took me far too long to realise that Knopfelmacher's letter was primarily aimed at the most powerful figure in the Australian Jewish community, Isi Leibler, once a close political friend of Knopfelmacher's – in the campaign to allow Soviet Jews to emigrate to Israel – but now a bitter enemy. Among the four letters attacking Knopfelmacher in the September issue of *Quadrant*, one was from Leibler, then the president of the Executive Council of Australian Jewry. Leibler claimed that the Jewish community almost unanimously supported the war crimes legislation. He would have preferred it if it dealt with all crimes against humanity and not only those connected with the Holocaust. The claim that the Jews were seeking vengeance and not justice – something Knopfelmacher had never and would never have argued – was plainly anti-Semitic. Leibler pointed out that he had discussions with the Israeli prime minister, Yitzhak Shamir, and other political leaders three or four times a year. The question of the Australian war crimes legislation had never been discussed. He objected most strenuously to the term used by Knopfelmacher: "pseudo ethnic fuhrers". "Did nobody at *Quadrant* blanch at the use of such language?" Knopfelmacher's letter might have been published in a journal under the "primatur" of the Stalinist cultural commissar, Zhdanov. In addition, Leibler pointed out that he "fully" endorsed "the views (if not the style)" of Bill Rubinstein's letter. And (just in case we hadn't noticed) he was "appalled and disgusted".

In his attack on Knopfelmacher, there was one detail of relevance concerning his relations with Israeli leaders that Leibler (of course) omitted. Leibler argued that Knopfelmacher's claim that some of Australia's Jewish leaders had "dual loyalties" was plainly anti-Semitic. As *Lone Voice*, Suzanne Rutland's recent highly sympathetic biography of Isi Leibler, reveals, however, while he was the most prominent leader of the Jewish community in Australia, Leibler had indeed worked for Israeli intelligence since 1959, following a "transformative meeting" with "the legendary Israeli spymaster" Shaul

Avigur. According to Rutland, for decades Leibler "acted unofficially *under instructions from Avigur and Levanon* [another senior member of Israeli intelligence], *becoming a de facto operative for Israel on foreign affairs* [my emphasis] ... Notably, unlike its American and British counterparts, Australian Jewry remained closely aligned with Israeli government priorities." Nor was Knopfelmacher's suggestion about the leaders of the Office of Special Investigations' corrupt commercial exploitation of the Holocaust as wildly speculative, even crazy, as I once believed. The head of the OSI, Neal Sher, whom I met with at the April 1988 meeting of the Victorian Jewish Deputies, later became the head of the International Commission on Holocaust Era Insurance Claims. According to Sher's 2021 obituary in *The New York Times*, "the New York bar suspended his licence" after "it was disclosed that he had submitted more than $100,000 in false claims for reimbursement of travel expenses".

I came under great pressure in 1989 to denounce Knopfelmacher. I did not. I could not. I did realise, however, that I could not publish him, in his present state of mind, on American Jews or Israel, and I wrote to him that I could no longer listen to his nightly telephonic diatribes against the Jewish American conservative intelligentsia (some of whom, not long after, as neo-conservatives, were critical in leading the United States into the catastrophic Iraq invasion).

On August 11, 1989, *The Australian Jewish News* published a 4,000-word analysis of the "*Quadrant* Controversy" by the journalist Michael Gawenda. Gawenda accepted the false Rubinstein claim that because I had not discussed (in an 800-word article) the difference between genocide and war crimes, I had indeed equated Hitler's Holocaust and Hirohito's war crimes. More importantly, he criticised me for publishing Knopfelmacher's letter. By now a new issue had been discovered. In our March issue we had published a short article on a French writer, Léon Daudet, by a Sydney friend of the magazine, Alister Kershaw, which had been accepted by Roger Sandall and put in the March issue by Peter Coleman without my knowledge. I am sure neither Roger nor Peter (nor I) had the faintest clue that Daudet was an anti-Semite and supporter of the anti-Jewish actions of the

Vichy government. Gawenda accepted that I had not read the Daudet piece before its publication, but nonetheless discussed its publication within the context of the preposterous question he and the *Jewish News* now raised: was Manne leading *Quadrant* to anti-Semitism and the racist right?

By now I was becoming angry. In the brief space Lipski allowed for my reply, I pointed out the centrality of the Holocaust to my political thought and to my teaching for many years, and the way in which it had led, naturally, to my work on behalf of refugees from totalitarianism in our own age – the Vietnamese "boat people".

On August 25, Rubinstein and Leibler were given the last words in the *Jewish News*. More than half of Rubinstein's attack on me concerned Daudet. Leibler made it clear that it was I who was leading *Quadrant* to the racist right. He had known Coleman for many years and had "the highest regard" for him: "Manne's co-editor ... is a man who could not conceivably be regarded as harbouring any trace of antisemitism or racial prejudice." Even though Coleman was still the co-editor of *Quadrant*, Leibler did "not believe that a number of items referred to above would have been published in *Quadrant* five years ago". (How, I wondered, had I forced Coleman to publish these articles and letters?) Shortly after, Leibler and Rubinstein achieved their greatest success. Without interviewing me or even reading the relevant articles in *Quadrant*, Pamela Bone wrote an article in *The Age* that suggested my co-editorship of *Quadrant* was a sign that racism in Australia was once again on the rise.

Through all this, I noticed, my co-editor had not discussed the issue with me and had maintained an eloquent public silence. Fortunately, I had an ally in the *Quadrant* office in Sydney, Robin Marsden. She had overheard telephone conversations between Isi Leibler and Peter Coleman, in which Coleman had let Leibler believe that I was solely responsible for the publication of both Knopfelmacher's letter and the Daudet article. In short, Coleman had betrayed me.

From the first, Coleman and I had not got along particularly well. An old friend of the magazine, Owen Harries, was now editing a conservative foreign policy magazine in the United States, *The National*

Interest. He encouraged us to republish an exciting new article that had come his way, Francis Fukuyama's "The End of History?". When I expressed reservations, Coleman looked at me as if I was mad. Fukuyama – rightly, I think – did appear in *Quadrant*. When Coleman read the editorial I wrote for our May issue – which accepted that Gorbachev was a genuine reformer but that his bold experiment was almost certain to fail – he was uneasy. The line of the neo-conservative intellectuals in New York, from which Coleman was accustomed to take his bearings, was that Gorbachev's reforms were deceptions, aiming at securing economic concessions from the West at a time when the Soviet Union had almost achieved, in the words of Norman Podhoretz, the editor-in-chief of *Commentary* magazine, "irreversible military superiority". Our compromise was the publication of my editorial "Can Gorbachev Succeed?", as usual unsigned, and in the body of the magazine a brief article from Podhoretz, "Grovelling to Gorbachev".

This was not our only disagreement. In mid-1989 a media-obsessed stockbroker took his life after reading a takedown of him in one of the weekend magazines. Coleman suggested that we create an annual *Quadrant* prize for an insensitive piece of journalism named after the author of the takedown. Having learned that the author was now severely depressed, I refused. Surely one suicide was enough. Coleman mocked my over-scrupulousness.

July 14 was the bicentenary of the storming of the Bastille, the event that was customarily taken as the beginning of the French Revolution. I spent several months reading the most influential interpreters of the meaning of the revolution – Edmund Burke, Alexis de Tocqueville, Karl Marx (and contemporary Marxists) and Hannah Arendt – for a talk I was to give on that evening to the Sydney friends of *Quadrant*. Coleman probably expected a witty fifteen minutes. What he got was a serious lecture lasting over an hour. He let me know by his silence that I had made a serious *faux pas*.

None of that mattered much but, perhaps inevitably, we finally arrived at a real disagreement. David Stove was a Sydney Andersonian, a close friend and ally of David Armstrong's in the vicious struggles that had split the philosophy department at the University of Sydney, and the author of a condemnation of almost all streams of new postmodern thinking in the humanities, in his famous (or notorious) *Quadrant* article "A Farewell to Arts". He was also a member of the *Quadrant* innermost circle and an author who could almost take it for granted that *Quadrant* would publish anything he wrote. It is fair to say that Stove was very intelligent, and equally fair to say that he was a genuine reactionary.

At the time of the war crimes controversy, Stove submitted an article called "Racial and Other Antagonisms". In many ways it was an almost intentionally foolish essay, for example describing "Anglo-Saxons" and "Celts" as contemporary "races" and ending with a petty personal attack on a minor female Sydney radio broadcaster. Its central argument about the origin of the antagonism he called "racialism" – Stove refused to use the newfangled term "racism" – was almost self-evidently false. Stove argued that no racial antagonism was ever groundless. In racial antagonisms, it could never be the case that one side was innocent and the other guilty. As he put it, "there could *not* be racial antagonism which depended *only* on false and irrational beliefs [his emphases]". His model for racial antagonism went like this:

> Suppose it could happen ... that Race A does not at first hate Race B at all, while B hates A, but only because of false and irrational beliefs which it has about A. Then, unless a fluke or a miracle prevents it, B's hatred of A will issue in treatment of members of A, of a kind which will cause A to hate B too ...

As almost everyone in our generation agreed, the most terrible instance of racial antagonism of recent times was the decision taken by those who controlled the German state after 1933 to rid the Earth of the Jews. According to Stove's argument, this decision could not have been grounded only on false and irrational beliefs. What, I wondered, might have been the Germans' true and rational beliefs about the Jews that preceded the Holocaust? Making too much money in business? Gaining too many university places in competitive examinations? Killing Christ? I would have been opposed to the publication of Stove's article at any time. However, as Stove's submission was made during the Rubinstein/Leibler attack on me for drawing *Quadrant* towards anti-Semitism and racism, I was not willing to take the consequences of a further attack while Coleman ducked for cover. I told Coleman I was entirely opposed to the publication of the Stove article, and tried to explain why. I thought he had agreed not to publish.

By late July 1989, I had decided that co-editing *Quadrant* with Peter Coleman did not work. I resigned from the co-editorship but told the board of directors, which was now chaired by Dame Leonie Kramer, that I was willing to assume the full editorship in 1990 if the magazine was brought to Melbourne. The board accepted my offer, although they decided not to inform Coleman about the move to Melbourne, presumably because they knew he would cause trouble. My most substantial achievement of the co-editorship appeared after my temporary retirement: a debate about the Vietnam War, stretching from Jim Cairns, the anti-war leader, on the left, to Brigadier Ted Serong, the legendary and secretive Australian war strategist, on the right, with Greg Clark, John Wheeldon, Coral Bell, Heinz Arndt, Kenneth Gee and Frank Knopfelmacher in between.

In late August, Robin Marsden told me that, despite our supposed agreement, Coleman was preparing to publish Stove on racial antagonisms. I asked her to send Dame Leonie the Stove article, and I outlined for Kramer the controversy over war crimes, Knopfelmacher and Daudet, with accompanying letters and articles. I told her that if *Quadrant* published Stove on racial antagonisms, as Coleman was planning to do, I would not be editor in the following year. Leonie supported me. As Coleman explained in his preface to a book of Stove essays, *Cricket versus Republicanism*, he was furious at those he called "the *Tartuffes* of cultural freedom". On November 9, on the day the Berlin Wall was breached, the committee of management (the board) appointed me editor of *Quadrant* on the understanding that I would move the magazine to Melbourne. Coleman was again furious about the move and the secrecy surrounding it. In *The Sydney*

Morning Herald on November 27, he conceded, in a phrase dripping with condescension, that I had "the makings of an editor". He believed, however, that the move to Melbourne would most likely prove fatal: "[T]he decisive move in burying [*Quadrant*] will have been made by a board of directors inexperienced in publishing and insensitive to the magazine's character, history, contributors, readers and friends."

*

The move to Melbourne was not easy. At first, we had no office. For a brief period, Ray Evans provided me with some space in the Melbourne headquarters of Western Mining. Ray had a booming voice, and his habit at work was to use a speakerphone. I was surprised to discover that, from the head office of one of Australia's most powerful mining corporations, Ray Evans was organising David Kemp's bid for Liberal Party preselection for the seat of Goldstein and the unseating of one of the most prominent "small-l" Liberal Party parliamentarians, Ian Macphee. This was like a scene from a play by Berthold Brecht, or perhaps the Marxist collective at the nearby Pram Factory.

While I was put up at Western Mining, I was invited to a lunch with a prominent critic of the provision of foreign aid to developing countries, Lord Bauer, a short Jewish man with an exaggerated Oxford accent. In another scene that might have come from a Brecht or Pram Factory play, I recall the clinking of the glasses and the fine white wine we drank while listening to a group of wealthy – or, in the case of Hugh Morgan, mega-wealthy – white males as they laughed together while agreeing about the folly of providing aid to the impoverished peasants of Africa and South Asia.

In fairness to Ray, he threw himself into assisting with the move. For a time, the few significant possessions of the Sydney office – like the back numbers of *Quadrant* – were stored in the garage of his modest home. Ray himself helped assemble the shelves in our new permanent office, on the ground floor of a terrace house in Fitzroy where my La Trobe friend John Carroll lived. I owe gratitude to Ray for something even more precious than all this. It was in conversation with him that I learned about the ideological extremism of those at the heart of the Australian neo-liberal movement. In one conversation Ray tried to convince me that the right to vote should be restricted to reasonably substantial property owners. He was not joking. Ray Evans was not a snob but he was an influential ideologue. Together with John Stone, a former head of Treasury, he was the driving force behind four right-wing societies engaged in elite opinion formation: the H.R. Nicholls Society (on anti–trade union industrial relations law); the Samuel Griffith Society (on anti-republicanism and constitutional law); the Bennelong Society (on a return to Indigenous assimilation and anti-self-determination) and the Lavoisier Group (on climate change denialism), all analysed in an excellent study called *Political Troglodytes and Economic Lunatics* by a former student at La Trobe, Dominic Kelly.

At the time I began editing *Quadrant* in Melbourne, the magazine's financial situation was rather desperate. It owed a Sydney bank some $30,000. Apart from small and falling revenue from subscriptions and newsagency sales, it relied on a greatly reduced grant from the Literature Board of the Australia Council ($14,000) and on annual grants of around $10,000 from a few corporations, most of which were mining companies with representatives on the board: Ray Evans from Western Mining; George Littlewood from CRA (later Rio Tinto); and Peter Chew, recently retired from Shell (which, incidentally no longer funded *Quadrant*). By far the most important financial support, I now discovered, came indirectly from Rupert Murdoch's News Limited, represented on the board by Richard Searby. A Greek-Australian-owned printery in Sydney owed News a considerable sum. One means of paying its debt off gradually was printing *Quadrant*. I never learned when this arrangement began. Robin Marsden warned me that if I valued my life, I should not criticise the printer's work.

When I took over the editorship, I thought we could not afford couriers. For quite some time, I drove from our home in the hills northeast of Melbourne to Glen Waverley, where our copy was typed onto disks by a young mother. I would later pick up the disks and deliver them to the sole secretary in our Fitzroy office, Ruth Rosenberg. I was rather rattled. This was the only time in my life when I was involved in a (happily minor) traffic accident. Apart from Ruth, I also received unpaid administrative assistance from a wonderfully generous woman, Chris Browning, a Roman Catholic married to a former ASIO officer, and before long editorial assistance from a curious young conservative, George Thomas, who had an interest in regional American poetry. His work was of such a high standard and his needs were so obvious that before long we found a way to pay him a modest salary. (Amazingly, as I write, George Thomas remains with *Quadrant* still.) For my own part I received an annual stipend of $20,000. I spent two days in Fitzroy editing *Quadrant* and three teaching at La Trobe's politics department. The great poet Les Murray accepted my invitation to become literary editor. Poems, stories and criticism arrived regularly at the Collingwood Post Office. I met Les only once or twice, and in those early years our relations were distant but amicable.

I outlined my ambitions for *Quadrant* in the March 1990 editorial, "The End of the Cold War and Us". In 1989 the world had experienced the astonishing collapse of all communist regimes in Eastern and Central Europe, the beginning of the disintegration of the Soviet Union, and the discrediting of communist China, most recently by the massacre in Tiananmen Square. I repeated what I had argued in the March 1989 editorial: that the end of the Cold War represented a vindication of *Quadrant*'s stubbornly anti-communist worldview, often deeply unpopular at least among the intelligentsia, and that one of our purposes in the post–Cold War world was to engage with the frequently shallow and intolerant new currents of thought on the left. But I now made explicit my conviction that we should do so not by engaging in the tit-for-tat of the culture wars but by demonstrating where there was shallowness and intolerance through what I called "the quality of our writing". In addition, I welcomed new debates on the right:

> During the course of the Cold War anti-Communists ... agreed to bury their differences in order to work together in a common cause. *Quadrant* represented one such community of

convenience. Now, however, the old anti-Communist coalition seems certain to fall apart. This is no bad thing. Conservatives and liberals; religious thinkers and agnostics; moral absolutists and relativists – belong to very different worlds of value and discourse. The pages of *Quadrant* would be a fine and civilised place for some of our differences to be debated.

What I meant by the quality of writing was illustrated by monthly instalments of short passages, sometimes journalism, from some of my favourite authors, whom we called "The Modern Moralists" – Fyodor Dostoyevsky on the soul's need for punishment after crime; Samuel Johnson on envy; Sigmund Freud on aggression; Aleksandr Solzhenitsyn on love in the Gulag; Karl Kraus on "Tourist Trips to Hell", day trips at the cut price of 117 Swiss francs to Verdun and other blood-drenched battlefields of the Great War, a dress rehearsal for the commercialisation of the Holocaust; Edmund Burke on Jean-Jacques Rousseau, "the philosopher of vanity ... who sends his children to the hospital of foundlings. The bear loves, licks, and forms her young: but bears are not philosophers"; Simone Weil on affliction; Hannah Arendt on the paradoxical, often deadly "politics of compassion" in her extended comparison of the French and American Revolutions; George Orwell on Malcolm Muggeridge's *The Thirties* and what Orwell called "the limits to pessimism", the unanticipated discovery of patriotism when one's country is under threat, which "even at its stupidest and most sentimental ... is a comelier thing than the shallow self-righteousness of the left-wing intelligentsia"; Michael Oakeshott on the limits of rationalism; G.K. Chesterton on the family.

Another way I tried to affirm the importance of quality writing in disputes over values was the monthly column that Raimond Gaita called "Turnings of Attention". In the column, nothing was predictable, nothing was banal. Gaita was fearless and sometimes disconcerting. In one column he called Martin Luther King's most famous speech, "I Have a Dream", "deeply corrupting". King had made the idea of justice hostage to confidence in its future success, "like a soldier whose courage is dependent on his assessments of the prospect of victory". I believe some readers sensed Gaita's originality, his depth and – the first and most important thing I had noticed about him – his purity of spirit.

Concerning trends in contemporary philosophy, Gaita could be scathing. The idea that Peter Singer et al. represented philosophy in the Socratic tradition was a travesty. "Philosophers now flirt with power and the attractions of an urbane worldliness to an extent which makes the emasculation of the subject little short of inevitable," he wrote.

> [P]hilosophers who have been to the forefront of the argument to relax the conditions under which it is permissible to kill people and who pioneered a new genre called "practical ethics" have not made academic philosophy less insular. Quite the contrary: they have extended the arrogance and insularity of the worst kind of academic professionalism beyond the academy ... nor do they show a sense of awe in the face of the questions they have raised ...

Even though he believed an article of Elizabeth Anscombe's (in 1958) had made it possible for philosophers once again to discuss the virtuous character, Gaita feared that, given the tenor of contemporary philosophy, this would soon be reduced to what would be called "the argument from the virtues" in the way that there was now talk in philosophy about "the 'argument from the sanctity of life' in those books which speculate when abortion and infanticide are permissible". In one column Gaita wrote about the loss we faced because there was no obvious secular concept that could replace "the sanctity of life", an idea that he insisted was not available to those without religion. "We may say that all human beings are precious, or that they are ends in themselves, or that they are owed unconditional respect, or that they possess certain inalienable rights. These are, in my judgment, ways of whistling in the dark."

In one column, Rai wrote about the bold talk and the cowardly behaviour of fellow academics: "'Speaking truth to power'. It has a heroic and self-congratulatory ring about it. It presupposes courage and a spirit of scrupulous truthfulness. How extraordinary, then, that anyone should speak in that way ... after the servile surrender of universities to state power in Australia and the United Kingdom." Gaita explained what he meant by this surrender in another column, "The Universities: Audits of Efficiency":

> University administrators comply readily to the demands of government, and they speak, as do governments, without comprehension of what they are destroying ... [G]overnments have acted according to their convenience and the universities have tried to roll with the punches, with an ever-diminishing sense of what they are defending. Now they propose things which even the most brutish ministers of education would have been embarrassed to say publicly only ten years ago.

There is no doubt that Gaita was a disconcerting presence to those who hoped that *Quadrant* would move seamlessly from the Cold War to the culture wars, where the right could continue to launch their standard attacks on the left. In Peter Coleman's words, "As soon as the Cold War ended, according to Irving Kristol, the real cold war began ... the war against American style liberalism." In "Beyond Left and Right", Gaita expressed the hope that many of us who had been involved in the intellectual battles of the Cold War would "once again talk to one another, acknowledging what they have in common and acknowledging, with a new sense of freedom, what they had previously felt compelled to deny ... Whether or not our freedom from embattlement to think new thoughts will be fruitful is unforeseen."

Rai was not a religious thinker but was attempting to establish the idea of good and evil as what he called "an absolute conception", without it being dependent on a belief in God. Because of the complexity of his prose, an inevitable consequence of the complexity of his thought, but even more because of his independence from the conventional camps of left and right – and also because it became obvious that I regarded what he was doing as a part of what I hoped to achieve as *Quadrant* editor – before too long there emerged from Perth a movement that called itself GROG, standing for "Get Rid of Gaita". To my mind, though, writing something of genuine interest, depth and originality in "Turnings of Attention", month after month, year after year, represented an extraordinary intellectual achievement.

Malcolm Muggeridge, a former editor of *Punch*, once remarked that magazines should be judged not so much by what they published but by what they did not. Not long after I became editor, David Stove submitted an anti-feminist essay called "The Intellectual Capacity of Women". Its argument was captured in its first line: "I believe that the intellectual capacity of women is on the whole inferior to that of men." The inferior intellectual capacity of women was explained by a kind of kindergarten evolutionism. The chief task of women was to give birth, and then to breastfeed and care for their babies. "[A] woman does not need to use her brains to have a baby, and doesn't even need to use them much in order to see the infant through the period of its most extreme helplessness." Hence the intellectual inferiority of women.

Anne was outraged by Stove's article, as was I. During the editorship of my chief predecessor at *Quadrant*, Peter Coleman, this essay would have been published. He wrote the preface to Stove's collection *Cricket versus Republicanism*, where the piece eventually appeared, and described Stove as "an essayist in the great tradition" and as a "hero not of our time", without expressing even one word of criticism of this essay or any others. In my letter of rejection to Stove, I wrote that there was one demanding role in history where women were called upon to perform the same duties as men. Elizabeth I and Catherine the Great were among the most admired monarchs of England and Russia. This was not the true explanation for my unwillingness to publish Stove's essay. No matter how plausibly it was argued, I would never have published an essay claiming that women were intellectually inferior to men.

What did I think worth publishing? It was important that *Quadrant* analysed the reasons for the end of the communist experiment in Europe, as we did with essays of Eugene Kamenka and

Knopfelmacher, and the nature of what was briefly called "the new world order" at the end of the Cold War. Our most important contributors on this topic were Owen Harries, the editor of *The National Interest* and Australia's most level-headed and penetrating analyst of international relations, and Coral Bell, whom I found delightful to deal with. It was clear that while communism had collapsed in Europe, in China the Communist Party had observed the mistakes of Gorbachev and shown, at Tiananmen Square, a willingness to keep a hold on power by brute force, the most traditional of means. This was analysed for *Quadrant* by Pierre Ryckmans, under the *nom de plume* Simon Leys. It was already clear that Ryckmans was the most perceptive of all Western China watchers.

By mid-1990 a curious argument had emerged from a group of senior Australian journalists – Paddy McGuinness, Murray Sayle, Phillip Knightley and Max Suich – that to describe the events at Tiananmen Square as a massacre was, in the words of McGuinness, "misleading nonsense". It was suggested that the death toll was not nearly 10,000, as the early estimates had it. In the editorial of June 1990, I pointed out that in the prelude to the 1905 Revolution in Russia – the infamous "Bloody Sunday" – the number of people killed by the tsarist army was thought to have been 1,000, the same number Amnesty International now believed to have been murdered at Tiananmen Square. "We belong to a generation that lives under the shadow of Auschwitz and the Gulag," I argued, "and which gazes indifferently every other night at the sight of terrible suffering on the television set. Our massacre standards are high. Our moral palates are jaded."

I was an enthusiastic supporter of the freedom of the European nations that had been suppressed under communism, in particular the Baltic States and Ukraine. I was particularly critical of the cautious way the American president, George H.W. Bush, greeted this springtime. Three weeks before the sudden collapse of the Soviet empire, Bush had visited Kiev. "His speech to the Ukrainian Supreme Soviet," I argued in September 1991, "delivered an unprovoked rebuke to the subject nationalities of the USSR in an accent even Mr Gorbachev would have feared to adopt.

"Americans," he warned, "will not support those who seek independence in order to replace a far-off tyranny with a local despotism; they will not aid those who promote a suicidal nationalism based upon ethnic hatred." It is a genuinely disgraceful fact that a mere three weeks before the Russian President [Boris Yeltsin] emerged as the liberator of the subject nationalities of the USSR, the American President had spoken in Kiev as their enemy. When news of the collapse of Communist Party rule throughout the USSR reached the ears of George Bush he was reported to have said that he found in these events "nothing adverse". The maligned Ronald Reagan would not have responded thus ... A great revolution has occurred. The future will bring many problems. But, for the present, celebrations are in order.

My instinct as editor was to encourage spirited argument within the *Quadrant* circle. We published an essay by Colin Jory on B.A. Santamaria's seventy-fifth birthday. "[T]here could surely be no more remarkable Australian alive; and certainly none who has exerted so beneficent an influence for so protracted a time," he wrote. The prominent Catholic intellectual, practising psychologist and still closeted gay man Ronald Conway responded. There was much to be praised about Santamaria – his role in "vanquishing" the communist threat and in exposing "the pure greed" of some "free-marketeers". However, "[e]ven those who like and admire him can lose patience with his stubbornly embalmed innocence of human variety and complexity". Conway wrote about his "years of professional frustration at hearing a distinguished Australian swallow medieval fustian about aspects of private morality and package it with all the skills of an accomplished modern ideologist".

The most pressing problem facing the nation in the early 1990s was the recession, with foreign debt of $150 billion, uncontrolled inflation and 1 million unemployed. For that reason, in a general magazine with an interest in politics, the issue could not be ignored.

In the first issue of 1991 we published a debate between John Carroll and Ray Evans on the oldest question of the Australian federation, protectionism versus free trade. In May 1991 we featured a forum on the future of the Australian economy, with substantial essays from C.D. Kemp, the founder of the IPA and an economic adviser to Menzies in the early post-war years; John Stone, the former Treasury secretary; Gregory Clark, an exile in Japan and son of the great Keynesian economist Colin Clark; Hugh Morgan; B.A. Santamaria; T.M. Fitzgerald, the left-liberal economic journalist and founder of the high-quality independent magazine *Nation*; Peter Costello, the economic rationalist Liberal Party parliamentarian and co-founder of the H.R. Nicholls Society (and future treasurer in the Howard government); Bob Catley, a former Marxist but now an ALP backbencher situated in the Keating-esque economic rationalist mainstream; and Terry McCrann, the economics journalist and associate editor of Rupert Murdoch's *Herald Sun*. The issue carrying the economic forum was the most successful, in sales and new subscriptions, since I had become the sole *Quadrant* editor.

In 1989 Paddy McGuinness had claimed that *Quadrant* had "missed the economic bus", for its failure to join in the nearly universal mainstream campaign of the 1980s in favour of free market reforms – deregulation, privatisation, industrial relations reform, the withdrawal of all forms of protection. In my editorial in May 1991 I accepted the criticism, in part. During the 1980s, *Quadrant* had not shown any sustained interest in the Australian economy. It was, however, inconceivable in my view that a magazine in which conservatives, liberals and social democrats had once "rubbed shoulders" would now simply join the economic rationalist chorus. Australia was entering a deep recession. "Especially, at such a time," I argued, "*Quadrant*'s role is not to propagate the certainties of any orthodoxy but rather to encourage what this country so manifestly lacks – intelligent and open-ended debate."

Throughout the 1980s the supporters of the free market had monopolised mainstream economic discussion to a degree that seemed to me scandalous. In addition, several important liberal and conservative voices, especially among the older generation – like W.C. Wentworth, B.A. Santamaria and C.D. Kemp – were, for different reasons, strongly opposed to the stranglehold over public discussion of the Australian economy. I thought it important that there was somewhere for such people to express the reasons for their disquiet and their dissidence. I realised that free marketeers were an important part of the *Quadrant* circle. Indeed, on the *Quadrant* board there were no representatives from manufacturing – where opposition to the Hawke government's tariff removal timetable was found – but three representatives of the mining interest, the most enthusiastically free-market sector of the economy. The more I read about aspects of what was still called in Australia "economic rationalism", and especially about its ideological self-certainty, the more sceptical I became. It seemed to me that my most useful contribution as editor was to encourage genuine debate. My even-handedness was so scrupulous that, following the publication of Michael Pusey's much-discussed *Economic Rationalism in Canberra*, I commissioned two reviews, one from a likely admirer, Hugh Emy, the professor of political science at Monash University, and the other from a certain disparager, John Stone, who began his review by joking that I had sent it to him as a punishment.

At the end of the Cold War, some of the earlier hostility to my anti-communism within fashionable intellectual circles fell away. In 1991, for the first time ever, I was invited to speak at the Melbourne Writers Festival, on a panel discussing literature and communism. At the end of my talk, which was published in *Quadrant*, I argued, almost as an afterthought:

> Today the *laissez-faire* Right alone possesses self-confidence and social vision. Adherents of the doctrine of *laissez-faire* are almost as devoted to Adam Smith as the Left once was to Karl Marx ... Some seem almost as immune to the consequences of market failure as the Left once was to the disasters of Communism. To put the point simply, the ideological vacuum created by the collapse of the Marxian socialist vision has been filled by a new historical and economic triumphalism on the Right. This seems to me, in general, an unhappy turn of events. The present atmosphere

is helping us to avert our gaze from the psychopathic elements of social life in Western societies ...

As a member of the editorial advisory board, Paddy Morgan – once more the defender of the James McAuley tradition – wrote a letter demanding that I be removed from the editorship of *Quadrant*. The comparison of the pro-communist left and the laissez-faire right was apparently another of my obscene false analogies. I immediately called for a telephone meeting of the editorial board. My editorship was supported by everyone – Martin Krygier, John Wheeldon, Tony McAdam and Greg Sheridan.

More serious opposition to my editorship came from two members of the committee of management, Heinz Arndt and Ray Evans. After I published an extract from F.R. Leavis's attack on C.P. Snow's once fashionable argument about the "two cultures" – the sciences and the humanities – Heinz Arndt smelt a rat. Leavis had argued: "Who will assert that the average member of a modern society is more fully human, or more alive, than a Bushman, an Indian peasant, or a member of one of those poignantly surviving primitive peoples, with their marvellous art and skills and vital intelligence?" This was too much for Arndt. In a letter-to-the-editor, he asked why I had resurrected Leavis. "I should be grateful. But it troubles me, Sir, that I am not sure about your motives for resurrecting Leavis's fulminations." And: "Is this, Sir, a new editorial policy aimed at better balance for and against economic liberalism?" Yes, Sir, it was.

In "Those Terrible Eighty Years", C.D. Kemp had taken apart the neo-liberals' caricature of Australia's economic performance since Federation, defended the role that tariff protection had played at various moments of Australia's economic development, and shown why Maynard Keynes, an "interventionist" bogeyman for the neo-liberals, could rightly be spoken of as the architect of Australia's post-war "golden age". In the period between 1945 and 1973, when Keynes' influence in Australia and indeed throughout the Western world was greatest, growth in Australia was impressive and both inflation and unemployment negligible. For Kemp, unemployment was a tragedy and the casino capitalism of Australia in the 1980s a disgrace. In one of his *Quadrant* articles, "A Patron Saint for Economists", he wrote of a story told by Keynes about the painting of a "down and out" worker that the great British economist, Alfred Marshall, hung in his room in college as a reminder of what was at stake at the end of his technical studies.

One day Ray Evans trudged from Western Mining's headquarters in the city to *Quadrant*'s office in Fitzroy. He asked me not to publish anything of C.D. Kemp's in the future. Why? Ray told me that David and Rod Kemp, both now Liberal Party parliamentarians and neo-liberal missionaries, found their father's articles politically embarrassing. I ignored him. On another occasion, in exasperation, Evans warned me aggressively: "We are paying you to do a job." "Paying" was a considerable exaggeration.

During the early months of 1992, hostility on the right to my editorship of *Quadrant* was obvious and growing. In April, *Quadrant* hosted a dinner to celebrate the retirement of the conservative *Age* columnist Michael Barnard. Both B.A. Santamaria and John Stone attended. I told the journalist Peter Ellingsen that our dinners were normally "very pleasant, interesting and intelligent affairs". This one was not. The level of tension was high and obvious (to everyone except Barnard). By this time, I strongly supported John Carroll's decision to edit a volume against economic rationalism. One of Text Publishing's directors, Di Gribble, convinced me that it would sell better if I was co-editor. The result was *Shutdown: The Failure of Economic Rationalism and How to Rescue Australia*. Because I recognised the difference between conducting a debate fairly and participating in it on one side and with conviction, in late June I resigned from the *Quadrant* editorship. The author's note accompanying my essay in *Shutdown* described me thus: "Robert Manne ... edited *Quadrant* from 1989 to 1992."

Peter Ellingsen outlined what now happened in a long article, "Rapture in the Right", published in *The Age* on July 22, 1992. Even though *Quadrant*'s circulation had increased from around 3,000 to nearly 5,000, and it had escaped from what Roger Sandall had called its "cultural ghetto" and was now widely regarded as the most important Australian conservative publication, there were members of the board who wanted me gone. Ray Evans did not comment to Ellingsen on what he called a confidential question for the board. George Littlewood told Ellingsen: "[P]olicies that closet and protect industry are not healthy ... new blood coming in as editor is a good thing." There were members of the board who didn't want me to leave: Martin Krygier and Tom Gregory certainly; probably David Armstrong; most surprisingly and most significantly, the chair, Leonie Kramer, who believed my odd views about the Australian economy could be explained by the differences between financial business in Sydney and manufacturing business in Melbourne.

A crisis meeting of the board took place in August in Sydney. I was asked to leave the room. The meeting lasted an unusually long time. I never discovered what exactly was said. When I was invited to return, I was told that the board had not accepted my resignation. Heinz Arndt on the spot and, shortly after, Ray Evans, left the board. George Littlewood, Peter Chew of Shell and Richard Searby remained. For my part, I resolved privately no longer to seek money from the miners.

[11.]

Quadrant 2: History Wars (1993–1995)

BOB SANTAMARIA WROTE SEVERAL ARTICLES for *Quadrant* while I was editor. While we were not personally close, our relations were always cordial. We held similar views about the former communist regimes in Europe and the present regimes in Asia. Although the Australian Communist Party no longer mattered, I admired the role his "Movement" had played in the struggle during the late 1940s and early 1950s against its influence in the Australian trade unions. I shared his view of the role of stable families, and like him was alarmed at the rapidity and trajectory of social change in an age of divorce and drugs. I also shared Santamaria's opposition to euthanasia, although for different reasons, but not to abortion, and I regarded his ultra-conservative version of Catholicism as none of my business.

On one occasion Santamaria invited me to address a weekend country gathering of the Movement. The program announced six lectures. I was amused when I discovered that I was to deliver one and Santamaria the other five. When a young woman questioned something he had said, I observed a flash of anger and a determination to maintain ideological discipline among his troops. To my surprise, Santamaria also invited me to deliver one of the talks at a meeting in Melbourne in May 1991 on the fiftieth anniversary of the Movement. I described Santamaria as "one of the great post-war Australians". He was not only an almost unequalled political strategist, courageous, shrewd and consistent, but also – and this was less well known – in all dealings with political allies, courteous, charming and even, strangely enough, "modest" and "diffident". When he and Frank Knopfelmacher fell out in the 1980s, over the ego wounds inflicted by Santamaria in his autobiography, *Against the Tide* – his romanticisation of James McAuley and failure even to mention Knopfelmacher – I was an interested but detached observer. Following their reconciliation in the 1990s, at a time I no longer was able to talk to Knopfelmacher, who believed I had become an agent of Mossad, I was immensely impressed by the solace Santamaria offered during his final, dark, lonely years. Following Knopfelmacher's death, Santamaria wrote a fine and honest obituary for *Quadrant*.

By the early 1990s, at the time of deep recession, Santamaria and I had come by separate paths to oppose the dominance of the free-market philosophy. Sometime in 1992 he invited John Carroll and me to a discussion about the formation of a new political party – inspired by him, supported by whatever remained of the Movement and led by Malcolm Fraser. I have almost no memory of these discussions, which are summarised by Paddy Morgan in Santamaria's edited correspondence, *B.A. Santamaria: Running the Show*, which also includes a long fax Santamaria sent to me in September 1992. All I recall is that Santamaria was interested in the phenomenon of the "Reagan Democrats", the new conservatism of the white working classes. He argued that the economic discontent of the losers in the age of neo-liberalism could be redirected from the party the Australian working class had traditionally supported (Labor, now under Paul Keating) and from the party that was presently ignoring their needs (the Liberals, now under John Hewson) to a socially conservative party with a protectionist and interventionist program centred on their real economic interests. My only memory of all this is a remark I made during our discussions. There was one big difference between Ronald Reagan and us, I said. Reagan controlled one of America's traditional political parties, while we controlled absolutely nothing.

Not surprisingly, Santamaria's hopes for a new political party – which he apparently referred to as "the Malcolm Fraser Group" – soon faded. His political instinct nonetheless was right. Within five years there was a new Australian party supported by a section of the white working classes. Its name was One Nation and its leader was not Malcolm Fraser but Pauline Hanson. In this new party, economic protectionism was conjoined with racism, something Santamaria always opposed and I always feared and loathed.

Shutdown was published in September 1992 and launched by both Malcolm Fraser and Bill Kelty; I recall Kelty and Terry McCrann falling into heated private argument. *Shutdown* was a publishing success. It sold well; two extracts and two comments appeared over four days in *The Age*; discussions took place over two nights on the Victorian edition of *The 7.30 Report*.

One *Shutdown* reader, several months after publication, was Kerry Packer. One-third of the way through the book, perhaps on a whim, Packer decided that what Australia needed was a new protectionist and interventionist political party led by John Carroll and me. He invited – or, perhaps more accurately, summoned – us to a meeting that took place one evening in the deserted restaurant of an imposing East Melbourne hotel owned by Lloyd Williams (best known today for his Melbourne Cup–winning racehorses). Packer was accompanied by his young son, James. The purpose of the meeting soon became clear. Packer had recently lost a business opportunity to a Canadian competitor who had been strongly supported by the Canadian government. Packer had not been supported by his.

Before we got down to business, we ordered meals. Packer asked for something or other and a helping of green peas. The waiter told him that, unhappily, there were no green peas in the kitchen. Packer was appalled. A white-faced Lloyd Williams apologised cravenly. Instructions were issued for a green pea search to be conducted in the kitchens of other nearby hotels. Between these two mega-wealthy individuals, it was clear where the power lay. As the discussion progressed, it also became clear that neither John nor I was willing to leave our university role to lead a Packer-financed anti-economic-rationalist party. James Packer uttered not one word.

The meeting turned out well for me, however. I was at this time trying to expand *Quadrant*'s subscriber base and free the journal from mining money. Perhaps unwilling to have wasted a trip to Melbourne, Packer decided to donate $50,000. Details concerning the gift were handled by a garrulous, cynical, high-spirited and thoroughly entertaining Packer retainer named Peter Barron, one of the most colourful characters I have ever met. Before working for Packer, Barron was a member of Keating's political base, the ALP's notorious New South Wales Right. Through his connection with Packer and Channel 9, Barron claimed credit for the victory of the Labor Party's "true believers" in 1993. I was pleased to be able to report the $50,000 Packer donation to the *Quadrant* board. This was five times Western Mining's no-longer-pursued annual grant. My only contribution to Packer's anti-economic-rationalist campaign was an article for the "Wrong Way: Go Back" issue of his glossy and shortly defunct *Australian Business Monthly*, edited, oddly, by the yachting commentator Bruce Stannard. Kerry Packer exerted no pressure on *Quadrant*. Indeed, I sometimes wondered whether he recalled the gift.

In the first half of 1993 I wrote several columns for *The Age*, edited at the time by Michael Gawenda, the journalist who, four years earlier, had speculated at length in *The Australian Jewish News* on the question of whether I was a racist before deciding that probably I was not. We now became friends. By this time, almost singlehandedly, Paul Keating had placed the issue of the republic on the Australian political agenda. On May 4, I wrote a column with the headline: "Why I Am Not a Republican". One of Keating's most influential allies was Paul Kelly, editor-at-large at *The Australian*. For Anzac Day, 1993, *The Australian* published, over the first two pages of its "Weekend Review", a powerful left-wing case for the republic, David Day's "Elusive Nation: Our Search for Identity". Day argued that "the maturing of Australia's national consciousness is reaching its final flowering in the coming republic, with the swelling republican chorus drowning out the death rattle of the remaining monarchists". The following weekend *The Australian* published an even longer article by the head of the Australian Republican Movement, Thomas Keneally. In mounting his case for the Australian Republic and in explaining his own republicanism, Keneally vividly recalled one dimension of Australia's recent past: the bitterness of the Protestant–Catholic sectarian divide and the depth of many Irish Australians' loathing of the British monarchy. He cited the example of his grandfather, "Old Mick", who had refused to stand up in the cinema when the national anthem, "God Save the King", was played.

In my column, I argued that political movements like the one now working towards the republic "were not shaped by the mass of people but by relatively small groups who care passionately". Perhaps with the recent contributions of Day and Keneally in mind, I argued that two groups who cared passionately about the republic were the left and the "self-consciously Irish" Australians. The third group were members of "the ethnic intelligentsia", who had memories of anti-monarchical or anti-colonial struggles in their homelands.

My discussion of the reasons why some Irish Australians were prominent members of the republican movement was not unsympathetic:

> Their folk memory is suffused with stories of harsh British rule in Ireland – of Cromwell and the famine and the Easter Rising of 1916 – and of the sectarian struggles and the Protestant ascendancy in Australia ... For the first time in our history the Australian elite is generously (and rightly) peopled by descendants of the Irish. In part at least, republicanism is their revenge.

I felt that I understood the politics of Irish Australians. Several of my teachers and then friends from university days were Vincent Buckley, "Dinny" O'Hearn and members of the ALP Club, Michael Crennan and Terry Tobin. Some identified passionately – even frighteningly, in the case of Vin – with the struggles of the Irish Catholics against the Unionists in Northern Ireland. Buckley and O'Hearn were both anti-monarchists on anti-British grounds.

Following the publication of this column, two republicans, the Irish Australian Susan Ryan and Malcolm Turnbull, who of course belonged to none of my three ideal types, argued against me very forcefully but civilly and rationally. Tom Keneally went berserk. In an ABC Radio interview with Terry Lane and in a lecture broadcast directly afterwards, Keneally claimed that I had argued that "there was some fatal mechanism in our [Irish Australians'] brains which stopped us from being mainstream Australians"; that I believed that Irish Australians were "unfit to participate in the general Australian debate"; that I had claimed that the Irish Australian involvement in the republican debate was akin to a "Fenian plot"; that I was a "white supremacist" who had tried to revive "the ugly bone of sectarianism"; and that I was thus a far more "dangerous" person than others who had argued against the republicans, such as the Liberal Party politician Bronwyn Bishop and the RSL president Bruce Ruxton. My views had been "said about particular racial groups by people far more sinister than the editor of *Quadrant*, but that is racism".

For the first time in my life, I took to the law. In the letter sent by Tanya Cirkovic & Associates, mostly written by me, we argued that all Keneally's claims were entirely false and some grossly defamatory. I was Jewish. I had lobbied for the entry of refugees from Indochina following the Vietnam War. There were hundreds of my students at La Trobe University who could provide evidence that there was not a white supremacist or racist bone in my body. In answer to Keneally, I would like to have added, in mirth but in truth, "Some of my best friends are Irish Australians." We did not now demand damages but would in the future if he did not desist.

In his attacks, Keneally had frequently referred to me as "the *Quadrant* editor". This was possibly revealing. The September 1977 issue of *Quadrant* had demonstrated that Keneally's wartime novel set in Yugoslavia, *Season in Purgatory*, had plagiarised extensively from *Island of Terrible Friends*, the novel of a fellow Australian, Bill Strutton. (Readers who doubt this can easily check; *Quadrant* has been fully digitised.) The lawyer's letter worked. Indeed, some years later Tom Keneally invited me to join with him in the leadership of a progressive political campaign. I declined.

I was at this time a genuine conservative but of a somewhat peculiar kind. I read with intensity *Reflections on the Revolution in France* and other works of Edmund Burke, the founding father of contemporary European conservatism – who alas was a close friend of Adam

Smith, the author of *The Wealth of Nations* whom almost every contemporary neo-liberal claimed was the founding father of the system of ideas to which I was opposed. I had read the major novels of Fyodor Dostoyevsky and had come to regard his most overtly political novel, *The Possessed*, as astonishingly prescient about the character type that would come to lead both Bolshevism and Nazism. I now read for the first time his journalism, collected in *A Writer's Diary*, where I discovered that possibly the greatest of all novelists was a jingoistic Russian nationalist, an Islamophobe and an anti-Semite. The world of ideas was not a simple place.

I was invited to respond to the "Toast to Australia" proposed by Bronwyn Bishop for the Victorian branch of the Australia Day Council on January 26, 1993. I did so by expressing my gratitude to the country that had offered refuge to my parents, whose own parents had been consumed in the monstrous furnace we now called the Holocaust. I told those at the meeting that, as a young Jewish child of refugee parents, I could "remember no single instance – not one – where the oddity of my background led to any social unpleasantness, let alone any act of discrimination". The audience almost purred in pleasure. I suggested there were three features that helped explain my attachment to Australia. The first was Australia's British heritage – once again the audience purred. I continued:

> Language (in some ways the deepest inheritance of all); literature; the understanding of the rule of law; a tenacious notion of private property; distrust of the tyrannical state; belief in, and experience of, parliamentary government; political parties; trade unions and social clubs; a passion for sports and hobbies; social tolerance and suspicion of fanaticism; a slight feeling of superiority to foreigners; a certain Protestant sectarianism and Irish Catholic anti-establishmentarianism; a self-deprecating humour; an expectation of ample meals; little interest in cuisine. Need I go on?

The second feature was not an inheritance but a repudiation of the British system of class. Australia had been settled by waves of lower-class migrants from the United Kingdom and Ireland. They created a society of what the historian John Hirst would call the "egalitarianism of manners", where snobbery and class difference was softened. They also created a distinctive polity – what the journalist Paul Kelly had recently called "the Australian Settlement" – offering "full employment, all-round protectionism, minimum wages and the impartial judicial arbitration of industrial disputes", where, at least until recently, I argued, Australia was able to avoid "the extremes of wealth and poverty" of Britain, the United States and Europe.

The third feature Australia offered was what I called "space" What had been fashioned here was:

> ... a kind of common man's paradise where peasants or rural labourers could become farmers and where city workers could aspire to generous-sized houses set on substantial suburban blocks with room to raise poultry or run a dog or cultivate a garden ... the capacity to play, tinker and potter; to raise a family in comfortable surrounds.

My conservatism of this time was instinctive and untheorised. It reflected the impress of Edmund Burke and Fyodor Dostoyevsky when I was thinking of Europe in what Eric Hobsbawm called "the age of catastrophe", and of George Orwell, especially his great wartime patriotic essay "The Lion and the Unicorn", when I was thinking about Australia. I could not yet see the centrality of two things that, as Orwell would have put it, were in front of my nose. My reply to Bronwyn Bishop's toast made no mention of the White Australia policy, the rigorously policed exclusion until the late 1960s of Asians and other peoples of colour. Even more, it made no mention of the most basic fact of the British settlement in Australia: the systematic and often brutal dispossession of Indigenous peoples.

*

On May 8, 1991, Peter Ryan, the former director of Melbourne University Press, lunched with members of the Seminar on the

Sociology of Culture at La Trobe. Peter mentioned that he intended to write an essay on his old friend Manning Clark, whose six-volume history of Australia was MUP's most successful and lucrative work. It would not be kind to Manning and was certain to anger the Australian intelligentsia, he said, but it had to be written. Peter asked whether *Quadrant* might be interested. I said that I was.

Two weeks later, unexpectedly, Manning Clark died. I heard no more about Peter Ryan's essay until he sent it to me in early August 1993. I published it in our September issue, which carried a characteristically brilliant caricature of Clark on the cover by my close friend John Spooner, cartoonist at *The Age*. Spooner received his advance copy of *Quadrant* in late August. He showed it to Michael Gawenda, who realised, as I had not, the unusual degree of interest it was certain to excite. (As knockdown evidence of my misjudgement and naivety, I had not asked our Greek printery in Sydney for additional copies that month.) Gawenda put an article on the front page of *The Age* about how Australia's best-known academic publisher had subjected Australia's best-known historian – his friend and his publishing house's most successful author – to withering critique.

Peter Ryan's essay on Manning Clark provoked a wild fortnight-long newspaper and radio controversy, involving even the prime minister. It occasioned, in whole or in part, two books: the bitchy *Suspect History* (1997) by Humphrey McQueen, a Maoist, and an academic monograph called *History Wars* (2021) by the New Zealand historian Doug Munro, which was impressively scholarly but, at least in my view, imperceptive regarding Ryan's motivation and character.

Peter Ryan's essay dismissed Manning Clark's *A History of Australia*, whose six volumes he claimed to have read three times in full. As one volume followed another, Manning's history of Australia had descended further and further into self-parody, achieving "the insubstantiality of thistledown". It was written in highfalutin, mock-Biblical language – "trying to tell Australian history in the style of an Old Testament prophet or of the chorus of a Greek tragedy". Ever since the first volume, Manning had been famously accused of writing a "History Without Facts". Over time, according to Ryan, things on that front got worse. The emblematic instance here was the claim, noticed by a Melbourne University Press storeman, that the most famous racehorse in Australian history, Phar Lap, had won the Melbourne Cup not once but twice. When asked to explain why he didn't read Clark, his colleague Professor John La Nauze, who exemplified what Clark called the "dry-as-dust" historian, explained that he hadn't time to read fiction.

According to Ryan, Clark vastly exaggerated the possibility of revolutionary violence in Australian history, where, in one of his favourite hyperboles, "blood will stain the wattle". If there was blood on the wattle, it was not the result of class warfare but of the dispossession of the Indigenous peoples of Australia, a subject Clark for the most part ignored. Ryan argued that Clark's history had begun with a "weighty and even noble vision", where three intellectual currents of late-eighteenth-century European thought – Catholicism, Protestantism and the rationalism of the Enlightenment – contended. By the end, as John Hirst had pointed out in a recent *Quadrant*, it descended into a standard left-versus-right Punch and Judy Show, where Manning "barracked" for the "Young Tree Green" of Australian radical nationalism and jeered at the "Old Dead Tree" of Austral/British Empire sycophancy.

Nothing in Peter Ryan's critique was especially original. What was unusual was that the criticisms came from Manning Clark's friend and publisher, and that they were interlaced by knockabout anecdotes of their friendship – their drunken escapades together, including a time, before Clark became a "faintly tedious teetotaller", when he had emptied an entire bottle of sherry over Ryan's head; Clark's regular Monday-morning self-pity sessions that Ryan had to soothe; his petty meanness with money when, at the end of an evening, there was a bill to pay, like the substantial fare for the taxi bringing a drunken Clark from Carlton to rural Croydon; his cunning way of disarming criticism in advance by attention and flattering correspondence; his outbursts of envy of academic colleagues in the elite Research School and not the General Studies section of the Australian National University, where he was employed; and, perhaps most importantly of all, his self-conscious creation of himself as an Australian Character, with broad-brimmed hat, waistcoat, pocket watch and walking stick.

Ryan was aware that, with these anecdotes, he was open to criticism. "Such disclosures of a man's indiscretions would be outrageous if made about a private citizen," he noted. "But the drive of Manning's life was to be a *public* citizen." More importantly, he claimed that "no attempt to evaluate this *History* can succeed without some comprehension of its remarkable author". The quality of character that undermined his history was what Ryan called "the deadly sin of pride" and what, in writing in his defence, I called "vanity", a word Peter thought captured what he was driving at even more precisely.

Ryan was attacked by a formidable battalion: Prime Minister Keating; the art critic Robert Hughes, from New York (before he read the essay!); Stuart Macintyre, the Ernest Scott professor of history at the University of Melbourne; Don Watson, one of the authors of *Manning Clark's History of Australia – The Musical*, which Ryan had mercilessly lampooned; and literally dozens more literary and historical luminaries. There were several standard lines of criticism, all documented at length by Doug Munro in *History Wars*. Ryan was a coward, having waited until his friend's death before unloading on him. Ryan was cruel, indifferent to the pain he was willing to inflict on Clark's family, and especially his loyal (and long-suffering) wife, Dymphna. Ryan was a traitor, having turned upon a man whom he had treated in life as an intimate friend, and a hypocrite, having never criticised to his face a historian he had published and praised for three decades but clearly secretly despised. He was supposedly driven by envy, having written one good book in his early twenties on his experiences in New Guinea, *Fear Drive My Feet*, and then nothing more of any worth. Don Watson called him "a cannibal", having grown fat on a salary from a publishing house enriched by the sales of an author whose body of work he had begun to devour. And, finally, Ryan had lost touch with the world of academia, having vastly exaggerated both Clark's influence on the work of the contemporary "dry-as-dust" historians of Australia and his place on the undergraduate curricula they set. He had significantly overestimated Clark's reputation among the historians of Australia and underestimated the number of hostile, if civil, reviews of his work that had been published by Australian historians during the past thirty years.

On several occasions, I defended Peter Ryan as honestly as I was able. He was not a coward who had waited until Manning Clark died before publishing his essay but one of the bravest men I knew. Few academics would risk the opprobrium, the scorn and even the hatred that he knew he was bound to face in publishing this essay. For calling him a coward, Ryan challenged Stuart Macintyre to a fistfight. And he meant it. Cowardice is also one of the chief lines of interpretation favoured by Doug Munro, despite the fact that Peter Ryan knowingly risked the rage of the larger part of the Australian intelligentsia. As to his supposed cruelty: was it not ridiculous, more than two years after Manning Clark's death, to require the maintenance of a moratorium on critique of his work? Was Clark criticised for the pain he caused the family of Sir Robert Menzies when he described him as amounting to "nothing"?

I was also very sharply criticised for publishing Peter Ryan's essay. Stuart Macintyre argued that I was "duplicitous" when I argued that I hoped the Ryan essay would force Australian historians into an open and public defence of Manning Clark's *History* – one that went beyond the standard vague comparisons to the great nineteenth-century literary histories, like Edward Gibbon's *Decline and Fall of the Roman Empire* and Thomas Carlyle's *French Revolution*. Peter Craven argued that I had timed the publication of the Ryan essay to coincide with the publication of Michael Cathcart's condensation of the six volumes, with my "unrivalled ... skill at making rapid interventions in the media". (When I'd decided to publish Ryan's essay, I'd had no idea that the Cathcart abridgement existed, let alone that its publication was imminent.) More generally, I was accused of "hunting" for Manning Clark. In the first five years of editing *Quadrant*, I had published a brief article by a former student of Clark's, John Barrett, and relatively short passages on Clark in an essay on Australian history by John Hirst and in the Australian Association of Cultural Freedom's annual Latham Lecture by Geoffrey Blainey – all of which, incidentally, had been greeted with silence from the Australian history professoriate. In his defence of Manning Clark in *Suspect History*, Humphrey McQueen's weapon of choice was attempted character assassination via ridicule. Because I once wrote, assuming the existence of a sophisticated audience, of Dostoyevsky's capacity to take us to the heart of darkness, McQueen claimed that I was not familiar with Dostoyevsky, my favourite novelist, or with Joseph Conrad's *Heart of Darkness*, the subject of a class I had taught for several years.

In truth, I never considered not publishing Peter Ryan's Manning Clark essay. Before turning to Manning, he had written superb pieces for *Quadrant* on the poet A.D. Hope and the politician and historian Sir Paul Hasluck, both friends. As in his Manning Clark essay, he had interlaced anecdote with critique. These effectively refuted the claim that his Clark essay was driven by envy, as many argued. Alec Hope and Paul Hasluck were more considerable writers and more famous persons than Peter Ryan, and yet he expressed for them nothing but an unambivalent, perceptive, even perhaps exaggerated praise.

Although I was not a Manning Clark expert, I also happened to agree with Ryan's judgement. As I was preparing to teach a course on twentieth-century Australian political culture (with John Hirst), I had recently read volume six of Clark's history very carefully and with growing incredulity. How could someone regarded as Australia's greatest historian write something so childish? I was not influenced by the fact that Clark was a man of the left. One of the historians I most admired was Eric Hobsbawm, a former communist and a Marxist still. I read Clark's sixth volume around the time I was struggling my way through the appallingly translated but masterly five-volume history of Russia by Vasily Klyuchevsky, one of the greatest works of history I have ever read. Klyuchevsky was trying with every fibre of his being to understand the political, social and economic history of his country. The comparison with Manning Clark was painful.

Because there was so little candour among Australian historians about the quality of the later volumes of Clark's history, I did not know that even his defenders, including Humphrey McQueen and Stuart Macintyre, recognised the hopelessness of volume six. If Patrick White's publisher had submitted a similarly dismissive essay, no matter how interesting, I know that I would have rejected it. I did not feel certain about Peter Ryan's motivation. Over coffee with the publisher at Text, Michael Heyward, I speculated that Ryan might not have forgiven Clark for his lofty lack of interest in Ryan's terrifying wartime experience in Papua New Guinea. An acquaintance of Ryan's overheard and reported this back to him. He was angry.

There was a touch of ambivalence in Ryan's essay that got lost in the trench warfare following publication. Manning Clark, he told us, "could teach as naturally as a thrush could sing". He had made Australian history truly interesting. Even more intriguingly, towards the conclusion of the essay, Ryan made a comment I found difficult to interpret then and find difficult still: "Never to have known him would, in retrospect, have been an unthinkable deprivation." By the time he wrote this, Ryan had turned himself from a post-war socialist into a conservative curmudgeon. He was, however, a man of vivid imagination throughout. Did he see in his friend a life lived to the full without repudiating temptation or suppressing the flaws and contradictions in his nature, the kind of life Peter Ryan himself might have lived but had steadfastly turned his back upon? In the controversy that followed the publication of the essay, the only contribution that sensed the tension in Ryan came from a letter-to-the-editor sent to *Quadrant* by Helen Garner:

> I do feel I can remark on Mr Ryan's tone. It provokes in me (and no doubt in many others) the painful, almost shameful embarrassment that always accompanies the public spectacle of a person helpless in the grip of his own unconscious – someone who is dumping his shadow on someone else. Perhaps if Mr Ryan were prepared, even a little, to address the source of this rage in himself he might be able to present his criticisms in a form which would invite a decent response.

*

As it happens, shortly after the Peter Ryan/Manning Clark affair, Helen Garner found herself in an even larger and more bitter politico-cultural controversy swirling around *The First Stone*, the extraordinarily successful book she wrote on an incident in the life of Ormond College at the University of Melbourne.

On October 16, 1991, the college had held a rather riotous end-of-year Valedictory Dinner. The Master, Dr Alan Gregory, was accused of having twice squeezed the breast of one student on the dance floor and, later in the evening, of speaking lasciviously and fondling a second female student in his office. Garner represented an older generation of 1970s feminists, women who had been profoundly affected by the idea of sexual liberation. At the centre of her book was dismay with the way the students responded: making a formal complaint to the college; when that failed, going to the police and taking Gregory to court; and when that failed, taking the case to the Equal Opportunities Commission. This succeeded. The commission required that the college issue an apology, effectively forcing Gregory to resign.

Garner was even more critical of the behaviour of some of the students' allies. During the long struggle between the Master and the students, a leaflet circulated: "If attacked by Gregory, please – do not panic – call the police. There is no guarantee his next crime will not be rape or battery." The two students were supported, or perhaps led, by one of the tutors at the College, Dr Jenna Mead, who named herself by writing a long article on the affair for the magazine *RePublica*. By dividing Mead into six or so different people (to minimise legal risk) Garner unintentionally exaggerated the conspiratorial nature of the affair.

I believed that what had interested Garner in the Ormond College Affair was a rather simple question, phrased in such a way that it answered itself. Was what Garner called "a nerdish pass" sufficient ground for a career and a life to be destroyed? *The First Stone* was written before the #MeToo movement that opened all our eyes, including mine, to the ubiquitousness of male sexual misbehaviour.

Feminism was one of the main fields of battle in the culture wars in Australia that had succeeded the Cold War. Over *The First Stone*, the literary world in Australia divided neatly on a left–right axis. The left supported Jenna Mead. The right supported Helen Garner. The editorial I wrote was equivocal. In an age of new-found sexual freedom, if Alan Gregory "merely" did what the students allege, he had indeed been punished disproportionately. According, however, to an older understanding, if the Master of the college, "charged as he was with the duty of care over a new generation of undergraduates", did "as much" as was alleged, then it amounted to considerably more than a "nerdish pass". We lived in an age "of sexual transition, where unprecedented freedom and disabling uncertainty about codes of behaviour co-exist uneasily". That was why I thought the controversy following the publication of *The First Stone* interested so many of us so deeply.

The dean of social sciences at La Trobe, Graeme Duncan, a first-rate political theorist, author of *Marx and Mill*, offered to review *The First Stone* for *Quadrant*. His review, which appeared in the same issue as my editorial, was decidedly pro-Mead and anti-Garner. It was clear that he had relied on Jenna Mead for several claims. On August 29, 1995, Alan Gregory sent me a not-for-publication letter complaining about both Duncan's review and my editorial. "I was dismayed to find coverage of the so-called 'Ormond Affair' in your May edition, and some serious errors pertaining to myself," he said. It was untrue that, shortly after the Valedictory Dinner, there were, as Duncan had claimed, five student complaints about the Master's behaviour. It was untrue that the two students sought a swift and confidential settlement. Male–female relations at Ormond College were not at "a low ebb".

And so on. Gregory asked for a retraction of certain claims and an apology. I asked Duncan about these matters. In these cases, he told me, his only source was Jenna Mead. This seemed a curious way to write a review, I thought. I wrote to Dr Gregory on October 12, answering his complaints as best I was able. In essence, I argued that where a matter of fact was in dispute between himself and Mead, I was in no position to know who was telling the truth. I offered him space in *Quadrant*.

Gregory answered five days later. To my offer, he replied:

> I am not a good writer of this type of thing. Mead has shown she is – and her capacity to suggest and make innuendo is brilliant if evil ... Given the detail necessary my style would sound the death knell ... [T]he whole affair has been extremely damaging and harmful both to myself and my family. I am virtually unemployable ... My disappointment was not only in errors made, and some serious ones, but that a journal, the philosophical position of which I respect, has been infiltrated by Mead. Although I have never seen Mead laugh I can quite imagine her chuckling at her triumph.

I think Gregory underestimated his own literary talent.

Gregory enclosed an unprintable letter-to-the-editor sent to *The Australian* by Peter Tregear, the student who was the "next door neighbour" of Jenna Mead at Ormond College between 1990 and 1992. Tregear outlined the origin of the conflict between Gregory and Mead – it was an article for an Ormond College magazine Mead had deemed racist and sought to censor in such an unbalanced way that Gregory threatened to sack her. He pointed out that Jenna Mead was the person discussed in *The First Stone* who had danced topless at the Valedictory Dinner; and that she had held a victory party in her room when a court found against Gregory (before the judgement was overturned on appeal). Throughout the affair, according to Tregear, Jenna Mead's conduct had been "unconscionable".

In 1997 Jenna Mead published the anti-Garner volume she had edited called *bodyjamming*. In the introduction, she referred to a 1995 debate involving herself and me that had been suggested by Graeme Duncan at La Trobe and organised by the student-run Politics Society. According to Mead, the students in the audience came well-prepared. There was a curious look on their faces Mead did not understand:

> Robert Manne turned on me and accused me of the feminist conspiracy ... Judith Brett ... also a member of the Politics Department, confirmed this line of interrogation by asserting without a single

shred of evidence so far as I can tell, that the Master of Ormond "had been denied natural justice." I then understood the looks on the audience's faces. These people had come to see me nailed.

Mead's account bore no relation to the meeting I remembered. I recalled that the Politics Society had made a tape-recording. In an *Age* and *Sydney Morning Herald* opinion piece, having listened carefully to the tape, I wrote:

> [Dr Graeme Duncan] and the two other speakers were, on balance, far more sympathetic to Mead than to me ... At no stage of the meeting did I accuse Jenna Mead of leading a feminist conspiracy. At no stage did Judith Brett argue that Alan Gregory had been denied natural justice. Her intervention concerned an unrelated question, the intrusion of law into private life. There was not the slightest feeling that anyone had come to see Jenna Mead nailed ...

In both "content and spirit", I continued, the tape of the meeting "reveals an utterly different meeting from the one Jenna Mead, no doubt sincerely, remembers having attended ... Mead was a central player in the Gregory affair ... [Her] interpretation of what occurred during our one and only encounter strikes me at least as unintentionally illuminating."

A quarter of a century later, Helen Garner told me how much that piece had meant to her.

*

Nationwide literary controversies are rare in Australia. In 1995 there were two – over Helen Garner's *The First Stone* and Helen Demidenko's *The Hand that Signed the Paper*. Unsurprisingly, within the literary world 1995 became known as the year of the "two Helens". While I was principally an observer in the former, in the Demidenko case I became a central player.

Helen Demidenko was a twenty-four-year-old University of Queensland student who told the world that she was the daughter of a working-class Ukrainian father and Irish Catholic mother. In 1992 Demidenko won *The Australian*/Vogel Literary Award for a first novel written by a young writer with her manuscript on the Holocaust in Ukraine. From a poem of Dylan Thomas, she called her book *The Hand that Signed the Paper*. Winners of the Vogel were guaranteed publication by one of Australia's foremost publishers, Allen & Unwin. *The Hand* was duly published in 1994.

Virtually every review was favourable, including one by *The Sydney Morning Herald*'s chief fiction critic, Andrew Riemer, a secular Jew who, along with his family, had narrowly escaped the last terrible chapter of the Holocaust, the round-up of the Jews of Budapest for transport to Auschwitz-Birkenau. Almost every reviewer was impressed by the novel's lack of affect, even its coldness. Demidenko was interviewed enthusiastically by Vic Alhadeff for *The Australian Jewish News*, who, as he later admitted shamefacedly, had not yet read *The Hand*.

In 1995 Helen Demidenko won the most prestigious fiction prize in Australia, the Miles Franklin Award. Two of the judges were connected to *Quadrant*: Dame Leonie Kramer, who was of course the chair of the *Quadrant* board, and Jill Kitson, a good friend of mine, several of whose ABC interviews with writers I had published in *Quadrant*. Jill had also been one of the Vogel judges and was the most important Helen Demidenko champion. On its back cover, she described *The Hand* as "[a] seriously truthful account of terrible wartime deeds that is also an imaginative work of extraordinary redemptive power". Soon after the Miles Franklin, Demidenko received the Gold Medal from the Australian Literature Society. She was by now a literary celebrity and also, with her long blonde hair, her embroidered peasant costumes and her exuberant folk dancing, a pantomime Ukrainian. Especially impressive was her apparent bravery. Demidenko hinted, vaguely but unmistakably, that her novel was based upon dark secrets of her family.

In June 1995, in *The Age*, Pamela Bone, the journalist who four years earlier had wondered whether I was partly responsible for the rise of racism in Australia, argued that *The Hand* excused without possible justification those Ukrainians who were involved in the murder of the Jews and suggested that it was an anti-Semitic novel about the Holocaust. "[T]here is no other side to the Holocaust ... I think I know where the author is coming from, and I do not much like it."

It was only after reading this article that I became interested in *The Hand*. Both the Stalin-engineered Ukrainian famine of the early 1930s and the Holocaust were close to the centre of my fields of interest, and to my heart. I read and then re-read *The Hand*. I could scarcely believe what I found. The central character was a young Queenslander, Fiona Kovalenko, a typical soft-left university student except for two family complications. Her father, Evenhy, was involved in the Babii Yar massacre, where, above a ravine on the outskirts of Kiev, 33,000 Jews were shot in three days. Her uncle, Vitaly, worked as a guard in the Warsaw ghetto, where he bayoneted a baby as an act of mercy, and then in the extermination camp at Treblinka, in Poland, where 800,000 Jews were gassed in three or so years. Neither are greatly fussed about their involvement in perhaps the most terrible crime in the history of humankind. Fiona's father keeps photos of piles of corpses from Babii Yar in his bedside table; her uncle still wears gold-rimmed spectacles taken from one of the Jews murdered at Treblinka. There is in the novel no remorse, or even awareness of the meaning of its absence.

In my reading, however, things were worse than this. *The Hand* is a *roman à thèse*. Its thesis is based on the idea of an ethnic cycle of revenge. The Jewish Bolsheviks persecuted the Ukrainians in the famine, whom they looked down upon as no more than animals. When a Ukrainian peasant begs a Jewish doctor, Dr Judit – i.e. Dr Jewess – to help save her baby, Judit tells the mother, "I am a physician not a veterinarian." Because of the arrogant, contemptuous and murderous behaviour of the Jewish Bolsheviks, when the Nazis arrive in Ukraine, the native peasants, like the Kovalenko brothers, are delighted to seize the opportunity to murder Jews – in the cases of Evenhy and Vitali, at Babii Yar and Treblinka. The novel is set in contemporary Queensland at the time of the Australian war crimes trials. The Kovalenko brothers are under threat of prosecution. *The Hand* argues that these trials are the next stage in the cycle of Jewish–Ukrainian ethnic revenge.

The Hand, in my reading, was astonishingly and recklessly inaccurate, merging fact and fiction – Demidenko called her book "faction" – in a manner only historians could pick apart. It argued that the supposed cycle of Ukrainian–Jewish revenge began with the brutish behaviour of Jewish Bolsheviks in Ukraine. In fact, Ukrainian hostility to the Jews living in their midst was centuries old and, before the Holocaust, had climaxed with the pogroms of 1918–20, where between 50,000 and 100,000 Ukrainian Jews were murdered. Most disturbing to me was the fact that near the centre of the argument of *The Hand* was the idea that Bolshevism – i.e. Soviet communism under both Lenin and Stalin – was an expression of Jewish political power.

The idea of "Jewish Bolshevism" was perhaps the single most important strand in the exterminatory ideology of the Nazi Party, what the historian Norman Cohn had called their "warrant for genocide". In *Mein Kampf*, Hitler wrote: "Communism is in fact nothing but an attempt by Judaism to take over the world." On January 30, 1939, he warned that if Jewry once again plunged the world into war, the result would be not the "bolshevisation" of the Earth but the annihilation of the Jews. (It was at that moment that my teacher, Frank Knopfelmacher, had decided to leave Europe.)

As criticisms pointing out the large and small historical errors of *The Hand* began to be published – by Gerard Henderson, Jacques Adler and Stephen Wheatcroft – Helen Demidenko turned on her critics and defended herself by revealing to the world what the Jews had done to her family. In a televised argument with Henderson on the ABC's leading current-affairs program, *The 7.30 Report*, she informed viewers that "most of my father's family, including my grandfather, were killed by Jewish Communist Party officials".

Wherever their power extended, soldiers or secret police serving the Nazi German state had scoured the cities, towns and villages in search of Jews – from babies to the aged – so that they could be shot on the spot or transported to the special-purpose extermination camps that had been established in Poland. These events had come to be called the Holocaust. Now, a novel that had invented excusing reasons for the lower-level murderers in Ukraine and that had revived, as if fact, the idea of Bolshevism as an expression of Jewish political power had been regarded by three sets of literary judges as the finest novel or piece of literature published in Australia during the past year. All this shook me more deeply than I found easy to explain to others, or even to understand in myself.

I did not for a moment think that the judges or the enthusiastic readers of *The Hand* were touched by anti-Semitism. I had, however, assumed that there existed within the Australian literary community at least a basic knowledge of the history of the Holocaust and an understanding that the Holocaust was not merely a recent chapter of Jewish history but an event of civilisational significance. I had also assumed that a novelist who chose the Holocaust as their subject would only be taken seriously if they grasped its gravity and its meaning. And I assumed, finally, that members of the Australian literary community would find it easy to understand why, for their fellow Jewish citizens, almost all of whom had lost members of their families, the Holocaust was still an open, untreatable and extraordinarily painful wound. As praise was showered upon Helen Demidenko and *The Hand*, it seemed to me that all my assumptions were false.

I entered a state I had never experienced before and have never experienced since, one I described as "cultural destabilisation". I set to work, rather obsessively, to try to show why those who praised *The Hand* were mistaken. By mid-August 1995 I had prepared a long article on *The Hand* for the September issue of *Quadrant*, as had Rai Gaita. My emphasis was on history: *The Hand*'s apparent ignorance of both Ukrainian–Jewish relations in the *longue durée* and the Nazi ideology of exterminatory anti-Semitism. Rai's emphasis was on the frightening emptiness of *The Hand*'s moral landscape, its creation of a flat world without weight or meaning, from which the ideas of both justice and remorse had been expelled.

When the September issue of *Quadrant* was close to going to press, the wheels fell off the Demidenko carriage. On August 19, David Bentley, a journalist at Brisbane's *Courier-Mail*, reported that

Helen Demidenko was not the daughter of a Ukrainian taxi driver and an Irish maid, as she had claimed, but of British migrants who had come from Scunthorpe before settling in Brisbane. Helen's surname was not Demidenko but Darville. She had not made her way up from an impoverished working-class school and suburb. Her parents belonged to the solid middle class, and she had been educated at a reasonably expensive Lutheran private college.

The news came through just in time for me to write a new opening paragraph for the Demidenko article in *Quadrant*. With certain unfriendly academics in mind, like McKenzie Wark, a columnist for *The Australian*, I commented, rather tartly: "Even post-modernist geographers would, I imagine, be obliged to concede in the end that Scunthorpe is not in ... Ukraine." I was pleased that news about Helen Demidenko's ethnic fraudulence arrived after I had finished the article for *Quadrant* but in time for a new opening paragraph. It was important to distinguish the problems with *The Hand* as a work of literature from the new problems flowing from the strange behaviour of its author.

It was not long before several instances of minor plagiarism were noticed. The book's very first line had been lifted from Thomas Keneally. There were several similar snatches of plagiarism – from Graham Greene, Robin Morgan, Robert Lowell, Patrick White, James McAuley, Toni Morrison and Anatoly Kuznetsov. Helen Darville's lawyers defended her here on the entirely irrelevant ground that no breach of copyright law had occurred. It was unlikely but remotely possible that Darville had a photographic memory and remembered phrases or sentences.

There was, however, not even a remote possibility of photographic memory in the most amusing instance of plagiarism. While Brian Matthews was travelling in a remote corner of Europe, his Adelaide office received a fax from Helen Demidenko. She explained that her friend, "Michelle", had noticed similarities between certain passages in an article she had written for *RePublica* and a piece written by Matthews about his experiences as a schoolteacher. As Brian commented, Michelle was right on the money. Long passages had been lifted and slightly adapted so carelessly that their original meaning was distorted.

The supporters of *The Hand* responded to the evidence of her ethnic hoax in different ways. David Marr conceded that some of her behaviour, and especially the claim that Jews had murdered a large part of her father's family, was a disgrace. Jill Kitson argued that the excellence of *The Hand* was even more astonishing now that we had learned that it was entirely imaginary. Frank Devine, a former editor of *The Australian*, came out fists swinging. He described Isi Leibler's triumphalist television appearance, following the unmasking of Helen Demidenko, as "the unacceptable face of anti-antisemitism". Leonie Kramer was silent – in one of Frank Knopfelmacher's aphorisms, a sphinx without a secret. Michael Gawenda told me that when, in the early days of the controversy, he had asked her, on the phone, for a comment, she could scarcely recall what *The Hand* was about. I suspected that in agreeing to award the 1995 Miles Franklin to Helen Demidenko, she had winged it.

Even after the unmasking of Helen Demidenko, the controversy over *The Hand that Signed the Paper* raged on. Although, on balance and eventually, the right supported Demidenko on anti-political-correctness grounds, while the left attacked her on anti-racism grounds, the pro and contra camps did not follow as neatly as usual the characteristic left and right pattern of the culture wars. David Marr was an ally of Frank Devine; Gerard Henderson of Guy Rundle. I was aware that Andrew Riemer was writing a book for Allen & Unwin in defence of Demidenko, the principal target of which would be the "totalitarian" leaders of the anti-Demidenko "witch hunt". I believed that the success of *The Hand* was a cultural accident but of a revealing kind. I knew that I would not be at ease unless I tried to convince members of the literary community that the book three groups of judges had celebrated was slovenly written, historically ignorant or consciously deceptive, and, in what I saw as its moral-revisionist interpretation of the Holocaust, ideologically anti-Semitic. With the encouragement of Michael Heyward and Di Gribble of Text Publishing, I decided to write an alternative to Riemer.

In Rochedale, Brisbane, I spoke to Helen Darville's headmaster at Redeemer Lutheran College, Robin Kleinschmidt; to her history teacher there, John Harms; and to her former boyfriend Paul Gadaloff, who insisted that Helen's motivation was to break the Jewish stranglehold over the interpretation of the Holocaust and, in a phrase he used on several occasions, to challenge "the Jews' monopoly of the speaking position in Australia". In Sydney I spoke to one of the Vogel judges, the novelist Roger McDonald, who was so disturbed about his role in the making of Helen Demidenko that when Allen & Unwin sent him a copy of *The Hand* he threw it straight into a rubbish bin. I also spoke to Stephanie Dowrick, the fiction publisher at Allen & Unwin who had dealt with Helen Demidenko. When problems arose, Demidenko had warned Dowrick: "The Jews are not going to get away with this one." As Dowrick commented, "[I]t was so shocking, so disgusting that a young person would say such a thing." She resolved never to speak to Helen Demidenko again.

The title of my book on the Demidenko affair was *The Culture of Forgetting*. It came from a conversation with Di Gribble at Text in which I'd used the phrase. As it happened, the book was very well received. Apart from essays by two of the literary awards judges involved – Adrian Mitchell of the Miles Franklin and Ken Stewart of the Literature Society's Gold Medal – the only seriously negative review was by Frank Devine, in *Quadrant*. By commissioning him, I was not only, or even mainly, covering my tracks. Foolishly, I hoped I could convince even him.

The most lucid and intense review came from Inga Clendinnen in *Australian Book Review*. Although we had been colleagues at La Trobe for twenty years – she in history, me in politics – Inga had barely spoken to me, a notorious conservative. After she had fallen ill, she had been forced to leave her field of scholarship, the Aztecs, and to write books that did not require travel or archival research. In her review, Inga pointed out that "while Manne has devoted much of his life to the study of the Holocaust, most of us who also recognise it as a great fact of history have not". Inga decided now "to face the Gorgon", as she put it. The consequence was *Reading the Holocaust*, one of *The New York Times*' "Best Books" of 1999. In its introduction, she wrote that "the immediate stimulus" was the Demidenko affair, and in particular my analysis of its meaning. "Reading Manne's book, I was both moved and ashamed," she explained.

The Culture of Forgetting was a pivotal moment in my relationship to the local intelligentsia. The widely acknowledged arbiter of matters literary in Australia, the critic Peter Craven, very openly changed his mind on Demidenko after reading the historical argument in *The Culture of Forgetting*. When I spoke about the affair at the 1996 Melbourne Writers Festival I was very warmly received. I was no longer "that fellow Manne".

During the Demidenko controversy, the only public comment Dame Leonie Kramer made was in a letter to *The Sydney Morning Herald* on August 29, 1995. "When the dust has settled," she wrote, "I hope that someone will analyse the reasons for the sustained and vitriolic attack on the book and its author. The whole episode calls into question our claims to be a tolerant and fair-minded society." As she was the chair of *Quadrant*'s board and I was its editor, the situation was, to put it mildly, a little delicate. As I explained to a journalist at *The Australian Jewish News*, almost a year later: "I'm sure [her letter] wasn't meant personally but I took it personally because if I'm editing a journal of which she is chairman, and if she thinks that my attitude is one that undermines Australia's traditions of tolerance and fairmindedness, then one by definition is in a difficult situation."

Shortly before *The Culture of Forgetting* was published, I wrote to Leonie with notice of its impending arrival. There was not a cross word between us. I had no idea what she was thinking.

*

On August 24, 1996, the Brisbane *Courier-Mail*, edited by Chris Mitchell, devoted the best part of eight broadsheet pages to an astonishing discovery: Professor Manning Clark, Australia's most admired and influential historian, was "an undiscovered member of the communist world's elite", who had been "awarded with the Soviet Union's highest honour, the Order of Lenin". Helpfully, it included photos of other Order of Lenin winners: János Kádár, Kim Philby, Fidel Castro, Nicolae Ceauşescu, Walter Ulbricht and Ho Chi Minh.

The Courier-Mail interviewed two high-ranking KGB defectors, Oleg Gordievsky and Mikhail Lyubimov. Neither had ever heard of Manning Clark. They were, however, asked a different question: to be awarded the Order of Lenin, what must Manning Clark have done, what must he have been? Gordievsky claimed he must have been "not only an extremely significant agent of influence but possibly something more – 'a very, very important agent'". Lyubimov went further. Being awarded the Order of Lenin has "got nothing to do with agent of influence; it's got to do with a spy". The front-page claim that Manning Clark was a Soviet spy was removed from the paper's second edition. The accusation it settled upon was that Clark was an extremely effective "agent of influence" who had worked secretly for the Soviet Union for half a century. In doing so, he had betrayed his country.

How had *The Courier-Mail* discovered that Manning Clark had been a recipient of the Order of Lenin? There were only two eyewitnesses, one dead and one alive, both of whom were known to me.

The dead eyewitness was Geoffrey Fairbairn, a delightful, romantically inclined, usually alcohol-affected, anti-communist historian. (On one occasion Geoffrey had tried to shock the Melbourne Club by bringing as his guests a Vietnamese and a Jew – Dr Dan, the former South Vietnamese ambassador to France, and me.) Geoffrey had seen his colleague, Manning Clark, wearing what he believed was an Order of Lenin medal in 1970 at a function at the Soviet Embassy in Canberra. He was shocked. He told the anti-communist journalist Peter Kelly about Manning and the Order of Lenin but swore him to secrecy.

The live eyewitness was *Quadrant*'s literary editor, Les Murray. At a dinner party at the home of a Canberra poet, David Campbell, Murray had seen the Order of Lenin on Manning Clark's chest. Les was quoted on the front page of *The Courier-Mail*: "Manning was wearing a very impressive decoration. I recognised it as the Order of Lenin. How did I know it was the Order of Lenin? Because I have always had an interest in gongs, decorations, heraldry. I recognised it straightaway."

Once Peter Kelly learned of Les Murray's story, he decided to break his promise to Geoffrey Fairbairn. With the sportswriter Wayne Smith, Kelly was the principal author of *The Courier-Mail*'s exposé. Within a day it had begun to fall apart. The family of Manning Clark let it be known that Manning did indeed have a Soviet medal with Lenin's face on one side. It had been given to him in thanks for the talk he gave during the celebrations in Moscow in 1970 on the centenary of Lenin's birth. *The Courier-Mail*'s exposé rested entirely on the capacity of Geoffrey Fairbairn and Les Murray to distinguish the Order of Lenin from another, more modest Soviet medal. Or rather, as Geoffrey was now dead, it rested entirely on Les Murray's expertise on "gongs, decorations, heraldry".

In mid-1996 I had moved as a columnist from *The Age* to *The Australian*, on Paul Kelly's recommendation. Recently it had established an ambitious monthly magazine, *The Australian's Review of Books*. I wrote a long article for it that mocked *The Courier-Mail*'s nonsense but discussed the role Manning Clark's flirtations with the Soviet Union and his fantasies about the reconciliation of Christ and Lenin had played in undermining his history of Australia. The article was well received by some of the most prominent Australian historians across the political spectrum. I received extremely thoughtful private letters from the more conservative historians Allan Martin and Ian Hancock, the centrists Geoffrey Bolton and Geoffrey Serle, and, most surprisingly to me, from Don Watson of the left.

Allan Martin wrote about the consequence of Clark's ultra-sensitivity to criticism:

> [W]e mostly shied away when asked to write about him; he cocooned himself (consciously or unconsciously) in a kind of protective cushion which few felt like piercing. When they did the result was whole-hoggism, of which my old friend Peter Ryan is the most notorious example.

Don Watson wrote:

I would have found more good to say about him and I think there are excuses for the undoubted decline in his work, but I greatly admired your article this week on Manning Clark and am grateful for it. I think most of what you say is sadly true. Perhaps more importantly, by separating the flaws and failures of his work from the idiot campaign which has just been run against him, you have made it easier for those of us who are amiably disposed towards Clark personally to be critical of his writings and actions without feeling we have joined in a massacre of the relatively innocent.

Stuart Macintyre did not write to me but published a column in *The Australian* that, while disagreeing with my interpretation of Clark's long flirtation with Soviet communism, praised me for my willingness to challenge the most recent episode in the anti–Manning Clark campaign. I was wrong, Stuart argued, when I claimed that Peter Ryan had displayed "civic courage". However, "[f]or Manne to reject the allegations of disloyalty against a figure with whom he is in such strong disagreement is indeed an act of civic courage, honesty and generosity that does him credit". (A quarter-century later, I went to the funeral service for my friend of undergraduate days David Fitzpatrick. With a certain intensity that I did not at the time understand, Stuart greeted me warmly and shook my hand firmly. He knew I had recently lost my voice to cancer. I did not know that it was not long before cancer would take Stuart's life.)

I have no doubt that many of the old anti-communist *Quadrant* circle hoped that I would support *The Courier-Mail*. Chris Mitchell lobbied me, but to no effect. As it turned out, the most significant reaction came from Les Murray. In my Manning Clark article for *The Australian Review of Books*, I described Les as "the great Australian poet". I claimed that he was right to be appalled when he saw that Clark was wearing a medal of a regime that was responsible for destroying "tens of millions of innocent lives". I argued, however, that *The Courier-Mail* had erred in two ways. It had not contacted the Clark family prior to its publication. If it had done so, it would have discovered the nature of the medal Geoffrey Fairbairn and Les Murray had seen. "Nor does it seem," I continued, "that the *Courier-Mail* took even the most obvious steps to check whether Murray could be certain that he had seen an Order of Lenin and not perhaps some other medal bearing Lenin's portrait."

Les did not take even the mildest and most indirect criticism easily. As I was soon to learn.

[12.]

Quadrant 3: The Politics of Race (1996–1997)

BY 1996 I HAD FOUND MY WAY TOWARDS what I hoped to achieve with *Quadrant*. The magazine had no single, overwhelming political purpose of the kind it had during the Cold War. It was no longer embattled or dedicated to struggles against the left. It was decidedly not at war with the new cultural movements of the 1960s – feminism, environmentalism, sexual liberation, gay rights and animal protection.

Rai Gaita continued to comment on contemporary affairs from his distinctive anti-consequentialist position. His columns provided the backbone of his later book *A Common Humanity*. When his father died, we published the talk Rai gave at the funeral. Not long after, he wrote *Romulus, My Father* for Text Publishing, an almost instant classic. John Hirst had by now written several revisionist essays on Australian history that were eventually collected in his *Sense and Nonsense in Australian History*. Our foreign policy commentators were still mainly "realists", most significantly Coral Bell and Owen Harries. From Owen's American magazine, *The National Interest*, we republished an article by Adam Garfinkle that offered a prescient warning about the perils to peace of NATO's eastward expansion. Earlier, I wrote about the failure of Western policy in the former Yugoslavia and then, as tensions rose in Crimea, a column about the possibility of a catastrophic Russia–Ukraine war. We continued with forums – those on the Vietnam War and neo-liberalism were followed by forums on the future of the Liberal Party and the new *Race Discrimination Act*.

In an editorial I argued strongly against making it unlawful to "offend" or "insult" one or another ethnicity. With the emergence of a new politics of race following the election of Pauline Hanson, however, I changed my mind.

Quadrant did not have any settled line on the republic. The most influential article we ran was John Hirst's "A Conservative Case for the Republic". In an editorial I called "Why I Am No Longer Not a Republican", I discussed my reasons for conversion to the republican cause. Sir William Deane had recently been appointed by the Keating government as Governor-General of Australia. As President of Australia, someone of his calibre might be liberated from the constitutional requirement, as a representative of the British Crown, to say nothing of possible political interest. Sir Zelman Cowen, who had published a book of his speeches, and who had coined the phrase "explaining the nation to itself" regarding his own speech-making as governor-general, let me know how deeply this argument had offended.

In June 1994, Anne wrote for *Quadrant* a quite wonderful essay on early motherhood, which I believe was one of the finest essays published during my time as editor. I realised she had a writer's voice with a capital V. I was determined to support her. Our lives now changed so that her distinctive voice could be heard. Following that *Quadrant* essay, first *The Australian* and then *The Age* offered her a column. By now, Anne was also contributing a series for *Quadrant* called "Tales of a Country Girlhood", later collected as *So This Is Life* for Melbourne University Press. Her early motherhood essay led eventually to *Motherhood*, published by Allen & Unwin. It drew attention to the powerful work of feminist economists on the care economy, and raised the question of the need for paid parental leave, given the poor quality of market-based, for-profit childcare, which, under the culture of the new capitalism, Anne argued, was becoming or had already become "McDonaldised". To raise the question of the quality and consequence of institutional for-profit childcare for babies and infants took considerable courage. As I write these words, the ABC's *7.30* is, at long last, analysing institutional childcare in Australia. Following the first of three segments, on the risk of serious injury and in one case death, the program received an outpouring of 1,000 responses from viewers. *Motherhood* was the first of several works that developed an original analysis of the destructive impact of the new culture of neo-liberalism, the contemporary privileging of paid work as a marker of status and the rise of narcissism. This analysis had an important impact on my thinking. Anne's writing combines an empathetic imagination with forensic analysis, seen most recently in the remarkable *Crimes of the Cross*, about child sexual abuse by a clerical paedophile network in Newcastle.

The tenor of *Quadrant* by the mid-1990s was no longer right-wing, but it was still, in part, conservative. In the early years, Sir Paul Hasluck had published his series of past and present observations – on gambling, on religion, on speech – that he called "Then and Now". Until the end of my editorship, Peter Ryan contributed a curmudgeonly column each month, always independent and usually interesting. And John Carroll defended traditional conservatism, often through criticism of paintings, with elegance and ingenuity but with perhaps (as I now see things) too little empirical research. One of my favourite articles was Pierre Ryckmans' single-page satirical takedown of Bill Hayden's desire to dispense with the elderly. We also by now published writers of the left. Gregory Clark argued with Santamaria over communism and with Gaita over the left and the Vietnam War. Dennis Glover, a Labor speechwriter and future novelist, wrote for us a comparative review of the memoirs of two left-wing Australians, one of whom, Tom Uren, had steered clear of communism, while the other, Bernie Taft, had been hopelessly compromised by it. Allan Patience contributed a delicate article on gay love across ethnic lines. An American scholar resident in Australia, Anne Waldron Neumann, wrote articles on popular culture – on *The Simpsons* and *The X-Files*.

Some of the essays I most treasured seemed to arrive out of nowhere. A Bendigo gentleman named B.J. Coman submitted "A Short History of the Rabbit in Australia", which was soon to become a book published by Text. The general editor of *The Australian Dictionary of Biography*, Professor John Ritchie, sent us a brief, warm and evocative memoir of almost photographic accuracy on the lives of the "ordinary" working people (not working-class) of suburban Melbourne in the early post-war years, which he called "Come Outside and Play". And from the eco-feminist Val Plumwood there came an extraordinary essay on the experience of having been hunted by a crocodile while canoeing in the Northern Territory. How she arrived at *Quadrant* I do not know. Martin Krygier published essays on Poland and the rule of law that led to his invitation to deliver the ABC's Boyer Lectures in 1997. *Quadrant*'s promiscuous political position was captured by the title of one of his essays, "In Praise of Conservative-Liberal-Socialist Democracy", which continued the argument (and consciously echoed the title) of an essay by the great Polish political theorist Leszek Kołakowski. Perhaps most importantly for the future of my editorship, Rai Gaita and I wrote several essays on the two most critical Indigenous issues of the 1990s: native title and the "Stolen Generations". Although always open to different opinion, *Quadrant* came out strongly on the side supposedly supported by the left.

There was interest in the new *Quadrant*. By 1997, we sold – by subscription and in newsagents – between 5,000 and 6,000 copies, double the number of our left-wing rivals, *Meanjin* and *Overland*, at their peak.

*

Between its election loss in March 1993 and landslide victory three years later, I wrote a dozen or so articles on the Liberal Party in my regular fortnightly column for *The Age* and then *The Australian*. By use of detailed opinion polls and the empirical electoral research of the ANU political scientists Ian McAllister and Clive Bean, I tried to show that the strange Liberal Party electoral defeat of March 1993, at a time of both severe recession and recent Labor Party leadership turbulence – the Hawke–Keating rivalry – was above all else due to the Liberal Party's embrace under Dr Hewson of a radical program of "economic rationalism". Hewson had promised "the most significant revolution that this country had seen in decades". What a majority of Australians wanted, I argued, was not revolution but security and stability. Both Labor and the Liberal Party were involved in dismantling the Deakinite "Australian Settlement" – with programs of financial deregulation, privatisation, tariff reduction and reform of the centralised industrial relations system. Labor, however, was in general one step behind the Coalition. This meant that it could accuse its opponent of flint-heartedness and economic lunacy before it adopted nearly identical policy reforms. By such political sleight of hand, the Liberals appeared to be the party of radical reform and Labor the party of caution and the middle way, overturning the general pattern of party politics in Australia over the decades.

After 1993, I argued, the Liberal Party suffered a prolonged crisis of identity and of ideological division. One line of division was between the party's wets and dries – between those who urged caution on the economic front because of the supposed anti-zealotry lesson of 1993 and those who wanted to continue with the Hewson reformist drive. The latter group drew from 1993 the lesson that the Liberals had, if anything, been not too radical but too timid in its revised "Fightback!" package on the eve of the election. I supported those who advocated caution. As I argued on November 24, 1993: "Contemporary Australians are, in general, not ideological but existential conservatives" and "more economic nationalist than economic rationalist".

The other division was between the party's conservatives and liberals. The conservative Liberals, I argued, favoured the "Reagan Democrat" strategy of wooing the working class – the traditional electoral base of Labor – by rejecting the progressivist program of Keating Labor: the republic, Aboriginal reconciliation, multiculturalism, Asian immigration, environmentalism, female emancipation and gay rights. The liberal Liberals favoured an "inclusivist" strategy, able to attract voters among those who supported aspects of the Keating social agenda, albeit with more moderation and what they thought of as common sense. I believed that the party should pursue both the conservative and the liberal strategies: "If the conservatives follow the 'Reagan Democrat' strategy, and the liberals the strategy of 'inclusivity', and if in the process both shed the habit of intolerance ... such diversity will strengthen and not weaken them in their common cause."

I welcomed the downfall of Hewson on anti-economic-rationalist grounds and foolishly (as I now think) blamed the progressivist Canberra press gallery for the demise of Alexander Downer's woeful, "loose-tongued" leadership attempt. Downer's leadership was finally destroyed when, in late 1994, he described the domestic violence section of "The Things that Matter", a moderate post-Hewson Liberal Party program, as "The Things that Batter". I believed that, in his idea of the "broad church", John Howard had found the right balance between the party's wets and dries, and between its liberals and conservatives. Although I had not voted for Dr Hewson in 1993, I did vote for John Howard in March 1996, as the editor of the country's most important conservative magazine was, I recognised, supposed to do.

I published two *Quadrant* editorials on the meaning of the 1996 election. In April I argued that Howard's landslide election victory "represents the triumph of pragmatism over ideology" and "of character – of persistence in the face of adversity and, even more, of the capacity to mature and to learn". Howard had confided to Liz Jackson, of ABC TV's *Four Corners*, that his aspiration as potential prime minister was for Australians once again to feel "comfortable and relaxed". Keating mocked Howard mercilessly for these words, claiming that he wanted to return Australia to the soporific Rip Van Winkle days of Sir Robert Menzies. Howard, I argued, grasped the mood of "middle Australia" more accurately than Keating.

The most dramatic 1996 election result appeared to be the victory of the disendorsed Liberal Party candidate Pauline Hanson in the once solidly Labor seat of Oxley, in Brisbane. She had won the largest swing in the nation, her one credential being the preposterous claim in a letter-to-the-editor of a local newspaper that Australian Aboriginals were unduly privileged. In my April editorial, I argued that the Canberra press gallery was exaggerating the significance of "Hansen's [sic]" victory. Had not Howard moved speedily against her? I urged the new government to honour "*Mabo* without equivocation but to extend its meaning beyond symbolism by hard-headed policy-making in the areas of Aboriginal health, housing and education", and to support the republican cause. "Only a conservative government can negotiate the passage to the republic," I concluded. What was I thinking? In my party-political commentary in the years between the fall of Hewson and the rise of Howard, there was an element that I now see as strained and inauthentic.

By the May edition of *Quadrant*, I had changed my mind on the meaning of the 1996 election. In Kalgoorlie, Western Australia, the disendorsed anti-*Mabo* and anti-multicultural former Labor parliamentarian Graeme Campbell was returned with a larger vote than he'd won as the endorsed ALP candidate in 1993. In Leichhardt, Queensland, the National Party member Bob Burgess had described citizenship ceremonies as "dewoggings". He increased the National Party's primary vote from 14 per cent in 1993 to 20 per cent. The independent member for Kennedy, in Far North Queensland, Bob Katter, who spoke of "slanty-eyed ideologues who persecute ordinary average Australians", increased his two-party-preferred vote by 12 percentage points. "But even he was outdone by Pauline Hanson," I wrote (having now learned how to spell her name). The once esoteric concept of "political correctness" had moved from the arguments of the right-wing intelligentsia to the political mainstream. The Keating government – which I described as "half Manning Clark and half Milton Friedman" – was "attuned to the preoccupations of the political elites [but] remote from the thinking of ordinary Australians". In June 1996, a new (and ultimately insignificant) political party was formed for country people who had been forced by the Howard government to surrender some of their weapons following the Port Arthur massacre. In *The Australian* of June 24, 1996, I argued that over the past twenty years Australia had passed through a great cultural revolution, part of which was the end of White Australia and the recognition of the meaning of the dispossession of the Aboriginal people. Resistance to this revolution had prepared the ground for "the birth of a new and ugly political party". In analysing what had occurred in the 1996 election, I recognised, finally, belatedly, something I had left out of my "Toast to Australia": the force of Australian racism.

In September 1996, Pauline Hanson delivered her maiden speech. Hanson spoke once more of Aboriginal privilege, of Australia being "swamped by Asians", and of the tyranny over ordinary people exercised by the politically correct left-liberal elites. She spoke to an almost empty House of Representatives. One response was a bipartisan vote in the parliament condemning racism. Outside parliament, however, large parts of the nation cheered her on. In the December issue of *Quadrant*, I called Hanson our first "anti-politician", someone who represented the losers in the age of globalisation, and those who opposed the profound revolution in sensibility – over questions of race, sex and gender – that had come to be called the "Sixties". The great sociologist Max Weber wrote that one type of political authority was exercised by those who possessed a magical quality he called "charisma". I argued that what Pauline Hanson possessed was a "negative charisma":

> We think of a charismatic politician as eloquent. Pauline Hanson is, by contrast, almost painfully inarticulate. We think of charismatic politicians as inspiring. Pauline Hanson's mood is of sullen resentment and stubborn defiance. Her negative charisma is expressive not of hope for the future but of bitterness about the present. In her inarticulateness, in her sulkiness, in her ignorance – for which she is not only forgiven but, I think, admired – she has become for a considerable part of Australia ... a symbol of nostalgia for an old world which has been lost and of deep-seated discontent with the new world which has taken its place.

I doubted that her negative charisma would survive if a political party formed around her. I was wrong. In 1997, the party of Pauline Hanson, One Nation, was born. Eventually, at its height, it won eleven seats in 1998 in the small Queensland Legislative Assembly. A rather creepy and anonymous member of the right-wing intelligentsia of Adelaide (whose identity I was able to establish but did not publish) wrote a manifesto called *Pauline Hanson: The Truth*. He argued that the "New Class" of left-wing intellectuals was conspiring to take control of Australia through three strategies: "Asianisation" through a mass-migration program; "Maboism", breaking down society through land rights and other needless concessions to the Aboriginals, whom he claimed were cannibals; and the disarmament of patriotic Australians through post–Port Arthur gun control. In a column in *The Australian* about *Pauline Hanson: The Truth*, I addressed the conservative intelligentsia, and in part my former self:

> Many will find their own ideas – on the new class, political correctness, *Mabo*, multiculturalism, Asian migration, the High Court – absorbed, simplified, systematised and radicalised. Because of this, I do not believe it is illegitimate to ask the conservative intelligentsia whether they agree with me in condemning the Hanson movement. Do they support the political movement bearing Hanson's name? Are they neutral in regard to it? Or, will they publicly oppose it?

In response to my clarion call, I received ... one letter, from the anthropologist Les Hiatt.

*

I had hoped that the Howard government would establish warm relations with Australia's Indigenous peoples. It was not to be. On December 23, 1996, the High Court handed down its *Wik* judgment, finding that native title was not necessarily expunged by pastoral leases. The government produced in response something it called "The Ten Point Plan", which most Aboriginal people rejected. At a Melbourne meeting, and with great insensitivity to the occasion – it was the thirtieth anniversary of the 1967 referendum, which had finalised the passage to full Indigenous citizenship – Howard vigorously defended his Ten Point Plan, which the leader of the Nationals, Tim Fischer, argued with even greater insensitivity contained "bucketloads of extinguishment". Many members of the audience rose and turned their backs on Howard. He shouted back angrily. This moment became an enduring symbol of the poisonous relations between the Howard government and Indigenous Australians.

In May 1997, *Bringing Them Home*, the report of the Human Rights Commission's National Inquiry into the Separation of Aboriginal and Torres Strait Islander Children from Their Families – which had been chaired by the president of the Human Rights and Equal Opportunities Commission, former High Court judge Sir Ronald Wilson, and the Aboriginal and Torres Strait Islander social justice commissioner, Mick Dodson – was published. The report was from the outset treated with hostility by the Howard government, which refused to offer an apology to the children, known outside the report as "the Stolen Generations". And it treated with contempt the carefully argued claim in the report that the policy and practice of Aboriginal child removal in the years between 1910 and 1970 constituted an act of genocide.

In 1996 and 1997, *Quadrant* published several articles and letters favourable to the Howard government's Indigenous policy. However, because of Rai Gaita and me, *Quadrant* was by now, on balance, strongly critical of the government's response to the High Court's *Mabo* and *Wik* judgments. In the first issue of 1997, Rai wrote a powerful essay called "Not Right". The right had attacked the *Mabo* judgment and especially the supposedly emotive language of justices William Deane and Mary Gaudron, who had claimed that the dispossession of the Aboriginals had bequeathed to all Australians "a legacy of unutterable shame". "A dispassionate judgment is not one," Rai argued, "which is uninformed by feeling, but one which is *undistorted* by feeling." He found it instructive that the right had reduced "a proper sense of shame to maudlin self-abasement". And with prescience – a quarter-century before the Uluru Statement from the Heart and Indigenous Australians' call for the establishment of a Voice to Parliament – he argued that their "deeper anger reflects their reasonable belief that the Coalition's policies are insensitive to, and perhaps an intentional assault upon, their determination to find their own voice – a voice with which to speak with non-indigenous Australians about their participation in the political life of Australia".

With my fortnightly column now appearing in *The Australian*, I therefore supposed myself for the first time to be directly addressing a considerable number of conservative politicians and public servants and members of the right-wing intelligentsia. On April 8, 1997, I tried to find an explanation for the right's moral blind spot when it came to thinking about the dispossession, the burial ground on which the foundations of contemporary Australia had been built. The political judgement of the anti-communist right had been vindicated by the outcome of the Cold War. This had led them to an overconfident "reflexive anti-Leftism". It was the left that had recognised the meaning of the dispossession. There was, however, in its "identification with the injustice done to the Aborigines", an element of "rancour in regard to their own society, a taking of pleasure in its denigration, in a systematic exaggeration of its shortcomings and underestimation of its virtues". Conservatives were repelled by this rancour and unambivalently proud of Australia. "What is finest about their attachment to their country, paradoxically, then, leads such conservatives to avert their gaze from the terrible story of Aboriginal dispossession, from their country's legacy of shame."

I now think this argument was far too kind. In an earlier column in *The Australian*, I had paraphrased a distinction – between guilt and shame – outlined by Rai. Individuals cannot bear guilt for the actions of others or their forebears. As a part of a collectivity, however, just as they can reasonably be proud of the actions of earlier generations – in John Howard's case, say, for the courage and endurance of the Gallipoli soldiers – so can they reasonably feel shame about wrongs done to others in the past life of their nation, including in its creation. Pride about the past without acknowledging the possibility of shame was a form of jingoism. By liberating conservatives from the false idea of present individual guilt for past wrongdoing in the history of the nation, Rai's distinction between guilt and shame proved of fundamental importance in the national conversation about the dispossession, preparing the ground for the near-universal acceptance of Kevin Rudd's 2008 apology to the Stolen Generations, a landmark in the moral history of Australia.

Bringing Them Home was in my view flawed – in the unhelpful historical account it offered, in its failure to outline with sufficient clarity that the removal policy was concerned exclusively with mixed-race children, and in its uncertainty about the numbers of removals, in estimate ranging from one in three to one in ten. Its tremendous power, however, lay in the heart-stopping testimony of the Indigenous witnesses who had been separated from their mothers, families and communities as babies or children. The report made it clear that the children had not been removed for social welfare reasons, as most Australians probably assumed, but in order to sever their connection with their Aboriginality. Children were fed the lie that they had been abandoned (their parents were frequently refused permission to visit them), they were punished for speaking in 'language', and their Aboriginality was systematically denigrated.

With *Bringing Them Home*, the confidence I had expressed about the history of the country that had provided my parents with refuge was severely shaken. I wrote that the policy of Indigenous child removal was "in essence an exercise not in misguided paternalism but in racially inspired social engineering". The policy ambition of the two most influential "Chief Protectors of Aborigines" in the interwar period, A.O. Neville in Western Australia and Dr Cecil Cook in the Northern Territory, was the "absorption" of "half-castes" into the white population by removing children from their mothers, families and communities in a program they both called "breeding out the colour". In my view it was "legalised kidnapping". I reproduced some of the most revealing expressions of the racist mindset that justified the removals, like this remark of James Isdell, the West Australian Protector in the early 1900s: "I would not hesitate for one moment to separate any half-caste from its Aboriginal mother, no matter how frantic her momentary grief might be at the time. They soon forget their offspring."

In its last moments, the 1996 ABC TV series on the dispossession, *Frontier: Stories from White Australia's Forgotten War*, quoted a sentence of A.O. Neville, in addressing the first ever meeting of all senior state and territory Aboriginal administrators, in Canberra in 1937: "Fifty years hence ... are we going to have a population of one million blacks in the Commonwealth, or are we going to merge them into our white community and eventually forget that there were any Aborigines in Australia?"

Because of its resemblance to a passage I knew almost by heart from *Eichmann in Jerusalem*, Hannah Arendt's great book about the trial of the Nazi bureaucrat who had charge of the logistics of the Final Solution, Neville's comment genuinely startled me. Arendt believed Eichmann should be executed. In explaining why, she outlined the nature of the crime of genocide more lucidly than anything I had read: "It was when the Nazi regime declared that the German people not only were unwilling to have any Jews in Germany but wished to make the entire people disappear from the face of the earth that the new crime, the crime against humanity – in the sense of the crime against the human status – appeared." She called this "an attack on human diversity", an idea that gave meaning to talk of "mankind" or "humanity". The Nazi regime believed that it had "the right to determine who should and should not inhabit the world".

Despite the vast and self-evident differences between the work of A.O. Neville and Adolf Eichmann, only intellectual dishonesty would have allowed me to pretend that there was no similarity between Neville's determination to "merge" Australian Aboriginals into the white population and Eichmann's pivotal role in implementing Nazi Germany's "Final Solution" of "the Jewish problem". The conceptual overlap became perspicuous by a simple interchange: just as Neville believed he and his fellow administrators had the right to determine that the Aboriginals of Australia should not inhabit the world, so did Eichmann hope that, one day in the future, his fellow Germans would have forgotten that the Jewish people had ever existed.

Frontier identified the conference at which Neville's comment had been made. I wondered whether it had somehow been taken out of context. At the time, the La Trobe University Library had an outstanding collection of government papers, both international and Australian, collected and collated by a dedicated librarian, Ann Miller. The verbatim proceedings of the "Aboriginal Welfare" Conference that had been held in Canberra in April 1937 over three days were available. Neville's sentence had not been taken out of context.

On the contrary, the ambition of absorbing the Aboriginals into the white society, by both biological and social means, had dominated discussion for a day and a half and formed the conference's first and most important resolution.

Naturally, as I was reading the conference proceedings at the time the nation was discussing *Bringing Them Home*, I was interested in what they might reveal about the policy of Indigenous child removal. Neville gave a detailed account of what was happening in Western Australia. All "half-caste" children – a term that included all non-"full-blood" Aboriginals, including "quarter-castes" and "one-eighth-castes" and every other combination of bloodline – were taken away from their mothers and the Aboriginal camps by the age of six. By the age of twelve or thirteen, in Neville's view, it was much too late. So far as humanly possible, all connections between children and their mothers, families and communities were severed. After a very basic education, the boys were principally sent into rural labour and the girls into domestic service. If the girls fell pregnant to white men, even several times, it was of little consequence. Within two years, their babies were taken from them, and the girls sent back into service.

Critical to Neville's policy was state control over Indigenous marriage. Marriages between "half-caste" girls and "full-blood" males were unlawful. Ideally, "the girls" were made suitable for marriage to white males. Within four or five generations, Neville argued, their Aboriginality would be altogether bred out. Dr Cecil Cook from the Northern Territory had very similar views and policies. In the southern states, where there were now very few or no "full-bloods", the methods for merging the "half-castes" into the white population were different – more social than biological – but the ambition was the same. Indeed, everyone present agreed that the principal policy ambition of the Commonwealth ought to be the eventual "absorption" of all Aboriginals who were "not of the full-blood" into the white population. And so it was resolved.

What, then, of the "full-bloods"? Here opinions differed. Neville was convinced, based on the historical record, that their destiny was either to join the "half-caste" population or, "no matter what we do, they will die out". Cook believed that if nothing was done to help the "full-bloods", "we shall see the black race vanish". From the politico-demographic point of view, this might be the desirable outcome, but he believed it to be "callous". Professor John Burton Cleland of South Australia thought that, from his angle of interest – the scientific – everything should be done to save the "full-bloods" still living in the wild. "They are unique and one of the wonders of the world." Joseph Carrodus, for the Commonwealth, came closest to the conference consensus: "Ultimately if history is repeated the full bloods will become half-castes." Which, of course, led to Neville's question: did Australia want to have a million blacks in fifty years' time or eventually forget that there were ever any Aboriginals in Australia? For all senior administrators of Aboriginal affairs, that question answered itself.

What shocked me most of all were the many forms of a taken-for-granted racism that peppered their conversations. At the Canberra conference, participants spoke without self-consciousness of "superior" and "inferior" races. Professor Cleland described the Aboriginal as "a grownup child who will have to be protected and nursed". Dr Cook thought the task of policy was "to make the coloured girls acceptable as whites". Neville was puzzled that the mothers of the quarter-caste children he had institutionalised had given him "some trouble": "Although the children were illegitimate, the mothers were greatly attached to them." He allowed the mothers to visit the institution; "The mothers were then eventually content to leave them there, and some eventually forgot all about them." Participants spoke in pseudo-scientific language. They categorised the mixed-race Indigenous people with zoological terminology, as "half-castes", "quadroons" and "octoroons". Neville claimed that studies had shown that the Australian Aboriginals were of Caucasian and not Negroid stock. This meant that the prospects of "breeding out the colour" without the danger of a "throwback" towards the black were excellent. There was talk of racial menace in the north. According to Cook, "If we bring them under our influence they will breed, and their numbers increase until they menace our security." The conference participants discussed the racial troubles in the United States, including the lynching of blacks by whites. Cook thought we were fortunate that, in Australia, "the aboriginal native is regarded with contemptuous tolerance". I was surprised to discover that "half-castes" in the Northern Territory could gain certain privileges if they proved worthy of something called "a certificate of exemption". I was even more surprised that one conference resolution supported, "for humanitarian reasons", the use of neck chains when bringing Aboriginal prisoners and even witnesses to court. This was in 1937.

I do not think there could have been a better way of discovering the depth of the racism of old Australia than eavesdropping on the discussions over three days of the most senior and experienced administrators of Aboriginal affairs, which took place not in the distant past but a mere sixty years ago. Like many conservatives, I had until that moment believed that those on the left were most likely exaggerating the racism of old Australia, taking pleasure in the moral failings of their country through the kind of rancour that Orwell had observed among the intelligentsia in wartime Britain. Auberon Waugh had coined a word for this – "pilgerism" – inspired by the left-wing Australian journalist John Pilger, whose documentary on the Australian Aboriginals, *The Secret Country*, I had lampooned in *The Herald* a few years before. An afternoon's reading had changed my mind on the question of Australian racism, forever.

In the latter half of 1997 Rai Gaita and I wrote a series of articles in *Quadrant* (and, in my case, also in *The Australian* and then in *The Sydney Morning Herald* and *The Age*), on *Bringing Them Home* and, in particular, its most controversial finding, that in the removal of the Indigenous children from mothers, families and communities, the crime of genocide had occurred. Although we wrote the articles separately, our argument at this time was almost identical. Our starting point was Hannah Arendt's concept of genocide in *Eichmann in Jerusalem* and A.O. Neville's question at the 1937 Canberra conference. I argued that those of us who were trying to understand the nature of the crime involved in the removal of the Indigenous children were often misled because the Holocaust was our model for the crime of genocide:

> When we use the word genocide we tend to think first of the Holocaust. Because of this, two rather different ideas – mass murder on a vast scale and the intention to eliminate a distinct people – are collapsed into one ... There can be vast acts of State-inspired mass murder, such as Stalin's crimes, which are not genocide. There can be deliberate policies of a State, aimed at the elimination of a people, which do not involve even one killing. If *Frontier* was accurate it [was] inescapable that in at least one period of our history something genuinely terrible – genocide in the Arendtian sense – had been contemplated by those who held power over Aboriginal affairs.

At the Canberra conference, all the leading Aboriginal administrators had resolved to try to merge the "half-caste" Aboriginal population into the white, while most believed that, in the *longue durée*, the "full-blood" population was destined to die out. Rai challenged those who denied that genocide could be committed without one murder by asking our many critics whether they disagreed with the idea that if an entire population of a particular people were sterilised, the crime of genocide would have taken place.

Our critics also claimed that because the removal of Indigenous children had been undertaken with "good intentions", the charge of genocide was foolish in the extreme. I pointed out that in attempting to rid the Earth of the Jews, the Nazis believed that their intention – the liberation of humankind from the centuries-old Jewish menace – was good. Rai argued that it was not possible to characterise the removal of Indigenous children as motivated by good intentions if those responsible for the policies felt and expressed for the mixed-ancestry children and their people, as manifestly they did, a "racist contempt". As I had elsewhere pointed out, in his 1947 book on the subject of "breeding out the colour", *Our Coloured Minority*,

A.O. Neville had described the "half-caste" human products of the Aboriginal camps as "weedy, under-nourished semi-morons with grave sexual appetites".

Together, Rai's writing and mine had some effect. In his column on matters literary on September 24, 1997, "Inspirational Speech Puts PM to Shame", Peter Craven wrote:

> Drusilla Modjeska ... took as her theme the stolen generation of Aboriginal children. It was a beautifully written speech ... She acknowledged what Robert Manne had said on this subject and she used the distinction between shame and guilt articulated by the philosopher Raimond Gaita, but she did this with a formal intensity and with a richness of personal reflection that made this one of the great speeches in this country's history.

On the other hand, I had never received so much hostile and even hate mail as I did during 1997. One of the letters I published, in response to Rai's essay "Not Right", came from T.A. Pitsikas, a West Australian *Quadrant* reader unknown to me:

> Given Mr Gaita's privileged position with *Quadrant*, his piece appears to contain an unsubtly coded message from the new *Quadrant* that the left should join with it to rout the right, who can perhaps be defined in part as *Quadrant*'s former contributors and supporters. If this is *Quadrant*'s present agenda it would be ethical to come out with it frankly.

Apart from many letters like this, most of the hostility to my editorship took place behind the scenes. The exception was the literary editor I had appointed in 1990, the great poet Les Murray.

*

My long Helen Demidenko essay had been published in the September 1995 issue of *Quadrant*. On September 4, 1995, Les Murray sent me a very friendly postcard:

> Qdt Sept. issue is v. good, tho' it has too much abt. me in it. I like the way you allow Bruce King his opinion [in a long pro-Demidenko letter-to-the-editor] when yours is so passionately different. That's the mark of our sort of civilization. Congrats on your essay.

Almost exactly one year later, on September 3, 1996, Les sent a card to me and the assistant editor, George Thomas: "Thanks for your sympathy and concern while I was ill. I'm well on the mend now, with just a touch of intermittent balance trouble from the anaesthetic." My Manning Clark essay in *The Australian's Review of Books* was published a month later, in which I suggested that, as Les was the only living witness to Manning Clark's supposed Order of Lenin, it would have been prudent of *The Courier-Mail* to make sure he could tell the difference between this highest of all Soviet honours and other similar medals. A fortnight after, on October 23, Les sent another postcard:

> I'm troubled: reviews of literary books which I've never seen regularly appear in Quadrant, while those I send typically languish for months or years before they see print. I enclose a typical appeal from one of "my" reviewers, one for whom *Quadrant* is his only hope for respectable publication in our otherwise solid leftist culture. So: am I becoming a back number in the *Quadrant* operation? Do my acceptances of non-fiction prose carry any weight now? Or what? Please let me know. I sent you a package of material this morning: should it be my last?

This was the first angry message from Les I had received after seven co-operative years. In reply, I told Les we had published almost all the critical essays he sent "reasonably promptly", except for a couple from one of his regular authors, Karl Schmude, that were not really literary, such as a review of two books on the Habsburgs, one of which had been published five years ago. Furthermore:

> Do you realise you have not sent us a review of a novel for three years? Perhaps there are other articles which you think trespass

on your patch. If so, could you please let me know. Or perhaps you have other more general complaints about my editorship? If so, I'd like to know what they are.

Les responded on November 20. He asked me to explain to the author of the Habsburg review why we weren't going to publish it. He explained that he was "bored by nearly all Aust. novels". He claimed he had no "cavil" with my editorship, except that I had "belaboured Demidenko too much; never persuaded me she was anti-Semite".

On December 10, 1996, Les sent a postcard, this time addressed only to George, accompanied by an article from Hal Colebatch on Manning Clark. Colebatch's hatred for Clark was frightening and disordered. In 1994 he had published a poem in a magazine called *The Horatian*:

> Earth, receive a putrid pest:
> Manning Clark is laid to rest.
> He dared not fight, nor dared he rob:
> He lied to try to please the mob.

The poem continued in this vein, describing Clark as a "spirit screeching hate and spite", a "slivering liar and coward", a "craven snivelling shit" and a "neurotic gangrenous freak". It concluded: "His flesh is like his spirit rotten: / Let them both stink and be forgotten." In the article that Les now sent to George, Colebatch claimed Clark was an anti-Semite who had written "most admiringly of Labor politician Frank Anstey's anti-semitic tract *The Kingdom of Shylock*". I noticed later that Colebatch's essay was dated December 1, 1990. It seemed to me to have been sent by Les as an act of war. Nonetheless, I took the submission at face value. On March 19, 1997, Les sent George another card. "I hope you & all the good Qdt folk I'm not at feud with are doing very well!" I wrote at once, explaining why I couldn't publish an article that claimed Manning Clark was an anti-Semite. "I don't think a matter like this is just cause for argument, let alone a feud," I concluded. "How about calling it off?" Les now let fly.

In a postcard, he wondered "when you & Mr Gaita will consider your position regarding the history of Quadrant and its function as a sanctuary for writers in Australia otherwise silenced by totalitarianism ... I hope you won't expect me to resign, or go quietly, if you try to push me out."

On May 21, 1997, Les sent George (not me) a poem on Pauline Hanson that was, he claimed, "Relevant, Current, of course, & wd. be best used soon, I'd say". The poet was "Alexander Farr-Cornell", someone of whom no one had ever heard, or would ever hear in the future. It was the first truly fascistic submission I had received as *Quadrant* editor. David Stove was merely a reactionary.

> **Watching Mrs Hanson**
> She's burning before me / Jade eyes unblinking / Hard like she's marble / Mouth hardly moving
> She stands like she's naked / Walks like a virgin / Talks like a novice / Voice like a razor
> I've seen her tremble / I've heard her whisper / I've felt her power / Burning before me

Finally, on June 9, Les sent me (not George) a long letter. He listed our differences in ascending order of gravity. There was, first, "the attitude to Jews of the traitor Clark". Then my criticism of Helen Darville, where I had led the pack:

> More seriously, from my point of view, you had started taking the received leftist line on Aborigines, letting the man Gaita trumpet against dissent on this matter. I began to wonder, if the Melbourne Left succeeded in duchessing you & getting you to bring Quadrant over to them. If Humphrey [McQueen] and the rest could by blandishments so obvious ... carry the citadel of Quadrant ... they'd have won all the high ground ... How do I know you've been getting duchessed? Not so much because of the Gaita stuff etc. but because of your extraordinary statements to members of the Qdt Board that my tastes in poetry are perhaps

too narrow and traditional for me to be the best editor of poetry for the journal ... [T]hat's a familiar Melbourne line ... Unlike your new, or I hope merely recent friends, I do know what is good, in my field. Now we have reached a real core of feud, and I await your comments on it with interest.

There was a P.S. in Les' letter: "I had Ramona [Koval] up here from ABC Radio National the other day checking for possible ways to depict me as antisemitic ... so perhaps that's to be the future Melb. Line against me." All this was paranoid fantasy. I had never spoken one word with Humphrey McQueen. Indeed, we were currently involved in serious dispute over Manning Clark. I had never spoken critically, on the board or elsewhere, about Les as poetry editor. I had never spoken to Les' fantasm, the Left-Wing Poets of Melbourne, about him or indeed about anything. I wondered which board member had spoken thus to Les.

I now recognised that my relations with Les were over. I should have dismissed him at once and then informed the board. As I had appointed him as literary editor without reference to the board, I believed I had the right to dis-appoint him. I decided instead to test the waters on the board. I wrote to Leonie on July 21, 1997, enclosing Les' letter. I explained that Les and I were obviously finished, and that I intended to outline what had happened at the next meeting of the board and "to ask [it] to agree to my appointing a new literary editor". I should have enclosed the fascistic poem about Pauline Hanson, but didn't. The board met on August 31. Only four members were present: Leonie, David Armstrong, Tom Gregory and Martin Krygier. I was "in attendance". It was agreed that we would either remove Les as literary editor (the option I favoured) or offer him the position of poetry editor, which we believed he would refuse (Leonie's option). The minutes of the meeting read:

> After considerable debate about the merits of the two options, it was decided that both the Chairman and the Editor would discuss the situation with Richard Searby before a final decision was to

QUADRANT 3: THE POLITICS OF RACE

be made and to hold a telephone discussion with members of the board to decide which alternative to adopt.

On September 17, I spoke on the phone with David Armstrong, who told me that Les and Leonie had spoken and that Les had refused the offer of poetry editor. The following day I faxed Leonie:

> I spoke with David last night. I was surprised to hear that you had spoken to Les Murray and that Les refused the offer of the Poetry Editorship. The Committee of Management agreed at its last meeting that if Les Murray refused this offer his relationship with *Quadrant* would be over. Is this the case?

Leonie replied on the next day:

> Les has *not* refused the offer of the Poetry Editorship. He is not happy with the suggestion that we split the poetry and review responsibilities, and he wants to continue as Literary Editor. After discussing this with David, Richard and Peter [Chew], I've concluded that the disagreement between you and Les is too small a point on which to settle this and other matters relating to *Quadrant*, and that it is certainly not the time to take quick action. Since the Committee did not, as I recall, make any decision about what action would follow, I think we should have a full Committee meeting (including the new members) as soon as possible, to discuss this and a range of other matters.

This was an extraordinary fax. The board had decided there were only two options. Either Les would accept the poetry editorship or he would be removed altogether. It had been agreed that, given his paranoid letter of June 9, in which he accused me of selling *Quadrant* out to the Humphrey McQueen/Melbourne Poets left, if I were to continue as editor he could not continue as literary editor. Why had Leonie not discussed this matter with my two allies on the board, Tom and Martin? And what were the "other matters" concerning

Quadrant that Leonie believed we needed to discuss? I wrote at once to Richard Searby. I explained that while everyone on the board had expected Les Murray to turn down the offer of the poetry editorship, Leonie and David thought that his "refusing a reasonable offer was in the interests of *Quadrant*":

> It was implicit in our long conversations at the Committee of Management meeting that relations between Les Murray and myself had broken down and the only real question was the best way for a break to occur. Leonie's fax suggests that Les Murray's unwillingness to accept the poetry editorship does not constitute a refusal. This rests on there being a difference between unwillingness to accept an offer and a refusal of it. This is not a distinction I have previously encountered. However, as Les Murray is deemed not to have refused the offer and as the matter between us (which will determine whether or not I go on as editor) seems to Leonie "too small" she has opted for a meeting of the Committee to resolve an issue which was previously resolved, without ambiguity.

In mid-September, something peculiar occurred. In a Kate Legge article in *The Weekend Australian* of September 13/14, under the headline "Witch-hunt", Les was quoted thus:

> "This is women's business" ... He has been bitten once too hard recently. His defence of Darville in verse drew fury from the literati, notably Quadrant editor Robert Manne, who found her book anti-Semitic. Murray, who is Literary Editor of Quadrant, says Manne "stopped speaking" to him and he no longer receives copies of the magazine.

Every claim here was a lie. I had said nothing about Les's poem on Demidenko/Darville. I had not stopped speaking to Les. It was Les who had begun sending material to George Thomas and not to me, and who had refused to call off what he had labelled "a feud". As our records showed, the September issue had been posted to him as usual.

Both Leonie Kramer and David Armstrong knew that Les was lying. And yet both were so concerned about what I might say that Leonie rang the *Quadrant* office and David spoke to me urging me not to reply to what they knew to be Les's falsehoods. Why? I ignored their advice.

I decided to resign as *Quadrant* editor. I discussed my decision with three people. First, and most importantly, as always, with Anne. She had long despised several people I worked with at *Quadrant*, beginning with Peter Coleman and, after one encounter, Hal Colebatch. She would have liked me to have considered staying on. Anne believed that *Quadrant* was opening a new space on political and cultural questions, and publishing, for the first time, many women writers. But she knew that the decision had to be mine. Martin Krygier also very strongly supported the kind of magazine *Quadrant* had become while I was editor. He was extremely distressed about the behaviour of Les Murray, Leonie Kramer and David Armstrong (someone he told me recently that he loved). He knew he would break all connection to the magazine should I resign. But because of his father's seminal role in the creation and management of the magazine for thirty years, the severance was enmeshed in a filial relationship and was considerably more painful for him than it was for me. Rai, of course, also supported me. He believed that *Quadrant* would either collapse or cease to be of interest to anyone not belonging to the right.

I was shocked by the petty behaviour of Australia's greatest poet and by the duplicity of the chancellor of the University of Sydney. I had no stomach for a protracted fight with the board, only half of whom supported me. I also realised that my politics had changed since my appointment. If the old guard on the board wanted a predictable and polemical right-wing magazine, of the kind *Quadrant* had gradually become in the 1980s under Peter Coleman, so be it. I did not realise the strength of the support for what I was doing with *Quadrant* until I had resigned. And by then it was too late. If I had known, it is possible I might have come to a different decision. The board meeting was scheduled for November 12.

In the interval, the Manning Clark issue returned. In an article for *The Australian* on June 7/8, 1997, "The Battle for History's High

Ground", I acknowledged that some of the criticism of Clark was "politically inspired or even grossly unfair". Without mentioning Hal Colebatch, I commented, in parenthesis, "I have in mind one campaigner who claims his work is antisemitic". Colebatch named himself and put his case in a very long letter-to-the-editor. Colebatch's principal evidence consisted of sentences in which Clark, in his characteristic literary style, paraphrased the views of Labor Party figures in the early years of the twentieth century. "[B]y selecting particular sentences from Clark's paraphrases of the views of Deakin, Bruce and Menzies," I wrote in answer to Colebatch, "one could as easily 'prove' that Manning Clark was a defender of the 'Yarraside' bourgeoisie as an anti-Semite." Colebatch omitted mention of Clark's claim, in *The Quest for Grace*, that the Nazi pogrom on *Kristallnacht* played a central role in his political formation: "Hitler and his ministers were wicked men: the imagination in their hearts was evil."

I had asked Sam Lipski and Peter Ryan about Colebatch's accusation. Sam thought, if anything, Clark was a "philo-semite", and knew he had been a friend of several Israeli ambassadors. Peter believed that in their thirty-year friendship Clark had not uttered even one anti-Semitic syllable. Something quite unexpected then happened. Manning Clark's widow, Dymphna, wrote me a private letter. "I must thank you for your careful and thorough refutation of Hal Colebatch's calumnies concerning Manning's alleged anti-Semitism," she said. Dymphna enclosed an article of Clark's from *The Jewish Herald* of September 20, 1946, headlined "Some Observations on Anti-Semitism", and concluded: "This letter is written to you personally and is not for publication. I thank you again for your sense of fair play in this matter."

The *Quadrant* board assembled on November 12 in the Chancellor's office at the University of Sydney. Leonie Kramer and David Armstrong had recruited the novelist Christopher Koch. Martin Krygier, Tom Gregory and I had recruited the eminent defamation lawyer Terry Tobin QC (who was married to one of Santamaria's daughters, Bernadette). I announced my resignation at the beginning of the meeting. A formulaic vote of thanks was passed. And then there followed an hour of criticism of my editorship – from Kramer, Armstrong, Chew and Koch – not one word of which had been heard until then. I wrote this summary for *The Age* and *The Sydney Morning Herald*:

> Under me *Quadrant*, I was informed, had become "politically correct". It had lost its good old boots-and-all polemical edge. It had become far too obsessed with questions of Aboriginal justice. I was wrong not to publish a particular article which argued the case for root-and-branch assimilation of a people called "the Antipodeans". *Quadrant* had become a voice for post-modernism and moral relativism ... It was even, God forbid, the kind of magazine that academics in the humanities faculties of contemporary Australian universities might read with interest or pleasure.

I failed to mention that Leonie had also criticised me for publishing essays on gay love and popular culture.

I wrote to Richard Searby, who was not present at the meeting, about that hour of criticism: "I had not previously thought that this kind of thing was the province of the board. Had I not resigned at the beginning of the meeting I would have resigned at its end." Given that my critics indulged in their carefully prepared criticism when there was no longer any point, I have only one regret: that I did not speak plainly about Leonie Kramer's duplicitousness and Les Murray's support of Pauline Hanson's racism.

Martin Krygier had followed events very carefully. He wasn't sure whether Leonie et al. wanted me to resign or, in his word, were "sleepwalking" to the inevitable result, believing that, with a sharp clip over the ears, they could turn me into a more right-wing editor, somehow reconciled with Les Murray. Following the meeting, Martin, Tom and Terry Tobin resigned from the board. In his resignation letter, Terry expressed astonishment that at the meeting Leonie had circulated a letter from a subscriber who was unhappy that *Quadrant* did not support Pauline Hanson on the question of Asian immigration.

What happened next came as a surprise. For a fortnight, events surrounding my resignation were extensively reported in *The Age*, *The Sydney Morning Herald* and *The Australian*. There were very many letters-to-the-editor and several opinion columns, from Peter Craven, Ramona Koval, Anne Waldron Neumann, Michael Duffy, Frank Devine, Christopher Pearson, Peter Coleman, Gerard Henderson, P.P. McGuinness and Greg Sheridan, who, with his characteristic overstatement, wrote: "The resignation of Robert Manne as editor of Quadrant magazine is a catastrophe for Quadrant and a minor tragedy for Australia. It represents an ugly moment in the politics of the Right and probably a significant 'dumbing down' of conservative intellectual life in this country."

From Coleman's column, it became obvious that he had been working secretly against my editorship. "If the board finds a good editor it must back him or replace him quickly," he wrote. "With Robert Manne, it backed him for far too long and then tried to shackle him." For the only time in my life, I received scores of personal letters, a thick manila folder's worth, many obviously heartfelt. They came from several people closely associated with *Quadrant* over the decades – Robin Marsden, my associate editor, and both Peter and Lee Shrubb. They came from people across the political spectrum – from Archbishop George Pell on the right to the Marxist political economist Ted Wheelwright on the left. There were letters from some of Australia's most distinguished academics, Frank Jackson, Jerzy Zubrzycki, Geoffrey Brennan, Jamie Mackie. The most succinct was Jenny Teichmann, from Cambridge: "May your enemies perish ..." In his beautiful, spidery calligraphic script, Pierre Ryckmans sent a long fax that began: "I just learned that you felt compelled to resign from *Quadrant*. The news is utterly distressing and unintelligible." Two of those "Melbourne Poets" who, I had discovered, haunted Les' paranoid imagination – Peter Steele and Chris Wallace-Crabbe – neither even remotely left-wing, composed verse for the occasion. Another, Alan Wearne, commented: "What the Australian poetry world has known for ages the rest of the country is only now discovering: that Les Murray is both a bully and a sook." The editor of

Meanjin, Christina Thompson, sent Leonie a stinging rebuke, a copy of which she sent to me: "The immediate consequence of [Robert Manne's] dismissal can only be a loss of credibility and influence for the magazine. Worse than this, however, is the impression it leaves that intellectual honesty does not pay." There were also many letters from readers of *Quadrant* not known to me. What I discovered, alas too late, was that there was support and understanding for what I was trying to achieve in my editorship of *Quadrant*.

I could almost admire the elegance of the way Dame Leonie Kramer extricated herself from the political awkwardness of my departure from *Quadrant*. In response to my Fairfax column, she wrote a letter-to-the-editor:

> All those members of the committee of whom he is critical praised his editorship, acknowledging that he came to *Quadrant* when its fortunes were at a very low ebb, restored its reputation and recruited new contributors and readers. Accordingly, it is very disappointing to find Mr Manne speaking of those members of the committee whose views, in some areas, differed from his own, in the terms he uses.

So, with Leonie having orchestrated the events that all but ensured my resignation, it was not I who had cause to be disappointed in her, but she who was disappointed in me.

Part IV
Culture Wars

[13.]

Denialism and the Right

I DELIVERED THE STEPHEN MURRAY-SMITH LECTURE in November 1997. My topic was the history of the Stolen Generations. The invitation came from Stephen's widow, Nita Murray-Smith, who appeared genuinely delighted that I had accepted. I became aware, however, of discontent within the younger left-wing team that now produced Stephen's magazine. How could *Overland* listen to such a notorious conservative? Perhaps for that reason the only people who dined with Anne and me after the lecture were Mietta O'Donnell and her partner, Tony Knox. The lecture appeared nonetheless to go down well. My final *Quadrant* was the January/February 1998 edition. As a parting gesture, I included the text of the lecture.

Shortly after reading *Bringing Them Home*, I decided to conduct research into the history of Indigenous child removal. I applied for an Australian Research Council grant and was awarded a little under $60,000, which allowed me to employ an experienced and much-published historian, Dr Heidi Zogbaum, to share in the research in the state archives across Australia. Until the 1967 referendum, the states were responsible for Indigenous policy and practice; the commonwealth government was responsible only for what happened in the territories – the ACT, which was of almost no importance in this research, and the Northern Territory, which was. The years between 1998 and 2004 were the only time where I was without what might be called a home magazine. As a result, during these years I published in

The Age and *The Sydney Morning Herald* not only a fortnightly column but also the kinds of essays I had written for *Quadrant* in the past, and would publish in the future in Morry Schwartz's *The Monthly* from the moment of its creation in 2005.

In early 1999, what was regarded as a Stolen Generations test case for approximately 700 Territory Aboriginals who had been removed as babies or children was about to begin. The North Australian Legal Service, assisted by Holding Redlich in Melbourne (to whom I offered some unofficial historical advice) sought substantial damages on behalf of their clients, Lorna Cubillo and Peter Gunner – for "wrongful imprisonment" and for breaches of duty of several kinds they were owed by the commonwealth, including its duty as guardian and its duty of care. On February 27, 1999, both Fairfax papers published a 4,000-word article of mine that provided a brief history of child removal in the Northern Territory, from its origins to the late 1950s. It was largely based on details I had just discovered in the Australian Archives. *The Sydney Morning Herald* found an excellent title for the essay: "The Whitening Australia Policy". What I hoped to convey was both the depth and the kind of racism involved. The removal policy in the Territory began with a letter in 1911, at the time the Commonwealth took over from South Australia responsibility for the Northern Territory, from the Acting Administrator of the Territory, Samuel James Mitchell, to his minister in Canberra:

> One of the first works to be undertaken is to gather in all the half-caste children who are living with Aborigines. The police could do most of the work. No doubt the mothers would object and there would probably be an outcry from well-meaning people about depriving the mother of her child but the future of the children should I think outweigh all other considerations.

What was intolerable was not that these children were neglected or rejected but that those with European blood should be allowed to live in the degraded conditions of the Aboriginal camps. By their removal, they could be saved. This was explicit in a letter Prime Minister Stanley Bruce sent to the South Australian premier in 1927:

> There are at the home at Alice Springs a number of quadroons and octoroons under five years of age who could hardly be distinguished from ordinary white children. My colleague is assured that, if these babies were removed, at their present early age ... they would not know in later life that they had Aboriginal blood ...

Especially in the early days, the state of the "half-caste" children's homes in both Darwin and Alice Springs were almost unbelievably dreadful. In 1927 the superintendent at the Kahlin Aboriginal Compound in Darwin described the *three-bedroom* cottage where *seventy-six* babies and children lived: "The building is not only too small, but it is very much out of repair ... the floor is rotten ... the shower is out of order ... In the kitchen the stove is unfit for human use ..." Two years later a Reverend Davies visited the other "half-caste" Northern Territory home in Jays Creek, close to Alice Springs, and recorded: "The accommodation exhausts my power to paint adequately ... The children lie on the floor ... The ration scale has been deplorable ... The whole place makes me boil that such a thing can be tolerated in a Christian country." The absurdity of the common argument among the defenders of the policy – that the "half-caste" children had been removed over social welfare concerns – could scarcely have been clearer.

My article also documented the justification offered by the Chief Protector in the Northern Territory during the interwar years, Dr Cecil Cook, for the removal and subsequent treatment of all mixed-ancestry Aboriginal children: both the ambition to "breed out the colour" and, his darkest nightmare, the prospect that if his racial engineering plans failed, the small number of Europeans in the Territory would be overwhelmed in the future by a new hybrid race comprised of what he labelled "multi-colour humanity" – "half-castes", "Asiatics", Pacific Islanders and low-grade whites.

After the war, the physical conditions of the removed children in the Territory improved, at the Retta Dixon Home in Darwin and at St Mary's in Alice Springs, but not the inhumanity. In my article I quoted the 1950 report of a patrol officer, Ted Evans, about his work at Wave Hill station: "The removal of the children was accompanied by distressing scenes the like of which I wish never to experience again." It also quoted the words of a 1951 speech in which one of the most respected friends of the Indigenous Australians, Dr Charles Duguid, claimed that the removal of the "half-caste" infants from their mothers was "the most hated task of every patrol officer".

Sir Paul Hasluck had launched *Quadrant* after it had moved to Melbourne, and had contributed several fine observation pieces on the changes that had taken place in the morals and manners of Australia over his lifetime; invariably, the past was preferred to the present. I was rather discommoded to discover in the commonwealth archives not only Hasluck's unambiguous support for the child removal policy as post-war minister for territories in the Menzies government, but also, when controversy arose over the minimum age at which the children might be taken from their mothers, his pencilled note on a policy paper that settled the question: "The younger the child is at the time of the removal the better for the child." The response of the Aboriginal mothers to the removal of their babies and children was principally known from their actions rather than their words – the fact that they frequently hid their children in the bush when news of the imminent arrival of police or patrol officers reached a settlement, and often darkened the skin of their "half-caste" infants with charcoal. In the Queensland government archives I came upon one of the rare instances where the lamentation of an Aboriginal mother had been recorded by a sympathetic public servant. On May 27, 1999, on what was by now called "Sorry Day", both Fairfax papers published my story of Nellie Bliss and her fourteen-year-old son, Walter.

I had learned in these archives that the pioneer of the "half-caste" child removal policy, not only in Queensland but in Australia more broadly, was the Northern Protector of Aboriginals, the English anthropologist Dr Walter E. Roth. It was Roth's practice to use the police to locate "half-caste" children living among tribal Aboriginals, to arrange for their trial before a magistrate on the *charge* of being "a child born of an Aboriginal or half-caste mother" under Queensland's astonishing 1865 *Industrial Schools Act*. After a perfunctory trial, the guilty parties were transported to one of the state's so-called industrial schools. Roth had become aware of a fourteen-year-old "half caste" boy, Walter, "loafing around" in an Aboriginal camp near Cardwell, where he lived with his "full blood" mother, Nellie Bliss.

Shortly after Roth's February 1903 instruction to the police to arrest and imprison Walter ahead of his trial, the Cardwell Shire clerk, William Craig, learned of Nellie's despair. He sent a telegram at once to the Queensland home secretary:

> Mother half-caste boy Walter weeping outside lock-up says she will kill herself by inflicting blood letting gashes and starving herself if son taken. May I acting on her behalf pray you to instruct police to return boy pending further inquiry.

Craig followed with a letter that expressed as eloquently as anything I have read the inhumanity of the child removal policy:

> It is an unassailable and incontestable fact that Aboriginals treat all children they come in contact with or nurse – half or full blooded or white – with universal kindness. The mother and her Aboriginal husband are endeared equally to the half-caste children, as to the full-blooded, briefly because it is the child of the mother and the family group ... Their children are always well fed if they have food. The beating of children is unknown.

Because of the grief of the mother and the inconsolable sobbing of her son, Nellie was allowed to enter Walter's prison cell and to nurse him back to health. He was then released, awaiting trial. With Craig's encouragement, Walter was convinced by Roth to go on board a government steamer, anchored at Cardwell, on the promise that it was a mere legal formality. He was immediately arrested. Recognising that he had been deceived, Walter tried to jump ship but was restrained by native troopers. He was then transported to the Yarrabah Industrial School. Craig had been warned by Nellie's husband: "The Government too much tell im lie, he all day want to steal im blackfellow's picanniny." Craig wrote to the Queensland home secretary: "[T]he old blackfellow knew the character of the government officials better than I did ... Do you dare assert that under English law you have a better right to this boy than the mother who reared and fed him?" For seventy years, this was precisely what the Protectors of Aborigines or the Native Administrators did assert. Fifteen months after Walter had been removed to Yarrabah, Nellie approached Craig. He wrote down her words, which, more than a century later, echo still: "Master, you write im letter longa govt and tell him me too much cross [sorrowful] me cry all day longa my boy, you tell im quick fellow send im longa me."

In early 2002, *Rabbit-Proof Fence*, Phillip Noyce's fine film about the Stolen Generations, was released. It was based on the true story of three young "half-caste" sisters, Molly, Grace and Daisy, who escaped from the Moore River Native Settlement, the West Australian detention camp for Aboriginal adults and children where they were confined, and made their way home to Jigalong, 1,000 miles to the north. Because of the material Heidi Zogbaum had found in the West Australian archives, I was able to document the film's historical accuracy. In 1904, on the advice of Walter Roth, the West Australian government made the Chief Protector of Aborigines the guardian of all Indigenous children up to the age of sixteen. On January 15, 1909, the Chief Protector, Charles Gale, provided James Isdell, a so-called Travelling Protector, with the legal authority to collect all "half-caste" children in the north of Western Australia. Isdell regarded it as a "great scandal to allow any of these half-caste girls to remain with the natives". By May 1909, he was able to report that the East Kimberley region had been "cleared up". Isdell was contemptuous of the opinion of liberal sentimentalists who were concerned about the breach of the bond of love between a mother and her children.

He believed the native mothers' attachment to their babies was no deeper than that of a bitch for her newborn pups. In the unforgettable words from *Bringing Them Home* that I have already quoted, Isdell informed Gale: "I would not hesitate to separate any half-caste from its Aboriginal mother, no matter how frantic her momentary grief might be at the time. They soon forget their offspring."

By 1931, the year when the Jigalong sisters were removed, the West Australian Chief Protector was A.O. Neville, played in *Rabbit-Proof Fence* by Kenneth Branagh. Noyce showed Neville lecturing a white audience on his principal mission and theory: how the colour of the "half-caste" babies and children could be bred out by the removal of the children from native camps, and by state control over their education and employment and, even more importantly, over whom they were permitted to marry. This was entirely accurate. It also showed Neville choosing lighter-skinned children for transfer to the Perth "quadroon" home of Sister Kate Clutterbuck, known as "Sister Kate's". Although in fact "Sister Kate's" opened two years after Molly, Grace and Daisy escaped from Moore River, the dramatising of the idea of choosing quadroons for special treatment was also historically accurate. The greatest moment of the Rudd government was, by general consensus, the prime minister's 2008 apology to the Stolen Generations. I hope that my articles in the Fairfax press, drawn from material Heidi and I had discovered in the government archives of the Northern Territory, Queensland and Western Australia, played even a small role in revealing this history. I learned at this time that perhaps the greatest ever ruckman in the history of my beloved Geelong Football Club, which I had followed with undiminished passion since the age of four, Graham "Polly" Farmer, had been brought up at "Sister Kate's". That might have helped explain something I had noticed, how his eyes often seemed to be looking into the middle distance, almost blank.

Shortly after my resignation from the editorship of *Quadrant*, Leonie Kramer asked me to allow the newly appointed editor, Padraic McGuinness, to write an editorial on the future direction of *Quadrant*. In his lengthy editorial, one-third concerned public policy and the Aboriginal peoples. This underlined the fact that I had lost the confidence of the *Quadrant* old guard, in particular over the question of the Stolen Generations and genocide. Although McGuinness did not mention Rai or me in this editorial, when he described the recent discussions of Indigenous history in *Quadrant* as "mawkish" and "sentimental", it was obvious he was referring to us.

I always regarded McGuinness as a strange man behind whose rough manner and apparent tough-mindedness there seemed to lurk a fear of expressed emotion or feeling. For both Rai and me, there was almost nothing more central than the belief that where moral questions were concerned, it was vital that both head and heart were fully engaged. As it turned out, to my increasing dismay and, yes, anger, political questions concerning the Indigenous peoples of Australia, and in particular the Stolen Generations, dominated the first three years of McGuinness' *Quadrant*. I was later criticised and even lampooned – by the chorus of the right-wing commentariat, and even by some left-inclined historians like Henry Reynolds, Inga Clendinnen and Bain Attwood – for my supposed claim that there had been a systematic right-wing "conspiracy" led by the McGuinness *Quadrant* to deny the moral gravity or even the existence of the policy of Indigenous child removal between 1900 and 1970. What I documented was not a conspiracy but an open campaign. These ideologues and historians had almost certainly not read the magazine as closely as I had.

In May 1998 the resident anthropologist at the neo-liberal IPA, Ron Brunton, argued in *Quadrant* that regarding the question of genocide there was no difference between the Stolen Generations and what he called the "unconceived generations" – that is to say, between state officials forcibly removing mixed-ancestry Aboriginal children from their mothers and communities and state officials providing Indigenous women with contraceptive advice. And in September 1998, in an attack upon Rai, the New Zealand–born Thatcherite political philosopher Kenneth Minogue argued that the many millions of Australians who had been moved by what they had learned about the Stolen Generations following the publication of *Bringing*

Them Home had been "pioneered in the grief for the death of Princess Diana"; that there was no "plausible" policy alternative to the removal of mixed-ancestry children from their mothers, families and communities (a curious position for someone usually critical of the "nanny state"); and that "from the no doubt limited perspective of the surfer on the beach the Aborigines are a pretty incompetent lot" (an opinion it was difficult to believe Minogue did not share).

And on it went. In 1999 and 2000, on Indigenous politics in general, McGuinness' *Quadrant* published articles attacking post-assimilation Aboriginal policy by Gary Johns on the dangers of reconciliation, where he advised us to "read the fine print"; by Ron Brunton on the Hindmarsh Island Bridge "hoax"; by the former assimilationist Peter Howson (Aboriginal Affairs minister in the McMahon government) on the wicked folly of his nemesis, H.C. "Nugget" Coombs, who had outmanoeuvred him in the corridors of power with his policy of Aboriginal self-determination; by the former Marxist Geoffrey Partington on the failure of post-assimilationist Aboriginal education; and by the former Sydney University extreme leftist Keith Windschuttle on the sinister plot of pro-Indigenous activists for nothing less than the "break-up" of Australia. In addition, on the Stolen Generations in particular, McGuinness published articles by a public servant who had worked in the Territory, Reginald Marsh, and, once more, Peter Howson, both of whom argued that the mixed-ancestry children who had been removed had not been "stolen" but "rescued" from the rejection of the traditional societies into which they had been born. Howson was, incidentally, a racist of the old school. In his 2000 submission to the Senate inquiry on the Stolen Generations, he argued that Aboriginal society was a Hobbesian nightmare where life was "solitary, poor, nasty, brutish and short" and on the edge of "extinction" (despite having dodged that bullet for 40,000 to 60,000 years). According to Howson, it was no surprise that when the British missionaries and the pastoralists arrived, first the women and then the men "seized the opportunity to escape" from conditions of "brutality and sudden death" so as to experience "the inestimable benefits of civilization". Following the commonwealth government's victory in the Cubillo/Gunner Stolen Generations test case, where it was cleared of unlawful behaviour in the removal of two Northern Territory children, McGuinness published five long and celebratory articles. In 1999 and again in 2000, McGuinness also convened seminars on the Stolen Generations.

The campaign in *Quadrant* might not have mattered much were it not that the themes developed at length there were supported by dozens of articles by a relatively recent phenomenon in Australian newspapers: an ideologically right-wing commentariat, found especially throughout the Murdoch-owned newspapers but also in Fairfax. The popularisation of the arguments that first appeared in either Ron Brunton's IPA pamphlet *Betraying the Victims* or in *Quadrant* was achieved by the phalanx of such columnists: Frank Devine and Janet Albrechtsen in *The Australian*; Christopher Pearson in the *Australian Financial Review*; Padraic McGuinness and Miranda Devine in *The Sydney Morning Herald*; Piers Akerman and Michael Duffy in *The Daily Telegraph*; Andrew Bolt in the *Herald Sun*; and Ron Brunton and, on occasion, Duffy in *The Courier-Mail*.

At McGuinness' second Stolen Generations seminar, which was called, characteristically, "Truth and Sentimentality", one of the speakers, Keith Windschuttle, went one step further into denialist territory, arguing from a 35,000-word article he had composed that historians led by Henry Reynolds had exaggerated vastly the number of Aboriginals killed on the frontiers by the British settlers, whose compassionate restraint could best be explained by their Christian values and their deep-seated belief in the rule of law. In the final three issues of *Quadrant* in 2000, McGuinness published Windschuttle's article in its entirety under the title "The Myths of Frontier Violence". At this point, something in me cracked.

In 2000 or thereabouts I encountered Morry Schwartz, an idealistic and inventive publisher who financed his publications through upmarket property development. From the first moment, we clicked. Before meeting Morry, I had supposed that he must be a tough or even ruthless operator to succeed as a developer. I could not have been more wrong. Morry is one of the kindest people I have ever met, with the sweetest nature and the quickest mind. Morry and I began discussing a new venture – he was never at ease without something fresh on the boil – that was only gradually taking shape. Eventually it became a long-form essay, of 20,000 words or more, concerning an issue in Australian public life. At first it was called *The Australian Quarterly Essay*. After a complaint from people associated with the once important but in truth long dead magazine of public affairs *The Australian Quarterly*, Morry's new child became *Quarterly Essay*, a far more arresting title. It would also be the father of a monthly magazine, called *The Monthly*, and the grandfather of a newspaper appearing on Saturday, called – what else? – *The Saturday Paper*. (Morry's paper appeared in print at a time when print newspapers were being digitised across the globe. All right-thinking people, including me, thought the new paper an impossibly romantic dream with zero chance of survival. It has recently celebrated its tenth anniversary.)

After Keith Windschuttle's three denialist essays were published, I suggested to Morry a *Quarterly Essay* on the right-wing campaign to discredit *Bringing Them Home* and the idea of the "Stolen Generations", the term invented by Peter Read and embraced by Indigenous Australia. Peter Craven, who already edited two annual anthologies for Morry – *The Best Australian Essays* and *The Best Australian Stories* – was appointed editor of *Quarterly Essay*. His assistant was the remarkable Chris Feik. Chris and I have worked together since 2000 on innumerable projects. I often say that it has been my good fortune to have worked with two of the most talented Australian book editors of the past four decades: Michael Heyward and Chris Feik.

On the eve of the publication of the almost-40,000-word essay we agreed to call *In Denial: The Stolen Generations and the Right*, my one-time opinion-page editor at Eric Beecher's Melbourne *Herald*, Andrew Bolt – a journalist I once would have described, borrowing Winston Churchill's description of Clement Attlee, as "a modest man with much to be modest about" – made front-page tabloid headlines across Australia with a despicable article about one of the most loved

Indigenous leaders, Lowitja O'Donoghue. When she was an infant, Lowitja's white father, an Irish stationhand, had seized Lowitja and her four siblings from their Aboriginal mother and delivered them to a South Australian "half-caste" mission, the Colebrook Home at Quorn. In explaining these circumstances to a journalist she assumed to be objective, even sympathetic, Lowitja had commented that she was not so much stolen as cruelly removed from her Aboriginal mother by her white father, who perhaps feared prosecution under recent South Australian law. Lowitja was one of the most eloquent and tireless advocates for the Stolen Generations. Accordingly, the advertising banners of newsagencies in Victoria announced Bolt's and the Murdoch papers' scoop: "LOWITJA: I WASN'T STOLEN". (Prime Minister Howard was on commercial radio in Melbourne that morning. He described Bolt's report on the front page of the *Herald Sun* as "highly significant".) Within weeks, the truth about Lowitja's removal was reported in *The Australian* by Stuart Rintoul, Lowitja's future biographer. Thirty years after her removal, relatives at Oodnadatta recognised Lowitja from her face. They told her where her mother lived. It was several weeks before Lowitja was able to make the journey to her mother's settlement. She learned that, every day for several weeks, her mother had stayed by the roadside, awaiting the arrival of her daughter. "They soon forget their offspring", indeed.

In Denial was published on April 1, 2001. After outlining Bolt's report and offering a sympathetic but quite tough critique of the weaknesses of *Bringing Them Home*, I told or retold four unusually well documented stories of the removal of stolen children: 'Walter'; Margaret Tucker; Lorna Cubillo and Michael Smith. I decided to retell these stories, from several states and territories and across the decades, to show how different were the circumstances of removal, how varied the life consequences, but how common the depth of the injustice experienced.

For Fairfax, I had already sketched the woeful conditions of the interwar half-caste homes that made a mockery of the claim that the children had been removed over a concern for their physical well-being. Another central argument of the Stolen Generations denialists was that the children had been "rescued" and not "stolen" from the Aboriginal camps, where, so it was said – for example, by the commonwealth public servant Reginald Marsh – that they had no place within the moiety system and thus faced ferocious, lifelong and even life-threatening rejection. In part, this argument was refuted by evidence from those, like Bill Harney, who lived among Aboriginal communities in the Northern Territory for much of his life. In his memoir, *North of 23 Degrees*, Harney wrote of a station "where, amidst laughter, swimming or maybe hunting with their father and mother, these little half-castes would live among their own peoples, tended by all the tribe and particularly by a mother who watches over her child and tends to its wants". What was more, having read thousands of pages of contemporary records concerning child removal, I had not found even one instance where rejection by the tribe was given as the justification. If that was wrong, the onus was on the denialists to produce the evidence. The argument about the rigidity of the moiety system also made no logical sense. The children were removed across Australia. In Victoria, New South Wales and much of South Australia and Western Australia, mixed-ancestry Aboriginal children were removed decades after the collapse of traditional society and the moiety system.

The archives disproved several claims made by the denialists. Let two instances suffice. In the lecture Douglas Meagher delivered at the *Quadrant* "Truth and Sentimentality" seminar, he bloviated at *Bringing Them Home*'s defamation of the Aboriginal tenor Harold Blair, when it claimed that his Aboriginal Children's Holiday Project of the early 1960s – for Indigenous kids in the Queensland camps to spend some weeks of vacation with white families in Victoria – was used as a means for permanent separations. Such "dreadful accusations", according to Meagher, were typical of the authors of *Bringing Them Home* and the lack of "rigorous analysis". Harold Blair was a fine man and a friend of Meagher's father, Ray, who had served as minister of Aboriginal Affairs in the Bolte government in Victoria.

In the Queensland archives I discovered an interesting correspondence. On July 22, 1962, Harold Blair wrote to the superintendent of the

Cherbourg Aboriginal Settlement on behalf of the Children's Holiday Project. Blair pointed out that he had already been offered assistance:

> [S]ome from families wanting children for holidays and others offering permanent homes either as adoptive or foster parents ... I immediately thought of you as the man most qualified to advise me of the best means of arranging these visits and of the possibility of, and procedure for, procuring children for fostering and adoption.

On February 5, 1963, Harold Blair and a Mrs Molly Pettett visited Cherbourg and discovered four mothers they thought might be willing to hand over their children permanently. Using the Holiday Project as a way of effecting fostering or adoption was strongly supported by the Queensland Director of Native Affairs, Cornelius O'Leary, who, however, thought there were few Aboriginal mothers who would be willing to part with their children. Blair's proposal concerned the superintendent of the Victorian Aboriginal Welfare Board, Philip Felton. On February 19, he replied to a letter from Blair: "The arrangement of a short holiday is a very different matter from their permanent placement under foster home conditions." Blair was not deterred. In March, the handover of the four Cherbourg children took place in a blaze of publicity, on Melbourne television. *Bringing Them Home*'s discussion of the Harold Blair Holiday Project was not one of its "dreadful accusations" but, in essence, accurate.

Bringing Them Home had discussed the plans of both Dr Cecil Cook and A.O. Neville "to solve the problem of the 'half-caste'" through a program they both called "breeding out the colour". In one of his *Quadrant* editorials, Padraic McGuinness pronounced:

> Did some bureaucrats in areas of policy-making advocate the steady disappearance of Aborigines by assimilation of mixed bloods and the inevitable disappearance of full-blooded Aborigines attached to their own culture and way of life? Yes, there is clear evidence of that. But was this the basis for policy

in any specific State or Territory ...? Is there any Government policy statement or internal policy document, as distinct from views expressed by individual bureaucrats however senior, to this effect? No-one has found one.

This was straightforwardly wrong. As I discovered in the Canberra archives, on February 7, 1933, Dr Cook had written to a senior official in the Department of the Interior outlining the settled Northern Territory policy of "breeding out the colour". He thought this policy ought to be adopted throughout the commonwealth. The minister, J.A. Perkins, agreed. The Department of the Prime Minister, Joe Lyons, was approached. It was willing to place Dr Cook's policy on the agenda for the next Premiers' Conference. A memorandum was produced defining commonwealth policy as the encouragement of "the marriage of half-castes with whites or half-castes, the object being to 'breed out' the colour as far as possible". As it turned out, the commonwealth's policy was not presented to the Premiers' Conference, almost certainly because of the opposition of the Queensland Chief Protector, J.W. Bleakley – not to the racism of the proposal but to miscegenation, sexual relations between superior and inferior races. Nonetheless, "breeding out the colour" remained commonwealth policy until at least 1938. When the Union of South Africa inquired about Australia's current policy regarding mixed-race marriages, the Department of the Interior sent Dr Cook's long "breeding out the colour" memorandum of 1933. This was still, after all, the age of absorption. And how did McGuinness respond to this evidence? Silence.

Why had so much energy been spent on the denial of injustice to the members of the Stolen Generations and their mothers, families and communities? In the conclusion to *In Denial*, I argued:

> Of all the questions concerning the injustices experienced by the Aborigines after the dispossession, Aboriginal child removal – perhaps because it concerned a violation universally understood, the separation of mother and child – was the one which most deeply captured the national imagination. After the publication of

Bringing them home many Australians were astonished to discover what had happened so recently in their country's history and what they had previously failed to understand or even to see. This story had the power to change forever the way they saw their country's history. Considerable numbers of Australians were not affected in a similar way ... Their scepticism about the injustice done to the stolen generations, which was reflected in the anti-*Bringing them home* campaign, was the most important cultural expression of a growing atmosphere of right-wing and populist resistance to discussions of historical injustice and the Aborigines.

In Denial was launched by Lowitja O'Donoghue and Paul Keating in Melbourne at 11.00 am on April 6, 2001, in time to make that evening's television news. What has stayed with me was the affection, even the love, Lowitja and Paul felt for each other despite, or perhaps because of, the tough negotiations they had been involved in over the Keating government's *Mabo* legislation. The launch was covered for *The Age* by the very fine journalist Michael Gordon (whose book on the Keating government I had reviewed years earlier with unjustified harshness), and for *The Australian* by the future biographer of Lowitja O'Donoghue, Stuart Rintoul. I was pleased that Lowitja thought I had captured the experience of the members of the Stolen Generations in the line she quoted about those with:

> ... so little capacity for empathy that they genuinely cannot imagine the harm inflicted on a child taken from the warmth of a family to a loveless institution where their skin colour is regarded as a cause of shame, or what depth of grief and bitterness and powerlessness is experienced by mothers and families who are robbed of their children by welfare workers or police.

An edited version of Keating's carefully crafted speech was published. My favourite lines were Keating's description of Howard's use of the word "practical", as in "practical reconciliation", as "an anti-matter particle designed to obliterate the noun it's meant to describe", and his brilliant, devastating description of the anti–*Bringing Them Home* brigade:

> Is there anything in contemporary Australian life more outrageous than the sight of the most powerful figures of Australian conservatism cloaking their well-nourished frames in the rags of the powerless? The men who control the national government, who declaim from the opinion columns of every newspaper, who stack each government-controlled board in the land, who draw their funding from the largest corporations in the country, claiming to be the victims of a conspiracy to silence them.

Keating's description of his incapacity to advance the great cause of reconciliation since Howard's victory in 1996 became on the following Saturday morning *The Age*'s advertising banner: "KEATING: MY BIGGEST REGRET". I got a copy of the banner from my local Hurstbridge newsagent.

In Denial was reviewed favourably in the expected places. In *The Age*, Henry Reynolds approved, although not without a gentle punch in the stomach: "Both sides of this debate see conspiracies where they may not exist in any highly organised manner." To reiterate, *In Denial* did not suggest a conspiracy – an idea that began with Andrew Bolt – but an open and public campaign. On balance, even the three reviews run by *Overland* were favourable. Most interesting for me was that by the Indigenous author Melissa Lucashenko:

> I pick up *In Denial: The Stolen Generations and the Right* gingerly. More Migaloo words, and these from a powerful conservative. Slightly nauseous with nervous tension (will the attacking words leap off the page? Will he too pull on a mask, and begin to kick the corpse?) I begin to examine Manne's arguments. It isn't long before I can relax; Manne can see the connections, he knows the score. He's still Migaloo of course – and in several instances wrong – but the sickening rank hypocrisy of the Bruntons, the McGuinnesses and the Duffys is absent here.

In Denial was in the bestseller lists for three months. It was republished as a short book and won a Queensland government prize for a work advancing public debate. We used the award money to build a feed shed for our horses, which my daughters, Kate and Lucy, christened, with a plaque, "The Peter Beatty [sic] Shed".

Even after Peter Craven and Chris Feik had, rightly, taken a little of the sting out of some of my language about the anti–*Bringing Them Home* brigade, *In Denial* was still an angry essay. On some occasions it was enough to simply quote the words of the columnists, like Andrew Bolt's description of Sorry Day as "celebrations of guilt" where "tens of thousands" of people "mooched" around signing Sorry Books, or Piers Akerman's description of Cathy Freeman, whose grandmother had been removed to Palm Island, as "a child-person". On others I added a comment. Without a scintilla of evidence, as they say, Christopher Pearson had described the woman who had mothered Lorna Cubillo – her mother's sister, as her mother had died at birth – a "call girl". In response I wrote: "The abuse by the pompous and the privileged of the powerless and the dispossessed is not a pretty sight." In one of his columns, Michael Duffy had described the non-Indigenous pro-Aboriginal intelligentsia as "white maggots" who were trying to "suck the blood" of the Aborigines. In another he argued that "the process of depriving us of our history is psychologically dangerous for many people". And in several others, pointing to the influence of Jewish academics (Colin Tatz but especially me), that the "growing links between Jewish and Aboriginal Australians could have a profound effect on how all Australians come to view our past". Putting these ideas together, I wrote: "Perhaps Jewish maggots might in the end do even more damage to their country than Anglo-Irish maggots." All members of the brigade returned fire and, knowing that readers were not likely to be able or bothered to check the sources, time and again claimed to have been misrepresented. On June 2, 2001, *The Courier-Mail* published a generally hostile 7,000-word article by Chris Mitchell's current wife, Deborah Cassrels, "History of Manne", where even Helen Demidenko/Darville was interviewed and allowed to claim that I knew "little" of history and "nothing" of literature.

It was interesting that I was often, inaccurately, regarded as the leading proponent of the genocide claim. Hostility to both Rai and me over this issue extended well beyond the right. In the short-lived *Australian's Review of Books*, in her essay "First Contact", Inga Clendinnen outlined a position that I'm sure was commonly held. Inga described the claim of genocide by the authors of *Bringing Them Home* and its supporters as:

> ... not only ill-judged, but a moral, intellectual and (as it is turning out) a political disaster. I am reasonably sophisticated in various modes of intellectual discussion, but when I see the word "genocide", I still see Gypsies and Jews being herded into trains into pits, into ravines, and behind them the shadowy figures of Armenian women and children being marched into the desert by armed men.

There is only one answer here. The crime of genocide has been outlined in international law. It specifies that one means by which the destruction of a nation, ethnicity, race or religion can be accomplished, "in whole or in part", is by "by forcibly transferring children of the group to another group".

Not long after the publication of *In Denial* I was approached by a man I did not know, who lent me a book that he believed would interest me: Margaret Morgan's *A Drop in the Bucket: The Mount Margaret Story*, a memoir that told the story of the Western Australian Mission to the Aborigines of the Reverend Rod Schenk, who was supported by the famed friend of Indigenous Australians Mary Bennett. Schenk had read the proceedings of the 1937 Canberra Conference of Aboriginal Administrators. His conclusions were identical to mine. Schenk understood that, at the conference, his nemesis, A.O. Neville, had articulated a policy for the elimination of the Aboriginal people. In 1937, Raphael Lemkin's word "genocide" was not yet known. Schenk therefore spoke of Neville's genocidal ambition as "the 'die-out' and 'breed-out' policy".

*

Keith Windschuttle had suggested that the scholarly work pioneered by Henry Reynolds on the bloodstained history of the settlement of Australia was a left-wing fabrication. Australia's most popular historian, Geoffrey Blainey, had given a name to this new school in an essay in an issue of *Quadrant* that I had edited: "black armband history". Prime Minister Howard was highly interested and obviously sympathetic. The campaign led by McGuinness to destroy the credibility of *Bringing Them Home* and to deny the injustice suffered by the Stolen Generations seemed to me the beginning of something new, and something of genuine ideological significance. Without a history that Indigenous and non-Indigenous Australians could share, the prospect of reconciliation would, I believed, be lost. It was for this reason that I had decided to write *In Denial*.

In late 2002 Windschuttle published the first of a promised (or, in my view, threatened) three-volume work he called *The Fabrication of Aboriginal History*. The first volume dealt exclusively with Van Diemen's Land, or Tasmania. The man with whom I had co-edited *Quadrant* in the first eight months of 1989, Peter Coleman – someone with zero knowledge of Australia's frontier history, as he was soon to prove – wrote the first review of *Fabrication* in the December issue of McGuinness' *Quadrant*. He argued that, because of the left's supposed stranglehold over Australian contemporary political culture, "[m]ost reviewers will ignore this book. Or, if they do notice it, it will be only to rubbish it. I hope I am wrong."

He was. At the book's launch on December 9, Windschuttle expressed his surprise at the way *Fabrication* had so far been received: "[M]y book has had a rather good press over the past two weeks." In 2000, Padraic McGuinness had accorded Windschuttle "a huge amount of space" to outline his case, and had defended him when Windschuttle's critics were at "their most ferocious". In Windschuttle's opinion: "If anyone ever writes an intellectual history of Australia in the late twentieth century, one of its most significant events would have to be Paddy's takeover in 1998 of the editorship of *Quadrant*. Under his regime, topics that were previously taboo became debatable again."

One widely reported comment at the launch occasioned in me both pain and shame. According to Professor Claudio Véliz, the convenor of the small, weekly lunchtime gatherings at La Trobe I had attended regularly over several years, the treatment of the Indigenous peoples during the settlement of Australia – where in many regions entire groups and their cultures had been almost totally wiped out – was, at least in comparison to other colonial adventures, little more than a "nuns' picnic". I had accepted that Véliz-ian tone of voice for too long.

My decision to respond to *Fabrication* was, as social scientists say, overdetermined. *Fabrication* was an even worse book than I had imagined, reactionary and absurd in almost equal measure. In Tasmania, the entire "full-blood" Indigenous people had been almost entirely wiped out within the space of some forty years. It was for this reason that nineteenth-century humanitarians took particular interest in the British settlement of Tasmania, and that Raphael Lemkin, the Polish Jewish lawyer who invented the term for a crime previously without a name, wrote a short history of the genocide in Tasmania. Indeed, in the 7,000-word attack *The Courier-Mail* had launched following the publication of *In Denial*, Deborah Cassrels had written: "[N]o Australian would deny the genocide committed against Tasmania's Aborigines."

Windschuttle would have none of this. According to his version, the Indigenous peoples the British settlers encountered on their arrival in Tasmania in 1804 had no attachment to the country on which they foraged and hunted, no word for "land" and no concept of trespass. The violence that took place following the arrival of the British was small in scale and was not an instance of an indigenous people defending their territory by a warlike action against invaders. Rather, they were natural-born murderers and thieves, and the violence was a result of the vicious behaviour of the Indigenous raiding parties in search of the highly prized "consumer goods" brought by the settlers. Windschuttle claimed that in the years between 1804 and 1847 the exact number of both Indigenous and non-Indigenous deaths could be known. Indigenous 'Tasmanians' had killed 182 settlers. The British settlers had killed 118 Indigenous 'Tasmanians'. (Later he amended this figure to 120.) Apparently, no Indigenous fighters died of their wounds. Apparently, too, the British shepherds, sealers and timber cutters, many of them ex-convicts, reported dutifully to the authorities in Hobart every time they killed an Indigenous Tasmanian, despite the fact that, except for a brief period of martial law, the Indigenous Tasmanians were British subjects whose killing might be found to be murder.

Of course, Windschuttle could not deny the extinction of all the "full-blood" Indigenous peoples of Tasmania. But for this the British settlers were blameless. Apart from death brought about by lack of immunity to European disease – a matter assumed by Windschuttle for which, unlike with killings, no evidence was, apparently, either needed or produced – the Indigenous peoples were, in Windschuttle's words, "the active agents of their own demise". He claimed that the Indigenous Tasmanians were too foolish to accept the great gift of "civilisation" the British generously offered, that their men were "misogynists" who frequently prostituted their women, and that they were so primitive a people – having not even discovered how to light a fire or clothe themselves in kangaroo fur (just two examples of Windschuttle's ignorance of contemporary scholarship) – that their survival could best be explained as a 30,000-year period of "good fortune".

Windschuttle argued that self-hating left-wing historians had falsely claimed that the British settlers in Tasmania were guilty of the crime of genocide. They aspired to the break-up of Australia. By close inspection of the footnotes of three prominent historians of Tasmania – Henry Reynolds, Lyndall Ryan and the late Lloyd Robson – what Windschuttle claimed he could demonstrate was not that the historians had made some mistakes, as they had, but that they had deliberately, scandalously, almost unprecedentedly falsified the record – that is to say, fabricated the Aboriginal history of Australia. Windschuttle was seemingly unaware that, as Bain Attwood would soon demonstrate, neither Reynolds nor Ryan had argued that genocide had occurred in Tasmania.

Fabrication unleashed what was probably the most ferocious Australian literary battle since Helen Demidenko's *The Hand that*

Signed the Paper. It had some serious support. Geoffrey Blainey told the starchily conservative American magazine *The New Criterion*, for example, that *Fabrication* was "one of the most important and devastating [books] written on Australian history in recent decades". Several conservative supporters of Windschuttle, including Peter Coleman and Chris Mitchell, who had recently been appointed editor-in-chief of *The Australian*, did at least recognise that *Fabrication* was a cold book, without pity for the tragedy that had taken place in Tasmania.

For their part, *Fabrication*'s enemies regarded it as, in the words of the late Stuart Macintyre, a historian unattracted to hyperbole, "a shocking book". Mark McKenna thought that *Fabrication* read "like a Social Darwinist writing letters home to England", and that, "[l]ike an actuary with an abacus, Windschuttle strolls through the landscape of Tasmanian history counting the dead". Henry Reynolds thought *Fabrication* was the most "biased and cantankerous" historical work to appear in this country since G.W. Rusden's three-volume *History of Australia*, published in the 1880s, although even Rusden, he argued, could not match "Windschuttle's vilification of the Tasmanian Aborigines". With the publication of *Fabrication*, he said, "the concept of savagery has been reborn". In late 2003, the journalist and academic Matthew Ricketson added up the number of newspaper articles concerning *Fabrication*. There were ninety-eight.

In preparing my Windschuttle column I noticed something odd. In the nastiest chapter of *Fabrication*, Windschuttle mentioned *Sick Societies*, a book by the American anthropologist Robert Edgerton. I discovered that its six pages on Tasmania had several clauses or sentences almost identical to clauses or sentences in two or three pages of *Fabrication*. On more than a dozen occasions Windschuttle had lifted them from Edgerton without quotation marks or footnotes. In *Fabrication* Windschuttle had written a short sermon on the importance of footnotes. And he had attacked the scholarship of Lloyd Robson, Henry Reynolds and especially Lyndall Ryan with unrestrained brutality. With Windschuttle's sermonising and ruthlessness in mind, I decided I would point out what I had found. My column concluded thus:

When I read the relevant section [of *Sick Societies*] I discovered several occasions where Windschuttle, without attribution, seems simply to have copied out Edgerton's words almost verbatim or provided slightly altered paraphrases. Here he has comprehensively fallen short of the standards he requires others to meet. An old remark about the goose and the gander comes to mind.

With these words, to my surprise, a fierce plagiarism controversy, lasting several weeks, erupted. Windschuttle threatened: "I'll sue the bastard." He argued that whatever apparent similarities existed between his text and Edgerton's it was because both had drawn on the same research, of the anthropologists, Ling Roth and Rhys Jones. The anti-Windschuttle camp was silent. The pro-Windschuttle camp pretended it was, in Roger Sandall's words, "a malicious diversion".

Why would the High Priest of La Trobe do anything so shabby? In his sneer that Windschuttle's business is "corpse minimisation" we find the reason. For Manne is in the rival business of "corpse maximisation", having made a career out of insinuating the holocaust concept wherever it will give him a moral advantage.

Sensing my vulnerability over Edgerton, Chris Mitchell decided to republish in *The Weekend Australian* Deborah Cassrels' entire 7,000-word article that he had published eighteen months earlier while editor-in-chief of *The Courier-Mail*. The headline this time was "Evolution of Manne" and the subhead: "[He Was] Doing What He Always Said Was Wrong – Bullying – Helen Darville". (Anyone interested in this minor matter, which did me some harm, can google "Keith Windschuttle and Robert Edgerton: A Comparison of Texts.")

When *Fabrication* appeared, Henry Reynolds had argued that it would eventually be answered, but in articles in academic journals that would not appear for years and that no one outside the profession would read. Around this time, I had agreed to edit a series of books within Morry Schwartz's stable that we called Black Inc. Agenda. A scholarly analysis of Windschuttle in an accessible book aimed at the intelligent general reader seemed the perfect way to begin. Two of Windschuttle's targets – Lyndall Ryan and Henry Reynolds – agreed to contribute chapters. Reynolds' "Terra Nullius Reborn" was devastating. Windschuttle argued that the Aboriginal Tasmanians had no word for "land", ergo no sense of belonging anywhere. Reynolds showed that in the most important Indigenous Tasmanian dictionary – Plomley's *Word List*, a work that did not appear in Windschuttle's bibliography – there was a page and a half of words the Indigenous Tasmanians used for "country".

I had become friendly with the novelist and Tasmanian patriot Richard Flanagan over the Demidenko matter. Richard now told me of a PhD candidate named James Boyce, who had already written an astounding essay in answer to Windschuttle. As soon as Chris Feik and I read James' "Fantasy Island", we knew it was the finest overview of Windschuttle's counterfeit coin ever likely to be written. Although almost twice the length of the other contributions, it needed to be published in full. Boyce's essay was the first chapter of *Whitewash*. In her superb review of the book, Inga Clendinnen called James Boyce's debut "thrilling". (Not even Windschuttle was able to deny its quality; "I only wish his obvious talents had been devoted to a better cause," he said.) Inga also provided a wonderful characterisation of Windschuttle's collective portrait of the Indigenous Tasmanians, a people "who lurk at the periphery of civilised settlement like escapees from a Swiftian nightmare, natural-born criminals so maladapted to their environment that their survival for 35,000 years could rationally be explained only as a rather extended period of good luck".

Whitewash was published nine months after *Fabrication*. In "Pack Attacks Replace Intellectual Debate" in *The Sydney Morning Herald* of September 1, in what was possibly the most poisonous article about me ever, Paul Sheehan accused me of "reputation rape": "[I]t's not debate. Last week Manne was back to his old habits. In the wake of the significant impact of Keith Windschuttle's book ... Manne has rushed into print with 18 others, with a book whose purpose is to dismember Windschuttle's reputation." In "Standover Left Axes Debate", an article in *The Australian* of September 6, 2003, Christopher

Pearson supported Sheehan's case and called me "the most conspicuous example of moral narcissism in the commentariat". There were several columns and editorials like this, especially in *The Australian*. And very many letters, on balance hostile.

Peter Coleman was chosen to review *Whitewash* for *The Australian*. Coleman had previously argued, in *The Adelaide Review*, that apart from two proven massacres of Aboriginals 100 years apart, at Myall Creek and Coniston, "several other massacres ... have been alleged". Several? Alleged? At latest count, there were 400 massacres for which the evidence is sound. The ignorance of Aboriginal history of an influential Anglo-Australian, who had been an editor of both *The Bulletin* and *Quadrant* and a parliamentarian, including the leadership of the New South Wales Liberal Party and a period in the federal House of Representatives, was both astonishing and instructive. His claim was that while "steady progress" had been made towards what he called "practical reconciliation", "[t]he rancour of *Whitewash* may set back the cause. But it will not stop it." According to Coleman, those who recognised the brutality of the dispossession of Indigenous Australians were the enemies of reconciliation. Those who denied the brutality and the tragedy were its champions.

Time and again I had argued that there could be no reconciliation between Indigenous and non-Indigenous Australians without rough agreement on the history of the only truly violent series of events in Australian domestic history: the dispossession of the Aboriginal population and its often-terrible aftermath. This was the reason I became involved in Australia's Indigenous history.

[14.]

"Howard Hater"

IN OCTOBER 1998, ON THE EVENING of his victory in the federal election, John Howard made a comment that immediately struck me as curious: "I also want to commit myself very genuinely to the cause of reconciliation with the Aboriginal people of Australia by the centenary of Federation [January 1, 2001]. We may differ about the best way of achieving reconciliation, but I think all Australians are united in determination to achieve it."

Howard's pledge, as I argued in a chapter of a book I edited, *The Howard Years*, did not seem to be insincere or motivated by narrow political ends. Yet he was no friend of Aboriginal Australia. In his first term, Howard had rejected many of the recommendations of the Human Rights and Equal Opportunity Commission's *Bringing Them Home*, most famously that the commonwealth government owed an apology to those mixed-ancestry Indigenous Australians who had been removed as babies or as children from their mothers, families and communities. Unlike Paul Keating with *Mabo*, Howard had entirely excluded the Aboriginal leadership from the negotiations over amendments to the native title legislation following the unanticipated High Court decision in *Wik*: that native title might have survived even over the vast lands held on a pastoral lease. In 1997, at a meeting of the Reconciliation Council on the fiftieth anniversary of the 1967 referendum, as I have noted earlier, many Aboriginal audience members stood and turned their backs on Howard as he began to harangue them over his Ten Point Plan. Yet even with John Howard, there was, or at least appeared to be – regarding the long British settler destruction of Aboriginal society – what one early colonialist had called a "whispering of the heart".

As it turned out, the whisper in Howard's heart was almost inaudible. In July 1999, the newly elected senators took their seats. One was an Aboriginal man, Aden Ridgeway, a member of the Democrats. Howard negotiated with him in secret. What emerged was a reconciliation motion that Howard put before the parliament on August 26, 1999. The motion acknowledged that "the mistreatment of many Indigenous Australians over a significant period represents the most blemished chapter" of Australia's history. Because of that "mistreatment", the motion continued, the parliament was asked to express "its deep and sincere regret".

I thought this motion was disgraceful. A "blemish" was, in common language, a superficial imperfection. What had happened to the Indigenous peoples of Australia following the arrival of the British was nothing less than catastrophic. To express "regret" about that catastrophe rather than to offer an apology suggested that the present generation of Australians bore no responsibility for the tragedy that their forebears had visited upon the Indigenous peoples.

In explanation of his refusal to apologise to members of the Stolen Generations, Howard had argued many times that the present generation could not be held responsible for the actions of earlier generations. On several occasions I had inquired of Howard, in response, whether that meant that the Emperor of Japan could not apologise to the families of the Australian diggers who, as prisoners of war, had been starved, tortured and worked to death by the Japanese in the Second World War? Silence. There were very many historical catastrophes for which present generations of Australians might feel "regret", but for which an apology would make no sense. Was there no difference between our relation to, say, the Irish potato famine or slavery in the United States, for which we bore zero responsibility, and the destruction of Aboriginal society in Australia brought about by the actions of several earlier generations of Australians, from which, in addition, present generations of non-Indigenous Australians were the obvious beneficiaries? Once again, silence.

In my regular Fairfax column, I called what Howard and Ridgeway had put before the parliament the "regrets and blemishes" motion. The father of the reconciliation movement, Patrick Dodson, who had recently retired in dismay and disgust from his position as leader of the Reconciliation Council, called – with the role of *Quadrant* in the anti–*Bringing Them Home* campaign in mind – the Howard/Ridgeway motion "the Paddy McGuinness apology".

I never regarded "reconciliation" as the right descriptor for the ambition to bring about better relations between Indigenous and non-Indigenous Australians. In contemporary times, the idea of reconciliation fitted circumstances in which both sides in a brutal civil conflict – between, say, the Protestants and the Catholics in Northern Ireland, or the Afrikaners and the African National Congress, representing the Black majority in South Africa – had committed violent acts of terror and reprisal for which they might offer apology. In Australia, given the overwhelming imbalance of forces and the inevitability of the outcome, in my view only one side needed to apologise; the task for the other was to find in their hearts the willingness to forgive.

Others did not share my misgivings. Over a decade, those citizens hoping for some kind of moral settlement between Indigenous and non-Indigenous Australians had worked together in an organisation called the Reconciliation Council. I was invited to attend a council meeting in early 2000 that was addressed by Charlie Perkins, "the grand old man of Aboriginal politics", as I called him, who made a dramatic late entrance with the aid of a walking stick. He was known at the time to be dying. As I wrote soon after: "I have never heard a speech of such eloquence, fury and dismay." By May 2000, the Reconciliation Council had found their form of words for the "Declaration" that was to be presented by Geoff Clark, the leader of the ill-fated Aboriginal and Torres Strait Islander Commission (ATSIC), to the prime minister of Australia, John Howard, at the Sydney Opera House on May 29. The Reconciliation Council hoped the Howard government would then formally accept the Declaration at a grand and solemn national ceremony that would mark the 100th anniversary of Federation, January 1, 2001.

Within a day of receiving the draft Declaration, in a brief media release, the Howard government killed it off. It explained that the government could not accept respect and recognition for "continuing customary laws, beliefs and traditions". It could not accept reference to an Aboriginal "right to self-determination within the life of the nation". And most importantly, it could not accept the key sentence of the Declaration, the Reconciliation Council's very deftly worded attempt to take Australia beyond John Howard's motion of blemishes and regrets: "As we walk the journey of healing, one part of the nation apologises and expresses its sorrow and sincere regret for the injustices of the past, so the other part accepts the apologies and forgives."

On May 27, perhaps 200,000 Indigenous and non-Indigenous Australians walked across the Sydney Harbour Bridge in support of reconciliation. To no end. Aboriginal Australia played a key role in the sparkling open and closing ceremonies of the Sydney Olympic Games in September. The Aboriginal runner Cathy Freeman first lit the Olympic flame and then won gold in the 400-metre race, which for many of us was the most glorious moment in the history of sport in Australia. In the centenary of Federation celebrations in Sydney, which I described in my regular Fairfax column as being unusually dismal (once more to the anger of the principal Murdoch tabloid right-wingers, Andrew Bolt and Piers Akerman), the movement towards reconciliation played no part. Ten years of discussion, and ten years of hope, had come to nothing.

*

From 1989, a relatively small number of boats of asylum seekers reached Australia. First to arrive were some 300 Cambodians, who were imprisoned under new Hawke government legislation. When the legislation was challenged, the High Court judged this "mandatory detention" to be lawful, so long as the purpose was administrative and not punitive. The initial legislation contained a time limit for permissible detention of unlawful arrivals of 273 days. As time ran out, in amended legislation, the limit was removed. Eventually the Cambodians agreed to go home on the understanding that they would shortly be allowed to return to Australia as migrants. This episode was barely reported. So far as I can remember, I knew nothing about the battle between Gerry Hand, the Hawke government's Immigration minister, and the lawyers representing the Cambodians. I certainly wrote nothing about it.

In the mid-1990s, during the Keating prime ministership, several hundred Sino-Vietnamese and Chinese asylum seekers reached Australia by boat. So far as I am aware, none was detained or allowed to present a case before a court or a tribunal claiming refugee status. All were returned to China. The repatriation of the Chinese took place in even greater obscurity than the compromise over the Cambodians. It was years before I became aware of the swift deportation of the Chinese boat arrivals.

In 1999 a new wave of boats reached Australian territory, this time bearing Shia Hazaras fleeing from the Sunni Taliban regime in Afghanistan, Iraqis fleeing from the police state of Saddam Hussein and, in smaller numbers at first, people fleeing for a variety of political and religious reasons from the Iranian theocracy. Australia was a signatory to the United Nations Refugee Convention. It was self-evident that the overwhelming majority of the Afghans, Iraqis and Iranians were likely to be, according to the convention's definition, genuine refugees. As convention refugees, they could not be repatriated in the ways the Cambodian and Chinese boat arrivals had been.

My interest in the new wave of Middle Eastern and Central Asian refugees is easily explained. I had not forgotten that both my parents were refugees who had made new lives because of the generosity of Australia during the first prime ministership of Robert Menzies. I suppose my father might have been able to settle in South Africa if Australia had not accepted his refugee application. He had the good fortune to be out of Austria at the time of the *Anschluss*. However, if my mother had not been accepted as a refugee by Australia a few weeks before the outbreak of the Second World War, it was possible that she would have been transported to the Lodz ghetto and then either died of disease like her mother or been gassed at Chelmno like her father.

There was, however more to my interest in the plight of refugees than this family history. During the Cold War, one of the most important ethical absolutes of the anti-communist movement was support for refugees from communism. In part this was a matter of principled belief in human rights. In part it was a matter of ideological politics. Because of my concern for the situation of refugees, in the late 1970s, as we have seen, I had spent three or four highly enjoyable years as president of the Victorian branch of the Indochina Refugee Association, trying to persuade the Fraser government to provide homes for reasonable numbers of Vietnamese, Cambodians and Laotians who had fled from the victorious communist regimes. Those fleeing from communism – voting with their feet, as we regularly called it – provided the camp of anti-communism with convincing evidence for the superiority of the kind of society we championed – liberal, democratic capitalism. The millions of escapees from communism in the post-Stalin era – from Hungary, after the revolution of 1956 was crushed by Soviet forces; across the Berlin Wall after 1961; from Czechoslovakia, after the Soviet Army's invasion in 1968; and, in greatest numbers, from the countries of Indochina after 1975 – were not only settled in Western societies without grumble but were welcomed, even celebrated. Support for refugees from communism was one of the unbending principles of my teachers, Frank Knopfelmacher and Vincent Buckley.

Despite considerable public unease, the Fraser government treated the 2,000 Vietnamese who arrived in Darwin by boat in the late 1970s with generosity. All were provided with hostel accommodation, English language lessons, free medical attention and assistance in finding employment. Repatriation was unthinkable. If they had not been treated generously, the fiercest criticism would have come from the anti-communist right, from Bob Santamaria and the National Civic Council (NCC), and from the intellectuals associated with *Quadrant*. As late as June 1989, following the events of Tiananmen Square in Beijing, where Chinese Communist Party soldiers had shot and its tanks had (literally) crushed hundreds of pro-democracy student demonstrators, Bob Hawke, with tears in his eyes, had offered political asylum to all students from communist China then in Australia.

It was clear that the Afghans, Iraqis and Iranians who arrived from late 1999 on Australian territory – most commonly Christmas Island or Ashmore Reef – had fled from regimes no less cruel and brutal than the refugees from the Soviet bloc and Indochina. With some notable exceptions – professors William Maley, Chandran Kukathas and Martin Krygier – most leading members of the anti-communist movement offered no support to these refugees. When Owen Harries, one of the most prominent and intelligent Australian anti-communists, argued in favour of harsh treatment for the new wave of refugees, I wrote a letter-to-the-editor of *The Australian*:

> There was a time when Owen Harries and I were both members of Australia's anti-communist intelligentsia. In those days, both of us fought tenaciously for the rights of refugees from communist countries. Those presently fleeing from the Taliban or from Saddam Hussein's Iraq are fleeing from regimes considerably more oppressive than those who fled a generation ago from post-Stalin Eastern Europe or the USSR. It fills me with considerable anger to observe the former members of the anti-communist intelligentsia now turning their backs on refugees. I once believed, quite naively, that Owen Harries was an anti-communist because he believed in human rights.

By August 2001, some 10,000 asylum seekers from Central Asia and the Middle East had reached Australia. Most had made their way to Indonesia via Malaysia, and then had purchased an extraordinarily dangerous passage to Australia on Indonesian fishing boats that had been hired by professionals in the so-called people-smuggling business. The asylum seekers were mandatorily detained under the earlier Labor government legislation. As a signatory to the United Nations Refugee Convention, Australia was obliged to assess their claims.

The principal detention centres – Villawood in Sydney, Maribyrnong in Melbourne – were soon overcrowded. New detention centres were built in remote Australia – at Port Hedland, Port Augusta and Woomera. There was no time limit on the detention. It frequently lasted not weeks or months but years. The detention centres became sites of great suffering – of suicide, attempted suicide, hunger strikes and self-harm. As an expression of their powerlessness, their voicelessness, inmates began to sew their lips together. There were occasional riots that had to be put down by force, and some short-term mass escapes. Families were detained together. Children witnessed adults slashing their wrists or being wrestled to the ground by guards. They frequently observed their parents falling ever more deeply into depression.

The tribunals eventually determined that almost all the Afghans and Iraqis were genuine refugees, but the Howard government decided to offer only temporary protection visas. Those receiving such visas were effectively prevented from travelling outside Australia. They were barred from applying for visas for members of their families. Because within three years their cases would be reviewed, they now lived in fear of deportation. Unlike those of the Afghans and the Iraqis, many Iranian cases failed. As the Iranian government refused involuntary repatriation, the unsuccessful Iranian asylum seekers, too frightened to return to Iran, effectively faced imprisonment for life. As the solicitor-general, David Bennett, once put it, according to law their detention could last "until hell freezes over". I visited a ward at Glenside, Adelaide's psychiatric hospital, set aside for such Iranians. The atmosphere was heavy with despair.

One visitor to Australia's detention centres in 2002 was Louis Joinet, the chairman of the United Nations Working Group on Arbitrary Detention. According to him: "[A] system combining mandatory, automatic, indiscriminate and indefinite detention is not practised by any other country in the world."

Shortly after the election of the Howard government in 1996, I had been appointed to a Citizenship Committee by the supposedly "small-l" liberal Philip Ruddock, the minister for Immigration. (It was on that committee that I met, happily, Donald Horne and, unhappily, the mean-spirited Gary Johns.) With the support of Howard, Ruddock did everything in his power to turn public opinion against the asylum seekers. He claimed that they were insolent and entitled, demanding "two-in-one shampoo" and free "orthodontic" treatment – things, Ruddock helpfully pointed out, many Australians would be delighted to receive. Ruddock claimed that whole villages were planning to set out for Australia, by clearest implication in search not of political asylum but of a better economic life. Ruddock's department produced a film that sought to convince potential asylum seekers not to come to Australia, a land of snakes, crocodiles and sharks, and whose people had loose moral values about which no Muslim parent could feel comfortable.

On August 13, 2001, I wrote a column about a six-year-old Iranian child, Shayan Badraie, whose condition I had learned about from a lawyer/activist, Jacquie Everett. Shayan was so traumatised by what he had witnessed in Villawood that he no longer spoke or ate or drank. He had been sent to Sydney's Westmead Hospital on numerous occasions, to be rehydrated, and then returned to Villawood against the strongest medical advice. Secret film of Shayan in a catatonic state, cradled in the arms of his father, was smuggled out of Villawood and shown on the ABC's *Four Corners*.

Ruddock let it be known to friendly journalists – like Paul Sheehan and Andrew Bolt – that Shayan Badraie's difficulties were to be explained not by the scenes of horror he had witnessed in Woomera and Villawood but by the fact that Shayan's father had remarried and that his stepmother had given birth to a new baby. In a television interview, Ruddock on four occasions referred to Shayan not by name, and not even as "he", but as "it". Ruddock's language was remorselessly abstract, playing the role George Orwell identified in one of his most brilliant essays, disguising the meaning of what he was doing from others and even from himself. Asked to justify the way he had treated Shayan, Ruddock said:

> Well, I do look at these issues in the context of humanitarian considerations and there are a broad range of issues that I have

to look at, firstly in terms of whether or not we give up a refugee place that could otherwise go, in this case to four other people, whose circumstances would, I suspect, be far more compelling.

I wrote about all of this. Serving on the Citizenship Committee under Ruddock's ministry became, over time, increasingly awkward.

Why was the Howard government treating the new wave of refugees with such cruelty? There was a considerable amount of loose talk concerning the return of the White Australia policy. I argued that it was inconceivable that Australia would ever again refuse all migrants of colour but that the shadow of the White Australia policy was still influencing what was now taking place. The Immigration department was driven by what had been called a "culture of control". With the Vietnamese refugees of the late 1970s and 1980s, I had become aware that the Fraser government was more politically comfortable selecting tens of thousands of refugees from the archipelago of camps scattered across South-East Asia than it was with the 2,000 who arrived spontaneously by boat. The new post-1999 waves of asylum seekers were manifestly, dramatically, outside Immigration department control. Its increasingly harsh deterrent policies were the response.

I also believed, however, that the question of race did still matter. In 2000 I suggested a thought experiment to an audience at the Sydney Writers' Festival. Imagine that thousands of persecuted white Zimbabwean, former Rhodesian, farmers arrived in Australia by boat, uninvited. Was it conceivable that the government would impose upon them, and that the public would tolerate, a regime involving years of mandatory detention in spartan desert camps surrounded by spotlights and razor wire, with the prospect, at best, of temporary visas, and no right for them even to apply to be reunited with wives and children? The question answered itself. To a small extent, this idea caught on among the critics of the government's policy. Ultimately, it probably affected nothing.

*

At the beginning of 2001 it appeared certain, according to all the opinion polls, that the Howard government would be defeated at the election due later in the year. Gradually, with one compromise economic measure after another, its prospects improved.

Despite the harshness of the government's deterrence policy, the number of asylum seekers from the Middle East and Central Asia arriving on Australian territory by boat continued to rise. In the third week of August, some 1,000 asylum seekers reached Christmas Island and Ashmore Reef, many more than in any week in Australian history. When news arrived of one boat with 345 asylum seekers on board that had just reached Australia, John Howard was criticised strongly by Neil Mitchell on Melbourne commercial radio. What, Howard asked, were we supposed to do? For a humanitarian country like Australia, turning boats away by force (as some South-East Asian countries had notoriously done) was simply not possible.

A few days later, on August 26, a Norwegian cargo ship, the *Tampa*, picked up more than 430 asylum seekers, principally Afghans, from an Indonesian fishing boat that was sinking. The asylum seekers pleaded, then demanded, that the captain, Arne Rinnan, turn back to Australia and take them to their planned destination, Christmas Island.

Rinnan was informed by the Howard government that his ship was not permitted to enter Australian waters. He defied the instruction. The stand-off between Howard and Rinnan dominated Australian news reports for several days. Australian SAS troops boarded and seized control of the *Tampa*. The asylum seekers were transferred to an Australian transport ship, HMAS *Manoora*. Frenzied diplomatic negotiations took place. New Zealand agreed to settle 150 of the *Tampa* asylum seekers. Eventually, the remainder were transferred to a bankrupt Pacific island, Nauru. For its service, Nauru was well rewarded by the Australian government.

In Australia, very many refugee supporters were outraged. During the *Tampa* drama, I attended a meeting of republicans at one of Melbourne University's colleges and, to the anger of the convenor, peppered the speaker, Robert McClelland, the Labor Party's shadow attorney-general, with hostile questions about the pathetic capitulation of his party and its leader, Kim Beazley. He explained that all Labor Party members were being made aware by angry telephone callers of the overwhelming enthusiasm for Howard's action.

At the height of the drama, the *Herald Sun*, the most popular Victorian newspaper, asked its readers whether they thought the asylum seekers on board the *Tampa* should be allowed to land: 615 thought they should, while 13,572 thought they should not. A new asylum-seeker policy was speedily improvised. Wherever possible, asylum seekers' boats – now called suspected illegal entry vessels, or SIEVs – were to be accompanied by an Australian naval ship back to Indonesia. Where this proved impossible, the asylum seekers were to be transported to the new detention camps on Nauru and New Guinea's Manus Island. In case some boats still managed to elude the Australian Navy, both Christmas Island and Ashmore Reef were excluded from Australia with respect to the operation of the United Nations Refugee Convention.

In the days following *Tampa*, Newspoll recorded a 5 per cent swing towards the Howard government. On September 11, 2001, the prime minister was in Washington. A day before he was due to speak at a joint meeting of the US Senate and House of Representatives, a rare honour, planes commandeered by al-Qaeda destroyed the Twin Towers in New York and damaged the Pentagon in Washington. On his flight back to Australia, on US Air Force Two, John Howard invoked the ANZUS Treaty for the first time in its history. Australia would support the United States in its hour of need. Newspoll recorded a second swing of 5 per cent in favour of the government. While at the beginning of 2001 the defeat of the Howard government at the federal election, due to be held by the end of the year, seemed assured, by mid-September Howard's victory seemed certain.

In early October, at the beginning of the election campaign, Ruddock became aware of a report from one of the naval officers involved in the new military repulsion policy that Iraqi asylum seekers were throwing their children into the ocean as a means of morally blackmailing Australia to accept them as refugees. Howard, Ruddock and the minister for Defence, Peter Reith, made sure that for several days the "children overboard" story dominated the news. The government's political logic was obvious. What kind of people were willing to sacrifice their children's lives to save their own? Did we want such people here?

Within a few days it became clear that the initial report was mistaken. No matter. Peter Reith released photos of asylum-seeker children in the ocean. He was soon informed by astonished naval officers, who had not lost their moral compass, that the photos concerned an altogether different incident. In mid-campaign, John Howard visited the ship from which the false report had come. He knew enough by now not to ask the captain, Norman Banks, about the children overboard affair. At the Liberal Party's formal election launch, Philip Ruddock was hailed as a hero. John Howard's remark – "We decide who comes here and the circumstances in which they come" – was greeted with wild applause. The sentence dominated the Liberals' campaign advertisements.

By now I genuinely did hate Howard. As he understood. On October 27, 2001, Paul Kelly interviewed the prime minister. Howard told Kelly that his place in history relied upon winning at the November 10 election. Victory would make him the second-longest-serving prime minister in Australian history. "There were people, and I don't just mean Phillip Adams and Robert Manne [he gives me a steely sidewards glance] who were saying, you know, 'He's got no world view and he's a cheap opportunist' ... if we win the election it is academic ..." Phillip Adams joked: "Manne was as surprised as I was by this strange declaration – and I can assure the PM, on behalf of us both, that he doesn't need to stick around for our sake." Howard won the election, not overwhelmingly but comfortably. His reputation was secure.

As a political commentator, I regarded Howard's 2001 election victory as one of the most accomplished and consequential pieces of retail politics in recent Australian history. Following *Tampa*, Howard had managed to gazump One Nation, by stealing their anti-refugee clothing, and to expose Labor's most telling and dangerous division since the time of Whitlam, between the educated and professional "progressives", who supported reconciliation, the republic, multiculturalism and humane treatment of refugees, and the party's old working-class base, who were, on balance, indifferent to the politico-cultural causes of the progressives and were probably no less delighted than Coalition voters with Howard's muscular anti-refugee policy. The number of votes that One Nation lost the Coalition gained. The election of 2001 was the first in which more workers and people on low incomes voted for the Coalition rather than for Labor.

As a citizen, I was angrier with an Australian government than ever before or since. In the year following *Tampa*, I spoke at several pro-refugee meetings and wrote a dozen or so columns, in defence of the new wave of Muslim refugees and against the actions of the Howard government – principally analysing their "children overboard" lies and the unspeakable conditions inside both the detention centres in Australia and the hellish camps on Manus Island and Nauru, which – scandalously, in my opinion – the government ensured no potential refugee supporter could visit.

I also for a time lost my political balance, taking more seriously than I should have a case being prosecuted by an embittered former Australian diplomat, Tony Kevin (who had looked after me extremely generously on a visit to Poland in 1994). Tony claimed Australian responsibility – not only indifference but something far more sinister, intentional complicity – in the fate of a dangerously overloaded Indonesian fishing boat, known as SIEV-X, which sank in international waters during the election campaign, with the death by drowning of more than 300 of its passengers. When I told Tony, over drinks at Jimmy Watson's Wine Bar in Carlton, that he might be wrong about the Howard government's clandestine involvement in the sinking of SIEV-X – which was to say, in a conspiracy to conduct mass murder – he looked at me as if I were insane.

What we knew for sure was, I believed, bad enough. One woman had lost her three daughters and a sister who were on SIEV-X with her. The woman was taken by the fishermen who rescued her to Indonesia. Her husband lived in Sydney on a temporary protection visa. When he asked if he might visit his grieving wife, he was told that he was perfectly free to visit her but must understand that, under the conditions of his temporary protection visa, he would not be allowed to re-enter Australia.

As I had in the case of Shayan Badraie, I asked, in anguish and in anger: what kind of country had we become? I wrote many columns against the now openly and aggressively anti-Muslim writings of the Australian respectable far right – such as my former *Quadrant* friend and contributor John Stone, who argued that Muslims had no place in a "Judeo-Christian" society like Australia, and my former opinion editor at the Melbourne *Herald*, Andrew Bolt, who claimed in one of his columns: "Unlike Mohammed, Christ did not slaughter unbelievers, execute women who sang rude songs about him, cut off limbs of apostates, sleep with a woman whose family he had just killed, have sex with a nine year old …"

On one political issue connected to asylum seekers I had changed my mind. I was no longer critical of Kim Beazley's capitulation to Howard at the time of *Tampa*. Beazley had supported all but one of Howard's post-*Tampa* acts – the one that granted legal immunity to every action taken by an Australian officer involved in the repulsion of asylum-seeker boats, even including murder. Had he opposed Howard root and branch, as the friends of the asylum seekers argued he should have, the result, I now believed, would not have been a Labor victory, nor even a close-run loss, but a Labor annihilation, which would have left the party with almost no prospect of winning government in 2004.

More significantly, I argued in February 2002 that it was more likely than not that the Howard policy of asylum-seeker military repulsion would be successful in its aim – stopping the flow of refugee boats to Australia. At that time, almost every pro-refugee voice argued that Howard's policy was almost certain to fail. By April 2002, at the end of the Pacific Ocean monsoon season, I was convinced that Howard had indeed "succeeded". Since early 2002, virtually no boats of asylum seekers had set out for Australia. This fact, I believed, had major implications for the 10,000 or so asylum seekers who were either living in permanent fear of repatriation on temporary protection visas, or imprisoned in the detention centres in Australia, their asylum cases having failed, or marooned on the Pacific island camps established after Tampa. Deterrence at the border had succeeded. The earlier deterrence measures were redundant. The cruelty still being inflicted by indefinite detention and temporary visas was therefore now entirely purposeless, cruelty without a reason. In addition, because of the success of Howard's military deterrence policy, the victims of the so-called Pacific Solution could be brought to Australia without risk. As I write, more than twenty years later, the final cohort of refugees and asylum seekers on Nauru, whose lives have been destroyed for no good reason, are being brought to Australia and to detention in cheap hotel rooms with windows that cannot be opened.

In 2004 I published a *Quarterly Essay* on the Howard government's refugee policies called *Sending Them Home*. Although no one among the friends of the refugees was allowed to visit Nauru, I was able to outline conditions there from two sources: correspondence received from the inmates on Nauru by one of the refugee supporters, Elaine Smith, and the extraordinary witness of a Dutch psychiatrist, Dr Maarten Dormaar, who had been appointed by the International Office of Migration to work with asylum seekers there. Dr Dormaar explained his decision to quit Nauru in a devastatingly powerful speech to staff on the island:

> Effective banning of media helps Australians to say, when all is over: "we have not known of it". Where else in recent history did people say so? ... The "processing centres" with their subjugated and desperate population under the tropical sun is like *The Heart of Darkness* ... 850 mostly young men and women are kept in a prison-like situation for no other offence than to get a more safe and fruitful life than they could have in their own country ... [T]he bare essentials of mental hygiene, like respect for a person's autonomy and integrity, are violated by those in power ... No self-respecting psychiatrist will accept work under these detention-like conditions.

I also tried to explain why Australia had an obligation to those asylum seekers who had reached our shores by analogy with the situation where a victim of sexual assault knocked on our door. Just as we could not turn the rape victim away by arguing that there were many others who had been treated more viciously than she had been, so was it not possible to dismiss the claim on us in the case of the 12,000 refugees who had reached Australian territory by reference to the plight of the 14 million refugees worldwide. In the case of both the rape victim at our door and the refugee who had managed to reach Australian territory, a "relationship" involving an obligation had been established. I called this relationship and this obligation "the ethics of proximity". This argument did not impress the new minister for Immigration, Amanda Vanstone, who called it "morally bankrupt" and "tokenism at its worst". "The ethics of proximity must seem twisted to people who have languished for years in refugee camps," she wrote in July 2004.

Although I was the sole writer of *Sending Them Home*, I had relied on one of my doctoral students and friends, David Corlett – the future presenter of SBS's highly successful series *Go Back to Where You Came From* – for some of the research on which the essay was based. Accordingly, I asked for his work to be acknowledged in the authorship thus: "Robert Manne with David Corlett". The general editor of *Quarterly Essay*, Peter Craven, was displeased. Already there were tensions between him and Morry Schwartz, particularly over Peter's attempt to lure the famous American critic Harold Bloom into the authorship of a *QE*. Morry wanted *Quarterly Essay* to deal with Australian questions. He also knew that I would not budge on a matter of honour. Morry sacked Peter, who put it around in literary circles not only that I was responsible for the sacking but also that I hoped to become the new editor of *Quarterly Essay*.

Astonishingly enough, Craven devoted most of a commissioned 4,000-word piece on Australian literature for *The Times Literary Supplement* to his sacking. Craven's article was vicious, playing on the trope of a vain property developer out of his depth in the elevated world of letters that Craven and his friends inhabited. Craven also suggested that Morry had mistaken Inga Clendinnen for a Nazi sympathiser because he had indeed, quite understandably, been upset with her description of concentration camps as *"gemütlich"* – cosy – in her very successful book *Reading the Holocaust*. Morry was furious about Craven's piece. His anger gradually subsided when the *TLS* published his dignified reply to the critic he now was able to describe in print, with Harold Bloom in mind, as "craven Peter".

*

Throughout my life, in the case of the invasion and occupation of a sovereign territory by a foreign power, I had consistently been in favour of defensive war. I supported even Margaret Thatcher's decision to force Argentina out of the nearby Falkland Islands, with its tiny British farmer population, which had the unexpectedly happy consequence of bringing down the military junta and restoring Argentinian democracy. I strongly supported the United Nations' decision to drive Saddam Hussein's Iraqi Army from Kuwait in the 1990–91 Gulf War campaign that was led by the United States. With less confidence (and although I wrote nothing), I also supported the ultimately disastrous post-9/11 United States decision to remove Afghanistan's Taliban government by force after it had failed to take action against al-Qaeda's military settlements on its territory.

By early 2002 it was becoming clear that for the George W. Bush administration, military action against the Taliban was not enough. A right-wing cabal, led by Vice President Dick Cheney and by those in charge of the Pentagon, Defence Secretary Donald Rumsfeld and his deputy, Paul Wolfowitz, had begun trying to convince President Bush just days after 9/11 to seize the opportunity offered by the understandably vengeful atmosphere in the United States and take out the brutal regime of Saddam Hussein – or, as they saw things, "finish the job" in Iraq that President George H.W. Bush had left unfinished at the end of the Gulf War. There was no evidence that Saddam Hussein had anything to do with the al-Qaeda attacks on New York and Washington. As one insider put it, the invasion and occupation of Iraq following 9/11 was like President Franklin Roosevelt declaring war on Mexico following the Japanese surprise attack on Pearl Harbor.

I read all I could on the balance of political forces inside the Bush administration. It became clear that the war party consisted principally of a group of right-wing Republicans who had come together during Bill Clinton's Democratic administration and formulated what they called the Program for the New American Century (PNAC). This supported a massive US military expansion, despite the fact that the Soviet Union and its East European quasi-empire – the enemy that had supplied the rationale for ambitious US military spending over more than forty years – had suddenly and unexpectedly disintegrated into its national parts. The ambition of the PNAC group was overwhelming American global military hegemony. It warned, as it turned out presciently, about the rise of China as a potential future rival to the United States. PNAC members were also strong supporters of the Israeli right-wing Likud Party, which was in the process of justifying the Jewish settlements on the occupied West Bank, and thus sleepwalking towards de facto annexation as the alternative to the "two state solution" pursued with considerable energy by the Clinton administration.

PNAC was based on an alliance between US imperial-militarists inside the Republican Party, Dick Cheney and Donald Rumsfeld, and neo-conservatives led by Paul Wolfowitz, former Democratic liberals who, in the words of Irving Kristol, had been "mugged by reality" and entered the Republican Party. The neo-con part of the PNAC alliance argued, in addition, for democratic regime change in Iraq that would somehow create the conditions for a Middle Eastern peace between the Jews of Israel and the Palestinians of the occupied West Bank. Even though there had once been differences of ideological emphasis between the Republican imperial-militarists and the former Democratic neo-conservatives, by the time of the formation of the PNAC group these differences had largely dissolved into a common muscular defence and foreign policy.

There was a particular reason why I was interested in PNAC, and dismayed by the role it was now playing in driving post-9/11 America to the invasion of Iraq. During the 1980s, the US ideological group to which I was most closely aligned were the liberal-democratic anti-communists. Following the collapse of the Soviet empire, many had become foundation members of the neo-conservative movement.

On my officially sponsored and financed trip to the United States in 1987, at my request I had dined in Washington with Irving Kristol and lunched in New York with Norman Podhoretz. Now, in 2002, I called to mind the explosive and seemingly slightly mad articles in *The Australian* that my old mentor, Frank Knopfelmacher, had written in 1970 after visiting the United States. According to him, the corruption of the New York intellectuals posed a clear and present danger to the future of America and, thus, the world. It did occur to me now that the successful PNAC campaign for an unprovoked, preventive war on Iraq – led by intellectuals both inside the Bush administration, like Paul Wolfowitz and Richard Perle, and outside it, like Podhoretz, the editor of *Commentary*, and William Kristol (the son of Irving), the editor of the neo-con house journal, *The Weekly Standard* – was precisely what Knopfelmacher had once prophesied.

By September 2002 I felt ready to write in my regular Fairfax column on the build-up to the invasion of Iraq. As there was no group on the left or the right from which I took my bearings, I had to think things through by myself. The Bush administration had just produced a new strategic doctrine as cover for the impending invasion. Within international law, one justification for military action was what was called "the pre-emptive strike", the right to take to arms in the face of imminent attack. In our age, as 9/11 had supposedly revealed according to the new Bush doctrine, so-called rogue states – belligerent dictatorships that hated the United States – might mount a surprise attack on the United States not only with conventional weapons but also with "weapons of mass destruction" – chemical, biological or nuclear – either openly themselves, or by the use of terrorist groups like al-Qaeda, to whom the weapons could be delivered in secrecy. Because such attacks could happen at any moment without warning, as 9/11 had shown, international law concerning the pre-emptive strike had to be extended to take into account the possibility of ambush with the most lethal weapons human beings had devised. In my column, I argued that, according to the Bush doctrine, there was nothing to distinguish between a pre-emptive strike and a "preventive war", something that, even at its most hawkish Cold War moments, the United States had excluded from consideration.

"Under the new doctrine," I wrote, "the US may not only go to war on the basis of an imagined threat.

> It also arrogates to itself the right to decide alone when such a threat exists ... If the right does not exist for others, the Bush doctrine amounts to an almost formal claim for US world hegemony. If, on the other hand, all states possess the same right, the Bush doctrine opens the way for the return to the jungle, where the powerful have the capacity to impose their will.

In applying the new Bush doctrine, the US argued that Iraq was one of a handful of existing rogue states. During its war with Iran from 1980 to 1988, Iraq, ruled over by a ferociously anti-American dictator, Saddam Hussein, had developed both chemical and biological weapons. Following its enforced withdrawal from Kuwait in 1991, it had been required to allow weapons inspectors on its soil to oversee the destruction of its WMD arsenal. In 1998 the inspectors had been thrown out of Iraq by Saddam. Accordingly, it was reasonable to assume that Iraq had retained some of its chemical and biological weapons.

In addition, intelligence existed – or at least so we were told – which revealed that Iraq was secretly developing a nuclear weapons capacity and forging links with al-Qaeda. In column after column, prior to the US, UK and Australian invasion of Iraq in March 2003, I argued that even if all this were true – and even if, as I believed, Iraq had indeed retained some WMDs – the justification for war still did not exist. Iraq had been under crippling economic sanctions and strict air surveillance since 1991. Saddam's regime in 2002 or 2003 was far weaker than it had been in 1990. Accordingly, Iraq posed no threat to Kuwait or to Israel, as supporters of war contended, let alone to the United States or one of its European allies. The only danger the regime of Saddam Hussein posed was to his own subjects, as demonstrated in the callous murder of tens of thousands of Marsh

Arabs and Kurds. If Iraq launched a direct attack on the US or one of its allies, or if evidence emerged that Iraq had handed WMDs to a terrorist group like al-Qaeda, which had unleashed these weapons against the United States or one of its allies, Saddam's regime would be "obliterated" instantly. As he must have known. Saddam might be a brutal dictator but there was no evidence that he was "insane".

Frequently, during the preparation for invasion, analogies between the Gulf after 9/11 and Europe in the 1930s were suggested. I regarded these analogies as ridiculous. Iraq under crippling economic sanctions and tight military surveillance since being driven out of Kuwait was a defeated state. Nazi Germany was, by the late 1930s, the strongest military power in Europe, having successfully broken every major arms restriction of the Treaty of Versailles. Saddam Hussein was a tin-pot dictator. Adolf Hitler was the charismatic *Führer* of a totalitarian state at the heart of Europe. And, to put it politely, the somewhat dim-witted George W. Bush was no Winston Churchill, whose penetrating intelligence and political courage had made him a hero of my generation.

It was self-evident by mid-2002 that if the United States and the United Kingdom went to war against Iraq, so would Australia. Why? Here history was helpful. During my studies at Oxford and in my early years at La Trobe, I had worked on the British foreign policy and military archives of the 1930s, including the records of the Dominions Office. Of the four principal dominions – Canada, South Africa, Australia and New Zealand – Australia was regarded by British policymakers as the most compliant, the one least likely to cause them any difficulty.

One incident I stumbled upon in the first volume of *The Documents of Australian Foreign Policy* illustrated what the British understood about Australia. In a meeting of early 1939, the British chiefs of staff decided that in the case of war against both Germany and Japan, Britain would concentrate its naval forces against Germany in the North Sea and allow the Pacific Ocean to be dominated by Japan. By mistake, the minutes of this meeting were sent to the office of the Australian High Commission. There could be no decision more important for the future of Australia than this. And yet, when the chiefs of staff asked the High Commission to return the minutes and not inform Canberra of their contents, the High Commission complied. In any other context, it occurred to me, the willingness of the Australian authorities in London to keep secret the knowledge of British plans to abandon Australia in the case of war against both Germany and Japan might be considered treason.

On November 4, 2002, I argued in my column that if there was indeed to be war against Iraq:

> Australia will line up alongside the US. Throughout this year, the Howard Government has followed every twist of US policy over Iraq like a faithful lamb ... In any explanation of Australia's Iraq policy, history weighs heavily. As its architect, John Howard has acted both as inheritor and, indeed, as the radical simplifier of the most fundamental foreign policy belief embedded in the Australian conservative tradition, namely that the only reliable safeguard for our security is to offer faithful and predictable support to the strategic policy of one or another of what Sir Robert Menzies famously called "our great and powerful friends".

The late Allan Gyngell captured brilliantly the essence of Australian foreign policy in the title of his masterly history, *Fear of Abandonment*. For a while, the Howard government pretended that even the pre-deployment of Australian troops in the Gulf prior to the outbreak of hostilities did not amount to a commitment to follow the Americans and the British into Iraq. Such dishonesty angered me.

In a column of February 10, 2003, I argued:

> If Australian troops were pulled out of the Anglo-American coalition at the very moment world opinion erupted over its intervention, this would represent such a diplomatic slap in the face to the Americans that our alliance with them would effectively be dead. Yet it is precisely in order to strengthen this alliance that our troops have been despatched.

What was happening to Australian policy after 9/11 and under Howard was a process I eventually called "the re-dominionisation" of Australia. At the time, this did not seem to matter much. As I write, however, the threat of war between the United States and China over Taiwan rises, at a time when Australia's embrace of the United States has become fully bipartisan. The alternative Labor Party foreign policy tradition of internationalism and greater independence has been abandoned, as it was not quite yet under the Labor leadership of Simon Crean, Mark Latham and even Kim Beazley. The process of re-dominionisation under John Howard might come to determine Australia's future.

The Anglo-American-Australian invasion of Iraq took place in March 2003. Within weeks, the regime of Saddam Hussein collapsed. For one brief moment, the war party in Australia, led by the Murdoch newspapers, cheered, and jeered at those who had opposed the invasion. In the words of one of *The Australian*'s triumphalist editorials, "The Coalition of the Whining Got It Wrong". At first, this mood, these words, stung. And yet not long after, it became obvious that almost everything predicted by those who had supported the invasion had proven false, and almost everything predicted by those who opposed it had come to pass. The people of Iraq did not welcome foreign occupation. In Baghdad and other cities, law and order collapsed, with the morgue in Baghdad soon choked with bodies. According to several studies, the wartime and post-war death rate in Iraq was extraordinarily high. Even more than under Saddam, there were problems with the supplies of food, water, medicines and electricity. Anarchy, not democracy, took hold. From the chaos of Iraq and also Syria, eventually a Sunni-Islamist movement, the Islamic State, or ISIS, emerged, which was more doctrinally fundamentalist than al-Qaeda, and more murderous, finding as its targets not only all Shia Muslims but entire small distinct civilisations within Islam, such as the Yazidi.

Most astonishingly, it gradually became clear that the regime of Saddam Hussein possessed no weapons of mass destruction, and that there had been no links between Saddam and al-Qaeda. The veteran US investigative journalist Seymour Hersh, among others, discovered that the PNAC group inside the Bush administration, dissatisfied with the intelligence provided by the professionals, had created their own intelligence bureau, the Office of Special Plans, led by a Cold War neo-con intellectual named Abram Shulsky. The OSP had cherry-picked from the raw data and willingly allowed itself to be conned by the fabricated intelligence fed to them by long-time Iraqi political exiles. The war against Iraq had been based upon a lie. It was not so much, as I argued, that the war party knew Saddam had no WMDs. It was rather that they exaggerated the importance of flimsy or fake evidence that suggested the existence of these weapons and links, and determinedly closed their eyes to the evidence that suggested otherwise.

Because of my opposition to the invasion of Iraq, personal insults had been thrown my way, not only by those I regarded as fools, like Andrew Bolt and Piers Akerman, but also by intelligent journalists like Imre Salusinszky and the foreign editor of *The Australian*, Greg Sheridan, who described me first as an "old friend" but then became more and more breathtakingly vicious as the nonsense of his commentary and claims on Iraq became ever clearer. I was determined not to simplify the ethical situation that faced both supporters and opponents of the invasion. In my conclusion to a chapter in the book of 2003, *Why the War Was Wrong*, edited by Rai Gaita, I wrote:

> Those who supported the war supported an action which originated in ideological fantasy and imperial hubris, which was justified on the basis of astonishing falsehoods, and which was, according to traditional understandings, both unlawful and unjust. Yet those who opposed the invasion, as I did, cannot wriggle away from the fact that, if our opposition had been successful, the disgusting regime of Saddam Hussein would still be in power in Iraq. From this simple unpleasant truth there is, I am afraid, no escape.

No words I wrote on Iraq had more influence than these.

By 2004, I was convinced that the invasion of Iraq was one of the greatest foreign policy disasters in the history of the United States and its Anglo allies. The reputations of George W. Bush and his chief lieutenant, Tony Blair, would never recover. In Australia, by contrast, John Howard's esteem and self-regard were almost entirely unaffected. And yet one aspect of his disgrace was even more obvious than theirs.

Before sending Australian troops to Iraq, Howard had made it even clearer than Bush or Blair that the only reason Australia was joining the Anglo-American invasion forces was to disarm Saddam – to discover and destroy the chemical and biological weapons he had supposedly retained in breach of both the 1991 Gulf War settlement and United Nations Security Council Resolutions. On the eve of the invasion, Howard had argued that "if Iraq had genuinely disarmed, I couldn't justify on its own a military invasion of Iraq to change the regime. I've never advocated that." As I pointed out in my chapter in *The Howard Years*, Howard had farewelled troops on HMAS *Kanimbla* with these words: "I believe it is right for the international community to try and disarm Iraq," and, on these troops' return, had welcomed them home like this: "You were sent in a just cause to liberate an oppressed people." This was not merely a lie. The "oppressed people" whom Howard now claimed Australian troops had been sent to liberate, whose suffering under Saddam he now documented in gruesome detail, were precisely the people – Iraqis fleeing from the regime of Saddam Hussein – whom Howard had claimed just two years earlier were so humanly debased that they were willing to throw their own children into the ocean and see them drown in if they could only gain asylum in Australia for themselves. Even though Howard now claimed – maybe even believed – that our troops had been sent to Iraq to liberate a people from the oppression of Saddam Hussein, when the fishing boats bearing Iraqis fleeing from Saddam could not be escorted by the Australian Navy back to Indonesia, their passengers were routinely imprisoned indefinitely in one of the hellish, sweltering, godforsaken detention camps on Nauru or Manus Island.

On the eve of the invasion, an analyst in the Office for National Assessments, Andrew Wilkie, a former soldier, had quit his post and approached Laurie Oakes, Channel Nine's chief political correspondent. Because of what he had learned from the United States and British intelligence, Wilkie believed that Iraq did possess some WMDs but that the Howard government had exaggerated both their number and the likelihood that Saddam would ever use them against a neighbour, let alone against the United States or one of its European allies. Howard had also misled Australians about the present state of Iraq's nuclear weapons program. Wilkie was also convinced that no sound intelligence showing links between Iraq and al-Qaeda existed. He hoped his appearance on Channel Nine would stir the national conscience and help halt the Howard government's march to a needless war. He believed that because of the genuine threat of al-Qaeda, if Australia joined the Anglo-American invasion of Iraq, Islamist terrorism would make Australians less secure, not more. Most importantly, he believed that the invasion of Iraq would take the lives of tens or hundreds of thousands of Iraqis. The Howard government sought to discredit Wilkie, with its by now characteristic dishonesty and cunning.

Someone passed an ONA analysis Wilkie had written on Iraq to Andrew Bolt that he was able to lampoon. Wilkie's paper referred to evidence supplied to Australia by foreign intelligence services. To leak it was a crime. As Wilkie still had friends inside ONA, he learned that shortly before Bolt's article appeared a member of Alexander Downer's staff had requested the Wilkie document. A federal police investigation was initiated. It came to nothing.

At the time of Wilkie's sensational resignation from the ONA and his public witness, I was still editing the Black Inc. Agenda series of books. We were able to convince Wilkie to write an account of his life inside ONA and the reasons he had resigned. Shortly before publication, an impressive legal team representing ASIO came down to Melbourne to discuss with Black Inc. the security implications of publishing Wilkie's book. It was a civilised and even sophisticated conversation on the balance, within a liberal-democratic polity, between the conflicting claims of freedom of the press and questions of national security. As the author of a book on the Petrov Affair and articles on Wilfred Burchett and the KGB's attempted recruitment of the former Labor Party secretary David Combe, I had always taken the claims about national security seriously. As did both Morry Schwartz and Chris Feik. We promised to think carefully about anything in Wilkie's book that concerned ASIO.

The early draft of Andrew's book had been sent to a few of us by email. There were some objections raised by ASIO on what seemed minor and peripheral matters. With Andrew's eventual agreement, *Axis of Deceit* appeared with some ASIO-requested unimportant changes. Sometime after, a couple of ASIO technicians arrived at my university office. With my permission, they found their way into the hard drive of my computer and removed the first draft of Andrew's book. The same thing happened to others who had emails of Andrew's first draft.

On the left, there was a little huffing and puffing about the supposed threat this posed to liberty. For my part, I was amused by the thought of foreign agents discovering and then searching carefully the first draft of Andrew's book on my university computer for the small amount of almost entirely innocuous material that had been "censored" by ASIO. Andrew struck me at the time as an intelligent, principled young Australian and as a patriot. I am not surprised that, after he moved to Hobart, he established himself as one of the nation's most popular and respected independent federal parliamentarians, a champion of many good causes, most importantly gambling reform.

Shortly before the 2004 federal election, I was contacted by Tim McCormack, professor of International Law at the University of Melbourne. When we met, Tim told me about a quite extraordinary case concerning Dr Bob Mathews, one of Australia's most distinguished WMD experts. Mathews had worked for Australian intelligence for thirty-five years and was presently in the Defence Science and Technology Organisation (DSTO). In 2002, as the march towards the invasion of Iraq gathered pace, Mathews believed that US and UK intelligence did not justify war. On several occasions he had been prevented by his superior at DSTO from sending a memorandum to this effect to the prime minister or his cabinet. Three days before the invasion, on March 17, 2003, at the time Andrew Wilkie was making the case against war to the largest possible audience, Mathews decided to send a letter to the prime minister of Australia not via the chain of command at DSTO but as a private citizen.

A year and a half later, on the eve of the 2004 election, Mathews wanted the story of what had happened to him as the result of his letter to the prime minister to become known. Because of my Fairfax column and my views on the invasion of Iraq, Tim hoped I could help. I contacted the defence reporter at Fairfax, Tom Allard. He was interested. Mathews provided Allard with a copy of his letter to Howard. On September 25, 2004, Allard reported its contents thus:

> Dr Mathews' lengthy critique called on Mr Howard to reconsider his position and take action to dissuade the US from its path ... There was not even circumstantial evidence to back the view that Saddam Hussein had substantial stockpiles of usable WMD ... If he did have WMD, and if Iraq were invaded, there was a "high probability" they would be passed on to terrorists. He said there was no chance of their falling into al-Qaeda's hands while Saddam remained in power [and that] "Australia would 'face an increased risk of terrorist acts" if it joined the invasion ...

John Howard was alarmed when he received Mathews' letter, not because he might be leading his country into a war without just cause but because of the possibility that Mathews might go public, as Wilkie had. A public servant, Jane Errey, was given the task of preparing a brief for the Defence minister, Senator Robert Hill, in case Mathews released his letter to the press. Disgusted, Errey instantly took leave, not wishing to be associated with spreading "propaganda". Mathews did not release his letter.

What happened next seems almost beyond belief. Because of his letter to Howard, Mathews lost his top security clearance. His right to travel overseas was strictly limited. Most importantly, Mathews learned that investigations were taking place as to whether he might be charged with an offence under the *Crimes Act* for passing classified material in a private letter to the Australian prime minister.

The impact of all this was devastating. Mathews was an anxious man and was described by colleagues as "mild-mannered" and "self-effacing". He was, however, principled. Mathews decided to tell his story to Philip Flood, the government insider who was appointed by Howard to investigate the question of Australia's involvement in the invasion of Iraq. One of Flood's key findings was, in the words of Tom Allard, "that there was no pressure on analysts to tailor advice to what the Government wanted to hear". Scandalously, Flood completely ignored the evidence given to him by Mathews, which contradicted this. As Ghassan Hage had observed shrewdly, the purpose of inquiries established by Howard, like the one of Philip Flood, was not investigation but exoneration.

Tom Allard's account was published on the front pages of both *The Sydney Morning Herald* and *The Age* on September 25, 2004. The leader of the Opposition, Mark Latham, criticised Howard, but formulaically. As if it were a matter of no account, Howard said that he had rejected Mathews' opinion. He added that "he would invade Iraq again, even knowing now that it had no weapons of mass destruction". Since Howard had told us without ambiguity on the eve of the invasion that he had taken Australia to war because of Iraq's WMD arsenal, and that he rejected the idea of an invasion for the purpose of "regime change", this was another outright lie. By Tuesday of the following week, September 28, the Mathews story was dead. As I concluded in a column on the eve of the 2004 election: "Allard's story did Howard no harm. In Britain, even now, a similar story would almost destroy Tony Blair." I was shaken by this experience.

*

In December 2003, Mark Latham defeated his rival, Kim Beazley, and replaced Simon Crean as the Labor Party's Leader of the Opposition. I was ambivalent about Latham. I recognised that he had the capacity to unnerve and even on occasion outmanoeuvre Howard, as he had, for example, over the reduction of parliamentarians' superannuation. In addition, unlike Crean, he interested the Australian people, with ideas like taking on the crisis of masculinity facing boys in contemporary society, or the benefit of parents reading their children bedtime stories. Such matters were, however, not enough to threaten Howard.

I argued that sometimes Latham sounded as if he was a member of a right-wing think-tank, on one occasion likening tariffs to racism. At other times, he answered Howard's conservative populism with a social-democratic populism of his own. Latham's framework for understanding Australian society was different from that of all previous Labor leaders. His imagined Australia consisted of "insiders" and "outsiders". His "insiders" were, on the right, "the top end of town" and, on the left, "the progressivist intelligentsia". His "outsiders" were, on the right, the aspirational small business suburbanites and, on the left, the traditional blue-collar working class. Latham promised to govern on behalf of his outsiders and against his insiders.

What this meant was that Latham Labor was effectively either indifferent or opposed to the causes of the left-liberal intelligentsia – Indigenous reconciliation, refugee rights, the republic, multiculturalism, feminism, gay rights and environmentalism. As he made explicit, his Labor Party had no room for "Phillip Adams" types (and therefore for me). Just as Tony Blair had refashioned the British Labour Party by ingesting aspects of Thatcher, so would Latham refashion the Australian Labor Party by ingesting aspects of Howard. As I argued, if Labor were to win government with Latham in October 2004, we would truly be able to say: "We are all Howardites now."

There was, I believed, one further problem with Mark Latham as Labor leader. By 2004 Australians were, on balance, more prosperous than ever before in history. The prosperity was, however, shadowed by anxiety over the very high levels of private debt, principally in the form of home mortgages. Howard understood both the anxiety and its cause. Labor under Latham claimed that Howard had shown that he could not be trusted – over the children overboard affair, for example, or Saddam's WMD arsenal, the cause of the invasion of Iraq. Howard turned the question of trust on its head by claiming that only the Coalition could be trusted to keep interest rates low. Because of middle-class voters' interest rate anxiety, what very many Australians were looking for in leadership, I believed, was caution and prudence.

Caution and prudence were, however, precisely the qualities Latham seemed to lack. He was by now principally famous (or notorious) for rugby-tackling a taxi driver who had displeased him. Except for a pre-election bone-crushing handshake of Howard captured by the television cameras, during the campaign Latham's minders imposed upon him a generally successful tight rein. The voters were unlikely to be fooled. Latham most likely seemed to them, or so I speculated, like "a larrikin on Mogadon, who would revert to type when the effect of the tranquilliser eventually wore off". The last thing the middle-class mortgage holders of 2004 wanted in their prime minister was "a buccaneer".

From this point of view, Latham's rival, the ever-cautious Kim Beazley, would have been a better choice as the Labor leader for the 2004 election. Howard had upended Beazley in 2001 with *Tampa*. In 2004 he outsmarted Latham over the question of the Tasmanian forests. Howard hinted, through his ultra-conservative minister Senator Nick Minchin, that he might soon announce a moratorium on any further logging in Tasmania. Latham took the bait. In the final week of the 2004 election campaign, he announced that Labor would end the destruction of the Tasmanian forests – something that, in truth, he probably cared not two hoots about. In my post-election column, I described what happened next. Howard announced:

> [I]n the interest of the workers, his government would allow logging to go on. The television pictures of Howard being cheered by left-wing unionists will remain with me as the most enduring image of the 2004 campaign. By his manoeuvre Howard gained two extra Tasmanian seats. More deeply, he sent a signal to traditional blue-collar voters on the mainland that ... the Labor Party had, after all, even under Latham, been captured by the left-liberal middle class and had abandoned its role as the party of the battlers ... The continued destruction of the magnificent, ancient forests, as a consequence of a low-grade political trick of this kind, is enough to make one weep.

"HOWARD HATER"

At the time of the October 2004 election, I was probably more hated by the right than at any time either before or since. Indeed, I was probably the most hated member of the left by those members of the right who were involved in the prosecution of the culture wars. My only competitors were Phillip Adams and Tim Flannery. Enemies in the newspapers included Andrew Bolt and Terry McCrann (the *Herald Sun*), Piers Akerman (*The Daily Telegraph*), Greg Sheridan, Chris Mitchell, Christopher Pearson, Imre Salusinszky and Frank Devine (*The Australian*), Gerard Henderson and Paul Sheehan (*The Sydney Morning Herald*), Michael Duffy and Ron Brunton (*The Courier-Mail*) and Paul Murray (*The West Australian*).

On the other hand, I was now probably more popular and influential among the group to which I now regarded myself as belonging: the left-liberal progressivist intelligentsia. Around this time, I appeared regularly on ABC Radio and occasionally on ABC TV; I was invited frequently to writers' festivals; I was the member of the academic left chosen by the *Australian Financial Review* for its annual discussions of "Power in Australia"; and I wrote a fortnightly column for both *The Sydney Morning Herald* and *The Age*. In detailed surveys conducted at this time by Michael Visontay for *The Sydney Morning Herald* and by Professor Richard Nile for *The Australian*, I was judged by my peers to be Australia's "leading public intellectual". When *The Bulletin* created a list of the hundred "smartest" Australians, a young Brian Schmidt was judged to be the smartest scientist and an even younger Eddie Perfect the smartest entertainer, while I was awarded the title of Australia's "smartest" social critic on account of my supposed stirring of the nation's conscience over Iraq, Aboriginal reconciliation and refugees. This *Bulletin* decision was greeted, in my case, with howls of hatred and contempt in lengthy columns by Andrew Bolt in the *Herald Sun* and Piers Akerman in *The Daily Telegraph*.

Following Latham's comprehensive defeat in the October 2004 election, I decided to give up my regular column in the two principal Fairfax newspapers. If I had something to say on public affairs, it would from now on usually be published in Morry Schwartz's new magazine, *The Monthly*, the first edition of which appeared in May

2005. As I explained on December 20, 2004, in my final fortnightly Fairfax column:

> I have been aware for the past several years that the issues in Australian politics that have preoccupied me – Aboriginal reconciliation, refugees, truth in government, the blind loyalty to America in foreign policy – have little traction in an electorate overwhelmingly concerned with personal and family security. This year the thought sharpened. If Labor were to embrace the views of those who think as I do, its electoral stocks would almost certainly be harmed ... The political needs of Labor and the human rights or foreign policy or environmental agenda of the left-leaning intelligentsia cannot at present be reconciled.

I added words that remained very important to me:

> Despite my concerns about its present political leadership and the narrowing of the popular mood, I still believe, as I always have, that Australia is a wonderful country. My warm wishes go to all those who read this column, even if only to disagree. My gratitude goes to all those who have not lost faith in the struggle, in these difficult times, to make it a more wonderful country still.

That wily old mountain goat, as I had called John Howard more than once, had not only defeated Mark Latham. He had also, at least temporarily, defeated me.

[15.]

"Oh Dear, Mr Rudd!"

THE QUESTIONS OF POST-KEATING Australian politics that troubled me most were reconciliation with the Indigenous peoples; humane treatment of those asylum seekers who had arrived by boat; Australia's participation in what I regarded as the illegal and immoral Anglo-American invasion of Iraq; the almost comical degree of political influence the Murdoch press had been granted (in large part by Paul Keating, alas); and, most recently and also overwhelmingly most importantly, Australia's commitment to the international struggle against global warming. By the end of 2004 I had given up hope that any would be confronted honestly while John Howard led the Liberal Party, and while Mark Latham's replacement, the affable but "ticker-challenged" Kim Beazley, led Labor. This did not of course mean that these questions no longer mattered to me deeply. I looked for ways of influencing opinion not directly, in analysis of the daily cut and thrust of parliamentary politics, but for the most part indirectly and in the longer term.

In early 2005 the ABC's *Four Corners* introduced us all to Rod Barton, an Australian intelligence officer who had been involved since 1991 at the centre of the sometimes very dangerous missions and always very complex politics that surrounded Iraqi compliance with disarmament provisions. According to these provisions, Iraq was required to destroy its entire once imposing arsenal of chemical and biological weapons. In mid-2004 the mistreatment of Iraqi prisoners of war – both by humiliation and torture – at the hands of relatively junior American soldiers at the Abu Ghraib prison became known. One question concerned the methods used during the interrogation of senior Iraqis. In parliament, Howard's minister for Defence, Senator Robert Hill, claimed that no Australians had been involved in interrogations. This was a lie. Barton had returned recently from Iraq and had informed Defence that he had conducted a five-hour interrogation of a senior Iraqi politician of his acquaintance.

And not only that. In late 2003 Barton had even for a short time become the de facto head of the CIA-led Iraq Survey Group and had reorganised its interrogation systems and processes. Barton was ropeable. He was now informed by Mike Pezzullo of Defence that what he had conducted was an "interview", not an "interrogation", a distinction that Barton had never before encountered and that Pezzullo could not satisfactorily explain. Hill also claimed that all Australian officers in Iraq had been instructed not to become involved in interrogations, something Barton knew to be yet another lie. By the time of his return from Iraq to Australia in early 2004, Barton had become suspicious about the methods being used by the Americans during the interrogation process. For these reasons, Rod Barton decided to go public – for an intelligence officer like him, a major and difficult decision. Hence the *Four Corners* program.

I spoke to Barton by phone and wrote a column (on February 22, 2005) for *The Sydney Morning Herald* and *The Age*. An editorial in Chris Mitchell's *Australian*, probably written by Imre Salusinszky, argued: "There are those in the coalition of the whining, such as Professor Robert Manne, who think the really big issue on Iraq is whether what Australian weapons inspector Rod Barton performed at Camp Cropper in Baghdad was an interrogation or an interview." The editorial went on to describe my column as an example of the characteristic "solipsistic twittering of the intellectuals". I did not believe the interrogation or interview question was "the really big issue of Iraq". Since late 2002 I had written perhaps fifteen lengthy newspaper columns on Iraq and a detailed chapter in Rai Gaita's *Why the War Was Wrong* on the forces inside the Bush administration responsible for the invasion decision. I would have been only too happy to compare my supposed "solipsistic twitterings" on what was happening regarding Iraq with *The Australian*'s jingoistic editorials or the reliably wrong-headed analyses of its foreign affairs editor, Greg Sheridan.

In 2005 *The Age* was edited by Andrew Jaspan, in later years the creator of the brilliant concept of *The Conversation*: academics writing on their fields of expertise for the intelligent general public. I suggested that I fly to Canberra to speak with Barton for an extended article. Andrew agreed. I learned from Rod Barton that he had gone to Iraq in 1991, at the end of the Gulf War. The grounds where the weapons hunt took place were so contaminated and littered with unexploded munitions that Barton and other weapons detectives believed them to be what they called "the most dangerous place on Earth". In 1996, after a brief and terrifying time in Somalia, Barton returned to Iraq as a part of a four-person UN team searching for any hidden biological weapons. One member was the British scientist David Kelly. He had leaked some critical information that threatened the reputations of both the British prime minister, Tony Blair, and the head of MI6, John Scarlett. Such was the pressure Kelly faced in the political crossfire between Blair and the BBC that he took his own life. Barton greatly admired Kelly and was badly shaken by the news.

In 1998 Saddam threw all UN weapons inspectors out of Iraq, including Barton. In 2002, however, as tensions between the Americans and Europeans over the possible invasion of Iraq mounted, Barton was employed by Hans Blix, the head of a new UN group – the United Nations Monitoring, Verification and Inspection Commission, or UNMOVIC – which was charged with assessing Iraq's compliance with the post–Gulf War disarmament demands. Barton was an eyewitness to the intense heat the Americans applied to Blix in the quest for reports that would help justify the already inevitable Anglo-American invasion. Blix and Barton met in the coffee lounge of the New York building where their office was located, a place they were confident American intelligence could not have bugged. Barton worked very closely with Blix, and even wrote the technical parts of his reports to the Security Council of the UN, which might determine whether the UN would support the invasion of Iraq. Every word mattered.

The invasion duly occurred in March 2003, as Barton had believed it would ever since President Bush's "Axis of Evil" speech in February 2002. Because of his reputation as a first-rate weapons detective, high-ranking Americans – including the deputy director of the CIA, John McLaughlin – were keen to have Rod Barton involved in the post-invasion search for Saddam's weapons of mass destruction. Because of the pettiness or rigidity of Australia's Department of Defence, which was willing to pay him only half of what he earned while working for the United Nations, Barton did not arrive in Iraq until late 2003. By then, the head of the CIA-led Iraq Survey Group (ISG), the once uber-hawk David Kay, had returned to Washington a defeated man, convinced that the WMDs that had provided the justification for the invasion of Iraq simply did not exist. As Kay's replacement, Charles Duelfer, had not yet arrived, Rod Barton found himself, curiously enough, as an adviser with no one to advise, and as the de facto leader of the Iraq Survey Group.

From photographs of facial abrasions, he came to suspect that Iraqi scientists involved in the earlier weapons program were being beaten before their interrogations in a hangar-like building known as Purgatory. Barton inspected the severely cramped and windowless cells at Camp Cropper, where senior Iraqis were imprisoned in solitary confinement. Especially as he believed that many of the weapons scientists had committed no crime under international law, he was disturbed. He was also suspicious about the reason for the death of Dr Mohammed Munim al-Izmerly, one of the Iraqi scientists he knew (and whom he despised for having conducted live experiments on prisoners condemned to death). According to a newspaper report, the autopsy on Al-Izmerly showed signs of his having been severely beaten. Barton was also a witness to the last, comical American attempts to convince themselves that the elusive, missing weapons of mass destruction would soon be found. When Kay had decided to return to the US, his tail between his legs, he had famously claimed to the ISG staff that their work was "85 per cent done", an encoded admission of defeat. Barton watched with astonished amusement as the visiting head of the CIA, George Tenet, addressed the members of the ISG involved in the forlorn Iraqi WMD wild goose chase. Tenet inquired: "Is our work 85 per cent done?" His audience roared back: "No!" By the time of his return to Canberra, Barton had reached two conclusions. The imprisoned Iraqi weapons scientists were most likely being seriously mistreated. And the invasion of Iraq had been based on a lie.

Andrew Jaspan gave me almost 5,000 words for my article, but I believed that Barton's story deserved much more detail than I was able to cover. My friends at Black Inc. – Morry Schwartz and Chris Feik – supported my idea of inviting Barton to write a book on his career. In early 2006 we were able to publish, under the Black Inc. Agenda imprint, a book on a key chapter in early twenty-first-century history we called *The Weapons Detective*. By this time, Greg Sheridan's abuse of me was escalating, month by month, principally because I believed that the decision to invade Iraq, which *The Australian* under Chris Mitchell cheered, was a blood-drenched catastrophic stupidity. I was a great admirer of the quiet, precise and principled Australian intelligence officer Rod Barton.

*

In the years following the 2004 election, Indigenous Australians were for some time my principal interest. After reading everything I could lay my hands upon regarding the Stolen Generations, I moved to the historical studies of the dispossession – beginning with Charles Rowley's great trilogy on the destruction of Aboriginal society and its consequences, the many books of Henry Reynolds, but also the brutally frank descriptions of the methods used in the dispossession like Hudson Fysh's *Taming the North*, published as late as 1933. I turned from history to anthropology and was most affected by A.P. Elkin's *The Australian Aborigines: How to Understand Them*, especially the chapter on the mind-bendingly complex kinship systems determining permissible and impermissible relationships and, thus, ultimately marriage; by Ronald and Catherine Berndt's *Sexual Behaviour in Western Arnhem Land*; and by Phyllis Kaberry's *Aboriginal Woman: Sacred and Profane.*

Knowing something about political science and sociology, I concluded that anthropology was the most distinguished branch of the social sciences in Australia. In a critical review of a book by the Swedish journalist Sven Lindqvist, whose earlier work *"Exterminate All the Brutes"* had impressed me greatly, I summarised what I believed the anthropologists had discovered – to be sure, a very violent world, but also one "that was filled with economic purpose; leavened by playfulness, joy and humour, soaked in magic, sorcery, mystery and ritual; present at every moment with deep and unquestioning meaning". I argued that, in the "technical" sense, the world of the pre-colonised Aboriginal Australians was "enchanted", a hardly controversial claim that followed Max Weber's seminal understanding of the processes of "disenchantment", which had transformed the post-Enlightenment European mind. Andrew Bolt did not, of course, understand the Weberian reference and advised his *Herald Sun* readers to "[h]ear barking Manne start to coo when he describes not our own foul society but the 'enchanted' world of Aborigines before whites came". Christopher Pearson did understand what I meant in referring to Weber. However, in an article the sub-editors at *The Australian* accurately entitled "Myth of the Noble Savage", he advised his readers that "enchantment, in the technical sense, ought not to blind us to the often murderous realities of hunter-gatherer existence" – something I had explicitly pointed out in my brief review. What interested me was the explosion of anger on the right at the merest mention of the attractiveness of the world the English pastoralists had set about destroying, as if that were a matter of no account.

The book on Aboriginal Australians that had most influence on me was an out-of-print collection of the non-academic essays of the Australian anthropologist W.E.H. Stanner, *White Man Got No Dreaming*. After I'd tried and failed to purchase even a second-hand copy, Morry, Chris and I agreed to publish a slightly revised edition under the Black Inc. Agenda imprint that we called *The Dreaming & Other Essays*. The first essay in the collection, "Durmugam: A Nangiomeri", a portrait of one of Stanner's Aboriginal friends, was the finest essay by an Australian that I had read. It still is. One of Stanner's ideas explored in his 1968 ABC Boyer Lectures – "the great Australian silence" concerning the Aboriginal dispossession – had the power to change the way many Australians came to understand the history of their country.

Inga Clendinnen had drawn attention to *From Hunting to Drinking*, the near-contemporary study by David McKnight, an English anthropologist, on the evil brought by alcohol to the community on Mornington Island, which he had visited for thirty years. I was greatly affected by McKnight's ideas, but also by the courage of the young Indigenous lawyer and activist Noel Pearson, in his early essays on the misery drink, drugs and the dole had brought to so many remote Aboriginal communities, but which most well-meaning left-wing Australians refused to face.

In mid-2006 I made a decision that reflected my rather characteristic naivety. By this time the *Herald Sun* columnist Andrew Bolt, who understood nothing about the history of the removal of mixed-ancestry Aboriginal children from their mothers, families and communities, had written *seventy* columns denying the existence of the Stolen Generations. On *thirty-two* occasions in these columns (a check on Factiva revealed) he had described me as the leading Stolen Generations "propagandist". In a column in June 2006, Bolt had claimed that the left was frightened of debating with the right. As Bolt had first agreed to a debate on my "In Denial" *Quarterly Essay* in April 2001 and then pulled out, providing different and inconsistent explanations, I wrote a letter-to-the-editor of the *Herald Sun* pointing out Bolt's hypocrisy.

After I challenged him again to a debate, Bolt invited me instead to a commercial radio program under his control. Here he showed some cunning, asking me on air without warning to "name ten" members of the Stolen Generations. This is not the kind of list that trips off the tongue. If Bolt had asked me to name ten people who had died in the Armenian genocide of 1915 or the Ukrainian famine of the early 1930s, historical tragedies I had read a great deal about, I would not have done any better. (I reflected later that I should have asked Bolt to name ten Australian soldiers who had died during the Gallipoli campaign.) What I did, as the Melbourne Writers Festival was approaching, was to challenge Bolt to a public debate.

Bolt tried to wriggle out once again. As a condition, he asked me to name not ten but "a hundred" or even "hundreds" of members of the Stolen Generations. In other words, as a condition for agreeing to debate me, what Bolt demanded was for me to prove in advance and to his satisfaction that he was wrong. I asked him to define what for him counted as a member of the Stolen Generations. He refused. I then sent him some 260 names. Bolt finally accepted the invitation to a debate.

Seven hundred people turned up to the RMIT's Storey Hall. Bolt's little band of right-wing supporters had been busy. One of the members of the Stolen Generations, Margaret Tucker, who was near the head of my list, had written a profoundly moving book, *If Everyone Cared*, on her experiences after being removed from her school by the police in the presence of her distraught mother. Bolt claimed that Margaret was being brought up by an aunty, "sort of". The audience had no way of knowing that this was a lie.

In my talk I quoted an exchange in 1919 between a West Australian policeman in the north of the state and the Protector of Aborigines, A.O. Neville. According to Inspector Drewery: "This seizing and removing of children is obnoxious to the police. No neglect has been shown by the mothers." To which Neville replied: "If the duty of bringing in half-castes is obnoxious to the Police, it is strange that the Department has not previously been advised of this, in view of the hundreds of cases that have had attention." I quoted a statement in 1934 of the secretary of the commonwealth government's Department of the Interior: "It is the policy to collect all half-castes from the native camps at an early age and transfer them to the Government Institutions at Darwin and Alice Springs." If Bolt were a journalist and not a propagandist, these two quotations from the archives were alone proof enough that the Stolen Generations was no myth.

The quotations were not alone. Prior to the debate, I had hastily compiled a 46,000-word selection of documents drawn from memoirs and archives illustrating the numbers, policies and practices of mixed-ancestry Aboriginal child removal in twentieth-century Australia. In front of the audience, I presented Bolt with the document selection I had compiled and printed. He called what I had handed to him "bits of paper", apparently unaware that it is from the "bits of paper" in archives and memoirs that history is written. Even that most notorious historical denialist, David Irving, did not dismiss documents as "bits of paper".

Of course, I did not expect Bolt to acknowledge that for several years he had been misleading his readers on the question of Aboriginal child removal. I told the audience and, later, the readers of the Fairfax newspapers that the documents would be made available to everyone on the internet. Knowing exactly what Bolt now had in his possession, they would be able to hold him to account regarding all his future columns on the Stolen Generations. Nothing happened. Bolt continued writing his nonsense about the "myth" of the Stolen Generations.

My public life had been devoted in large part to a belief in the existence of the world I had read about as a young boy in which a British prime minister, having listened to the speech of a political opponent on a matter of fundamental importance, the protective tariff on corn, had turned to a cabinet colleague and told him: "You must answer this for I cannot." Despite all evidence to the contrary, none more extraordinary than the case of Andrew Bolt and the Stolen Generations, I was unwilling to abandon hope in the idea of a rational public square.

*

Readers of this memoir will be aware that at different times in my life and on different questions, two thinkers – Frank Knopfelmacher and Raimond Gaita – influenced me profoundly. There is a third, Anne Manne – the author of *Motherhood*; *So This Is Life*; *The Life of I*; and, most recently, *Crimes of the Cross* – to whom I have spoken (and with whom I have laughed) in many conversations for the past almost fifty years. Several questions have woven their way through Anne's life and thought: the ongoing struggle for female equality; the shadow care economy; human interdependence and the importance of care, including care for the Earth; and the call upon us to see the world through the eyes of the vulnerable child, seen throughout her writing and most purely in her haunting essay "Ebony", about a girl starved to death by her parents. At the time when Anne was thinking about neo-liberalism's impact on the family policy and preparing a *Quarterly Essay, Love and Money: The Family and the Free Market*, on the cultural, psychological and political consequences of the neo-liberal age in which we now lived, we watched the emergence of the first apparently anti-neoliberal Labor leader together with some optimism.

In October and November 2006, Kevin Rudd published two articles in *The Monthly*: "Faith in Politics" and "Howard's Brutopia". Rudd described the political struggle between the Liberal and Labor parties as a "battle of ideas" between the "liberal" followers of Friedrich Hayek and the "social democratic" followers of John Maynard Keynes. He pointed to the contradiction at the centre of John Howard's politics: his economic individualism, which was based upon a market fundamentalism, and his social conservatism, based upon a defence of family and community. What Howard did not understand was that nothing was more destructive of family and community than the force of the market, once fully unleashed.

As his chief example, Rudd pointed to Howard's radical new industrial relations legislation, *WorkChoices*, which had been made possible by the Coalition's control of the Senate. The "new workplace relations system" treated human labour as a factor of production, and swept aside the traditional regulations allowing family and community to flourish. Unlike the market-fundamentalist Hayekian Liberals, Keynesian Labor sought a balance between the claims of the individual and of the community. While the Hayekians dismissed the idea of "social justice", social justice stood at the centre of Labor Party's support of vulnerable members of society. In "Faith in Politics", Rudd had declared that his greatest hero in the history of the twentieth century was the Lutheran German pastor, scholar and activist Dietrich Bonhoeffer, who wrote in favour not of a division between church and state, which had led so many of his fellow Lutherans to "quietism" and de facto support of Nazism, but of an activist Christianity, fully engaged in the struggle for social justice. True to his word, Bonhoeffer was member of the anti-Nazi Resistance movement, which had led to his execution.

The example of Bonhoeffer allowed – indeed, required – Rudd to speak with direct moral engagement in the defence of "the marginalised, vulnerable and the oppressed" – the impoverished peoples of the undeveloped world and the Millennium Development Goals; the asylum seekers (he even spoke of the lesson of the "the parable of the Good Samaritan"); and, by inference only in his Bonhoeffer essay, Indigenous Australians. He spoke in the moral language that had frightened Kim Beazley since *Tampa* and that was of no interest to Mark Latham. As part of his defence of what was vulnerable, Rudd included the Earth, which the contemporary Liberal Party under John Howard had disastrously failed to defend, even by signing the Kyoto Protocol. Defence of the Earth clashed with the Coalition's uncritical support of the foreign policy of United States of George W. Bush. Their Hayekian neo-liberalism blinded them to the enormity of the market failure. The impending catastrophe of global warming meant that future generations would bear the cost of our failure to take the vital action now needed.

Eventually, Rudd would discover that Max Weber was right in his lecture "Politics as a Vocation" about the differences between the politics in the real world (his "ethic of responsibility") and the politics of the saint (his "ethic of absolute ends"). For the present, I set aside all doubts and found myself in enthusiastic agreement with almost every word in these two articles. Since late 2004, after the electoral experiences of Beazley over asylum seekers and Latham over native forests, I had believed no Labor leader would speak like this. And that if a new leader of Labor spoke like this, they would be torn apart by Howard and his supporters and by the Murdoch press. On both counts

I was wrong. By November 2006, even before he took the Labor leadership from Kim Beazley, I was a Kevin Rudd supporter, and referred to myself, not entirely comically, as a "Ruddite".

On October 6, 2006, one week after the publication of Rudd's first *Monthly* essay on Bonhoeffer, I was involved in an ABC Radio National discussion of Australian politics with Gerard Henderson, who had already attacked me on hundreds of occasions and who, as I once pointed out, had followed my progress "with the attentiveness of a U-Boat commander and the generosity of spirit of a wounded Rottweiler". In our discussion I argued that Rudd's Bonhoeffer essay marked a seminal moment in Australian politics. Rudd had explicitly distanced the Labor Party from the kind of individualist society delivered by "neo-liberal" economics, and had spoken with the moral directness not found in any Labor leader since Paul Keating, but had done so in what I called the "timbre" of an active Christian, which was suited to our conservative times. "[I]t's been quite interesting that at the moment the heavy hitters in the Liberal Party haven't really known what to say about the Rudd intervention," I said. I argued that Rudd had the capacity to "bridge the gap" that existed between Labor's old, morally conservative working-class and outer-suburban base and the inner-city progressives who had been attached to Labor since Whitlam. On December 12, 2006, I published a column that outlined the reason for my support for Rudd more systematically:

> Speaking of Bonhoeffer and the meaning of faith in politics allowed Rudd to discover a language that has eluded all Labor leaders during the gradual Hansonisation of Australian public life over the past 10 years ... Because he has married the ideas of social justice and the defence of the family and community with the old idea of an intelligent, activist state and the more recent commitment to fiscal conservatism, he has begun to fashion what he thinks of as an unfamiliar centre ground of politics, potentially taking his party and his country to a new territory, beyond both left and right.

Because his task would be difficult, I concluded, "Rudd deserves ... not the customary carping of the intelligentsia but our wholehearted support".

Ever since the mid-1990s, I had believed that differences over issues concerned with "culture" were overtaking those concerned with "class" as the most salient division in contemporary Western societies. John Howard had demonstrated an almost unparalleled capacity to exploit Labor's support for the side of progress in those kind of "cultural" issues – sympathy for asylum seekers, Indigenous reconciliation, multiculturalism, feminism, support for Muslim, Asian and African immigrants, gay rights, and environmentalism, especially climate change. As these were the issues that divided the people I called "the elites" from those I described as "ordinary people", I appealed to the members of the left intelligentsia to understand Rudd's commonly criticised "me-tooism". As I argued in the October 2007 issue of *The Monthly*: "[B]ecause [Rudd] is an intelligent man [he] has worked out that a politics too far removed from the moral instincts of ordinary people will not succeed in the long run ... Rudd understands this. Phillip Adams does not. On this question, Rudd is right."

Nonetheless, I was convinced that if Rudd was elected Australia would be a better, kinder country. Australia would rejoin the world on the challenge of climate change; our "mimetic" foreign policy, which had taken us into Iraq, would be modified; our industrial relations laws would be softened; our universities would be better funded; the cultural warriors of the right would gradually be replaced from cultural boards; the public service might regain some of its former independence; and the gulf between the government and Australia's creative artists would be narrowed. I also believed that with a Rudd government the best-informed members of the intelligentsia, whose politics was generally but not entirely on the left, would once more be listened to.

Indeed, I was so keen for this last prediction to happen that, in the hope of the election of a Rudd government, I turned to those members of the intelligentsia whose writing had most impressed me and invited them to address those policy questions that, after eleven years of the Howard government, seemed most in need of fresh thought. I had never found commissioning a book easier, which was rather remarkable, given that if Howard won the election the work of the authors approached would be in vain. On a single day, August 1, 2007, two-thirds of the essays I sought were promised. I decided to give the book, if published, an epistolary, slightly comical title: *Dear Mr Rudd*.

If my argument – that, under a Rudd Labor government, Australia would become a different and a better country – could be criticised for anything, it was, as I put it, for stating the bleeding obvious. This was not Chris Mitchell's view. On October 27, 2007, *The Australian* published an editorial entitled, "Daydreaming Left Is in for a Big Surprise". I was the only left-wing daydreamer it was able to discover. Most of the left at the time were criticising Rudd for his political caution – over the false charges the Australian Federal Police had directed against a supposed friend of Islamist terrorism, Dr Mohamed Haneef, or over the government's "intervention" in the Northern Territory over the report into the sexual abuse of Indigenous children. According to *The Australian*, the "fantasists from the Left" had failed to notice that "the use-by date of Das Kapital is well and truly passed". Kevin Rudd was "fundamentally conservative". If anything, his electoral tactic had been "to outflank the Prime Minister on the Right":

> Of course, we may be wrong about Mr Rudd. He may turn out to be the most convincing actor ever to walk the Australian political stage. Prime Minister Rudd may withdraw Australia from the ANZUS alliance, shut down the coalmines, declare Australia a republic, make gay marriage compulsory and transform the nation into a wind-powered, mung-bean-eating Arcadia. But we think not ... [W]e will make one prediction. The agenda of a Rudd government is likely to be much closer to the position advocated in the editorial columns of this paper than the outdated, soft-left manifesto supported by our broadsheet rivals.

It was with the editorials about the daydreaming, psychotic left in mind that in *The Monthly* in 2008, I described *The Australian* under Chris Mitchell as "a newspaper that manages to combine the ambition of an ideologically engaged small magazine; the reckless take-no-prisoners, smart-aleck tone of an undergraduate publication; and the financial resources of an American-based global media empire".

*

The finest moment of the Rudd government, and very likely the only one that will be remembered, came early. On the first day the new parliament sat in February 2008, Rudd offered, on behalf of his government and his nation, a solemn apology to the Stolen Generations. I recorded that moment in a *Monthly* essay:

> Kevin Rudd delivered his speech in the presence of every living prime minister, except John Howard. He delivered it in the presence of large numbers of members of the Stolen Generations. In the lobby of the parliament, and in the public space between the old house of parliament and the new, thousands more Indigenous and non-Indigenous Australians listened to each word with rapt attention. Following his final words – "Let us turn this page together ... let us grasp this new opportunity to craft a new future for this great land, Australia" – a huge cheer erupted. It was the sweetest sound in public life that I have ever heard. In the politics of nations there are few transcendent moments. This was one.

There was only one false note. Rudd expressed a hope that the nation could now "move on". With something as dark as the policy and the practice of Indigenous child removal, I was convinced, we had rather to remember always, and not aspire to moving on.

Quite amazingly, only a few days after the Apology, *Dear Mr Rudd* was ready for publication. As expected, it was ridiculed by the Murdoch press. In its editorial, "Leftist Manifesto Good for a Laugh", *The Australian* argued that "Mr Rudd would be well-advised to give [the Left] sinecures where they can amuse themselves with utopian prescriptions to which he should pay absolutely no attention". This was also the view of one of the paper's regular columnists, Janet Albrechtsen, who described *Dear Mr Rudd* "as a manifesto of what not to do if he wants to win another election". She found particularly risible Professor Julian Disney's essay on housing, which began with these words:

> Affordable housing is crucial to a country. Without it, people are impoverished, families and communities eroded, jobs lost and the economy weakened. Yet a creeping crisis in affordable housing has been developing in Australia during the last decade or so with very little attention from most of our governments.

Disney was not the only expert ahead of their time. In 2008, most Australian international relations specialists thought that Australia would be able, relatively easily, to rely upon the United States for security and upon China for trade. This was not the view of Hugh White, who already foresaw China's rise to economic and, later, even military equality with the United States, and therefore that the chief task of Australian foreign policy should be:

> ... to initiate a deep and serious dialogue with Washington about the choices America faces as it responds to China's rise. American policy is drifting in a dangerous direction – towards an attempt to build a coalition of democracies designed to contain China's challenge to American primacy. This is a dangerous and futile idea.

Trying to convince the United States to find a way to share power with China in the Indo-Pacific would "require a diplomatic effort greater than anything Australia has attempted before. But what alternative do we have, and what do we have to lose?"

It was not only White who thought his way into the future. Kevin Rudd would have been wise if he had taken utterly seriously the advice of Patrick Dodson about the need for "a formal dialogue between Indigenous people and the Australian nation state", in the search for what he called "a policy and philosophical framework that can support the rebuilding of Indigenous communities and honour Indigenous people's place in the Australian nation". This idea found its form a decade later in the Uluru Statement from the Heart and the idea of Indigenous constitutional recognition via a Voice to Parliament.

The critics of *Dear Mr Rudd* regarded it as a left-wing manifesto. This was lazy. How could Harry Evans' spirited, old-style defence of the institution of parliament against the incursions of the executive, or Martin Krygier's parsing of the idea of the rule of law as Islamophobia threatened, or Geoff Gallop's rethinking of the federation, or, indeed, Anne Manne's original defence of the family from the point of view of the child, be seen as belonging to a left-wing manifesto edited, in the words of the *Australian Financial Review*'s Peter Ruehl, by "the country's foremost crackpot"? What I valued, always, were those thinkers who were not a part of any tribe and who were willing to think for themselves.

The purpose of *Dear Mr Rudd* was to suggest that lines of communication between the government and policy experts or public intellectuals, which had been closed during the Howard years, needed to be reopened. Rudd obviously had the same idea. To general amusement, 1,000 Australians were invited to a weekend "Ideas Summit" in Canberra in April 2008. The thousand met first in general assembly to greet and cheer the new prime minister. We then divided into hundreds. I chose Governance. Everyone was able to nominate an idea: I suggested the mandatory approval of parliament before going to war (except in a 9/11-style emergency). Because of the opposition of about twenty invitees, including Paul Kelly and Gerard Henderson, this failed to make it as what was called a "Top Idea". As time began to run out, confusion reigned among the Governance group. As I wrote in a piece for *The Monthly*:

> Often the loudest voices prevailed. Sometimes it was not even clear what the vote was about. Even though there was near-complete consensus about a two-stage program for the creation of a republic, at the very end of the meeting David Marr intervened

with a dramatic plea that the republic be included. He was told that the idea was actually at the top of our list.

Despite the chaos, I argued that on balance the Ideas Summit was a "Good Thing". During the Howard years, policy experts and public intellectuals who rejected the neo-liberal and neo-conservative governmental framework were not simply ignored, their ideas were treated as "illegitimate", almost un-Australian. "With the summit, this atmosphere vanished," I argued. The summit might have helped to satisfy Prime Minister Rudd's not inconsiderable appetite for approval and for praise. But it also acted as "a kind of political theatre, pronouncing the burial rites on one era and the birth of another".

There was one issue in the early days of Rudd government where I was concerned about the judgement of the prime minister. True to his word in the Bonhoeffer essay, as a modern-day Good Samaritan, Kevin Rudd had repealed many of the harshest elements of the Howard government's asylum-seeker policy. I was extremely pleased about the end of temporary protection visas and long-term detention in Australia. I was, however, worried about the government's abandonment of the Pacific Solution – the threat of naval escort to the point of departure in Indonesia of all asylum-seeker boats sailing to Australia, or, if that proved impossible, offshore detention on Nauru or Manus Island. I had argued since 2002 that, in its ambition to "stop the boats", the Pacific Solution had "succeeded", a fact I placed inside inverted commas. George Orwell once claimed that one of his qualities as a political writer was the capacity to face "unpleasant facts". I believed that the "success" of the Pacific Solution was one such unpleasant fact that the friends of the asylum seekers needed to face. In "What Is Rudd's Agenda?", published in November 2008, I argued:

> The hope of the government is ... that because of the success of the Howard government's brutal deterrence policy, people smugglers will continue to give Australia a wide berth. The new humanitarianism of the Rudd government's asylum-seeker policy is free-riding on the "success" of the Howard government's

inhumanity. The Rudd government is gambling on the fact that the shaky logical and moral foundations of its asylum-seeker policy will not be tested. Last month two boats arrived.

In my political life, there is hardly anything that has caused me as much private anguish as my argument about the dangers that the Rudd government might face by its abandonment of the threat of naval deterrence or offshore detention for asylum seekers setting out for Australia by boat. I wish I had argued it more often and more strongly. In 2009, some 2,800 asylum seekers reached Australia by boat; in the first eight months of 2010, the number was 4,000. Rudd sought to escape his policy failure by expressing the Good Samaritan's sympathy for the asylum seekers and by describing those who arranged their passage to Australia as "vermin".

The return of the boats was one of the reasons the Rudd government lost its early lustre. In October 2009, Australian naval officers pleaded unsuccessfully with seventy-eight rescued Sri Lankan asylum seekers on board an Australian customs vessel, the *Oceanic Viking*, to disembark on Indonesian soil. In a fortnight, the primary vote for Labor, as measured by Newspoll, fell by 7 percentage points. I described the incident as "*Tampa* in reverse": "*Tampa* convinced the Australian people that John Howard was strong; the *Oceanic Viking* that Kevin Rudd was weak."

*

The summer months of 2008–09 were difficult for me. During a holiday in New Zealand with Anne and our younger daughter, Lucy (Kate was now studying in the US), my voice continued to croak. Not long after our return, I went to an ear, nose and throat specialist, a doctor I came later greatly to admire. As soon as he poked his instrument down my nose to examine the vocal cords, he told me: "Cancer, I'm afraid." Throughout January and early February, on each weekday I drove from our cottage on the north-eastern outskirts of Melbourne to the Epworth Hospital in Richmond for radiation treatment. Soon my neck was burned raw.

Shortly before Saturday, February 7, the Victorian authorities warned about the extreme risk of bushfire. They were right. We learned from the Country Fire Authority (CFA) in the morning about a fire in East Kilmore. By the early afternoon we learned that it had spread to Mount Disappointment, still some 50 kilometres from our home. And then nothing more. In the late afternoon there was a strange roar to our north. It sounded like a massive train was passing through. I thought it was the wind. Overnight there were radio reports of deaths by fire at St Andrews, 5 kilometres to the north of our home. If the wind had blown in a slightly different direction, we might have been killed.

We soon learned of deaths a little further north of St Andrews, in Kinglake. We also learned that the entire nearby township of Strathewen had been destroyed, with more than two dozen deaths. Among the dead were several acquaintances, including a delightfully eccentric elderly couple near Strathewen who had dedicated their lives to the restoration of the land they owned to its natural state.

On "Black Saturday", 173 Victorians had burned to death. With appropriate warnings, many would still be alive. Anne and I became obsessed by one question: why weren't those in danger warned? In the days that followed, we both became increasingly astonished that the newspapers were not demanding an answer to this question. I phoned my old opinion editor at *The Age*, Paul Austin, without result. I then suggested to the editor of *The Monthly*, Sally Warhaft, that we commission a *Monthly* essay on the failure of the authorities to issue warnings. Eventually, she agreed.

We thought of Richard Flanagan. As I had known Richard since the Demidenko affair, and understood better than Sally what had occurred in country Victoria on Black Saturday, we agreed that I should call him. As it turned out, Richard was canoeing in the Tasmanian wilderness and was uncontactable. I had phoned David Marr several days before to congratulate him on articles he had written on the bushfires. Shortly after I learned that Richard was uncontactable, David rang. I asked him whether he might be interested in writing a long essay on the lack of warnings on Black Saturday. He was interested, although he had to ask his editor at

The Sydney Morning Herald for permission. I then phoned Sally, who was a great admirer of David's journalism, with the good news. She appeared to be delighted. When David did not get his editor's approval, we decided that I would write the article, which by now we both believed – or, at least, so I thought – needed to be written. I began research at once.

In January 2009, Kevin Rudd sent *The Monthly* a 7,700-word essay, a lengthy analysis of the global crisis that had been triggered in the United States with the September 2008 collapse of one of the great financial houses in the United States, Lehman Brothers. Rudd and the Treasury secretary, Ken Henry, had been fighting from the first moment against the threat of an Australian recession with a classically Keynesian policy of significant government spending: first cash gifts and then, most importantly, the funding of school buildings and home insulation.

According to Rudd, the sixty years since the end of the Second World War could be divided into two eras. In the first, the social-democratic era, economic thinking in the Western democracies was dominated by Maynard Keynes, and in the second, the neo-liberal era, by Friedrich Hayek. The current crisis signalled the end of neo-liberalism, which had failed because of what the financier-philanthropist George Soros had called its key idea – "market fundamentalism". Unlike the neo-liberals, social democrats believed in the need for a balance to be struck between private enterprise and public ownership. Unlike neo-liberals, the social democrats believed in the idea of an active state, involving regulation where needed and including the pursuit of "social justice", something anathema to Hayek. The threat of the political extremism of the right and left now threatened, as it had during the 1930s. It was once again the duty of social democrats to rescue capitalism.

At this moment of crisis, as Rudd pointed out, everyone had turned to government, recognising that it was only through state activity that solutions to the crisis could be found – the crisis that had been created, in part, according to Rudd, by neo-liberal delusion about deregulation. The neo-liberals believed that the free market alone could regulate the vast trillions of dollars of trade in so-called "derivatives", often bundles of ultra-vulnerable home mortgages, that one of the most successful financiers in the United States, Warren Buffett, had identified as potential "weapons of financial destruction". The crisis was also created, according to Rudd, by the benefaction neo-liberalism had pronounced over greed, and by the grotesque levels of inequality in the contemporary United States, where an American CEO now received several thousand times the salary of one of their workers. Just as Franklin Roosevelt had helped save capitalism during the years of the Great Depression with his New Deal, so would it now fall upon world leaders, led by Barack Obama, to save capitalism from the damage wrought by Hayekian neo-liberalism.

Exactly what shape the political economy of capitalism would take in the new post-neo-liberal era was not yet known. What was known, however, according to Rudd, was that in the new world there would be a vital role for state regulation, that a balance would have to be struck between the private and public sectors of the economy, and that the striving for social justice could not be ignored. Even more than all this, in the contemporary world, the greatest moral challenge, the looming threat of catastrophic climate change, could best be understood, in the words of Sir Nicholas Stern, as the most profound case of market failure in the history of humankind.

When Rudd's essay arrived, entirely unexpectedly, everyone at *The Monthly* was both surprised and delighted (as an email to me from Sally Warhaft confirmed). I was particularly pleased because, once again, I agreed with the essay's almost every word. And because, as it had turned out, it was not the daydreaming left but the delusional right that had experienced "a big surprise". Kevin Rudd turned out to be, to borrow the language of *The Australian*, the greatest actor who had ever strutted across the Australian political stage. Or, rather, as I wrote in *The Australian*, someone whose opposition to Hayek and neo-liberalism had been consistent from his maiden speech to the House of Representatives to his *Monthly* essay "The Global Financial Crisis".

Because Rudd's essay was greeted with ridicule and abuse by members of the Coalition and the Murdoch press, I suggested to Sally and the other *Monthly* editorial board members, Morry Schwartz and Chris Feik, that we should invite some leading writers to comment on it briefly. In a short time, we assembled a stellar cast, including Eric Hobsbawm, the Marxist author of the unmatched four-volume history of the world from the French Revolution to the present; the neo-liberal economist David Hale, well-known to Australian audiences; and John Gray, the former student and interpreter of Hayek who had moved on to a heterodox form of liberal conservatism. (To my amusement, the former communist Hobsbawm required and received $4 per word for his contribution!)

Since I had suggested most of the panellists and was the only member of *The Monthly* inner circle who had read their works, we agreed that I should write a brief anonymous introduction. It began: "*The Monthly* was surprised and gratified when Kevin Rudd offered us his analysis of the global financial crisis, earlier this year. We were, however, puzzled and disappointed by the quality of the media response to it." To my astonishment, Sally demanded that I remove the words "surprised and gratified". She could not explain why. When a fierce controversy erupted over this question, I came to believe that it must have been because she had been boasting around the town that she had commissioned Rudd's essay.

By now Sally had alienated every member of the *Monthly* editorial board, which no longer met. I had done as much as I could to help launch Sally's career, first employing her as the tutor in my course on Australian politics at La Trobe and later providing much assistance to her as editor. In return, she refused the only favour I had ever asked of her, to open the online space of *The Monthly* to a discussion with Gerard Henderson on the Australian anti-communists' silence (or worse) during the months in 1965–66 when between 500,000 and 1 million Indonesians had been murdered by the forces of General Suharto.

In our final phone conversation, on the "surprised and gratified" issue, Sally told me that it was too late to do anything as the pages she had unilaterally amended had already been sent to the printer. I had just been on the phone with Morry and, as I told Sally, I knew this simply was not true. She hung up. We never spoke again. For the next hour, I later learned, Sally screamed at Morry until the battery of his mobile phone ran dead. Her editorship was over. Thus began the most ridiculous controversy of my life.

The controversy occurred in three places: in the online publication *Crikey*, in *The Age* and in *The Australian*. It was triggered by a piece in *Crikey* by Jonathan Green, who at first relied on two anonymous sources, Gideon Haigh and Peter Craven. It was continued, principally, by reports in *The Australian* by Caroline Overington and by two long articles in *The Age* and in *Crikey* by Haigh, to which I replied in *The Australian* and *Crikey*.

According to the case mounted against me, I was principally to blame for Sally's removal. I was an "old bore" and "a once prominent public presence now grappling with a quickly descending twilight that has combined serious illness with a fading profile". In my ill health and approaching dotage, I was supposedly envious of a bright, young, independent woman, who not only edited *The Monthly* with brilliance and was almost alone responsible for its success, but who had even appeared at the 2020 Rudd Summit and on ABC TV's *Q&A*. It was claimed that I went behind Sally's back and commissioned pieces for *The Monthly* without her knowledge. This was based upon the David Marr muddle and was entirely untrue. In fact, because Sally felt overburdened she had asked me and I had agreed to guest-edit, unpaid, the entire July 2009 issue of *The Monthly*, and had accepted the offer made by Chris Feik and me that we work on the commissioning of book reviews and reviewers, although in no case without her knowledge and approval. It was also claimed that I was interested in the lack of bushfire warnings not because of the deaths of 173 Victorians, including several of my acquaintances, but because I expected a personal phone call from the CFA. As I later wrote, when this was suggested to me by Overington, "I am not usually lost for words. On this occasion I was." And so on. Morry was apparently so reliant on me for his beliefs and indeed was so "besotted" that he had gone along with my anti-Sally hostility, as he had when I'd wanted to credit David Corlett for his contribution to the *Quarterly Essay* titled *Sending Them Home*. For a while, I suppose, my reputation among the inner-city Melbourne left must have suffered because of the Sally Warhaft question. Luckily, I was not a part of that world.

Despite Kevin Rudd's ambitious, even grandiose agenda, in the public mind he was always most associated with the question of climate change, the issue that he had frequently described as "the greatest moral, economic and social challenge of our time". As soon as he became prime minister, Australia joined the countries of the Kyoto Protocol, a costless but necessary step. With the election of Rudd and Barack Obama one year later, the fantasy of a climate change movement led by George W. Bush and John Howard and based on voluntary emission reductions that would render Kyoto obsolete was spoken about no more.

By now, in my mind, action on climate change overwhelmed every other political question. As I wrote in *The Monthly* in November 2008: "Humanity's main chance now for avoiding catastrophe is for individual nations to take unilateral action on carbon dioxide and other greenhouse gas emissions, in the hope that their actions will have … a benign domino effect." I was, however, pessimistic:

> Climate change demands more of politics and international relations than they can deliver … Kevin Rudd has failed as much and as little as would every imaginable Australian prime minister. Even more than Rudd would find it comfortable to acknowledge, it is the crystal spirit and the wisdom and the courage of Dietrich Bonhoeffer that we now need.

From the dying days of the Howard government, Rudd had inherited the idea of an emissions-trading scheme. I argued that his government's plans for the reduction of emissions were a considerable disappointment – with generous financial compensation going to what were called "trade-exposed, emissions-intensive industries" and even to some "coal-fired electricity plants", and a likely general emissions-reduction target of a miserly 5 per cent by 2020, unless an international agreement for a more ambitious number emerged from the next international climate conference, to be held in Copenhagen in the northern winter of 2009–10.

The choice Kevin Rudd had to make was whether to look to the left or the right for the passage of his climate change legislation. In general, Rudd placed his government, ideologically speaking, on a ground he called "the reforming centre", between the troglodytes to his right and the zealots to his left. But in choosing to negotiate with the Coalition rather than the Greens for the passage of his emissions-reduction legislation, a gulf opened between Rudd's soaring rhetoric and his ultra-cautious policy that posed real political danger. So it turned out. In December 2009, Malcolm Turnbull lost the leadership of the Liberal Party to Tony Abbott, the natural successor to John Howard and the leader of the "denialist" wing of the Coalition, whose thinking was dominated by the lessons taught to him by B.A. Santamaria (except when it came to the question of capitalism). Abbott's rise was almost as lethal a blow to Kevin Rudd as it was to Malcolm Turnbull.

At Copenhagen, Rudd worked with all his energy for a global agreement with obligatory emissions-reduction targets for the countries of both the developed and undeveloped worlds. He left Copenhagen exhausted and empty-handed. Unsurprisingly, in the absence of a Coalition negotiating party, Rudd now relied on the Greens for the passage of his emissions-trading scheme. The Greens could not be convinced.

From the taxation review conducted by Ken Henry, Rudd chose to act on one item, a mining super-profits tax. The miners, however, had very deep pockets and the support of both the Coalition and the Murdoch press. A campaign for the removal of Rudd began in earnest. At the same time, the number of boats of asylum seekers were increasing. Tony Abbott's promise was that only a government led by him would have the courage to once again "stop the boats".

Then, in late April 2010, someone leaked to Fairfax journalist Lenore Taylor an astonishing decision that had been taken by

Rudd's small inner "kitchen cabinet" – the prime minister; the deputy prime minister, Julia Gillard; the treasurer, Wayne Swan; and the finance secretary, Lindsay Tanner. They had decided that the idea of an emissions-trading scheme would be abandoned for the life of the present parliament and not revived until 2012. According to Newspoll, support for the Rudd government at this point collapsed.

Even though I had no knowledge of the manoeuvrings behind the scenes, I believed that, following Rudd's apparent climate change surrender, his government was probably finished. An article I wrote for *The Monthly* argued: "In the history of Australian politics there has never been a collapse as dramatic, unexpected and as unnecessary as the one experienced by Kevin Rudd during the past two months." Rudd's mining tax proposal was "crazy brave". His climate change retreat looked like "cowardice" and as if Rudd believed in nothing.

> With Rudd there has been ... a permanent tension between past words and present performance, and an even deeper tension between an idealistic rhetoric drawn from people such as his hero, Dietrich Bonhoeffer, and a supposedly pragmatic political practice reflecting the advice of members of the Sussex Street school of cynicism from the New South Wales Labor Right, such as Senator Mark Arbib ... In politics it is easy to propose plans about education revolutions, reforming the tax or health systems, building submarine fleets and new broadband networks, closing the gap between Indigenous and non-Indigenous wellbeing, reducing global poverty and nuclear weapons, redesigning the architecture of the Asia-Pacific, combating climate change, or whatever. But without high-level political skills they can begin to resemble Walter Mitty dreams.

Eleven days after I had finished this article, which I had the sense to date June 13, Kevin Rudd was gone.

In just a couple of years I had moved from the optimism of *Dear Mr Rudd* to the despondency of "Oh Dear, Mr Rudd!" – something to do, I suppose, not only with politics but also with my brush with cancer, and with the recognition that my family might have died with a tiny change in the direction of the wind on Black Saturday. That had been followed by the faux martyrdom of Sally Warhaft, which had rendered me for a while an enemy of the people of Fitzroy and Balmain. I was, once again, "that fellow Manne".

[16.]

Good News, Bad News

A FEW MONTHS AFTER THE ELECTION of Julia Gillard's minority government, I decided to write a short comment on Julian Assange for *The Monthly*. Because of WikiLeaks' publication of hundreds of thousands of documents from the United States on the war in Afghanistan and the invasion and occupation of Iraq (including film of the massacre of fifteen innocent Iraqis), and of diplomatic cables from the State Department, Assange was at the height of his fame. Recently he had been named by *Le Monde* as its "Man of the Year" and by *Time* as its "Person of the Year". Despite the thousands of articles that had been written about him, it was not long before I realised, to my considerable surprise, that no one seemed to have understood either his intellectual origins in the "cypherpunk" movement, or to have grasped the political theory outlined in a short paper Assange had written, "Conspiracy as Governance", which had given birth to WikiLeaks. For almost every book or long article I had written previously, I had needed to travel to archives – to London on British diplomacy on the eve of the Second World War; to Canberra on Wilfred Burchett; to Canberra and Adelaide on the Petrov Affair; all around eastern Australia for the records concerning the Stolen Generations. In the case of Assange and WikiLeaks, all the research could be conducted from my study at home.

When I began, I knew almost nothing beyond the newspaper reports on Julian Assange or WikiLeaks. I had never, for example, heard of the cypherpunks. Nor was I well credentialled, to put it mildly, to write about the most significant political movement to emerge in the new age of the internet. I was the second-last member of the politics department at La Trobe to write on a computer and send emails, and I'd been the very last Fairfax commentator to telephone columns to the nearly extinct band of copytakers at *The Sydney Morning Herald*. When my article on Assange was published, a colleague at La Trobe was unkind enough to question whether I was indeed the author, while a friend of Assange's, who learned about my modest acquaintance with computers and the internet, was outraged. Within a few days of exploring Assange and WikiLeaks on the internet, I realised that there was a detailed article almost demanding to be written.

After the departure of Sally Warhaft, the small *Monthly* editorial board had migrated from Jimmy Watson's, in the heart of Carlton, to a swish wine bar in North Carlton that was very close to the location of my father's small furniture workshop, which I had visited as a young child. We discussed the essay at our new meeting place. Morry Schwartz was keen on publishing a very long essay; the new wunderkind editor of *The Monthly*, Ben Naparstek, whom I never understood, was decidedly less so.

At the time I began reading for the article, Julian Assange's exploits as a youthful computer hacker were well known. With two others, who called themselves the International Subversives, Julian had found his way into the communications of the US military and the Apollo space program. He had been taken to court by the AFP after the discovery that the Subversives had penetrated a Canadian telecommunications company, Nortel. Assange was well known, in part through *Underground*, a book he had had researched and helped write with a friend, Suelette Dreyfus, and in which Assange, hiding behind one of his many masks, called himself Mendax ("Liar"). What was not known was the role his association with the "cypherpunks" had played in his intellectual/political formation.

The cypherpunks were anarchists whose interest was the novel character of the struggle between the state and the individual in the age of the internet. Because of two breakthroughs – the invention in the mid-1970s of a brilliant new code that was called "private key cryptography", and in the early 1990s of a computer program known as PGP ("Pretty Good Privacy") – communications between individuals under a condition of unbreakable anonymity became possible. Because of what this situation offered terrorists, financial criminals and pornographers, the combination of private key cryptography and PGP was opposed by governments, most importantly the United States. But it was the uses to which impenetrable communications between individuals could be put that was at the centre of the discussions of the very lively cypherpunks email list.

All cypherpunks were, as anarchists, enemies of the state. Most were anarchists of the right, Ayn Rand–style economic libertarians. Some, however, were not. Many were intra-individual communication absolutists, opposed to even the smallest interference by the state. Especially after 9/11, some cypherpunks were willing to compromise, to the absolutists' outrage. Among these absolutists many schemes were discussed, most radically and famously one that outlined how a financial reward might be offered to the person who predicted correctly the date on which a despised politician would be assassinated. Only the assassin would be aware of the date. As all politicians would begin to live in fear in the new age of political assassination, the state would begin gradually to wither away.

Between late 1993 or early 1994 and 2002, as I discovered, Julian Assange was an active contributor to the cypherpunks' exchanges, more than holding his own against professors of mathematics or former Silicon Valley "Masters of the Universe" – no small accomplishment for a university dropout. When Assange became world-famous, one of the most radical and cantankerous cypherpunks, John Young – a supporter of assassination politics and the creator of *Cryptome*, a site for the publication of "leaks" damaging to the United States and its allies – decided to publish all Assange's cypherpunk postings. They showed Assange to have been a private communication absolutist whose politics were unusual for a cypherpunk, not libertarian-capitalist but of the anti-communist left.

Assange asked Young, his politico-spiritual father, for assistance as he was establishing WikiLeaks. Because Young, characteristically, began to suspect Assange was working for the CIA, he also decided to publish all WikiLeaks' internal foundation documents to which he had been privy.

The more I read, the more I warmed to Julian. He was a person of the left but also an anti-communist, as was I. In an instruction to his followers in June 2007, where he argued for the need to remain politically open, even to disillusioned members of the right, Assange scolded:

> OK, you guys need to keep the Progressive/Commie/Socialist agendas and rhetoric to yourselves ... Now, now, don't get your dander up: if I can pass by gross mis-characterizations of the existing world order as "capitalist" or "white supremacy", you can stay calm and listen for a minute.

Because he had published hundreds of thousands of secret American documents and cables, by the time I was researching the creation of WikiLeaks the world believed that Assange was a conventional anti-American. This seemed to me a mistake. After reading his cypherpunk interventions and his correspondence in the early days of WikiLeaks, I was convinced that if he had received documents from a Chinese equivalent to Chelsea Manning (born Bradley), WikiLeaks' American source, he would have published them with perhaps even greater relish. Assange had assured Young: "We are going to fuck them all. Chinese mostly ..."

There was a corrosive cynicism among many cypherpunks, especially its most authoritative voice, Tim May, the author of *The Cyphernomicon*, a kind of cypherpunk manifesto or even bible. Assange would have none of this. He accompanied many of his cypherpunk postings with the beautiful words of Antoine de Saint-Exupéry: "If you want to build a ship, don't drum up people together to collect wood and don't assign them tasks and work, but rather teach them to long for the endless immensity of the sea."

There was no value more mocked by the Ayn Rand/Hayekian cypherpunks than "altruism". On the cypherpunks list, Assange attempted a defence. "Everyone maybe self-interested, but some are self-interested in a way that is healthy (to you, or the people you care about) ..." Assange was greatly taken by the speech Aleksandr Solzhenitsyn, one of his favourite authors, had delivered following his expulsion from the Soviet Union, about the decline of "civic courage" among Western elites. Assange was contemptuous of those he called "the typical shy intellectual", supposedly the kind of left-wing academic he had encountered at the University of Melbourne: "The power of their intellect and noble instincts may lead them to a courageous position, where they see the need to take up arms, but their instinctive fear of authority then motivates them to find rationalizations to avoid conflict."

Assange regarded "courage" as the most important political virtue. And he regarded courage as "contagious". With WikiLeaks' publication of the Afghan war logs, the Iraqi incident reports and the 250,000 US State Department cables, Assange had taken on the most powerful nation in world history. As one after another of his closest supporters deserted him, he discovered that fear frequently trumped courage. At least one of his closest followers, Rop Gonggrijp, was honest: "I guess I could make up all kinds of stories about how I disagreed with people or decisions, but the truth is that [during] the period that I helped out, the possible ramifications of WikiLeaks scared the bejezus out of me. Courage is contagious, my ass."

The intellectual challenge facing Assange was to find a way to weaponise the new world of undetectable communications for the betterment of humankind. What he proposed was the establishment of an organisation well known to the general public. The organisation could receive information from state and corporation whistleblowers across the political spectrum, guarantee that the whistleblower's identity would be protected, and publish to the world without redaction or interpretation the information received. Assange assumed that the information his organisation published would be analysed enthusiastically and meticulously by the independent media.

In his key theoretical document, "Conspiracy as Governance", Assange argued that all contemporary states and corporations operated to some extent as exploitative conspiracies hiding the truth of their behaviour from those whose interests they pretended to serve or protect. Insiders were often privy to the self-serving conspiratorial behaviour of the state or corporation that employed them, from the flow of secretive internal communications, without which no organisation could operate with at least a minimum of efficiency. These insiders could, without fear of detection, forward the evidence of corrupt or exploitative behaviour to the organisation that had been established to receive it. The more corrupt the organisation, the more crippled it would be by its fear of insider leaks. Assange called the escalating fear of exposure via leaks a "secrecy tax". The more corrupt the organisation, the steeper would be the secrecy tax it would be obliged to pay.

What Assange was proposing involved a kind of political Darwinism, the triumph of the states and corporations that had the least amount of corrupt behaviour they needed to hide – the survival not of the fittest but of the least corrupt. He believed the information would ignite a worldwide non-violent revolution, or what I described in my article as a "moral revolution". Assange believed that the organisation he established – which he called WikiLeaks, following the astonishing success of the new-style encyclopedia Wikipedia – would pose a lethal threat to powerful states and corporations. Because he understood that freedom of expression was a sacred value in the age of liberalism, even if it was often more honoured in the breach than in the observance, it was vital that WikiLeaks should pretend to be nothing more than an "apple-pie press freedom project", whose revolutionary ambition and potential should for as long as possible be disguised.

In January 2007, the creation of WikiLeaks was announced prematurely. For once, Assange spoke the truth in public about the organisation he was about to launch.

> Principled leaking has changed the course of human history for the better ... Public scrutiny of otherwise unaccountable and secretive institutions pressures them to act ethically ... When the

risks of embarrassment through openness and honesty increase, the tables are turned against conspiracy, corruption, exploitation and oppression ... WL will provide a forum for the entire global community to examine any document relentlessly for credibility, plausibility, veracity and falsifiability ... WL may become the most powerful intelligence agency on earth, an intelligence agency of the people ... WL, we hope, will be a new star in the political firmament of humanity.

I know I was attracted to WikiLeaks in part because of the power of Julian Assange's prose. But there was more to it than that. In *The Monthly*, I wrote: "There are few original ideas in politics. In the creation of WikiLeaks, Julian Assange was responsible for one."

My 15,000-word essay on Julian Assange as a "cypherpunk revolutionary" was well received, both here and abroad, although some found it difficult to understand. In *The Age*, Martin Flanagan described it as "a mighty piece of journalism" but thought that while my prose was normally "smooth as butter", on this occasion it was "lumpy". Patsy Crawford of the Hobart *Mercury* reported: "I had a mate drop in. 'I've just read that Robert Manne article about Julian Assange. I couldn't understand a bloody word,' he shouted." Without warrant, as was his way, John Young posted the entire article on *Cryptome*. Although Young praised nothing and suspected everything, on this occasion – probably because his role during the creation of WikiLeaks had been noticed – he almost purred: "Thanks to Robert Manne for an exemplary essay and *The Monthly* for paying him 2 cents a word." (Why he thought I had been paid 2 cents per word, I have no idea.)

By far the most pleasing response to the essay came from Julian Assange. Although I was obviously an admirer, my essay was not without criticism. I had described Assange as "a fabulist" when writing about his early life, and the tone in his cypherpunk interventions as rather arrogant, sometimes "sarcastic", sometimes "brash", and sometimes contemptuously dismissive of others. The essay was published before Assange was accused by two Swedish women of rape. I noticed, however, that sometimes, when discussing women, his tone was "awkward in a Mills & Boon kind of way", but also at times "rather sinister" in what I would now call "a #MeToo kind of way". What I wrote was no panegyric. No matter. In a civil email, Julian pointed out certain minor errors of fact and interpretation, sometimes convincingly, sometimes not. After a detailed and courteous exchange, I promised that if the essay was ever republished, I would make several amendments – a promise I was able to keep. Julian then recommended the article to his supporters.

The Australian's gossip columnist, James Jeffrey, takes up the story:

> With more than 800,000 followers, WikiLeaks' Twitter account was always going to prove more than a match for *The Monthly*'s website. And so it proved yesterday when Julian Assange tweeted that Robert Manne's essay was "easily the best article" about him ... Without much further ado, *The Monthly*'s site crashed and would-be visitors were re-directed to this message: "Due to overwhelming demand ... we have posted the essay on Julian Assange here on our Facebook page in three parts."

One consequence of the Assange article was an invitation for me to appear in a film by one of the most celebrated American documentarians, Alex Gibney. By the time *We Steal Secrets* was released, in mid-2013 – in which I made a small and undistinguished appearance – Julian Assange had taken refuge inside the Ecuadorian embassy in London. Sweden was seeking his extradition. In the United States, a grand jury had been empanelled. Even before the film's release, Assange's supporters had launched a ferocious attack on the film and on Gibney. Assange understood the peril he would face if liberal opinion turned against him.

Within what could be described as the "moral economy" of the film, the balance fell heavily on the side of the journalists at *The Guardian* and *The New York Times* with whom Julian had fallen out badly and bitterly, and on the side of the former WikiLeaks insiders Daniel Domscheit-Berg and James Ball, with whom he had fallen out even more badly and bitterly. The most damaging accusation, from Nick Davies of *The Guardian*, was that Assange had placed the lives of the Afghans who had worked with the Americans at extreme risk through his carelessness (or worse) regarding the redaction of names. The most damaging accusation of the defectors was that he had turned WikiLeaks into an authoritarian, secretive and even corrupt organisation, a mirror image of those states and corporations it had been established to expose. The hero of *We Steal Secrets* was not Assange but Private Bradley Manning, the source of the hundreds of thousands of Afghan, Iraqi and State Department documents published almost in full by WikiLeaks and, after redaction and selection, by *The New York Times*, *The Guardian* and *Der Spiegel*, which had turned Assange into a global political actor. Manning, "human, all too human", had undermined the modus operandi of WikiLeaks – undetectable communication – by informing an underground hacker named Adrian Lamo that he was the source of the documents. Lamo had informed on Manning and Assange to the FBI. In *We Steal Secrets*, Gibney suggested that Assange's callous indifference to the wellbeing of Manning, who was wrestling with his trans identity, was the reason he turned to Lamo.

Gibney must have been stung by my *Monthly* review of his film. What followed was an intricate exchange between us, which was published online and almost as lengthy as my original article. The most important question was whether Assange's fear of extradition to the United States from either Sweden of the United Kingdom was fanciful, as *We Steal Secrets* suggested, or realistic, as I argued. The only time I became angry was at Gibney's suggestion that in refusing to go to Sweden to face the music Assange was behaving in a cowardly manner. In my view, in taking on the American state Assange had been brave, even crazy-brave. There was nothing cowardly about fighting against the prospect of spending the rest of his life in an American prison. My final comment showed how far my thinking had come since the end of the Cold War:

> In the age where our political elites have brought us Iraq, Wall Street, Fox News and passivity in the face of the impending,

foreseeable catastrophe of global warming, I must admit that I have come to admire highly fearless and intelligent political animals like Julian Assange.

I did whatever I could to support Assange. Two La Trobe University forums sponsored by the Ideas and Society Program, which I convened, discussed WikiLeaks. I accepted an invitation for an event at the Sydney Opera House with Glenn Greenwald, the journalist to whom Edward Snowden had turned after releasing a cache of documents that revealed the sinister reach of the post-9/11 American surveillance state; Alexa O'Brien, an idealistic American radical who had independently transcribed Manning's entire trial; and, from the Ecuadorian embassy in London, Julian Assange himself.

Gradually, my respect for Assange faded somewhat. At one of the La Trobe events, a young and impressive Englishwoman, Sarah Harrison, introduced herself. Soon after, she flew to Hong Kong as an agent of Assange and, remarkably enough, was instrumental in assisting Edward Snowden's flight from Hong Kong to Moscow, and in negotiating the terms of the protection Russia offered him. Harrison was in love with Assange but had been dumped. As it was now too dangerous for her to return to Britain, she had settled semi-permanently in Berlin. Assange's behaviour seemed cruel and, to use a hopelessly old-fashioned word, dishonourable.

And then there was politics. In 2016, WikiLeaks published material that was damaging to the US Democratic Party and Hillary Clinton and of very great value to Donald Trump, who referred to it gleefully on some 150 occasions. Russian intelligence was the most likely source. As I argued in *The Monthly* of July 2017:

> WikiLeaks was itself vulnerable to a radical form of corruption if the leaks it published came not from upright whistleblowers but from manipulative political actors, such as agents or intermediaries of an intelligence service. There was quite simply nothing in Assange's theory that might have dissuaded him from co-operating with Russian intelligence in its clandestine

anti-Clinton, pro-Trump operation. A revolutionary movement born of idealism and the hope of creating a better world has thus ended by assisting in the election of the most dangerous president in the history of the United States.

None of this prevented me from feeling intense pity as Assange's life drained away after he was transferred from the Ecuadorian embassy to British prisons while fighting extradition to the United States. As I write, after pleading guilty to one count of espionage, Julian Assange has made a spectacular and altogether unexpected return to Australia as a free man. This is good news indeed.

*

In late 2010, my political ally and friend Clive Hamilton, who had written *Scorcher* on climate change politics for Black Inc. Agenda, suggested a *Quarterly Essay* on *The Australian* under the editorship of Chris Mitchell. I was interested but, after some thought, realised that our approaches to the subject and styles would be so different that joint authorship would not work. I asked Clive if he would be okay if I wrote the essay alone. He was. So, after the Assange essay was complete, I began research.

I had long believed that, despite its modest sales, *The Australian* was the country's most important newspaper, which members of the political nation – politicians, public servants, journalists, academics, the engaged citizenry – no matter what their values and beliefs, were obliged to read. *The Australian* was the only paper Rupert Murdoch had created. It was his principal means of influencing the direction of the country of his birth, even more significant than his far more popular tabloids, Melbourne's *Herald Sun* and Sydney's *Daily Telegraph*. For this reason, *The Australian* was more generously resourced than any paper in the country.

It was a strange, perhaps even unique newspaper, having managed under the editorship of Chris Mitchell to combine the supposed depth of the broadsheets Murdoch had acquired – *The Times* and *The Wall Street Journal* – with the pugnacious "take-no-prisoners" aggression of his tabloids – *The Sun* (of London) and *The New York Post*. I decided to concentrate the analysis not on generalities but on the particularities of *The Australian*'s coverage of certain "ideologically sensitive" questions that I had been following, closely and aghast, for many years: the faux debate Mitchell's *Australian* had sponsored around Keith Windschuttle's reactionary *The Fabrication of Aboriginal History*; the jingoistic support it had offered the Howard government during the unprovoked invasion of Iraq, and its shameless response when the baselessness of the invasion was revealed; Chris Mitchell's obsessive and on occasion comical years-long arm wrestle with ABC TV's weekly fifteen-minute program *Media Watch*; the cruel decision to try to destroy the reputation of a young Indigenous academic, Larissa Behrendt, and the threatened defamation action against another young academic, Julie Posetti, on the basis of one or two entirely accurate tweets about a talk on climate change; the implicit denialism and the frightful intellectual muddle of the paper's coverage of climate change; its role in the breaking of Kevin Rudd after his article in *The Monthly* which pointed out the role played by neo-liberalism in the global financial catastrophe; and its open declaration of war against the rising force in Australian politics, the Greens.

By 2011 I had learned from considerable experience not to trust Chris Mitchell. For this reason, I decided to request an interview as a protection and in the hope that the request would be denied. Within two hours, Mitchell accepted. I thought it would be prudent if what happened was witnessed by someone I could trust. I suggested the Sydney journalist and academic who had recently written a book on Rupert Murdoch's politics, David McKnight, and who had co-edited with me a short book on the possible end of the neo-liberal era, *Goodbye to All That?* Mitchell refused on the ground that David was a former communist. I then suggested Morry Schwartz. Mitchell agreed.

Morry and I flew to Sydney on June 15. Because of the traffic we missed our flight and arrived at News Corp's headquarters a little later than planned. I hoped for an hour with Mitchell. What I was offered on arrival – or, more accurately, was confronted with – was a string of arranged interviews: two hours with Mitchell and *The Australian*'s so-called editor-at-large, Paul Kelly, followed by unrequested interviews with *The Weekend Australian*'s editor, Nick Cater (who, as Morry noticed, had placed the essays of a famous, unbendingly high-principled broadcast liberal on his desk); then with the daily editor, Clive Mathieson; the economics editor, Michael Stutchbury; the politics editor, Dennis Shanahan; and finally with senior reporter Matthew Franklin.

Only one thing on that day left a lasting impression. Paul Kelly had once been a fiercely independent editor-in-chief of *The Australian* and remained the country's most influential and accomplished political journalist, the author of the seminal political history of Australia in the 1980s, *The End of Certainty*. I was astonished at his apparently unfeigned deference to Chris Mitchell. And was even more astonished when Kelly explained to Morry and me, with his characteristic gravitas, that climate change was a purely technical policy question without a moral dimension. Our generation had discovered that, principally because our energy was produced by the burning of fossil fuels, we were responsible for the destruction of the benign condition of the Earth, for all future generations, *forever*. And here was Australia's most respected political journalist informing us, with his customary certainty, that climate change was not a moral matter. I am not easily shocked. On this occasion I was not only shocked but also deeply disheartened.

In early August 2011, Anne and I were participants at the Byron Bay Writers Festival. News Corp was a sponsor, having supplied a festival tent, along with which came Nick Cater. One of the events was a discussion about *The Australian* between Cater and me. I believed it would be dishonest (and dangerous) if in our conversation I did not make clear the conclusions of my *Quarterly Essay*, which was to be published the following month. Anne sat next to Cater's wife, Rebecca Weisser, then *The Australian*'s opinion editor and now editor of *Quadrant*. Recently, Wendi Deng had lunged at someone who threatened husband Rupert with a cream pie. Anne joked that one of them might soon need to similarly intervene. Weisser told Anne that she need not be concerned. Only the left was uncivil. Anne mentioned the case of Anders Behring Breivik, the right-wing extremist who had recently murdered dozens of young Swedish Social Democrats in cold blood. Silence.

One audience member that afternoon was the veteran journalist Mungo MacCallum. He reported in the *Lismore Echo* of August 11 what happened between Cater and me:

> Cater's patently absurd line was to insist that *The Australian* is not an organ of the right. It is central, mainstream, indeed really old-fashioned Liberal ... Cater kept on assuring his incredulous audience that the paper really believed in man-made climate change and in taking action about it, and was even in favour of a mining tax; it had said so in its editorials. When Manne pointed out that its treatment of both news and comment overwhelmingly opposed both propositions, Cater muttered that it was only an argument about what sort of action and what sort of tax. His derisory attempts at self-justification were greeted with well-merited loathing and contempt.

In front of this audience, Cater renewed an offer for me to write in *The Australian*. I declined. To do so, I said, would be to provide the paper with "legitimacy". I had no intention of being rolled out as an alibi every time the paper was accused of being right-wing.

In our relations, Cater had always been courteous. It was a mistake to humiliate him in front of a left-wing Byron Bay audience. Nick Cater now became an implacable enemy, without the pretence even of civility, let alone courtesy. On August 19, *The Australian*'s "Cut & Paste" column – which I described as "the daily compendium of *Schadenfreude* and spleen" – was devoted to mockery of my political journey from right to left: "I've been everywhere Manne, I've been everywhere: a salute to an intellectual wanderer." There were very many such "Cut & Pastes" to come.

That evening a "Great Debate" had been organised. The debaters were driven in a small bus to the venue, Byron Bay High School. I was one of the debaters; *The Australian*'s cartoonist, Bill Leak, whose journey had been from left to right, was another. He almost hissed his hatred at me. In July 2012, Scribe, the publishing house of my old Melbourne University friend Henry Rosenbloom, released a book of Bill Leak cartoons, *UnAustralian of the Year*. Its short introduction was published by Mitchell and Cater in *The Australian*. It shows as well as anything written about me the wisdom of Mark Twain's warning, not to argue with anyone who buys ink by the barrel. A short passage of Bill Leak read:

> [F]or now, such a Murdoch arse-licker have I become that I even saw fit to have a go at Robert Manne when he wrote that splendid Quarterly Essay about how *The Australian* is destroying public debate in the country. In hindsight, I see now that I really should have just dropped to my knees in awe of the comic genius Australia's Leading Public Intellectual had shown when he'd flicked the switch to parody, writing an impassioned plea for the suppression of free speech mocked up to look like a defence of it. *The Weekend Australian*'s editor Nick Cater asked him at the Byron Bay Writers Festival why he'd never accepted any of Cater's requests to have his views published in *The Australian*, and Manne responded by saying he didn't want to give that squalid rag "legitimacy" by writing for it. I witnessed that little exchange and fascist that I am, misinterpreted his answer as pompous and sanctimonious, when I really should have considered myself lucky to be there, able to gaze on admiringly while the great Manne put that Murdoch lickspittle in his place.

My *Quarterly Essay* titled *Bad News* was published in September 2011. A brief account of one of its arguments – concerning the debates about the dispossession of Indigenous Australians – is needed to understand what was to come. *The Australian* had provided space for a detailed debate on the first volume of Keith Windschuttle's promised trilogy, *The Fabrication of Aboriginal History*, with many reports and editorials favourable to him – to his surprise, as he acknowledged – and at least twenty columns of opinion, for and against. No work of

Australian history in recent decades had received this kind of attention. This was, I argued, a major failure of judgement. Following Windschuttle, it was possible for conservatives to believe that Indigenous "Tasmanians", and by extension Indigenous "Australians", were a hopeless lot whose problems during and after the long history of the dispossession were self-inflicted. It was not only possible; this was what an Australian prime minister, John Howard, and Australia's most popular historian, Geoffrey Blainey – both of whom had spoken or written enthusiastically of Windschuttle – now believed. Blainey reviewed *Fabrication* for the ultra-conservative New York magazine *The New Criterion*. His review was republished in *The Australian* on April 14, 2003. The final sentence read: "[Windschuttle's] book will ultimately be recognised as one of the most important and devastating written on Australian history in recent decades."

It was true that, under Chris Mitchell, *The Australian* was more interested in the Indigenous people than other newspapers. The problem was, as I argued in *Bad News*, that their interest was what I called "univocal", taking its bearings on Indigenous matters from only one school of thought, that of Noel Pearson, and showing extreme hostility to all those whom the paper associated with the left. This univocalism was best illustrated in another section of *Bad News*.

One evening, Bess Price, an Aboriginal supporter of John Howard's "intervention" in the Northern Territory, appeared on ABC TV's *Q&A*. There was almost nothing at this time that divided Indigenous opinion more deeply than this Howard action. Price claimed that all Indigenous women supported the intervention. That evening, Professor Larissa Behrendt, a left-wing Indigenous academic from the University of Technology, Sydney, was watching the American Western series *Deadwood*. In response to something about Price on *Q&A* from a friend, she sent a high-spirited, jokey tweet: "I watched a show where a guy had sex with a horse and I'm sure it was less offensive than Bess Price."

On April 14, 2011, Behrendt's tweet was the subject of a prominent front-page article in *The Australian*: "More Offensive than 'Sex with a Horse': Behrendt's Twitter Slur against Black Leader".

Strangely enough, the article was written by Patricia Karvelas, best known now as the accomplished, left-leaning presenter of both *Q&A* and ABC Radio's *RN Breakfast*. Karvelas' article was accompanied by an opinion column by Gary Johns, a former junior minister under Keating, now notorious as the most offensive opponent of the 2023 constitutional referendum for an Indigenous Voice to Parliament. Johns hoped that, as a consequence of the tweet, Larissa's academic position and others who worked for the Jumbunna Centre would be investigated by her university. Behrendt at once issued two apologies, one to be published by *The Australian* and the other to Bess Price. Karvelas described the public apology as "humiliating"; an editorial described it as "belated".

In reports, editorials, letters-to-the-editor and op-eds, one accusation followed another. In an opinion column, "Aboriginal Sophisticates Undermine Bush Sisters", Marcia Langton thought no Aboriginal elder had been treated with greater disrespect than Bess Price had been in Behrendt's now infamous tweet, described by *The Australian*'s gossip columnist as "the slur of the century". A binary that reflected *The Australian*'s editorial position on Indigenous matters shaped the discussion. Bess Price spoke as an authentic Indigenous Australian, who understood the crisis of life in the remote communities. Larissa Behrendt spoke as an out-of-touch, inner-city Indigenous academic – Langton even described her type as "sepia-toned" – interested only in symbolism and empty gestures. In fact, Behrendt worked regularly among the Indigenous people in several country towns of New South Wales and a remote settlement in the Northern Territory. One of Karvelas' reports falsely claimed that Behrendt had tried to prevent a fellow Indigenous academic from writing for the *National Indigenous Times*. In another, we learned that voices were calling for her removal from her Gillard government–commissioned investigation of Indigenous university education, for which it was claimed she was earning a daily fee of $641. In fact, she earned nothing; the fee went to her university. Unsurprisingly, the nastiest blow was delivered by Keith Windschuttle, who argued, without evidence, that Behrendt had not deserved either the scholarship that had taken her to Harvard or the doctorate from Harvard that she had been awarded.

I spoke to Larissa after my day at *The Australian*. She told me that waiting for the regular 4.00 p.m. call from Patricia Karvelas had been a torment. I asked her how she had been affected by her experience at the hands of *The Australian*. She could not speak.

Before *Bad News* was published, we decided to close down *The Monthly*'s editorial board, which I chaired, partly to reduce the chance that the magazine would suffer collateral damage from the counterattack *The Australian* seemed certain to mount. Because I wanted to be able to respond immediately, *The Monthly* created a personal blog for me on its website, called *Left, Right, Left*. Shortly before publication, we offered Fairfax extract rights, which they eventually accepted, although without great enthusiasm, or so it seemed to me. Within Fairfax there was, I surmised, a reluctance to treat *The Australian* as a culturally significant newspaper in the way I had in *Bad News*, and no pleasure taken in the prospect of the undignified mud wrestle with News Corp that seemed certain to arise as a result.

My first *Left, Right, Left* blog post came out on September 12, 2011, a week or so after the publication of *Bad News*. I was puzzled:

> [S]o far ... to my considerable surprise, the essay has been more or less entirely ignored by my enemies on the Right ... The pessimistic interpretation is that there is a view that the questions raised by the essay can be avoided by pretending that it simply does not exist ... The optimistic conclusion ... is that *The Australian* is preparing a careful and detailed response.

If *The Australian* maintained its silence, one of the arguments of *Bad News* – that the paper could not tolerate criticism – would seem to be disproved.

I need not have worried. *The Australian*'s first critique came from Paul Kelly on September 14. Kelly regarded it as scandalous that, after a two-hour interview with him and Mitchell, I had not quoted directly from either of them. To this I replied that my essay was based on almost ten years' close reading of his paper. Nor were direct quotes from interviews my style. In fact, as I might have argued, I had also interviewed Bob Brown for *Bad News* and not quoted directly from him either.

More importantly, Kelly claimed that, over climate change and other issues, I wanted to close down debate and to censor opinions with which I disagreed. Kelly informed me that the public was no longer willing to defer to experts. Here, as I replied, Kelly had simply misunderstood my essay. Unlike most academics, I had devoted my life to encouraging and participating in public debates. Over climate change, I had tried to show how ridiculous it was for those without scientific knowledge or training to enter a debate on questions of extraordinary complexity where they were clueless. In many areas, moreover, we did defer to experts – with cancer to oncologists, and with bridges to engineers.

What was most interesting to me was Kelly's undisguised anger. I was accused of "emotionalism"; of "dogmatism", both "faith-based" and "hectoring"; of "blatant intellectual censorship" and "schoolboy scribblings". "It is good," he argued, "that Manne's technique of handling opponents is put on the public record." This was all quite unlike Kelly's normally unruffled, authoritative, Olympian prose. He and I agreed to debate *Bad News* at Melbourne's Wheeler Centre in the following week.

On September 17, *The Australian* also published its first *Bad News* editorial. There was one issue that upset me and that I thought must be answered at once. The editorial claimed that, at our meeting on June 15, "Mitchell and the editor-at-large were assured the newspaper would be offered extracts. That we were not suggests a lack of good faith." This was a lie. On June 1, as I documented, Mitchell had emailed me: "[W]ould I be right to assume your piece was sold to Fairfax even before you approached me? If not, can *The Australian* bid for the rights to it?" To which I replied: "The question you raise of extract rights to the Essay is months away and will be handled not by me but by the publicist at Black Inc." I added: "At my insistence when I went to Sydney on June 15 I was accompanied by the proprietor of Black Inc., Morry Schwartz, as my witness. The question of extract rights was not discussed, as Morry will attest." After some wrangling, a weasel-worded, mendacious "clarification" was published a week later: "An editorial in *The Weekend Australian* on September 17 implied publisher Black Inc had offered the newspaper the rights to publish extracts from the latest Quarterly Essay." Not "implied" – it had stated that as a plain fact.

The Weekend Australian of September 17 was what Guy Rundle at *Crikey* called "a collector's piece for the ages". Guy advised readers to buy any issues they could lay their hands on. Alongside the editorial, "The Bad News on Good Faith", Bill Leak expressed his admiration with a cartoon of me sitting on the toilet, reading a copy of *The Australian*, shitting. When the reader reached the "Inquirer" section, they found a series of articles on *Bad News*, under the general headline of "Setting the Record Straight", beginning with Nicolas Rothwell, who, with characteristic elegance and superciliousness, defended *The Australian* without mentioning my essay, and ending with Chris Mitchell's more than 3,000 words, described by Rundle as "the jewel in the crown"; to call it a "ramble" would be "unfair to bushwalkers", he remarked.

Mitchell began with a lengthy attack on me for, once again, weaponising the Holocaust. There was only one problem here. In the entire 45,000 words of *Bad News*, the Holocaust was not mentioned. There were several simple errors of fact. *The Australian* had not published twenty-nine articles by climate change deniers over the past ten years, as Mitchell claimed. The number was closer to 200. My position on Indigenous politics was not the opposite of Noel Pearson's and Rosemary Neill's. I had praised Noel publicly and provided an endorsement for the cover of Rosemary's book *White Out*. In between Rothwell and Mitchell, there were lengthy articles on *Bad News* by Greg Sheridan; Michael Stutchbury, the economics editor; Chris Kenny, the prominent culture war columnist; and Graham Lloyd, the environment editor. Only two errors of fact were found. I had mistaken the date of Mitchell's divorce from Deborah Cassrels, and the name of the journalist who had tried to show that Mick Dodson was a hypocrite.

Kenny described climate change as a "hobby horse" of mine. It was obvious that I regarded it as the most consequential crisis our species had faced, possibly ever. What was painful was the imperceptive psychologising. Mitchell explained my current hostility to the right as a consequence of my "scarifying" and "humiliating" sacking as editor of *Quadrant*. There was, again, only one problem: as was reported many times, including in his own newspaper, I was not sacked. I resigned. Even more ridiculously, Sheridan claimed that "most of Manne's bitter and vituperative enmities concern some long-lost friend with whom he's fallen out". By 2011, I had lost only two close friends – John Carroll, over Howard, and John Spooner, over climate change. In neither case did I feel the slightest edge of bitterness. Only sadness and an understanding about the fragility of friendships when people who feel deeply about politics part ways. I had written not one hostile word about either man.

A day after the September 17 issue of *The Weekend Australian*, I wrote to Nick Cater requesting a right of reply. He refused. Several letters – from professors Michael Ashley, Martin Krygier and Clive Hamilton, and from authors Mark Aarons and James Boyce – defending *Bad News* and me were also not published. On September 20, I wrote to the chairman and chief executive of News Limited, John Hartigan, requesting a right of reply. If not granted, I told him, I would take my case to the Press Council. For some reason never explained, that same day Paul Kelly pulled out of our Wheeler Centre debate. The event went ahead nonetheless, with Max Gillies reading out the Kelly column. On September 22, Greg Baxter, News Limited's corporate affairs manager, replied on behalf of Hartigan. I had "abdicated" all rights because my *Quarterly Essay* had not reached the ethical standards News Limited required. Nonetheless, my right to reply was granted, so long as it met the industry's "best standards"! At 2.00 p.m. Cater emailed. My reply was due by 6.00 p.m. I told him I was happy to wait until the following weekend.

A Guy Rundle *Crikey* comment of September 22 got it right: "Coming up tomorrow – The Oz continues to not respond to the Manne essay." And not respond it did. In the month or so following

431

the publication of *Bad News*, *The Australian* published eight extended opinion columns, nine *Bad News*–connected "Cut & Pastes", three editorials and one cartoon. In addition, during this month, *The Australian* published thirty-three letters, thirty-one of which were hostile. These letters were as vicious as anything I had ever seen. According to John Kidd, my "intellectual arrogance" was "breathtaking" According to John McCarthy, it was not *The Australian* I disliked, it was "the Australian people". According to L.J. O'Donoghue, "given the rampant narcissism evident in the work, the professor must have dictated it to a stenographer. He wouldn't have had a free hand to write anything." And according to Ralph Hoskin, *The Australian* had not only "demolished" my "credibility" but "implied doubts" as to my "sanity". Peter Kelly, the ageing Cold Warrior who had helped convince Mitchell that Manning Clark was the spy of the century, recalled a remark of Frank Knopfelmacher's: "Manne will betray us all." I wondered idly whether it was okay for a paper to describe someone as an arrogant, un-Australian, naturally treacherous, possibly insane, narcissistic wanker.

During this month of battery, there was only one surprise: Matthew Ricketson's review of *Bad News* in *The Australian* was favourable. Stephen Romei, the books editor, was not someone who could be pushed around. And there was only one genuine amusement. "Cut & Paste" of October 11 quoted from an outside blog: "Can you imagine Robert Manne with a chainsaw?" For several years it was with a chainsaw that I had done my best to gather the family's weekly wood. At this time, Clive Hamilton said that I had "the hide of a rhino". It was not really true. On November 21, the chief orchestrator of *The Australian*'s campaign, Nick Cater, finally wrote a column on *Bad News*. He called me a "post-modernist" who had rejected the "Socratic" method of argument, and suggested that I was remiss in not having studied all editions of *The Australian* over the past forty-seven years.

In early March 2012, I received a phone call from a reporter at *The Australian*, Ean Higgins. He told me that, as a result of a "tip-off" from an anonymous academic, a "freedom of information" application had been registered regarding the non-fulfillment of promised outcomes of two Australian Research Grants I had been granted in 2000 and 2002, which had been used, according to the anonymous academic, for nothing beyond my two earlier *Quarterly Essay*s. Higgins asked me several questions that I answered as best as I could. I told him that, as I intended to write about his phone call, I had several questions that I would like him to answer, including the date of the lodging of the FOI request, and by whom it had been lodged. Higgins described my questioning of his paper as unusual. He would have to confer with his "editor".

I got to work at once and on March 6 published "Payback: The Bullying Tactics of the Murdoch Press" on *The Monthly*'s website and on the ABC's *The Drum*, edited at the time by Jonathan Green. I had no intention of allowing myself to be placed on the defensive by *The Australian* with one of their accusatory house styles – "Accused by a fellow academic of failing to fulfil the condition of two lucrative research grants, Professor Manne batted away suggestions ..." I pointed out: "In cases like this, when one of its editors whistles, its well-trained team of attack dogs – Andrew Bolt, Piers Akerman, Miranda Devine, Tim Blair et hoc genus – emerge from their various kennels, teeth bared, snarling, moving in for the kill." And I provided a summary of the results of the two ARC grants.

> [T]he publication by me and my research associates, of five books or book-length studies ... of one public policy monograph; of a 40,000 word online document collection; of several book chapters and academic journal articles; of very many influential newspaper and magazine articles in the *Washington Post*, the *Monthly*, the *Sydney Morning Herald*, the *Age* and the *Courier Mail* ... This is an outcome of which I am genuinely proud.

A News Limited solicitor, Jane Summerhayes, demanded, on behalf of Chris Mitchell, that both *The Monthly* and *The Drum* remove my post. Morry and Jonathan did not budge. In an *Australian* article of March 9, it turned out that the "editor" who had ordered the FOI request that Higgins had mentioned to me was the still seething man who edited the weekend paper, Nick Cater. Higgins remarked:

"I came to the conclusion with Nick Cater that this did look like a pretty solid publication list of Manne's." Mitchell complained that my article was obviously defamatory. He knew nothing about his own editor's FOI request: "[Manne's] got me, Goebbels-like, directing something deep, dark and sinister ... he's trying to deconstruct me."

*

During the period of Julia Gillard's government (2010–13), I was more involved in party politics than before or since. I met Kevin Rudd at least three times, twice when he was foreign minister and once when he had gone to the backbench after his February 2012 challenge to Julia Gillard had been defeated 71–31. One of the meetings concerned the section of *Bad News* dealing with Rudd and *The Australian*, which I had asked him to check for factual accuracy. The second meeting was over a proposal for La Trobe to become a participating campus of the United Nations University. Although in both these meetings he was the Gillard government's foreign minister, Rudd was open with me about his intention to destroy Gillard and return to his rightful position as prime minister.

Following the second meeting, La Trobe created, at Rudd's invitation, a posse of senior people to discuss with his department the United Nations University prospect. On the appointed day our group flew to Canberra and met with several members of the Department of Foreign Affairs and Trade. The first question we asked concerned finances. How much money would DFAT be able to set aside to support our bid? We were told that there was nothing. All further discussion was pointless. I realised that the only reason Rudd had feigned enthusiasm for my proposal was to have me as an ally in his campaign to replace Gillard.

Closer to the time of Gillard's surrender, I met with Rudd again. He told me there would be blood. I argued that although there was no chance of his winning the election following his return as prime minister, he could at least save some of the furniture. With Gillard, there would be an electoral catastrophe for Labor, far worse than either 1931 or 1975. Nonsense, I was told. Rudd was convinced he could win.

My attitude to the Gillard prime ministership was straightforward. In its first year I was a strong supporter of the wide-ranging deal struck between Julia Gillard and Greens leader Bob Brown, and hopeful that a new balance in Australian politics might have arrived – what Europeans called "the Red/Green Alliance" – where Labor and the Greens would realise that even though they were fierce rivals in the struggle for the votes of the inner-city professionals and students, if they were to achieve their ambitions, they must also rely upon each other. Labor relied upon the Greens for their second preferences in the House of Representatives election and for the numbers in the Senate needed for the passage of their legislative program. The Greens relied on the election of Labor governments if they were to push or even nudge Australia in the direction they desired, most importantly, but not exclusively, regarding the struggle against climate change. My description of the Greens' supporters as a "permanent oppositional moral-political community" appealed to the cultural warriors at *The Australian*, principally Chris Kenny, who referred to it on some twenty occasions.

In the second half of 2011, my attitude to the Gillard government changed. One of Gillard's promises to the electorate following her replacement of Rudd was that under her government there would be no carbon tax. Part of her deal with the Greens was for an emissions-trading scheme that involved a price on carbon. Under great pressure, eventually the prime minister agreed that this price might be called a carbon tax. Julia now became "Juliar". Both Tony Abbott, as leader of the Opposition, and News Corporation were jubilant. The campaign to destroy the Gillard government began in earnest. By the beginning of 2012 I had decided that Labor's only chance of survival, in the short term at least, was for Rudd to replace Gillard as prime minister. On January 23, 2012, I published a long blog entry outlining the Newspoll numbers of Rudd from his election to his removal, and the numbers of Gillard since her opinion poll collapse.

> Since April 2011 not once has the Gillard government polled as well as the Rudd government polled at its worst ... Kevin Rudd

> led one of the most popular governments in Australian political history. Julia Gillard is now leading one of the least popular ... Either the federal Labor government will agree to go quietly to an ignominious death. Or it will try to save itself by electing a new leader ... Here there are again two main possibilities. Either the federal Labor Party ... will in desperation try, and perhaps then try again someone new – like the lacklustre Stephen Smith or the quiet pigeon-fancier Greg Combet or the famously ambitious faction leader who part-orchestrated the Rudd assassination, Bill Shorten. Or it will return to the leader it destroyed ... [M]y recommendation would be for the return of Rudd.

I recognised that if Rudd returned, things would have to be different. Part of the reason for the coup that overthrew him were questions turning on character – his poor relations with his Labor colleagues and the public service. To acknowledge, understand and rectify this would require what George Orwell had once called "moral effort". Rudd would also need to mend his relations with the Greens and abandon his illusions about working with the Coalition. And, perhaps most importantly, he would need to go to the country with a social-democratic program – climate change action, of course, but also, perhaps, new money in the areas of mental and dental health, and the completion of the disability insurance scheme begun by Gillard.

In *The Australian*, Christopher Pearson argued that my article was almost certainly written with "the tacit approval of the Minister for Foreign Affairs". This was not the case. There was a sentence that, almost immediately, I regretted. I described Julia Gillard as "the least impressive" Australian prime minister since Billy McMahon, by which I meant she was lacking in vision about Australia's place in the world and its future. In an address at the National Press Club, Tony Abbott repeated my Gillard remark, to the amusement of the News Corp journalists there assembled.

Shortly before the election of 2013, Kevin Rudd replaced Julia Gillard as prime minister, thus preserving her reputation from the certain drubbing at the poll. Gillard had promised in 2010 that we would see "the real Julia". The world saw the real Julia only once, when she rounded spontaneously on Tony Abbott's faux feminism: "I will not be lectured ... by this man." It was such a brilliant speech, delivered off the cuff, that it made it clear what a pity it was that we did not see "the real Julia" more often. Rudd was duly defeated. In a lengthy *Monthly* article on Rupert Murdoch in the November 2013 edition, I outlined the scandalous manner of the News Corp papers' coverage of the campaign. Here, for example, was the Murdoch tabloids' collective portrait of Kevin Rudd:

> [Kevin Rudd] was "venomous", "a volatile, nasty man", "a self-addicted, twittering Facebook junkie", who thought that "rules are for other people". Not only during the campaign had he "trashed the Bible" and "slimed his faith" but also "trampled on the lowly". As a typical "class clown", "the more he tries to be like us, the less he is" and "the more you know him, the more you detest him". He was a "fake", "a narcissist", "hubris on steroids", "callous and manipulative" with no capacity for "empathy" and most accurately to be understood as a thoroughgoing "psychopath". Even his physical demeanour, we learnt, was rather disgusting. He "smirks". He "pouts". He "wants to stamp his little feet". He "flicks" his hair repeatedly. Not only is he "afflicted by a repetitive, involuntary twitch of his lower lip" but "his rotating hand movements have to be seen to be believed".

My article argued that Murdoch was driven by two passions: business and politics. In the United Kingdom, his most important weapon was *The Sun*. Margaret Thatcher described the support *The Sun* had given her throughout her prime ministership as "marvellous". In the United States, Murdoch had created in the very lucrative Fox News something genuinely original, "a 24-hour conservative-populist propaganda channel, where right-wing opinion and slanted news ... were delivered in a highly entertaining fashion". Fox was "currently tearing Congress and American society apart". As the principled neo-conservative David Frum remarked, "Republicans originally thought that Fox worked for us. Now we're discovering that we work for Fox."

Because Australia was a federation, I argued, there could be no single tabloid equivalent of *The Sun* of London. Because of our modest population, there could be no profitable conservative-populist propaganda channel like Fox News. Instead, by combining *The Australian* with a "hydra-headed" set of state tabloids, ideologically unified but reflecting the temper and the interests of the particular states – *The Daily Telegraph*, the *Herald Sun*, *The Courier-Mail*, *The Advertiser* in South Australia and *The Mercury* in Tasmania – what Murdoch had created in Australia was "an instrument at least equal in potential political influence to those fashioned in the UK and the US". By 2013, no Australian government could challenge Murdoch's political power. If one tried, it would be torn apart. Rupert Murdoch's newspapers had played an important part in the destruction of two Australian prime ministers – in 2010 and 2013 Kevin Rudd, and in 2015 Malcolm Turnbull. Long after losing office, both supported the idea of a Murdoch royal commission.

But it was far too late, I concluded. My article was called "Why Rupert Murdoch Can't Be Stopped". For Australian democracy, this was bad news indeed.

[17.]

On Borrowed Time

ON A FEROCIOUSLY HOT DAY IN THE EARLY SUMMER of 2005–06, while lying on a couch in the living room of our largely non-air-conditioned cottage, I read Tim Flannery's *The Weather Makers*. For most of my life before that day I had not attended closely to political questions connected to the so-called environment. When I became co-editor and then editor of *Quadrant*, I had even, rather lazily, included "radical environmentalism" in my laundry list of politically correct causes the right-minded post–Cold War coalition of social democrats, liberals and conservatives needed to challenge. Soon after, I changed my mind on this and so much else. But it was Flannery who woke me up.

During the period of the late Howard and then the Rudd and Gillard governments, I read many books, articles and reports on climate change. According to three methodologically different academic studies, some 97 per cent of climate scientists had arrived at a devastating conclusion. The source of the energy that had been responsible for the Industrial Revolution that had transformed the world over the last 200 years – the burning of fossil fuels, chiefly coal, oil and gas, releasing carbon dioxide, along with the emissions from other chemicals – was causing the global temperature to rise. In turn, this global warming was threatening to destroy the benign condition that had allowed human beings, other species and the natural world to flourish over the past 10–11,000 years. The phrase "existential crisis" is nowadays considerably overemployed. But regarding global warming and its consequences it seemed to me not only appropriate but almost obligatory. At the beginning of the Industrial Revolution there were 280 parts per million of carbon dioxide in the atmosphere. As I write these words, there are over 420. The increase in temperature has already almost reached the target set at the 2015 Paris Climate Conference for what was needed if we wanted our descendants to live on a habitable planet, 1.5 degrees Celsius.

In February 2006, I wrote the first of many *Monthly* and *Guardian* articles on the conclusions of the climate scientists. By now, in my view, climate change was the most pressing political issue our generation had to face, overwhelming by a very large margin everything else. Indeed, it seemed to me the most significant question that human beings had ever faced.

My first piece of writing that had any obvious influence was the section in *Bad News* on climate change and *The Australian*. The analysis relied on certain conceptual clarifications. The first was the distinction between the basic theory about climate change – the conclusion that global warming was indeed happening and that human beings were responsible for it, primarily through the burning of fossil fuels, which among the climate scientists was "consensual", although not necessarily unanimous – and the scores of particular questions about the future impact of global warming, where the models of climate scientists differed, like the rate at which extinction of the species would occur, or when the Antarctic and Greenland ice sheets or the Siberian permafrost would melt, or at what rate the oceans would become acidified and continental temperatures rise. The second clarification was the distinction between those who were qualified to reach conclusions about both these kind of questions – in general, those with higher degrees in one or other of the climate science disciplines, and who had published the results of their research in refereed climate science academic journals – and everyone else, who had no alternative but to listen to the experts. The third was the distinction between the kind of scientific questions where only expert opinion mattered, and the policy questions – what actions individual nations and the international community needed and were able to take in the light of both the consensual and non-consensual conclusions of the climate scientists – where all citizens could and indeed should become involved.

In an article on December 4, 2010, in which Chris Mitchell had been interviewed by Graham Lloyd, *The Australian*'s chief environmental reporter, Mitchell had argued that his paper had consistently supported the basic theory of the climate scientists and the responsible policy actions that flowed from their work at both the national and international levels. To test his claims, I conducted a Factiva search of every climate change article published by *The Australian* between January 2004 and April 2011. There were 880 articles, of which those unfavourable to the basic theory of climate change outnumbered the favourable by 700 to 180, a ratio of almost four to one.

I analysed the editorials separately, and showed the scores of occasions where Mitchell's *Australian* had mocked or cast doubt on the consensual conclusions of climate scientists and had opposed both the Kyoto Protocol, the only available proposal for international action, and various emission reduction trading schemes, the principal domestic Australian proposal for the reduction of carbon emissions between late Howard and early Gillard. Time after time, those who favoured radical climate action to save the Earth were insulted in *The Australian*'s editorials as "greenhouse hysterics", "prophets of doom", "antediluvians", "Luddites", "totalitarians", et cetera.

I then analysed the hundreds of opinion columns. The overwhelming majority of those without scientific credentials opposed the basic theory and the principal measures that had been suggested for practical action, both nationally and internationally. Why did it matter, I wrote, that Christopher Pearson thought carbon dioxide was most likely "a perfectly harmless gas", and that Janet Albrechtsen believed in "the real possibility of global cooling"? And what of the opinion columnists in Mitchell's *Australian* who claimed some scientific credential? "In the real world, scientists accepting the climate consensus view outnumber denialists ninety-nine to one. In the *Alice in Wonderland* of Chris Mitchell's *Australian* their contributions were outnumbered ten to one." In a different section of *Bad News*, I analysed the war *The Australian* had declared on the political party committed to radical climate change action, the Greens. On one occasion the paper forgot to pretend to fairness or objectivity: "[The Greens] are hypocrites; they are bad for the nation; and they should be destroyed at the ballot box."

In his critique of *Bad News*, as we have seen, Paul Kelly claimed that over climate change I wanted to shut down debate. Kelly had failed to see or to acknowledge that, as I wrote, "I was at pains to distinguish between the *scientific* questions about global warming where debate between laypeople is absurd and the *political* questions where vigorous debate between laypeople is vital." When he was replaced as editor-in-chief of *The Australian*, Kelly had explained to me that Rupert Murdoch wanted his paper back. Murdoch now not only had *The Australian* back, he had also captured Kelly.

For this reason, in October 2014, I wrote "Kelly Country", on *Triumph and Demise*, Kelly's most recent narrative on Australian contemporary political history, on the Rudd and Gillard years. My comment was not a review of *Triumph and Demise* – I had written extensively and critically on the period, agreeing with some of Kelly's judgements and disagreeing with others. Nor was it personally hostile. I could scarcely have offered higher praise for Kelly's earlier analysis of the Hawke/Keating years, which I called possibly the most significant political book on Australia of the past fifty years. I argued, however, that while *Triumph and Demise* had the strengths of his earlier works – "narrative drive, familiarity with detail, the insider's privileged access to the main players" – in this book "something has gone seriously wrong". That something was, first, Kelly's pretence that the often-violent hostility of Rupert Murdoch's newspapers – *The Australian* and the state tabloids – had played no part in the downfall of the Rudd and Gillard governments. This was not so much *Hamlet* without the Prince as *Othello* without Iago. And it was, second, Kelly's "juxtaposition throughout of perceptive analysis and specious pontification". To demonstrate Kelly's solemn-sounding higher bullshit, I chose his discussion of the politics of climate change:

Kelly must know that almost every scientist working in the field of climate, almost every national scientific institute and almost every major international institution – from the World Bank to the International Energy Agency – now regards the burning of fossil fuels as a potentially catastrophic threat to the future of humankind and other species. Nonetheless, on dozens of occasions Kelly spices his narrative with irrational pronouncements from the songbook of climate change denialism. He thinks that the warnings of the scientists are "alarmist"; that the problem of climate change is self-evidently not "a moral issue"; that climate change has become a Labor "faith"; that imagined catastrophes of the future provide "a poor basis for policy action now"; that only a political "mug" would call upon people to make a "sacrifice" for future generations; and, flatly, that "climate change was the priority for neither Australia nor the world at this point". Not one of these arguments is justified ... All reveal a profound ignorance of the work of climate scientists and its implications. All rest on nothing better than the prejudices of the contemporary Anglophone right. Not one could survive in a public debate outside the sheltered ideological workshop that now exists at the *Australian*.

Even by *The Australian*'s standards, the response to "Kelly Country" was disordered. On October 7, Nick Cater wrote: "Readers familiar with Manne's voodoo logic will know by now where the professor is heading: to the grassy knoll and the book depository, where shadowy figures lurk with loaded guns." Much more Cater-fuelled vitriol ensued – on October 8, 9, 15, 18 and 21. It climaxed with a piece from the literary critic Peter Craven, who was granted 4,000 words for an article on my Kelly comment in *The Monthly*. As I pointed out in a post called "The Revenge of the Kelly Gang", Craven described my comment as "a bit fantastical", as "inflamed outrage" and as "ludicrous misrepresentation". Paul Kelly possessed "the kind of worldly perspective that is remote from Manne". In Kelly's prose Craven divined "levelness of gaze and compassion". In mine he could see "a mirror that is capturing nothing but the rage of the viewer's face".

Craven did not like my admittedly hyperbolic description of Rupert Murdoch as a contemporary Iago. Murdoch had used his global newspaper and television empire to encourage the invasion of Iraq, the justification for which was false and the consequences of which were several hundred thousand deaths, millions displaced and homeless, and the savage chaos in which the evil Islamic State was born. He had never expressed even one word of remorse over Iraq. Murdoch was also one of the chief sponsors of climate change denialism in the United States (via Fox News), in the United Kingdom (via *The Sun*) and in Australia (via the state tabloids and *The Australian*). Perhaps Craven might understand that this mattered. I reminded Craven, who was after all a literary critic and not a political commentator, that years before either the invasion of Iraq or global warming awareness, the great British writer Dennis Potter, perhaps now most remembered as the creator of the wonderful television series *The Singing Detective*, in a devastating BBC interview on the eve of his death, had told us that he called his cancer "Rupert".

After 2006, climate change was my chief preoccupation. Wherever possible I drew attention to the books that had most influenced me: *The Weather Makers*, of course; NASA physicist James Hansen's lucid exposition of the hard climate science, *Storms of My Grandchildren*; Naomi Oreskes and Erik M. Conway's seminal history of the rise of the denialist movement in the United States, *Merchants of Doubt*; Michael E. Mann's partly autobiographical study of the denialist attack on his fellow climate scientists in the United States, *The Hockey Stick and the Climate Wars*; Naomi Klein's *This Changes Everything*, the most important book on climate change from the anti-capitalist left; Kari Marie Norgaard's *Living in Denial*, a study of the way in which, in a small Norwegian town, the unbearable knowledge of impending life-changing global warming was able to be evaded in daily life; George Marshall's parallel study *Don't Even Think About It*, about how the threat was evaded in daily conversation; and Clive Hamilton's socio-psychological lament, *Requiem for a Species*, which was so powerful that it captured the thinking of one of the contemporary world's most eminent sociologists, Bruno Latour, to whom Clive introduced me in Melbourne.

Strangely enough, the work that impressed me most deeply was Pope Francis' *Laudato Si'*. My explanation of its impact conveys how I saw things at this time:

> When I was young the intellectual milieu was shaped by the need to come to terms with the unprecedented crimes and the general moral collapse that had taken place on European soil following the outbreak of great power conflict in August 1914 – Hitler and Stalin, the Holocaust and the Gulag, the concentration camps and genocide, the tens of millions of deaths that had occurred in two unprecedentedly barbarous wars. For me the most important book on the contemporary crisis of civilisation was Hannah Arendt's *Origins of Totalitarianism* ... The book was important to me not only because of its formal arguments and insights but because it was written in a tone that seemed, unlike any other work I had read, to have risen to the extremity of the crimes and the breakdown it was struggling to understand and to explain.
>
> In our own age we are faced with a crisis of civilisation of equivalent depth but of an altogether different kind – the gradual but apparently inexorable human-caused destruction of the condition of the Earth in which human life has flourished over the past several thousand years ... During the past decade I have read scores of books and thousands of articles, many outstanding, examining from every conceivable angle and also trying to explain the wreckage we are knowingly inflicting on the Earth. It was however not until last week that I read a work whose tone and scope seemed to me, like Arendt's *Origins*, fully adequate to its theme. That work was Pope Francis's encyclical *Laudato Si': On Care for Our Common Home*.

In my article on *Laudato Si'*, I argued that, among the most influential voices who grasped the depth of the crisis we faced, there were two broad streams of thought. Those who represented the best of mainstream liberal-democratic-capitalist society, like Al Gore and Nicholas Stern, believed that global warming was "an unhappy but nevertheless innocent accident" from which, with sufficient "political will and technical ingenuity", we would emerge more or less unscathed and brush ourselves off, after which the Western story of human progress and limitless economic growth would continue much as before. Francis believed that the looming climate catastrophe represented something much deeper, a two-centuries-long crisis of industrial civilisation, connected to the malaise of growing but inadequately noticed material inequality, moral numbness and indifference, individual lives of meaninglessness and despair, and humankind's loss of contact with, and desire for mastery over, the natural world. Francis shared something with several of the contemporary authors I admired – the environmentally sensitive leftist Naomi Klein; the great sociologist of "liquid modernity" Zygmunt Bauman; and Václav Havel, author of *The Power of the Powerless*, with his "hostility to the technological-industrial-consumer society, profound democratic faith, and a notion of transcendence grounded in the idea of the human spirit".

Among contemporary climate change activists, Francis was closest to Bill McKibben, author of *The End of Nature* and co-founder of the activist climate change organisation 350.org (of which my younger daughter, Lucy, was to become CEO in Australia). Bill responded to *Laudato Si'* in the way I had: "This marks the first time that a person of great authority in our global culture has fully recognised the scale and depth of our crisis, and the consequent necessary re-thinking of what it means to be fully human." I imagine that he was moved by the hope in the human spirit that, despite everything, illuminated *Laudato Si'*. "No system can completely suppress our openness to what is good, true and beautiful," Francis wrote. And: "An authentic humanity ... seems to dwell in the midst of the technological culture, like a mist seeping gently beneath a closed door." Did Bill McKibben wonder, as I did, whether this vision was more than mere whistling in the wind?

What I sought to understand in the many articles I wrote were the reasons for the stunning success of climate change denialism. In 2011, a year after the collapse of the Copenhagen Climate Conference,

I wrote "Dark Victory" for *The Monthly*, an analysis of the way in which the fossil-fuel corporations and the conservative think-tanks had managed to capture one of the United States' political parties, the Republicans, and temporarily even silence the Democratic contender for the presidency, Barack Obama, who understood as well as anyone the nature of the climate crisis. The conversion of the Republicans to climate change denialism provided space for the emergence of the monster of narcissism, Donald Trump, whose climate change policy was captured in three words: "Drill, baby, drill."

It occurred to me that it was rather odd that the work of the social scientists – economists, students of international relations, psychologists, sociologists, students of mainstream and social media – had no place either in the reports of the Intergovernmental Panel on Climate Change or something similar. After all, the reasons why international society and individual nations had thus far failed to take necessary action to try to avert catastrophe were no less important than the diagnoses of the impending crisis provided by the climate scientists. For this reason, for a conference convened at the University of New South Wales, I composed a kind of *tour d'horizon* of the principal findings of the social scientists regarding humankind's failure to rise to the challenge of the climate crisis.

Sociologists had written about the character type most commonly found among the climate denialists – ageing, educated, white males, the so-called "Cool Dudes" – who found intolerable both climate science's challenge to the faith they encountered in their younger years – *man's mastery over nature* – and the discomfit they felt when their dominant position in the social hierarchy could no longer be assumed, something the sociologists called "system justification". One media study found that mainstream, quality broadsheets were so committed to publishing both sides of any controversial question that their "balance" became a form of "bias" regarding an issue where, on the question of whether humankind was responsible for climate change, there was only one side. Dan Kahan produced a complex theory of what he called "cultural cognition", which explained the rationality of choosing to believe in the opinions of experts already trusted, and how critical it had been for the conservative think-tanks to create a "Potemkin Village" of supposed contrarian climate scientists, or the mirage of what another study called "duelling scientists".

On the evening before I was due to deliver this paper, Guy Standing, the British sociologist in large part responsible for the identification of neo-liberalism's new underclass, "the precariat", mocked the subject of my talk in a taxi we were sharing, unaware that I was its author. Before I delivered my paper, in a place that was for me *terra incognita*, I was uncharacteristically nervous. After the talk, possibly contrite, Standing came forward to thank me.

None of the contributions to an understanding of societies' failure to respond to the climate crisis that I summarised – and there were dozens of other equally interesting studies – penetrated much beyond academic journals and conferences or university lecture theatres. I turned my paper into an article, "Diabolical", that the new editor of *The Monthly*, Nick Feik, kindly agreed to publish although it was probably both too academic for the magazine and in implication too pessimistic. As I saw things by now, the human future rested with the fossil-fuel-rich United States, one of whose political parties had been entirely captured by the denialists; with an increasingly authoritarian coal-rich China under President Xi Jinping, cornering the global market for solar panels and electric vehicles but continuing to create new coal-fired power stations at an alarming rate; with an oil- and gas-rich Russia under Vladimir Putin, whose economy relied on the export of fossil fuels; and with several undemocratic and illiberal Middle Eastern Islamic states whose astonishing displays of wealth arose exclusively from their sale of oil. Even the truest democracies seemed incapable of ending their exploitation of the fossil fuels discovered under their land and sea – the Norwegians with their oil; my own country with its coal and gas. I quoted Elizabeth Kolbert of *The New Yorker*: "It may seem impossible to imagine that a technologically advanced society could choose, in essence, to destroy itself but that is what we are now in the process of doing." Given that no country on Earth had prohibited the fossil-fuel corporations from continuing their search for coal, oil and gas, I argued that "an intelligent and observant Martian visiting the Earth and learning of our climate problem would be entitled to believe the human race insane".

*

In 2014 an Islamist military and religious movement that called itself "the Islamic State of Iraq and al-Sham" and became known as ISIS conquered Mosul, Iraq's second- or third-most populous city. By now it controlled territory the size of Belgium in Syria and Iraq. I had never heard of the Islamic State or ISIS before the fall of Mosul. Nor, I discovered, at an international relations conference that I attended in Canberra in June 2014, had almost anyone else, except perhaps for specialists in the contemporary politics of the Middle East and some intelligence officers.

The more I read, the more astonished I became. Unlike Stalin's Soviet Union, Hitler's Germany or Pol Pot's Cambodia, ISIS did not kill its ideologically determined victims in secret. It became notorious for the well-publicised massacres of Druze, Yazidi, Alawites and especially non-Sunni Muslims, the Shia: the stoning to death of adulterous women or those it deemed promiscuous; the murder of homosexuals by throwing them off tall buildings; and especially for its slaying by sword or by fire of Christians, Jews, Japanese and Muslim enemies it had captured. Details and photographs were displayed in ISIS's glossy monthly magazine, *Dabiq*, available in four languages.

Ever since my 1967 review of Norman Cohn's *Warrant for Genocide*, a history of *The Protocols of the Elders of Zion*, which had played a part in the decision to remove the Jews from the face of the Earth, I had been interested in the murderous potential of ideas. I became aware of a long, politico-theological Salafi jihadist guide that some scholars believed had provided ISIS with inspiration. Called *The Management of Savagery* by its English translator, it arrived at the conclusion that putting to death all human beings except faithful Sunni Muslims was an act of mercy, required by Allah. I decided to write about *The Management of Savagery* and the genesis of ISIS for *The Monthly*. After the article, Chris Feik suggested a short book. I agreed because

I did not think there was anything new that I could write about climate change. I joked – only to close friends – that I had turned to ISIS because I found the subject of climate change too dispiriting.

I applied to my book on ISIS the method I had used in studying WikiLeaks and the cypherpunk movement: total immersion, reading and thinking about almost nothing else for a period of several months. I was guided in my search for the origins of ISIS by a remark made by a Yemeni adherent: "The Islamic State was drafted by Sayyid Qutb, taught by Abdullah Azzam, globalised by Osama bin Laden, transferred to reality by Abu Musab al Zarqawi, and implemented by al-Baghdadis: Abu Oman and Abu Bakr."

I concentrated on the key political writings of Sayyid Qutb, *Milestones*; Muhammad Abd al-Salam Faraj, *The Neglected Duty* (an important stage in the genesis of ISIS ideology that the Yemeni had left out); Abdullah Yusuf Azzam, *Join the Caravan*; Ayman al-Zawahiri, *Knights Under the Prophet's Banner* (Zawahiri was the co-leader of al-Qaeda, and leader after the assassination of Osama bin Laden, and a more theoretical writer than Osama); Abu Bakr Naji, the possible author of *The Management of Savagery*; Abu Musab al-Zarqawi (who was a fighter, not an intellectual, but still the father of Islamic State, and one of whose letters to al-Qaeda possessed a sacred place and constitutional significance); and, for an understanding of ISIS, the fourteen very substantial editions of *Dabiq*. My book was a study in "cumulative radicalisation", a concept I borrowed from the study of Nazi policy towards the Jews, although in this case the cumulative radicalisation referred not to policies but to ideas.

One way of demonstrating the concept of cumulative radicalisation, I suggested, was with an outline of whom the key writers in the genealogy of ISIS believed ought to be killed.

> In his final days, Qutb was to justify violence by his Islamic vanguard if they needed to defend themselves against the repressive acts of the Egyptian state. Faraj ... plotted to assassinate the Egyptian President and other leading figures of the apostate and repressive Egyptian state. Azzam called upon all Muslims to

engage in defensive war against the Soviet Army and its Afghan communist supporters and, beyond that, against the armed forces of the Zionists and the Crusaders and the supporters of Israel ... In addition [to Azzam's targets], Osama bin Laden and Ayman al-Zawahiri called upon their supporters to kill, wherever possible, Jewish and American civilians ... Zarqawi and his successors [in ISIS] targeted all Shi'a Muslims, Alawites, Yazidis, Druze, and all the "apostate" Sunni Muslims who actively opposed the Islamic State. They also targeted those they regarded as serious sinners, like promiscuous women, adulterous wives, homosexual men, consumers of alcohol, drug takers, and so on. The only bridge too far for the murderous inclinations of the Islamic State was the general Sunni population.

A less precise way of demonstrating the idea of cumulative radicalisation in the genealogy of ISIS was to trace the character of the leading thinkers, from Qutb, a gentle scholar who was horrified by the violence of the wrestling matches he witnessed in the United States, to Zarqawi, the true founding father of ISIS, who was in thought and deed a bloodthirsty killer, especially of Shia Muslims, who was chastised for his brutality during the post-invasion Iraqi chaos by the leaders of al-Qaeda, themselves no gentlefolk, who were responsible for the murder of 3,000 innocent Americans on 9/11.

As I was about to submit the manuscript of the book I called *The Mind of the Islamic State*, the fifteenth edition of *Dabiq* was posted. A passage in one of the articles, which sounded as if it were written by a cocky young American member of ISIS, caught my attention:

> The clear difference between Muslims and the corrupt and deviant Jews and Christians is that Muslims are not ashamed of abiding by the rules sent down from their Lord regarding war and enforcement of divine law. So if it were the Muslims, instead of the Crusaders, who had fought the Japanese and Vietnamese or invaded the lands of the Native Americans, there would have been no regrets in killing and enslaving those therein. And since

those mujahidin would have done so bound by the Law, they would have been thorough and without some "politically correct" need to apologize years later. The Japanese, for example, would have been forcefully converted to Islam from their pagan ways – and if they stubbornly declined, perhaps another nuke would change their mind. The Vietnamese would likewise be offered Islam or beds of napalm. As for the Native Americans – after the slaughter of their men, those who favour small-pox to surrendering to their Lord – then the Muslims would have taken their surviving women and children as slaves, raising the children as model Muslims and impregnating their women to produce a new generation of mujahidin. As for the treacherous Jews of Europe and elsewhere – those who betray their covenant – then their post-pubescent males would face a slaughter that would make the Holocaust sound like a bedtime story, as their women would be made to serve their husbands' and their fathers' killers.

I have rarely encountered a political paragraph as foul as this, spitting contemptuously and flippantly at those in the present generation who have sought to understand and see truthfully the darkest and most shameful episodes in the history of the West and make reparation to the victims, wherever possible, in word and in deed. Readers of this memoir will understand why I found it unusually repellent.

The Mind of the Islamic State was favourably received, especially by comrades from the Cold War, anti-communist times, who thought I had finally come to my senses. I was particularly pleased by endorsements from Martin Chulov, *The Guardian*'s Middle Eastern correspondent, and Mark Danner, the American writer whose work on contemporary US foreign policy and political culture I had come to admire enormously. It was even published in the United States by Prometheus Books. And yet it encouraged no debate and was understandably ignored by the handful of scholars working on ISIS, who had spent their lives absorbed in the history of Islamic and Islamist thought.

Nonetheless, I had enjoyed the challenge of trying to understand Salafi jihadism, the most recent instance in the history of modernity of the ideologies – Nazism, Stalinism, Maoism, Pol Potism – where mass murder is the recommended road for the creation of a better world and the perfection of humankind.

*

In the spring of 2016, I felt a permanent lump in my throat. The specialist who had diagnosed the cancer on the vocal cord eight years earlier peered down my throat once again. And the result? Once again, "Cancer, I'm afraid." Two surgeons at the Epworth Hospital informed Anne and me that the choice was between the removal of the larynx or a certain, painful death. As I was about to lose my voice to who knew what, Anne asked me to record something for her. I wrote quickly. Here is, in very abbreviated form, what I wrote:

> It seems strange to be writing and then speaking this when at present you're a room or two away but I'll do my best. I'm now awaiting my fourth major medical experience in less than a decade. Oddly, I've never quite stopped believing in my undeserved good fortune in life. In part, I attribute this rather foolish view of things to the unconditional love of my mother. Even more, I attribute it to the good fortune that we met and then fell in love after my return from England.
>
> Neither of us, to put it mildly, had a conventionally happy childhood, although yours was infinitely more troubled in the ways that most matter than mine. Still, I believe in part that we were drawn to each other because we had learned about the vital human importance of care. It is interesting that even when I was a teenager I was aware that the kind of mental anguish and instability you had to learn to deal with [in your mother's mental illness] would have been a far more painful and frightening condition to confront than the debilitating physical illness of the kind that afflicted my mother over a decade. Bathing wounds was, I knew even then, far easier than attending to someone you loved who was in torment and who from time to time had lost her mind.

There are two main ways someone might respond to early experiences like these. One would have been bitterness and anger and cynicism. The other providing for others lovingkindness and attentiveness and steadiness. I know how supremely fortunate I have been because somehow, miraculously, you were able to choose the latter path. And not only me. My radical astonishment at what you were able to do for our daughters will remain for me for the rest of my life as one of the most luminous examples of what a human being can give to others and can be.

I think of the years when our daughters were both still at home as a kind of idyll, although of course there were all sorts of the usual kinds of problems that everyone faces from time to time. As a family we did manage to do a lot together and to have a great deal of fun. Of the hundreds of memories, I think of the daughters on one of our indifferent couches watching *Ballykissangel* or *Sea Change* with us, or all of us laughing together or swapping witticisms during a cooking or a talent show that I had been dragged into watching. You didn't need to be dragged because you were so effortlessly able to enter their world through your empathetic imagination, and to take pleasure in what it was that gave pleasure to them.

From all this came the book on motherhood which Rai always, and rightly, describes as a masterpiece. Although I hasten to add, only someone of the highest intelligence and imagination – the girl who topped Australian History in the state from a small country high school – could have turned those experiences into a book so original, so theoretically sophisticated but, above all other things, so wise and humane. It was followed by two outstanding books, the beautiful partial memoir, *So This Is Life*, and the extremely successful anatomy of narcissism, *The Life of I*.

We now face the darkest and most challenging three months of our lives together or maybe more. You want to hear my voice as it should be for the last time. This is why I have written this piece which only says what we both know. You are the most wonderful person I have known. My love for you, my gratitude, is too deep for words. It is that, above all things, which will keep me going during the next days and months and years.

In the days before the operation to remove my larynx, I spoke at a human rights conference at Griffith University on the cruelty of Australia's asylum-seeker policy; flew from Brisbane to Sydney for my final appearance on *Q&A*; and recorded a discussion of *The Mind of the Islamic State* for Radio National with Andrew West, who seemed stunned and upset when I explained why this was likely to be my last such broadcast. In Brisbane, I had dinner with Rai. A young woman who had been observing us, whom we didn't know and who didn't know us, came to our table. "What a beautiful friendship," she said. It was true.

It took ten hours or so with two surgeons to remove the larynx and repair the damage. A few days after, the plastic surgeon, on the morning round of the ward, noticed that something was very wrong. I was taken to the operating theatre immediately. It took another ten hours to remove the infection; without the second operation I would almost certainly have died. (I have told the story of my two months or more at the Epworth in an essay in *On Borrowed Time*.) I owe more to Anne for her lovingkindness and her strength than I will ever be able to repay.

I was allowed to return home briefly for Christmas, spent with Anne and our beloved daughter Lucy. Kate was now living in the United States. A few weeks after I had returned to hospital, a small platoon of surgeons, physicians, a speech therapist, a counsellor and of course Anne assembled to see whether the small silicon valve that had been placed in the wall of the stoma that led to my lungs would allow me to speak. Rather miraculously, it would. Although I spoke in the same tone as before, and not as the robot of my first fears, my voice had been reduced to what Anne kindly described as a Leonard Cohen whisper. Shortly after I had emptied the bottle of oxycodone the hospital had given me, in the area where my neck had been slit, I began to feel a tightness as if I were being strangled. The strangled feeling turned into a state of just-tolerable pain. My surgeon recommended a pain specialist, who prescribed a non-addictive opioid, palexia, and a neuropathic drug, gabapentin, pills that I still take. It was not long before I realised that the pain would be permanent.

I had long taken from J.A. Schumpeter the definition of an intellectual as someone who sought to influence the shape of things through the written and the *spoken* word. For some time after the removal of my larynx, I spoke at writers' festivals in Sydney, Canberra and Bendigo, and in the rainforest at Bellingen, following the publication of my essay collection *On Borrowed Time*. I accepted a radio invitation from Geraldine Doogue and even a television interview with Jane Hutcheon on the ABC's *Face to Face*. For his part, Phillip Adams phoned to apologise for not inviting me onto *Late Night Live*. He told me that one of his producers believed their listeners would find my voice "unendurable". I was a little shocked. Would the host of a television program tell a blind person with obviously damaged eyes that their appearance on television was impossible (unless they wore dark glasses) as viewers would find the sight unendurable? Around this time, I had agreed to deliver a formal lecture. Halfway through, exhausted by the physical effort now needed to speak at any length, I handed my script to the chair and asked him to read what remained. I decided that I would no longer accept the trickle of invitations to speak on radio or television or at public events. It was not long before such invitations almost altogether dried up.

There was more to this decision than the realisation that, for the first few minutes of anything involving speech, most of the audience would be thinking not about the character of my argument but about the unpleasant quality of my voice. Apart from the occasional book review for *The Monthly* or Fairfax newspapers, the old drive to contribute to the discussion of current events – which had lasted from 1975 to 2017 – deserted me. I felt I had done enough. I had written in *Bad News* that even those members of the political class who "loathed" *The Australian* "understand that they cannot afford to ignore it". For most of my adult life I would go to considerable lengths to find that day's copy of *The Australian*. I gradually stopped reading it, and eventually even my old friend, *The Age*, as well. The only exception to my withdrawal from public life was continuing to organise a forum on current affairs, "The Ideas and Society Program", which I had convened at La Trobe University since 2009. And here I learned a lesson about how far I had drifted in sensibility from most of my colleagues in the humanities and the social science faculties of the contemporary Australian university.

In 2019 I decided to convene a series of debates on questions central to Australian public life. The first debate was between professors Hugh White and Clive Hamilton on Australia's relations with China. Several of the major players in the national discussion about China turned up. Even though there was tension between the speakers and in the audience, I thought it was a great success. The second debate I planned was entitled: Does Australia Still Have a Problem with Racism? The question at this time was whether Australia had outlived its undeniably racist past, which had included both the White Australia policy and the Indigenous dispossession, or had allowed it to return with new dance partners in Pauline Hanson and John Howard. The former Australian Race Discrimination Commissioner, Dr Tim Soutphommasane, a Sino-Lao, Cambridge-educated political theorist, accepted our invitation, as did Tom Switzer, the director of conservative think-tank the Centre for Independent Studies.

Shortly after the advertisements for the event went out, an Australian right-wing terrorist murdered fifty Muslim worshippers in Christchurch, New Zealand. I changed the text of the event advertisement: "Has racism in contemporary Australia entered the political mainstream? Or is its influence found only among the far-right extremist groups and lone wolves?" I wanted the debate still a month away, to be held. What had happened in New Zealand made the question of the relations of Australia's racist past with its present even more urgent, or so it seemed to me.

This was not the view of many fellow academics. The majority of the members of the history department at La Trobe thought that "[f]raming this event in the current manner could be seen to validate a politics of denial about Australia's problems with racism". They also were "concerned" about the presence of Tom Switzer on the panel because of his "polarising views". A second petition was signed by forty-five staff and students at La Trobe: "We call on [the] organisers to reframe the discussion to focus on how Australia can better address the reality of structural and deep-seated racism. Additionally we call on [the] organisers to reconsider Tom Switzer as a speaker to the event."

Finally, a third petition circulated that was signed by more than 150 academics, principally from the humanities and social science faculties of Australian universities. I was genuinely shocked by the intellectual quality of this petition. It argued that "decades of debates about racism, immigration and related topics have exacerbated racism and Islamophobia, with real world effects ranging from daily microaggressions to hate crimes and murderous terrorism". The second name on the petition was that of Ghassan Hage, who had participated in a debate on Australian racism I had convened in 2009, and who therefore, as I wrote to the La Trobe vice-chancellor, John Dewar, "apparently believes that the debate he participated in a decade ago helped incite hate crimes and murderous terrorism".

In arguing against the idea of conducting debates, the petition reminded Dewar that "in the 19th century, white scientists debated whether black people were human". As I wrote to John, this "is like arguing that opera should be forbidden because Wagner's operas were anti-Semitic and an inspiration for Hitler". A far better discussion did go ahead after we added a Muslim, Tasneem Chopra, and a young Indigenous academic, Chelsea Bond (now Watego), to the panel. Evidently, in the eyes of many of those who had signed one of the petitions, I was, as of old, "that fellow Manne".

What was clear to me from all this was that many academics in the humanities and social sciences faculties of the contemporary Australian university were opposed to debates or even discussions whose terms they did not control on issues of greatest interest to the engaged citizenry. As Australia was still demonstrably a racist society, the academic signatories believed, even to debate the question of whether or to what extent it had escaped its racist past or allowed that past to be reborn was somehow to be complicit in racism. It was also clear that, for these academics, Tom Switzer – the former opinion editor at *The Australian*, who was currently the host of an interesting ABC radio program with access especially to leading American foreign policy "realists" – was not welcome on campus.

Of such censoriousness I believed no good would come. Nor was this the kind of university that the young boy who had tuned into the proceedings of the Australian parliament on his crystal set and taken the tram into the city to listen to the debates between communists and anti-communists on the Yarra Bank had once dreamed of joining. By now, Morry Schwartz had suggested I write a memoir, and I was researching in earnest, beginning with the task of finding out what exactly had happened to my grandparents.

Afterword

WRITING THIS BOOK HAS HELPED ME see aspects of my life with greater clarity. As soon as I experienced the role of teacher at a Temple Beth Israel Sunday School, I knew that teaching would be for me a calling. The only question was where I would teach. As a son who had looked after an invalid mother who relied upon me to bathe her wound, to wake in the night to help uncomplainingly with whatever she needed, I was never in doubt about the importance of family and the value of care. I believe it was because of my mother's unconditional love that I was prepared for a marriage that has endured and deepened, with perfect loyalty, for almost fifty years. For a marriage where the love for our daughters was almost fierce. From the youngest age I also experienced the pleasures of friendship, first with the son of the Scottish-Presbyterian family who invited the young Jewish boy in their neighbourhood to dance the Highland fling with them. But these are matters that this memoir is not about.

I can now see clearly the decisions I made that shaped my political life, which is the subject of this memoir. When I was in Year 9 I realised that, because of the formula the teacher used, I would receive a higher mark in woodwork – where my attempts to create even match-trays and bookends were unusually poor – if I failed to show up to classes. I had already decided, in the language of old Marxism, that I would be a worker of the brain and not of the hand. But of what kind?

AFTERWORD

As I set out for Oxford following my undergraduate years, I was already certain that, when studies there were completed, I would return to Australia. Raimond Gaita remembers conversations at that time in England where I explained that I was determined to go home so that I could contribute to public life in some way. Even though I was appointed as a history master in one of England's most prestigious public schools, I regarded the position as temporary.

At the time of my return from England, when the Americans had accepted defeat in Vietnam and at the mid-point of the Whitlam government, intellectuals played a far larger role in Australian political life than at present. Academics were under far less pressure to publish exclusively in specialist, refereed journals. High-quality literary-political "small magazines" – on the left, *Meanjin*, *Overland* and *Arena*, and alone on the right, *Quadrant* – still mattered. It was assumed that arguments of obvious depth over controversial questions of significance must be answered. Silence was regarded as an admission of defeat. The most important question of the age was whether the future belonged, as the left believed, to (reformed) communism or socialism or, as the right believed, to democratic capitalism and the open society. In the mid-1970s I entered this world with articles for *Quadrant*. Although I felt ever-growing scepticism about the capacity of argument to overcome entrenched economic and political power, this was one of my worlds until the cancer of 2016.

At the age of twenty-seven I was appointed to a tenurable (that is, lifelong) position at La Trobe University. I loved teaching. However, the determination to play some role in Australian public life, beyond the occasional *Quadrant* article, remained with me. In 1983, I applied for a position in the office of the leader of the Opposition, Andrew Peacock. I was accepted. I turned the offer down, for both political and family reasons. I did not admire Peacock. More importantly, I could not bear the thought of leaving Anne and our first-born child, Kate, for lengthy periods.

In 1985 an article for *Quadrant* on Australia's most consequential communist, Wilfred Burchett, ignited a fierce six-month-long left-versus-right debate. I was by now not only closely associated in the public mind with *Quadrant* but was truly hated by the left-liberal anti-anticommunist academic mainstream. By chance, as I was researching for a television miniseries about the Petrov Affair, the ASIO archives on this subject – the defection in 1954 of Vladimir and Evdokia Petrov, two intelligence officers inside the Soviet Embassy in Australia – had just been opened by the Hawke government. My book *The Petrov Affair* was favourably reviewed in Australia, even by the left-wing experts on intelligence.

I can see now that my public life had arrived at another turning point. One road was to continue with historical research on the Australian Cold War and to publish some hopefully solid books. The other was to grasp the opportunity to find, through writing, a role in Australia's political life. Following the publication of *The Petrov Affair* I was offered and accepted a weekly column in the Melbourne *Herald* and the editorship of *Quadrant*. I had chosen to play the role of what was commonly termed a "public intellectual" rather than the more usual role for academics of pure research scholar.

For a long time I rejected the term public intellectual. Intellectuals seemed to me *by definition* to be those writers who sought to help shape their nation's future by their interventions. To speak of a public intellectual seemed like speaking of hot fire or cold ice; the adjective was redundant. Eventually I abandoned my objection to the label. I believe that in the humanities and social science faculties of the universities there are two distinct ideal types – the research scholar, concerned with the advancement of knowledge and understanding, and the public intellectual, concerned with influencing the political life of society through their research and writing. I have always believed that there is a place at universities for both research scholars and public intellectuals.

I have also always tried to live according to a further distinction. If public intellectuals are permanent members of the university, as I have been since 1975, it seems to me that their work must always meet the standards of depth and integrity required of other scholars or scientists at the university. In Australia, most public intellectuals have confined themselves to their academic specialty – to take some of the most distinguished examples, Hugh White on defence, Anne Twomey on the constitution, Noel Pearson and Marcia Langton on Indigenous affairs, Ross Garnaut on economic policy, Raimond Gaita on moral philosophy. Some, however, like Tim Flannery, Anne Manne and Clive Hamilton, range more broadly. I belong to this group. I have written on an unusually wide range of subjects. It has always been my hope that academic scholars, expert in these subjects, would be able to read these contributions with interest and learn something from them. It is, of course, for others to judge whether in this ambition I have succeeded.

*

In writing this memoir I have become even more aware of the extent to which what happened to the Jews of Europe only five or so years before my birth determined most of the political questions that have concerned or disturbed me. During the Cold War I accepted that the political divide between totalitarianism and liberal pluralism had overtaken the customary division since the French Revolution between left and right. Totalitarianism included both Nazism and Soviet communism, whose principal difference was, as Frank Knopfelmacher taught, that while Nazism had been defeated and discredited, Soviet communism had not. For this reason, I was an anti-communist, not concerned with the Australian Communist Party, which by the time I began to write had lost almost all its influence, but with what looked to many of us as the struggle for the future between the Soviet bloc and the United States and its allies.

The Cold War was followed by the culture wars. Here, even while still editor of *Quadrant*, my political identity shifted from what was regarded as the right to what was regarded as the left, a relatively unusual drift. Most important here was my belated turning of attention to the brutal dispossession of Australia's Indigenous peoples. I also published a *Quarterly Essay*, many *Monthly* essays and newspaper columns on the Howard government's cruel treatment of refugees who arrived uninvited by boat.

AFTERWORD

Writing this memoir has also allowed me to see even more certainly that belonging to the Jewish people has been the most important element of my political identity. But it is so in a very particular, even peculiar, way. I have not attended a synagogue in decades. I have, as anxious Jewish leaders say, "married out". I do not believe in the Jewish (or any other) conception of God. I do not feel "love for the Jewish people", for the reason Hannah Arendt expressed during the controversy over *Eichmann in Jerusalem*. I feel love only for family and friends and, like Arendt, regard love for the Jewish people as a potentially dangerous form of "self-love". For better or for worse, I recognise that my political identity as a Jew is grounded in radical astonishment at what the Germans sought to do under the protective cover of war: to rid the Earth of the Jews. My political writing has moved from the Holocaust, Stalinism and Pol Pot's Cambodia to the Islamic State via the dispossession of Australia's Indigenous people. Behind all this has been profound anger and shock at the evil of which human beings were capable, and pity for the victims of an overwhelmingly greater power, a sympathy that began when as a child I discovered what had happened to my family and my people in the Holocaust.

In his *Remembering the Holocaust*, Jeffrey C. Alexander claimed that the world's memory of the murder of 6 million Jews has become a profoundly humanising, "sacred-evil", mythic event, acting as a protection to other peoples into the future. In my sceptical response to Alexander's optimism, my most important reservation was connected to the extraordinarily prescient insight of the Israeli philosopher Yehuda Elkana, a survivor of Auschwitz. There were, he suggested, two ways in which Israelis and, by my extension, all Jews, might think about the political meaning of the Holocaust. One way was: "Never again" – my own position. The other was: "Never again, to us". Within the second, Elkana suggested, lay the possibility of future catastrophe regarding Israel's relations with the Palestinians. It is the distinction "Never again" and "Never again, to us" that has divided Jews in Israel and the Diaspora, more deeply than at any time in my life, over the current Israeli campaign in Gaza that is aimed at the total destruction of the terrorist Islamist organisation Hamas, following the unspeakable murders of Israeli Jews on October 7.

That catastrophe has now arrived. For the innocent civilians of Gaza, of course, not only the deaths, mutilations and starvation, but also the lifelong psychic scars, especially for the children. Catastrophe will also almost certainly come for both Israel and the Jews of the Diaspora, but in a quite different way. Israel is becoming, even more than before October 7, a pariah state for much of the world. Because of the Diaspora's defence of Israel's anti-Hamas campaign in Gaza and apparent indifference to the suffering of innocent Palestinians, anti-Semitism – "the world's longest hatred", as it has been called – is now more pervasive and threatening to Jews than at any time since the Holocaust.

I have friends whom I love who have defended the Israeli campaign. I could not disagree with them more deeply. However, I understand the fear – the destruction of the Jewish state and the final triumph of anti-Semitism – that lies behind that support, especially among those whose grandparents or parents miraculously survived the Holocaust.

The Holocaust and the dwindling hope – "Never again" – has determined, directly or indirectly, almost all that I have written about over the years. But not everything. Eventually and far too late, I realised that the most disastrous consequence of the culture wars was the way corporate interests and right-wing ideologues had been able to use the struggles between left and right to manufacture doubt over climate change, the most important question facing us, not only now but ever. Will humankind act in time and with the necessary urgency to abandon the use of fossil fuels for the energy needs of our industrial civilisation? Or will we allow the benign condition of the Earth – for humans, other species and the natural world – that has existed over the past 10,000 years, to be destroyed? I hope to live long enough to see what the answer to this question will be.

July 1, 2024

Acknowledgements

Morry Schwartz suggested that I write a memoir. Without his invitation I doubt that this book would have been written. He and I have collaborated on many projects since we met in 2000. It has been my good fortune to have had Morry as a publisher and a friend throughout these years. It has also been my good fortune to work with Chris Feik, the presiding spirit at Black Inc. and La Trobe University Press. Chris is one of the most penetrating thinkers and finest people I have encountered during my long life. He has given his full attention to this memoir, to its very considerable benefit. Jo Rosenberg has been the memoir's principal editor. I have been impressed by her professionalism, courtesy and good humour throughout. She was ably assisted by a former Black Inc. managing editor, Julian Welch. Those I have had the pleasure of working with at Black Inc. over the years also include Sophy Williams, Caitlin Yates and Anna Lensky.

I have been associated with La Trobe University for almost fifty years. Accordingly, I chose La Trobe University Press as the publisher. Morry proposed an innovative model for the press to the former vice-chancellor, John Dewar. Even though financial times for universities were (as always, recently) tough, John agreed to its establishment. We are in his debt. On the editorial board Morry, Chris and I were joined by the talented scientist and science writer Elizabeth Finkel. My thanks to her. We are also fortunate that John's successor, Theo Farrell, a widely published author, has backed LTUP with enthusiasm. My present work at La Trobe, both with the press and as convenor of the Ideas and Society Program, has been supported by the professional and warm-hearted Leon Morris, Katie Phillis, David Evans and Tory Dillon.

There are many people I am grateful to have the chance to acknowledge as I near the end of my writing life. At high school I had three wonderful history and literature teachers: Bob Ewins; Joe Rich, author of the delightful memoir *Refugee*; and Denis Grundy. Two fellow students remained friends throughout the years: Jan MacDonald, who married Denis – both died too early – and the famous French teacher Ric Benson.

At university, as I have explained in this memoir, I was most influenced by Frank Knopfelmacher and Vincent Buckley. The most brilliant teacher I encountered was the Leavisite Sam Goldberg. The poet and Jesuit priest Peter Steele, also of the English department, remained a greatly valued friend until his death. Several friendships from university days have endured: Rai Gaita, of course, as readers of this memoir will understand, but also, until her death, the actor Jan Friedel and the writer Arnold Zable.

At Oxford, I enjoyed discussing the history of Europe with an old-style, learned Montreal Jew, Aaron Krishtalka, and was greatly encouraged by my thesis supervisor, R.A.C. Parker. I watched while Elijah Moshinsky, who attended the same high school as me, moved from a history doctorate to a career as a theatre director that soon took him to Covent Garden.

La Trobe University once had the most interesting politics department in the country. My heartfelt thanks go to those colleagues whom I also count as friends – Sanjay Seth, the postcolonial scholar who left us for professorships at universities in London and Edinburgh; Dennis Altman, one of the pioneers of gay liberation; Judith Brett, most recently the author of a magnificent biography of Alfred Deakin; and Gwenda Tavan, author of the definitive study of the slow death of white Australia. I relished the time spent with several doctoral students in politics – David Corlett, Russell Marks, Dorota Sacha-Krol, Aurelien Mondon and Dominic Kelly.

Among the frequent contributors to *Quadrant*, I admired several key political players in Australia's Cold War years – the founder of the Movement, B.A. Santamaria; the former Menzies minister and governor-general Paul Hasluck, who wrote a nostalgic but sharply observed "Then and Now" column; the creator of the then Keynesian Institute of Public Affairs, C.D. Kemp; and the most perspicuous watcher of Maoist China, Pierre Ryckmans, whose biography, *Simon Leys: Navigator Between Worlds*, was one of the first books published by LTUP.

ACKNOWLEDGEMENTS

During *Quadrant* days I worked closely with the incomparable caricaturist John Spooner. Through Spooner I also worked with the quirky and superb designer at Text Publishing, W.H. Chong, and then on several books with their remarkable chief editor, Michael Heyward, and publisher, Di Gribble. Criticism of neo-liberal economics drew Spooner and me together. Eventually, climate change forced us apart.

Even before *Quadrant* I began writing regular newspaper columns that continued for some twenty years. My thanks go to Eric Beecher for the initial *Herald* invitation, to Michael Gawenda and Paul Austin at *The Age* and, briefly, Julia Baird at *The Sydney Morning Herald*. With *Quadrant* came regular radio appearances and occasional television. I enjoyed sparring with Morag Fraser on Ranald Macdonald's local ABC program and being interviewed on alternate weeks by Norman Swan and Geraldine Doogue on ABC's Radio National. I abandoned my regular newspaper column for *The Monthly*. Thanks are particularly owed to three editors – Christian Ryan, John van Tiggelen and Nick Feik.

In my post–Cold War days, I have been proud to have been able to count as political friends three great Indigenous Australian leaders, Patrick Dodson, Mick Dodson and Noel Pearson. The scholars whose views on the different questions of the culture wars influenced me include Tim Soutphommasane, the Sino-Lao political theorist and former Australian race discrimination commissioner; Mark McKenna, advocate for the intertwined causes of the republic and Indigenous reconciliation and biographer of Manning Clark; David McKnight, political biographer of Rupert Murdoch and critic of neo-liberalism; A. Dirk Moses, genocide scholar and editor-in-chief of *The American Historical Review*; and Hugh White, the most perceptive analyst of Australia's defence challenge in the age of China's rise and America's decline.

Those I learned most from on the fraught subject of climate change politics were my daughter Lucy Manne, CEO of 350.org in Australia; David Ritter, who has led Greenpeace Australia Pacific with both courage and intelligence; and Clive Hamilton, author of the most challenging analysis of humankind's current situation, *Requiem for a Species*.

ACKNOWLEDGEMENTS

Our once close political friendship could not survive Clive's puzzling association with the anti-China movement, at a time when a hospitable Earth seemed to me to rest on co-operation between the United States and China.

My life and Anne's have been nourished by enduring friendships with couples – the moral philosopher Rai Gaita and his Israeli-born wife and Hebrew teacher, Yael; with Morry and Anna Schwartz, a lifelong supporter of visual artists; with Martin Krygier, the passionate rule of law scholar, and Julie Hamblin, a formidable and humane lawyer; with Mark Aarons, the author and broadcaster and former communist, with whom I came to share an understanding of Cold War history, and Robyn Ravlich, the stylish documentary radio program-maker; with Tim and Merridie Costello, both true Christians, fully engaged in the struggles of family, community and the world; and with the great Australian novelist Alex Miller and Stephanie Miller, the academic and editor of Alex's recent *A Kind of Confession*.

Our small family has always meant more to me than anything else. My nephew David, a distinguished and committed refugee lawyer and advocate, has been for many years one of my closest and most valued friends. I am immensely proud of my two beloved daughters, Kate, a feminist moral philosopher, and Lucy, a climate change activist, who are both, in their different spheres, fighters for justice and, even more importantly, wonderful human beings. Kate brought into our lives the legal academic and polymath Daniel, and our grandchild, Sophie, of joyful spirit and purest charm.

My greatest blessing in life is Anne. Those who have read this memoir will understand why. I admire Anne's intellectual achievement – four great books, all expressing different dimensions of her experience as an ultra-sensitive, inquisitive and startled young child. I know no one more perceptive or kinder of heart. I was a witness to the fierce and selfless love she gave to our daughters as they grew up, and to her unwavering attentiveness to her mother throughout her long, troubled life. Without Anne, my body might have survived the challenges of cancer; my spirit, most likely, would not have. I owe more to Anne than I find it easy to say or will ever be able to repay.

Previous Works by Robert Manne

AS AUTHOR

The Petrov Affair: Politics and Espionage, 1987

Agent of Influence: The Life and Times of Wilfred Burchett, 1989

The Shadow of 1917: Cold War Conflict in Australia, 1994

The Culture of Forgetting: Helen Demidenko and the Holocaust, 1996

The Way We Live Now, 1998

In Denial: The Stolen Generations and the Right, 2001

The Barren Years: John Howard and Australian Political Culture, 2001

Sending Them Home: Refugees and the New Politics of Indifference (with David Corlett), 2004

Left, Right, Left: Political Essays 1977–2005, 2005

Making Trouble: Essays Against the New Australian Complacency, 2011

Bad News: Murdoch's Australian and the Shaping of the Nation, 2011

Cypherpunk Revolutionary: On Julian Assange, 2015

The Mind of the Islamic State, 2016

On Borrowed Time, 2018

AS EDITOR

The New Conservatism in Australia, 1987

Shutdown: The Failure of Economic Rationalism (with John Carroll), 1992

The Australian Century: Political Struggle in the Building of a Nation, 1999

Whitewash: On Keith Windschuttle's Fabrication of Aboriginal History, 2003

The Howard Years, 2004

Do Not Disturb: Is the Media Failing Australia? 2005

Reflected Light: La Trobe Essays (with Peter Beilharz), 2006

Dear Mr Rudd: Ideas for a Better Australia, 2008

W.E.H. Stanner, *The Dreaming and Other Essays*, 2009

Goodbye to All That? On the Failure of Neo-Liberalism and the Urgency of Change (with David McKnight), 2010

The Words that Made Australia: How a Nation Came to Understand Itself (with Chris Feik), 2012

The Best Australian Essays 2013

The Best Australian Essays 2014

PREVIOUS WORKS BY ROBERT MANNE

PRINCIPAL ESSAYS

"Pol Pot (Regime) and the Persistence of Noam Chomsky", *Quadrant*, October 1979

"The Rise and Fall of the Communist Movement" in Robert Manne (ed.), *The New Conservatism in Australia*, Oxford University Press, 1982

"David and Goliath: The Media and Mr Combe", *Quadrant*, October 1984

"The Strange Case of Helen Demidenko", *Quadrant*, September 1995

"Christ and Lenin", (on the Manning Clark Affair), *The Australian's Review of Books*, October 1996

"The Stolen Generations", *Quadrant*, January 1998

"The Whitlam Revolution" in Robert Manne (ed.), *The Australian Century: Political Struggle in the Building of a Nation*, Text Publishing, 1999

"Explaining the Invasion" in Raimond Gaita (ed.), *Why the War Was Wrong*, Text Publishing, 2003.

"The Unknown Story of Cornelia Rau", *The Monthly*, September 2005

"Little America: How John Howard has Changed Australia", *The Monthly*, March 2006

"Pearson's Gamble; Stanner's Dream: The Past and Future of Remote Australia", *The Monthly*, August 2007

"On the Political Corruptions of a Moral Universal" in Jeffrey C. Alexander, *Remembering the Holocaust: A Debate*, Oxford University Press, 2009

"Why We Weren't Warned: The Victorian Bushfires and the Royal Commission", *The Monthly*, July 2009

"A Dark Victory: How Vested Interests Defeated Climate Science", *The Monthly*, August 2012

"The University Experience: Then and Now", *The Conversation*, October 18, 2012

"Primo Levi: An Appreciation" in Christopher Cordner (ed.), *Philosophy, Ethics and a Common Humanity: Essays in Honour of Raimond Gaita*, Taylor & Francis Group, 2013

"Diabolical: Why Have We Failed to Address Climate Change?", *The Monthly*, December 2015

"The Mind of the Islamic State", *The Monthly*, June 2016

"How We Came to Be So Cruel to Asylum Seekers", *The Conversation*, October 26, 2016

"On Borrowed Time", *The Monthly*, March 2018

Index

Aarons, Laurie 160
Aarons, Mark 214
Abbott, Tony 408, 435, 436, 437
Aboriginal Australians *see* Indigenous Australians
Aboriginal Children's Holiday Project 335–6
"Aboriginal Welfare" Conference. Canberra (1937) 303–4, 305–6, 307, 341
Abu Ghraib prison 383–4
Academics for Peace in the Middle East 204
Adams, Phillip 223, 361, 379, 381, 395, 456
Adler, Jacques 281
Afghanistan War (2001–21) 411, 415, 419
Akerman, Piers 332, 340, 352, 373, 381, 433
al-Qaeda 360, 366, 368, 369, 370, 372, 375, 377, 450, 451
Albrechtsen, Janet 332, 398, 441
Aliens Classification and Advisory Committee 34
Allard, Tom 377, 378
Alley, Rewi 153–4
ALP Club, University of Melbourne 67, 70, 75, 79, 80, 82, 85, 89, 229, 265
Angka (the Organisation) or Angka Loeu (the Organisation on High) 124, 125, 130
Angleton, James 182
Anschluss, Vienna 17–20, 21, 25, 39, 101
anti-anticommunism 128, 131, 153, 165, 166, 463
anti-communism 84–5, 90, 98, 119, 128, 140, 142, 152, 158, 163, 170, 175, 210, 220, 222, 223, 248–9, 256–7, 301, 354, 367–8, 405, 413, 414
antinomianism 234, 235
anti-Semitism 54–5, 61, 72, 84, 148, 157, 159, 202–3, 215–16, 217, 240, 241, 242, 267, 280, 282, 284, 310, 314, 316, 466
ANZUS Treaty 218, 360, 396
Appel, Marta 5
Arendt, Hannah 6, 32, 243, 249
  Eichmann in Jerusalem 83, 90, 99, 215, 303, 306–7, 465
  The Origins of Totalitarianism 82, 90, 445

Armstrong, David 148, 227, 231, 232, 243, 259, 312, 313, 314, 315, 316–17
Árnason, Jóhann 103
Arndt, Heinz 227, 245, 257, 259
Asian migrants in Australia 206–10, 268, 298–9, 317
ASIO 170, 171–4, 176, 178, 179, 180, 181, 182, 183, 185–6, 189, 190, 191, 375–6, 463
  "Operation Cabin 12" 172, 174
Assange, Julian 411–21
asylum seekers *see* refugees
Atlantic Charter 40
Attwood, Bain 330, 344
Australian Council for Overseas Aid (ACFOA) 128–9
Australia Council, Literature Board 227, 247
Australia Day Council, Victorian branch 267
Australian Association of Cultural Freedom (AACF) 147–8
Australian Greens 408, 422, 435, 436, 442
Australian High Commission, London 370–1
Australian Jewish Welfare Society 8, 30–1
Australian Jewry 240, 241
Australian Labor Party (ALP) 66, 169, 170, 176, 178, 180, 189, 207, 210, 218, 262, 294, 295, 316, 359–60, 363, 372, 378–80, 379, 382, 392–4, 396, 434–6
  New South Wales Right 264, 409
  The True Believers television series (1988) 184
Australian Research Council grants 323, 432–3
"Australian Settlement" 295

Badraie, Shayan 357–8, 363
Baltic States 97, 214, 220–1, 253
Barron, John and Anthony Paul, *Murder of a Gentle Land* (1977) 121, 126–7, 130, 134, 135, 136, 139
Barron, Peter 264
Barton, Rod 383–4, 385–7

INDEX

Bauer, Lord 246
Beazley, Kim, jnr 360, 363, 372, 378, 380, 383, 393
Beazley, Kim, snr 62
Beckett, H.C. 172, 173
Beecher, Eric 192
Begin, Menachem 204, 205, 213
Behrendt, Larissa 422, 426–8
Bell, Coral 245, 253, 291
Benson, Ric 60, 69
Beria, Lavrentiy 173, 180
Berlin Wall fall 223, 245
Bialoguski, Michael 172–3, 174, 180, 188
Bicentenary year, 1988 211–12
Bin Laden, Osama 450, 451
Binding, Karl and Alfred Hoche, *The Destruction of Life Unworthy of Living* (1920) 201
Bishop, Bronwyn 266, 267
Black Inc. 375–6, 387, 429–30; *see also Quarterly Essay; Monthly, The*
Black Inc. Agenda 346–7, 375, 387, 421
    The Dreaming & Other Essays 388–9
Black Saturday bushfires 402–3, 406, 410
Blainey, Geoffrey 207–8, 209, 272, 342, 345, 426
    All for Australia (1984) 208–9
Blair, Harold 335–6
Blair, Tony 374, 378, 379, 385
Blake, George 182
Blamey, Thomas 179
Bliss, Nellie 326, 327, 328
Bliss, Walter 326–8, 334
Blix, Hans 385–6
Bolt, Andrew 332, 333–4, 339, 340, 352, 357, 363, 373, 375, 381, 388, 389–91, 433
Bone, Pamela 242, 279–80
Bonhoeffer, Dietrich 393, 394, 400, 407, 409
Boyce, James 347, 431
Braham, Mark 238
Brett, Judith 277–8
Brezhnev Doctrine 222–3
Bringing Them Home report (Human Rights Commission, 1997) 300–2, 304, 306–7, 323, 329, 330–1, 333–4, 336–9, 340, 341, 349
Britain *see* United Kingdom
Brookes, Alfred Deakin 183
Brown, Bob 429, 435

Browning, Chris 248
Bruce, Stanley 8, 316, 325
Brunton, Ron 330, 331, 332, 339, 381
Buckley, Vincent 69, 75–6, 77–8, 83, 229, 265, 354
Bukovsky, Vladimir 164
Burchett, Wilfred 45–6, 73, 131, 132–3, 135, 148, 149–67, 171, 212
    Manne's essay in reply to McCormack's article 148, 153, 156, 158, 159–63, 165–6, 411, 462–3
Bures, Susan 213
Burke, Edmund 243, 249, 266–7, 268
Bush, George H.W. 253–4, 366
Bush, George W. 366–7, 368–9, 370, 374, 376, 393, 407
Butler, Eric 84
Byron Bay Writers Festival 423–5

Cain, Frank 189
Calwell, Arthur 34, 180
Camberwell High School 60, 232
Cambodia 112, 119, 123, 125, 171, 465
    ACFOA conference on human rights in Asia (1978) 128–32
    genocide denial 129, 132–40
    see also Democratic Kampuchea; Khmer Rouge; Phnom Penh; Pol Pot
Cameron, Clyde 141–2
cancer treatments and impacts on Manne 289, 401, 409–10, 453–7, 462
capitalism 63, 87, 88, 90, 171, 211, 212, 217–18, 222, 233, 234, 258, 292, 354, 403, 404, 414, 462
Captive Nations Council 214
Carroll, John 103, 112, 115, 233, 246, 254–5, 258, 262, 263, 264, 293, 431
Cassrels, Deborah 340, 343, 346, 430
Cater, Nick 423, 424, 425, 431, 432, 434, 441
Cathcart, Michael 272
Catley, Bob 255
Ceauşescu, Nicolae 223, 287
censorship 197–8
Chandler, David 124–5
Charles, Stephen 189
Charlesworth, Max 88
Chelmno extermination site 14–15, 16, 23, 354

474

INDEX

Chew, Peter 247, 259, 313, 317
Chiddick, John 104, 105
China 62, 74, 79–80, 123, 149–50, 156, 157, 159, 171, 222, 234, 236, 248, 353, 354–5, 367, 372, 448
    Cultural Revolution 122, 154, 167
    Great Leap Forward 122, 153–4, 167
    relations with Australia 218, 355, 398, 457
Chinese Communist Party 157, 163, 253, 354–5
Chomsky, Noam 124, 134, 137–9, 140, 144
Christchurch, New Zealand, mosque shooting (2019) 457
CIA 147–8, 182, 384, 386, 414
Clark, Dymphna 271, 316
Clark, Gregory 255, 293
Clark, Manning 187, 269–73, 297, 309, 310, 312, 315–16
    Manning Clark's History of Australia: The Musical 211, 271
    Order of Lenin 286–300, 309
Clark, Mark 154
Clayton, Walter 183
Cleland, John Burton 305
Clendinnen, Inga 103, 285–6, 330, 341, 347, 365–6, 389
climate change 113, 383, 393, 395, 404, 407–9, 420, 421, 423, 429, 431, 436, 439–40, 466
    books that influenced Manne 444–6
    denialism 247, 422, 441, 443, 444, 446–9
    Manne's writing 440–1, 442–4, 446–7, 448
Clinton, Hillary 420–1
Clutterbuck, Kate 329
Coady, Tony 165–6
Cohn, Norman, *Warrant for Genocide* 72, 449
Cold War 40, 41, 57, 90–1, 129, 147–8, 149–50, 152–3, 163, 171, 186, 187, 214, 217–18, 229, 230, 231, 234, 248–9, 251, 253, 291, 301, 464
Colebatch, Hal 310, 315, 316
Coleman, Peter 148, 152, 165, 177, 227, 232–3, 235, 241–6, 251, 252, 315, 318, 342, 345, 348
Combe, David 189, 376
Committee for Cambodian Refugees 128, 141
Committee of Patriotic Cambodians 125

communism 40, 47, 57, 58, 62, 75, 77, 79–80, 84, 88–9, 106, 147, 149, 152, 153, 163–4, 171, 175, 217, 222, 234, 248, 252–3, 293, 354, 462
    Knopfelmacher's standpoint 79–82, 83, 84, 233
    see also anti-anticommunism; anti-communism; Soviet communism; and names of specific communist parties
Communist Party of Australia (CPA) 66, 79, 80, 156, 160, 163, 164, 167, 169–70, 178, 183, 210, 218, 261, 464
Communist Party of the Soviet Union (CPSU) 58, 164–5, 220, 221; *see also* Soviet communism
concentration camps 5, 6, 7, 18, 21, 22–3, 31, 43, 44, 84, 90, 202, 279
Conquest, Robert 90, 121–2, 218
conservatism 113, 145, 169, 171, 194, 259, 262, 266–7, 293, 301, 339, 405
    The New Conservatism in Australia (Manne (ed.), 1982) 145, 171
Conway, Ronald 254
Cook, Cecil 302, 304, 305–6, 325, 336, 337
Coombs, H.C. "Nugget" 331
Corlett, David 365, 407
Costello, Peter 255
Cowen, Zelman 61, 99, 113–14, 292
Craig, William 327, 328
Craven, Peter 198, 272, 286, 308, 318, 333, 340, 365–6, 406, 443–4
Crennan, Michael 70, 265
Crittenden, Brian 113, 1009
Crocker, Sir Walter 188
Crockett, Peter, *Evatt: A Life* 189
Crozier, Laurie 128
Cubillo, Lorna 324, 332, 334, 340
culture wars 248, 251, 275, 284, 381, 395, 464, 466
Curtin, John 8
cypherpunks 412–15, 417
Czechoslovakia 25, 78, 81–2, 84, 163–4, 221, 223, 354

d'Abbs, Peter 86–7
Dalziel, Allan 177
Daudet, Léon 241–2
Day, David 264, 265
Dayan, Moshe 204
Deane, Sir William 292, 300

INDEX

Dear Mr Rudd: Ideas for a Better Australia (Manne (ed.), 2008) 396, 397–9
Demidenko (Darville), Helen
   The Culture of Forgetting (Manne, 1996) 285–6
   The Hand that Signed the Paper (1994) 278–85, 308–9, 310, 311, 314, 340, 344–5, 346
Demjanjuk case 217
Democratic Kampuchea 120–4, 130–1
   death toll 124, 129, 132–3, 153
   defence by left-wing intellectuals 122, 124–6, 129–30, 132, 133–40, 144
   Vietnamese invasion (1978) 121, 132, 135, 136, 137, 140, 143, 153, 166
Democratic Labor Party (DLP) 170, 179
Democratic Socialist Club, University of Melbourne 66, 67, 68, 73, 74, 84
Deng Xiaoping 222
Dening, Greg 102–3
Devine, Frank 284, 285, 318, 332, 381
Devine, Miranda 332, 433
Dewar, John 458
Disney, Julian 398
dissociation 51–2, 193
Dodson, Mick 300, 430
Dodson, Patrick 398–9
Dormaar, Maarten 364
Dostoyevsky, Fyodor 249, 267, 268, 273
Downer, Alexander 296, 375
Dowrick, Stephanie 285
Dreyfus, Alfred 148, 150–1, 157, 235
Duchamp, Marcel, "Étant Donnés" 196
Duffy, Michael 318, 332, 339, 340, 381
Duguid, Charles 326
Dulles, Allen 182
Dulwich College 99–100, 101, 462
Duncan, Graeme 187, 276, 277, 278

economic rationalism 145, 233, 255–6, 257, 258, 263, 264, 294; *see also* neo-liberalism
Edgerton, Robert, *Sick Societies* 345–6
Eichmann, Adolf 7, 20, 90, 215, 303
Eilish, Billie 199
Ellingsen, Peter 258–9
environmentalism 234, 291, 295, 379, 395, 439
eugenics 201
Europe, East-Central 149, 163, 166, 220, 221–3, 239, 248, 252–4, 367

Evans, Harry 399
Evans, Ray 113, 227, 246–7, 254–5, 257, 258, 259
Evans, Ted 326
Evatt Collection, Flinders University 178
Evatt, Herbert Vere 170, 174, 176, 177, 178, 180, 184–5, 189

Faine, Jon 53
Fairbairn, Anne 231
Fairbairn, Geoffrey 287, 288, 290
Fairfax press 319, 324, 326, 329, 332, 334, 351, 352, 368, 377, 381, 382, 391, 412, 428, 429–30, 456
Farmer, Graham "Polly" 329
Feik, Chris 333, 340, 347, 376, 387, 405, 406, 449
Feik, Nick 448
Felton, Philip 336
feminism 92, 196, 198, 234, 275, 291, 292, 295, 379, 395
First Nations Australians *see* Indigenous Australians
FitzGerald, Stephen 209
Fitzpatrick, David 61, 70, 289
Flanagan, Richard 347, 402
Flannery, Tim 381, 464
   The Weather Makers 439, 444
Flood, Philip 378
Foale, Jeffries 140–1
Foley, Sir Noel 227, 232, 233, 234
Fordham, Jan (later Friedel) 70
Foster, John 101, 102
Francis, Pope, *Laudato Si'* 445–6
Frankfurter, Felix 32
Fraser, Malcolm 107, 115, 142, 206–7, 209, 262, 263, 354
Freeman, Cathy 340, 352
Freud, Sigmund 51, 194, 195, 197, 249
Frontier: Stories from White Australia's Forgotten War (ABC TV series, 1996) 302–3, 307
Fukuyama, Francis, "The End of History?" 243

Gaita, Raimond 71, 81, 91, 98, 238–9, 291, 293, 391, 462, 464
   friendship with Manne 70, 88–9, 165–6, 455

476

on Indigenous Australians 301, 306, 307, 308, 330, 341
Quadrant columns and articles 249–52, 282, 291, 294, 300, 306, 308, 311, 315, 330
Why the War Was Wrong 373, 384–5
Galbally, R.T.J. 33, 34
Gale, Charles 328, 329
Garnaut, Ross 464
Garner, Helen 274
  The First Stone 275–6
Gaudron, Mary 300
Gawenda, Michael 241–2, 264, 269, 284
gay rights 234, 291, 295, 317, 379, 395, 396
Gaza 73, 205–6, 213, 216, 367, 465–6
Geelong Football Club 46, 48, 329
Gelber, Harry 188–9
Georgiou, Andrew 107
Gerasimov, Valery 222
Gibney, Alex 418, 419
Gillard, Julia 409, 411, 434–7, 442
global financial crisis 403–5, 422
global warming *see* climate change
Glover, Dennis 293
Goebbels, Josef 5, 10
Goldberg, Sam 77, 92
Gorbachev, Mikhail 212, 217, 219, 220–1, 222–3, 228, 239, 243, 253
Green, Cliff 171, 172, 184
Green, Jonathan 406, 433
Greens 408, 422, 435, 436, 442
Gregory, Alan 275–8
Gregory, Tom 227, 232, 259, 312, 313, 316, 317
Gribble, Di 258, 284, 285, 469
Grove, Robin 77
Grundeman, Albert 177
Grundy, Denis 60, 66, 69, 75
Grynszpan, Herschel 6, 7
Gudgeon, Mac 171, 184
gulag 127, 249, 253, 445
Gulag Archipelago, The (Solzhenitsyn, vol. 1, 1973) 99, 122,
Gulf War, 1990–91 366, 374, 385
Gunner, Peter 324, 332

Habonim 59
Haeckel, Ernst 201
Hage, Ghassan 378, 458
Hall, Richard 187
Hamas 73, 466
Hamel-Green, Michael 71, 85, 88

Hamilton, Clive 421, 431, 432, 444, 457, 464
Hanson, Pauline 210, 263, 292, 296, 297–8, 299, 311, 312, 317, 457
Harney, Bill, *North of 23 Degrees* 335
Harries, Owen 115, 242–3, 253, 291, 355
Harris, Max 210
Hasluck, Sir Paul 57, 273, 293, 326, 468
Hawke, Bob 171–2, 210, 213–14, 215, 218, 228, 256, 294, 352, 355
Hayden, Bill 207, 293
Haye, Valerie 145
Heenan, Tom 164
Heller, Ágnes 105–6, 110–11, 113, 196
Helmer, Michael 81
Henderson, Gerard 71, 87, 88, 104, 109, 233–4, 281, 318, 381, 393, 399, 405
Herald, Melbourne: Manne's column 192, 206, 209, 210, 211, 214, 219–20, 223, 233, 235–6, 306, 463
Herman, Edward 137–8
Hewson, John 262, 294, 295, 296, 297
Heyward, Michael 274, 284, 333, 469
Higgins, Ean 432–3
Hill, Jim 183
Hill, Ted 180
Hirohito, Emperor 236, 238, 241
Hirst, John 103, 111, 112, 162, 268, 270, 272, 291, 292
history of Australia 211–12
Hitler, Adolf 6, 10, 17, 18, 38, 50, 61, 83, 84, 95, 101, 105, 122, 135, 177, 202, 316, 370, 445; *see also* Nazi regime in Germany
Ho Chi Minh 88, 164, 287
Holocaust 46, 48, 72–3, 83, 132, 147, 200–1, 204, 242, 244–5, 267, 281–2, 285, 445, 452, 465
  commercialisation 237, 238, 241
  denialism 79, 202–3, 215
  influence on Manne 3, 63, 84, 91, 122, 466
  model for the crime of genocide 307
  not to be weaponised 216, 430
  war crimes legislation and trials in Australia 214–17, 235–8, 239, 240–2, 280–1
  see also Demidenko (Darville), Helen; Manne, Joachim (Chaim); Manne, Leonora (née Hötchner); Meyer, Friederike (Frida, née Munter); Meyer, Otto Joseph; Nazi regime in Germany

INDEX

Horvath, Robert 164
Howard, John 198, 296, 297, 301, 379, 380, 382, 383, 392, 393, 395, 396, 397, 399, 400, 407, 457
   Iraq policy 371, 372, 374, 375, 377, 378, 379, 422
   position on immigration and refugees 209, 210, 356, 357, 358, 359–62, 363, 364, 379, 400–1, 464
   position on Indigenous Australians 299, 300, 334, 338, 339, 342, 349–52, 426
Howson, Peter 331
Hruby, Peter 163–4
Hungary 221, 222, 354
Hungarian Revolution (1956) 57, 167
Hussein, Saddam 366, 369–70, 372, 373, 374, 377, 385, 386

Ideas Summit, Canberra (2008) 399–400, 406
Ieng Sary 127
immigration 207, 209, 395, 458; *see also* Asian migrants in Australia; refugees; White Australia policy
In Denial: The Stolen Generations and the Right (Manne, 2001) 333, 334–5, 337–42, 389
Indigenous Australians 57, 91, 113, 211, 212, 247, 299–308, 311, 317, 330, 331, 332, 342–8, 393, 396, 398–9
   apology to the Stolen Generations 301, 326, 329, 340, 350, 397
   dispossession 268, 270, 297, 300–3, 348, 350–1, 387–9, 425–6, 457, 464, 465
   genocide 300, 306–8, 330, 341, 343–4
   "half-caste" children's homes 325, 326, 334
   Mabo judgment 296, 297, 299, 300, 338, 349
   Manne's research into Indigenous child removal 323–9, 335–6, 337, 391, 411
   native title 294, 299
   reconciliation 295, 331, 338, 339, 342, 348, 349–52, 361, 379, 381, 382, 383, 395
   Stolen Generations 294, 300, 301–2, 304, 306–8, 323, 324, 330–2, 333–40, 342, 349, 387, 389–91
   Uluru Statement from the Heart 300, 399
   Voice to Parliament 300, 399, 427
   Wik judgment 299, 300, 349
Indo-China Refugee Association (ICRA) 141, 142, 144, 206, 242, 266, 354
Indonesia 91, 206, 355, 360, 362, 374, 400, 405
infanticide 199–200, 201, 250
intelligentsia 67, 79, 85, 89, 119, 140, 152–3, 165–6, 187, 194, 195, 241, 243, 248, 265, 269, 272, 286, 306, 318, 340, 368, 384, 395–6, 399, 400, 456
   different worldviews from "ordinary people" 211, 212, 395
   left-wing 121, 122, 124, 135–6, 137–8, 145, 187, 218, 234–5, 249, 298–9, 379, 381, 382, 395
   public intellectuals 112, 161, 220, 381, 399, 400, 425, 462, 463–4
   right-wing 121, 135, 234–5, 297, 298–9, 301, 354
International Scientific Commission (ISC) 149–50
Iraq Survey Group 384, 386–7
Iraq War (2003–11) 241, 366–75, 376–8, 381, 383, 384–7, 395, 411, 415, 419, 422, 444
   fear of weapons of mass destruction (WMD) 368–9, 372, 373, 374, 375, 377, 378, 379, 386–7
Iraqi disarmament 383, 385–6
Irish Australians 56, 211, 264–6, 267
Irving, David 202–3, 391
Isaac, Rhys 103
Isdell, James 302, 328–9
Islamic State (ISIS) 372, 444, 449–53, 465
Israel 59, 61, 202, 203–5, 213, 451
   migration of Soviet Jews ("refuseniks") 212, 213, 240
   oppression of Palestinians on West Bank and in Gaza 73, 204–6, 213, 216, 367, 465–6
   Six-Day War (1967) 73, 204, 213
Israeli Labour Party 59
Ivan the Terrible (Ivan Marchenko) 217
Ivanhoe East Primary School 53–7, 60
Ivanov, Valery 189

478

INDEX

Jackson, Frank 102, 318
Jackson, Nigel 79
Jakobovits, Lord Immanuel 238
James, Michael 104, 105, 108–9
Japan 41, 56, 74, 218, 236, 237, 350, 370–1, 452
Jaspan, Andrew 385, 387
Jewish Board of Deputies, Victorian Branch 214, 239, 241
Jewish Bolshevism 280, 281, 282
Jewish refugees, Australia 7–8, 26–7, 29, 30–1, 33–4, 37, 45–6, 50, 56, 58, 91, 104, 267, 353–4
Johns, Gary 331, 357, 427
Jones, Barry 114
Jones, Evan 77
Judaism as a religion of community 59
Judenhausen 9–10
Jupp, James 67

Kane, Jack 151, 158
Karski, Jan 32
Kartsev, Victor 156–7, 159
Karvelas, Patricia 427, 428
Kay, David 386–7
Keating, Paul 217, 262, 264, 271, 292, 294, 295, 296, 297, 338–9, 349, 353, 383, 394, 427
Kelly, David 385
Kelly, Dominic, *Political Troglodytes and Economic Lunatics* 247
Kelly, Paul 264, 268, 288, 361, 399, 423, 428–9, 431, 442
    Triumph and Demise 442–3
Kelly, Peter 287, 288, 432
Kelty, Bill 263
Kemp, C.D. 255–6, 257–8
Kemp, David 246, 258
Keneally, Thomas 264–6, 283
Kenny, Chris 430, 431, 435
Kent, Dale 112–13
Kent Hughes, Wilfred 84
KGB (earlier MVD) 151–2, 156–8, 159, 162, 163, 164–5, 167, 189, 287
Khmer Rouge 112, 119–22, 124–7, 128, 129–33, 134–40, 142, 143, 153, 166
Khrushchev, Nikita 58, 166
Kiernan, Ben 125, 126, 129–30, 131, 136–7, 142, 160, 162, 164, 165
Kirby, Michael 215
Kirsner, Douglas 71
Kislytsin, Philip 182
Kitson, Jill 279, 284
Knapp, Wilfred 95
Kneale, Bruce 41–2
Knightley, Phillip 164, 253
Kniss, Paul 151, 155–6, 163
Knopfelmacher, Frank 78, 84, 90, 102, 106, 148, 169, 179, 195, 218, 223, 228, 245, 253, 262, 281, 284, 354, 368, 391, 432
    and the Burchett debate 160, 165
    letter in *Quadrant* on war crimes legislation 238–41, 242, 245
    at Melbourne University 52, 67, 69, 72, 75, 78–83, 86, 89, 233–4
Koch, Christopher 316, 317
Koestler, Arthur, *Darkness at Noon* 78, 83, 156
Kohler, Alan 191, 192
Korean War 149–50, 152, 154–5, 158–9, 161–3, 166–7, 171
Kozower, Philipp 11
Kramer, Dame Leonie 227, 245, 259, 279, 284, 286, 312, 313–14, 315, 316–17, 319, 329
Kristallnacht 4, 6–7, 9, 17, 316
Kristol, Irving 218, 251, 367
Krotkov, Yuri 151–2, 156–8, 162, 163, 164, 165
Krygier, Martin 227, 231, 237–8, 257, 259, 294, 312, 313, 315, 316, 317, 355, 399, 431
Krygier, Richard 147, 148, 152, 227, 237, 238, 315
Kwiet, Konrad 215

La Trobe University 102–3, 194–5
    conversazione, Bundoora campus 114
    department of politics 103–6
    Ideas and Society Program 420, 457–9
    incident involving the Maoists and Spartacists 106–7
    Manne 102, 106–7, 108–11, 115, 248, 266, 462
    Rabelais student newspaper 105, 107, 109
    super-*conversazione* on the future of the university (1988) 115
    United Nations University proposal 434

INDEX

Labour Club
  Monash University 73, 74, 87–8
  University of Melbourne 66–8, 71, 73, 81, 82, 83–5, 87
Lane, Terry 198, 265–6
Langer, Albert 59, 136
Langton, Marcia 427, 464
Lanzmann, Claude, *Shoah* 216, 237
Laos 119, 138, 141, 157
Lasch, Christopher 147
Latham, Mark 372, 378–80, 382, 393
Lawrence, D.H. 197
Leak, Bill 424–5, 430
Leavis, F.R. 257
Left, Right, Left blog, *The Monthly* 428, 435–6
Leibler, Isi 212, 213, 214, 217, 240–1, 242, 245, 284
Lenin, Vladimir 122, 222, 281, 288
Leydin, R.S. 176, 184
Liberal Party 189, 246, 255, 258, 266, 291, 294–5, 296, 361, 383, 392, 393, 394, 408
Liberal–National (earlier Country) Party Coalition 170, 174, 176, 179, 189, 209, 210, 295, 300, 361–2, 379, 392, 405, 408, 436
Liffman, Michael 88
Likud Party 204, 239, 367
Lipski, Sam 169, 171, 205, 231, 236, 242, 316
Littlewood, George 247, 259
Lockwood, Rupert 177
Lodz Ghetto 3, 4, 11, 12–15, 21, 354
London 100–1
Lowen, Fred 50
Lowy, Cathy 88
Lucashenko, Melissa 339
Lyons, John 231, 232
Lyons, Joseph 337

Macartney, Keith 77
MacCallum, Mungo 424
MacDonald, Jan (later Grundy) 60, 69
Macintyre, Stuart 71, 165, 271, 272, 274, 289, 345
Macphee, Ian 246
Mahurin, Walker 151
Maly Trostinec 23
Mann, Thomas 37–8, 41
Manne, Anne 101–2, 184, 188, 194, 252, 315, 323, 391–2, 401, 402, 423–4, 453–5, 462
  marriage of Anne and Robert 115, 461
  writing 292–3, 391, 392, 399, 454, 464

Manne, David 40
Manne, Henry 16, 17, 20, 25–7, 59, 88, 267, 353
  ABC broadcasts 36–7, 40, 42, 47, 48
  categorised as "enemy alien" 28–9, 30, 39
  categorised as "refugee alien" 34–5
  death 50–1
  family life 48–50, 52
  furniture manufacturing business 26, 27, 37, 42, 47–8, 50, 51, 412
  migration to Australia and arrival in Melbourne 16, 17, 20, 25
  naturalisation 28–9, 30, 33, 35
  newspaper articles 29–34, 35–6, 37–44, 47
  work in the Monsanto chemicals factory 28, 35, 42, 49
Manne, Joachim (Chaim) 16–17, 18–19, 21, 23, 28
Manne, Kate (daughter of Anne and Robert) 115, 340, 454, 455, 461, 462
Manne, Kate Rosalie Marie (Kathe, née Meyer) 4, 6, 8, 26, 42, 45–6, 47, 48–50, 51, 52–3, 54–5, 58–9, 88, 267, 353–4, 453, 461
Manne, Leonora (née Hötchner) 16, 18–19, 26, 28, 39
Manne, Lucy 340, 446, 454, 455, 461
Manne, Ruth 27, 45
Manne, Siegmund *see* Mitchell, Siegmund 18–19, 20–1, 26, 28, 49, 50
Manning, Chelsea (born Bradley) 419
Mannix, Daniel 84
Manus Island detention camp 360, 362, 374, 400
Mao Zedong 88, 122, 153–4, 166, 167
Marr, David 284, 399–400, 402–3, 406
Marsden, Robin 228, 230, 231, 242, 245, 247, 318
Marsh, Ian 234–5
Marsh, Reginald 331, 335
Marshall, Graeme 166
Martin, Allan 190, 288
Marx, Karl 40, 61, 222, 243
Mathews, Bob 376–8
Matthews, Brian 283–4
Maxwell, Ian 76–7
McAdam, Anthony 160, 231, 257
McAuley, James 228, 229, 232, 257, 262, 283
McBride, Philip 175

480

INDEX

McCaughey, Patrick 88
McClelland, James 186–7
McCloskey, Mary 66
McCormack, Gavan 135–6, 148, 150–2, 155, 157, 158, 159, 160, 161–3, 164, 165–6
McCrann, Terry 255, 263, 381
McGuinness, Paddy 253, 255, 318, 329–30, 331, 332, 336–7, 339, 342, 351
McKellar, Michael 142, 143
McKibben, Bill 446
McKnight, David 389, 422
McQueen, Humphrey 147, 187, 269 273–4, 311, 312, 313
Mead, Jenna 275, 276–7
Meagher, Douglas 335
Media Watch 422
Menzies, Andrew 214
Menzies, Robert 8, 45, 150, 154, 170, 171, 173–4, 178–9, 189, 190, 210, 218, 272, 296, 371
Méray, Tibor 164
Meyer, Friederike (Frida, née Munter) 3–4, 6, 9, 10–11, 12, 14
Meyer, Hans 4, 6, 8, 46–7, 49, 50, 51, 59, 73, 101
Meyer, Otto Joseph 3–4, 6, 9, 10–11, 12, 16, 23, 200–1
MI6 182, 385
Middle East 204, 448, 449
Miller, Henry 197–8
Miller, John 105
Milner, Ian 182–3
Mind of the Islamic State, The (Manne, 2016) 449–53, 455
Minogue, Kenneth 330–1
Mitchell, Chris 286, 289, 340, 345, 346, 381, 384, 387, 396, 397, 421–3, 425, 426, 428, 431, 433, 434, 441
Mitchell, Samuel James 324
Mitchell, Siegmund (formerly Manne) 18–19, 20–1, 26, 28, 49, 50
Molotov, Vyacheslav 178, 180
Monash University 65, 70, 80, 124
Monthly, The 333, 392–4, 402–6, 422, 428, 437
    Manne's public commentary 192, 324, 381–2, 395, 396–7, 399–400, 402–3, 405–6, 407–8, 409, 411–12, 417–18, 419–21, 433, 443–4, 447, 448–9
    see also Left, Right, Left blog
Morgan, Hugh 113, 255

Morgan, Paddy 70, 71, 85, 87, 229–30, 231, 257, 262
Morrisby, Edwin 160–1
Movement, The 170, 261–2
multiculturalism 145, 209–10, 234, 295, 297, 299, 362, 379, 395
Mulvihill, Tony 206
Munro, Doug 269, 271, 272
Munz, Martin 84
Murdoch press 332, 383, 393, 397–8, 405, 408, 437–8, 444
"Payback: The Bullying Tactics of the Murdoch Press" (Manne, 2012) 433–4
Murdoch, Rupert 247, 421–2, 423, 437–8, 442, 444
Murray, Les 248, 287–8, 289–90, 308–15, 317, 318
MVD (later KGB) 169, 173, 174, 178, 181, 182

Nadel, David 59, 73
Naparstek, Ben 412
National Party 297, 299; see also Liberal-National (earlier Country) Party Coalition
National Union of Australian University Students 86
NATO countries 219, 291
Nauru detention camp 359, 360, 362, 364, 374, 400
Nazi regime in Germany 4, 6–7, 8, 10, 17, 26, 29, 37–8, 46, 56, 73, 77, 78, 79, 83, 104, 216, 236–8, 280, 316, 370
    policy of extermination of the Jews 31–4, 39, 43–4, 60, 63, 72, 90, 200–1, 202, 236, 241, 244–5, 281, 282, 303, 307
Nazi–Soviet Non-Aggression Pact (1939) 97, 111
Nazism 38, 77, 79, 83, 84, 99, 106, 111, 193, 238, 464
Neill, Rosemary 430
neo-conservatism 239, 241, 243, 367–8, 400, 438
neo-liberalism 59, 145, 191, 233, 235, 247, 257, 258, 262, 267, 291, 293, 330, 392, 393, 394, 400, 403–5, 422, 448, 469; see also economic rationalism
Neumann, Anne Waldron 293, 318
Neville, A.O. 302–3, 304–5, 307–8, 329, 336, 341, 390
New China News Agency 155, 162–3

481

"New Right" think-tanks 113
New Zealand, nuclear-free policy 218, 238
News Corp 422–3, 428, 437
News from Kampuchea 125–7
News Limited 247
nuclear disarmament 219–20
Nuremberg Laws, 1935 5

Obama, Barack 404, 407, 447
O'Donoghue, Lowitja 334, 338
Oeser, Oscar 78–9
Office for National Assessments (ONA) 375
Office of Special Investigations, US Justice Department 214, 217, 241
On Borrowed Time (Manne, 2018) 53, 455, 456
One Nation party 210, 263, 298, 361, 362
Orwell, George 41, 73, 78, 83, 89, 90, 138, 220, 235, 249, 268, 306, 357, 400, 436
O'Sullivan, Fergan 176, 177
Oxford University 92, 94–5, 98, 462
    Magdalen College 92, 93–4, 96

Pacific Solution 364, 400
Packer, James 263
Packer, Kerry 263–4
Panmunjom peace talks 149
Parker, R.A.C. 98
Parkes, Sir Henry 208
Paul, J.B. 171
Peacock, Andrew 115, 462
Pearson, Christopher 318, 332, 340, 347–8, 381, 388–9, 436, 441
Pearson, Noel 389, 426, 430, 464
Perkins, Charlie 351
Petrov Affair 169, 171–3, 178–80
    ASIO–Menzies conspiracy theory 169–1, 172, 173–4, 177–8, 184, 185, 188–9
    Document H 176, 177–8
    Document J 176–8, 189
    PBL miniseries (1987) 169, 171, 184
    The Petrov Affair: Politics and Espionage (Manne, 1987) 172, 179, 185–9, 192, 233, 411, 463
Petrov, Evdokia (later Anna Allyson) 169–70, 173, 174–6, 177, 179, 180, 181–2, 184–5, 189
Petrov, Vladimir 169–70, 172–4, 176–7, 180–1, 182, 189

Phelan, Diane 191–2
Phnom Penh 130
    evacuation (1975) 119–20, 122–3, 125–6
    Radio Phnom Penh 120–1, 123, 127
Pilger, John 164, 306
    The Last Dream (television documentary) 211–12
    The Secret Country (television documentary) 306
Pincher, Chapman, *Too Secret, Too Long* (1984) 183, 186
Podhoretz, Norman 218, 243, 368
Pol Pot 112, 122, 123, 124, 125, 132–3, 135, 136, 137–8, 166
    "Pol Pot and the Intellectuals" (Manne, 1979) 140, 144–5, 153
Poland 3, 4, 8, 28, 31, 36, 97, 221, 222, 280, 281, 294, 362
Polanski, Roman, *Chinatown* 195
political identity of Manne
    anti-communism 84, 90, 98, 140, 256, 355, 464
    conservatism 268, 299
    importance of belonging to the Jewish people 63, 84, 91, 465
    influence of Soviet communism 57, 122
    Oxford University influence 98–9
    public intellectual 112, 161, 220, 381, 425, 463–4
    reading of political works 82–3, 99, 266–7
    shift from left to right to left 74–5, 83–4, 87, 424, 428, 464
    at University of Melbourne 61–3, 66–7, 72–5, 77–8, 80, 83–90
Ponchaud, François, *Cambodge, L'Année Zero* (1977) 121, 123, 126–7, 130, 133, 134, 135, 136, 137, 139, 144
pornography 197–9; *see also* sex
Posetti, Julie 422
Potter, Dennis 444
Poynter, John 92
Price, Bess 426–7
Program for the New American Century (PNAC) 367–8
Office of Special Plans 373
Protestant–Catholic sectarianism 56–7, 265, 267
Pusey, Michael, *Economic Rationalism in Canberra* 256

INDEX

Quadrant 114, 144–5, 165, 166, 423, 462
   Anne Manne's writing 292
   Committee of Management 227, 229
   Editorial Advisory Board 229, 230–1, 232
   finances 227, 247–8, 263–4
   Manne as associate editor 228, 230, 231
   Manne as co-editor 148, 232–6, 242–5, 439
   Manne as editor 148, 162, 192, 232, 245–59, 261, 263–4, 266, 269, 272–7, 282–3, 285, 286, 291–4, 296, 308–19, 323, 342, 431, 439, 463, 464
   Manne's article on war crimes legislation 235–8, 239, 240–2, 245
   Manne's writing 111–12, 121, 133, 148, 152–63, 186, 197, 202, 206, 208–9, 228, 282, 283, 296, 298, 306–8, 462
   McGuinness's article on the future of *Quadrant* 329–30
   political position 293–4, 296–7, 298, 300, 306–8
   political questions concerning Indigenous Australians 300, 306–7, 330–2, 335, 336, 342
   quality of writing 248, 249–52
   Sandall's editorship 228–32
Quarterly Essay 333, 364, 365, 392, 407, 421, 423, 425, 430, 431, 433, 464
   Bad News (Robert Manne, 2011) 421–8, 429–32, 434, 440–2, 456
   Love and Money (Anne Manne, 2008) 392
   Sending Them Home (Robert Manne, 2004) 364–5, 407, 432
   see also *In Denial: The Stolen Generations and the Right* (Manne, 2001)

Rabbit-Proof Fence (film, 2002) 328, 329
Race Discrimination Act 291–2
racism 206, 207, 208, 210, 211, 242, 244–5, 263, 279, 297, 298, 302, 305, 306, 307, 317, 331, 337, 457–9
Rapke, Jeremy 236
Rath, Ernst vom 6
"Reagan Democrats" 262, 295
Reagan, Ronald 219–20, 223, 254, 262
Reconciliation Council 349, 351–2

Recorded Music Society 35
"refugee alien" classification 34–5
refugees 39–40, 91, 353–64, 379, 381, 382, 383, 393, 400, 455
   boatloads of asylum seekers 142, 206–7, 242, 353, 354, 358–9, 362, 383, 401, 408, 464
   from Cambodia 121, 126–7, 128, 130, 133, 134, 135–6, 137, 139, 141, 142–3, 206, 352–3
   camps, South-East Asia 142, 206, 358
   from Central Asia and the Middle East 353, 355–6, 359–61, 362, 374
   "children overboard" story 360–1, 362, 374, 379
   detention centres 356, 357–8, 362, 363–4, 374, 400–1
   from Indochina 141–2, 206–7, 209, 242, 266, 354, 358
   see also immigration; Jewish refugees, Australia
Reich Association of Jews in Germany 11
Reith, Peter 360–1
republican movement 264–5, 292, 295, 361, 379, 396, 400
Reynolds, Henry 211, 330, 332, 339, 340, 342, 344, 345, 346, 387
   "Terra Nullius Reborn" 347
Richards, Ron 173, 174, 183, 185–6
Rieff, Philip 194–6
Riegner, Gerhart 32
Riemer, Andrew 279, 284
Riga Ghetto 21
Rintoul, Stuart 334, 338
Robertson, Mavis 164
Robson, Lloyd 344, 345
Rodeck, Ernest 50
Rosenberg, Ruth 248
Rosenbloom, Henry 69, 70, 85, 169
Roth, Walter E. 326–8
Rowley, Kelvin 71, 187
Royal Commission into Aboriginal Deaths in Custody (1987–91) 212
Royal Commission on Espionage (1954–55) 170, 171–2, 176, 177, 178, 180, 185–6, 188
Rubinstein, W.D. (Bill) 217–18, 237–8, 239, 240, 241, 242, 245
Rudd, Kevin 301, 329, 392–401, 407–9, 434–7, 442
   "The Global Financial Crisis" (2009) 403–5, 422

INDEX

Ruddock, Philip 356, 357–8, 360–1
Rumkowski, Chaim 12–13
Rundle, Guy 284, 430, 431
Russia 420–1, 448; *see also* Soviet Union
Russia–Ukraine war 291
Russian Social Club, Sydney 173, 178
Rutland, Suzanne, *Lone Voice* 240–1
Ryan, Lyndall 344, 345, 347
Ryan, Peter 268–74, 288, 289, 293, 316
Ryan, Susan 109, 265
Ryckmans, Pierre 253, 293, 318, 468
Rydon, Joan 104, 105

Salisbury, Harrison 164
Salusinszky, Imre 373, 381, 384
Sandall, Roger 228–32, 241–2, 258–9, 346
Santamaria, B.A. 67, 75, 84, 104, 142, 160, 165, 170, 171, 177, 223, 233–4, 254, 255, 258, 261–3, 293, 354, 408
Sayle, Murray 253
Schanberg, Sydney 120, 122, 125, 144
Schenk, Rod 341
Schuschnigg, Kurt 17, 18
Schwartz, Morry 332–3, 346–7, 365–6, 376, 381–2, 387, 388–9, 405, 406–7, 412, 422–3, 430, 433, 459
Schwarzbart, Ignacy 32
Scott, John 105, 108–9, 162
Searby, Richard 114, 227, 247, 259, 312, 313, 314, 317
Second World War 56, 83, 89, 96, 97–8, 127, 183, 236, 370–1, 411
Seminar on the Sociology of Culture 112–13, 114, 162
Serov, Ivan 164–5
sex 60
    male sexual misbehaviour 275–8
    in Western culture 195, 197–8, 291
    see also pornography
Sharp, Geoff 89
Sheehan, Paul 347, 348, 357, 381
Shell Postgraduate Arts Scholarship 92, 95, 99
Sher, Neal 239, 241
Sheridan, Greg 229, 257, 318, 373, 385, 387, 430, 431
Shrubb, Lee 318
Shrubb, Peter 230, 318
Silber, John 115
Simon Wiesenthal Center 214, 239
Singer, Peter 102, 199–201, 250

Smith, Michael 334
Smyth, Eris Mary 131–2
Snowden, Edward 420
social class 57, 93–4, 95, 267–8
society, Australian 87–8
Soldatow, Alexander (Sasha) 60, 82
Solzhenitsyn, Aleksandr 99, 122, 249, 415
Sontag, Susan 134, 194, 196
South-East Asia 80, 142, 218, 358, 359
Soviet communism 57–8, 62, 83, 84, 122, 138, 164–5, 171, 220, 221, 233, 281, 289, 464
Soviet Embassy, Canberra 169, 173, 177, 181, 287
Soviet Union 3, 40, 77, 78, 79–80, 82, 90, 97, 99, 121–2, 127, 129, 138, 147, 158, 167, 182, 183, 288, 289, 354
    Cold War 40, 171, 217–18, 234, 464
    dissolution 163, 220–3, 239, 248, 254, 367
    glasnost 217, 228
    nuclear weapons 219–20
    perestroika 228
    relations with Australia 228
    relations with China 149
    see also KGB; Petrov Affair; Russia
Special Investigations Unit 217
Spooner, John 269, 431, 469
Spry, Charles 170, 171, 173–4, 175–6, 178, 179–82, 183–4, 185–6, 189–91, 192
Spry, Helen 191–2
Spry, Ian 190, 191, 192
Stalin, Josef 40, 46, 58, 78, 83, 84, 88, 97, 99, 106, 121–2, 149, 156, 166, 173, 220, 223, 238, 280, 307, 445, 465
Steedman, Pete 70
Steele, Peter 77, 318
Stephen Murray-Smith Lecture (1997) 323
Stone, John 113, 247, 255, 256, 258, 363
Stove, David 243–5, 245, 252
Strutton, Bill, *Island of Terrible Friends* 266
Stubbs, John and Nicholas Whitlam, *Nest of Traitors* 169–70, 184, 188
Students for a Democratic Society (SDS) 68, 71, 86, 87–8
    campaign for University of Melbourne strike 68, 72, 85–6
Suich, Max 253
Swain, Jon 120, 125
Switzer, Tom 457–8, 459

484

INDEX

Tampa asylum seekers 359–60, 363, 364, 380, 393
Tanter, Richard 131, 219
Tarr, Shane and Chou Meng 125–6
Taylor, A.J.P. 95, 96–7, 98, 99
Taylor, Lenore 408–9
Temple Beth Israel, St Kilda 59–60, 461
Thailand 120, 121, 128, 132, 135, 141, 142, 143, 206
Thatcher, Margaret 145, 209, 210, 366, 437
Theophanous, Theo 105
Thomas, Bill 67, 79, 80
Thomas, George 248, 309, 310, 314
Thompson, Christina 318
Throssell, Ric 188
Thwaites, Michael 174, 184
Thwaites, Vivien 143, 193
Tiananmen Square 222, 223, 248, 253, 354–5
Tibet 154, 167
Tighe, Margaret 201
"Toast to Australia" by Manne (1988) 267–8, 297
Tobin, Terry 70, 265, 316, 317
Tomlinson, Maggie and Jock 77
Toohey, Brian 187
totalitarianism 79, 83, 84, 90, 99, 145, 156, 175, 201, 216, 218, 219, 220, 222, 311, 464
Tregear, Ann 70, 94, 100, 193
Trendall, Dale 103
Trump, Donald 420–1, 447
Tucker, Margaret 334, 390
Turnbull, Malcolm 265, 408, 438
Twomey, Anne 464

Ukraine 79, 129, 221, 253, 279–81, 282–3; *see also* Russia–Ukraine war
Ung Huot 141, 144
United Kingdom
　Australia's British heritage 210, 211, 267–8, 270, 370
　relations with Australia 182–3, 218
　relations with the Soviet Union 97, 98, 99
　see also Iraq War (2003–11)
United Nations 149, 155
　Security Council 374, 386
United Nations Monitoring, Verification and Inspection Commission (UNMOVIC) 385–6
United Nations Refugee Convention 353, 355, 360

United States
　Cambodia 119, 133, 139, 144
　climate change denial 447, 448
　Cold War 90–1, 147, 150, 171, 217–18, 464
　Korean War fake germ warfare allegations 149, 151, 158, 159, 163, 166–7
　Manne's visit in 1987 218, 368
　nuclear weapons 219–20
　pressure for settlement of Indochinese refugees in Australia 207
　relations with Australia 371–2, 382, 398
　relations with China 372, 398
　relations with European nations suppressed under communism 253–4
　September 11, 2001 terrorist attacks 360, 366, 368, 451
　see also Iraq War (2003–11); Program for the New American Century (PNAC); Vietnam War (1955–75); WikiLeaks
universities 85–6, 91, 251, 395
　problems facing newer Australian universities 108–9
University of Melbourne 61, 65–78, 415
　community of scholar-teachers and students 68–9, 71–2, 91
　Farrago student newspaper 69, 70, 72, 79, 80–1, 85, 86–7, 88–9, 90
　Manne as German history tutor 101, 102
　political clubs 66–8, 69, 71, 73, 74, 75, 79, 80, 81, 82, 83–5, 86, 87–8
University of Sydney 72, 79, 244, 315

Vallentine, Jo 219
van Moorst, Harry 71
Véliz, Claudio 103, 112–13, 114, 115, 343
Venona breakthrough of Soviet code 183, 186
Vietnam 141, 452
　invasion of Cambodia (1978) 121, 132, 135, 136, 137, 140, 143, 153, 166
Vietnam War (1955–75) 66, 67–8, 71, 72, 73–4, 80, 85, 89, 90, 91, 119, 128, 133, 135, 139, 145, 153, 166, 171, 207, 245, 291, 293

INDEX

Wagner, Richard 38-9
Wake, R.F.B. 178
Wallace-Crabbe, Chris 77, 318
War Crimes Act and subsequent trials 214, 215, 216-17, 235-8, 239, 240-2, 280-1
Warhaft, Sally 402, 403, 404, 405-7, 410, 412
Warner, Denis 154-5
Warsaw Ghetto 12, 32, 280
Waten, Judah 63, 77
Waten, Pippa 63
Waterhouse, John 113
Waters, Joseph 160
Watson, Don 271, 288, 289
We Steal Secrets (documentary film, 2013) 418-19
Webb, Sidney and Beatrice, *Soviet Communism* 138
Weinberg, Mark 61
welfare state 58-9, 67
Wentworth, Bill 175
West Bank 73, 204-5, 213, 216, 367, 465-6
West, Nigel 187
Western culture 195-6, 196-7
Western Mining 113, 227, 246, 258, 264
Wheeldon, John 231, 245, 257
White Australia policy 207, 211, 268, 297, 358, 457
White, Hugh 398, 457, 464
white supremacy 84, 266, 414
White, Thomas 8
Whitewash (Robert Manne (ed.), 2003) 347-8

Whitlam, Gough 58, 68, 74, 141-2, 145, 150, 171, 361, 394, 462
Whitlam, Margaret 188
WikiLeaks 411-12, 414, 415, 416-17, 418-21
Wild, Ron 109, 110
Wilkie, Andrew 374-7
Wilkie, Douglas 206
Williams, E.N. 99-100
Wilson, Sir Ronald 300
Windschuttle, Keith 331, 333, 342, 427-8
   The Fabrication of Aboriginal History 342-6, 347-8, 422, 425-6
   "The Myths of Frontier Violence" 332
Winnington, Alan 149, 150
Wolfowitz, Paul 366, 367, 368
Wolfsohn, Hugo 102, 104-5, 106
World Jewish Congress 214

Yad Vashem 3, 11, 204
Yeats, W.B. 76
Yeltsin, Boris 164, 221, 254
Young, John 413, 414, 417
Young, Mick 207

Zable, Arnold 70, 71
Zhou Enlai 164, 199
Zogbaum, Heidi 323, 328, 329
Zygielbojm, Shmuel 32

Robert Manne is an emeritus professor of politics and vice-chancellor's fellow at La Trobe University, Melbourne. From the late 1980s he wrote regular, often controversial, columns on current affairs for *The Herald*, *The Age*, *The Australian* and *The Sydney Morning Herald*, and was a frequent commentator on ABC radio and television.

Between 1990 and 1997 Manne was the editor of *Quadrant*. Appointed as a well-known opponent of communism, he resigned over right-wing opposition to his call for uncompromising recognition of the crimes committed against the Indigenous peoples of Australia. Since 2005 he has written widely for *The Monthly* and *The Guardian*.

Manne is the author or editor of some thirty books, including *The Petrov Affair*, *Left, Right, Left*, *The Mind of the Islamic State*, *On Borrowed Time* and three Quarterly Essays. In 2005 he was voted Australia's leading public intellectual.

A fellow of the Academy of the Social Sciences in Australia, Manne was appointed an Officer in the General Division of the Order of Australia in 2023.

Printed in the USA
CPSIA information can be obtained
at www.ICGtesting.com
LVHW090051051224
798141LV00008B/45